Developing a Constitution for Europe

The European Union is presently at a crossroad. The prospect of enlargement has led to a project of comprehensive reform. Existing structures – originally designed for just six members – need to change. The Constitutional Convention has succeeded in forging a Draft Treaty Establishing the Constitution for Europe but these developments raise fundamental issues of legitimacy and democratic accountability.

This book aims to address the challenge of forging a legitimate Constitution for the EU and explores the questions:

- Does the EU need a constitution and, if so, what is to be constituted?
- Can such a constitution be made by a non-state entity?
- How could the constitution be made and what is the role of the Convention on the Future of Europe?

The authors aim to clarify the constitutional status of the EU, to take stock of the European Charter of Fundamental Rights and Convention of the Future of Europe as vehicles to foster and create a European constitution. *Developing a Constitution for Europe* should interest students and researchers of European Politics.

Erik O. Eriksen is Professor of Political Science at the University of Oslo and Professor II at the University College of Oslo.

John Erik Fossum is Senior Researcher at ARENA, University of Oslo, and Associate Professor at the University of Bergen.

Agustín José Menéndez is Ramón y Cajal researcher at the Universidad de León, Professor at the Instituto Universitario Ortega y Gasset and CIDEL fellow at ARENA, University of Oslo.

Routledge Studies on Democratising Europe
Edited by Erik Oddvar Eriksen and John Erik Fossum
ARENA, University of Oslo

Routledge Studies on Democratising Europe focuses on the prospects for a citizens' Europe by analysing the kind of order that is emerging in Europe. The books in the series take stock of the EU as an entity that has progressed beyond intergovernmentalism and consider how to account for this process and what makes it democratic. The emphasis is on citizenship, constitution-making, public sphere, enlargement, common foreign and security policy, and Europe society.

1. Developing a Constitution for Europe
Edited by Erik Oddvar Eriksen, John Erik Fossum and Agustín José Menéndez

2. Making the European Polity: Reflexive Integration in the EU
Edited by Erik Oddvar Eriksen

Developing a Constitution for Europe

Edited by
Erik Oddvar Eriksen,
John Erik Fossum and
Agustín José Menéndez

Routledge
Taylor & Francis Group

LONDON AND NEW YORK

First published 2004
by Routledge
2 Park Square, Milton Park, Abingdon, Oxon, OX14 4RN

Simultaneously published in the USA and Canada
by Routledge
270 Madison Avenue, New York, NY 10016

This edition published in paperback 2005

Routledge is an imprint of the Taylor & Francis Group

Typeset in Baskerville by Taylor & Francis Books
Printed and bound in Great Britain by
Antony Rowe Ltd, Chippenham, Wiltshire

British Library Cataloguing in Publication Data
A catalogue record for this book is available from the British Library

Library of Congress Cataloging in Publication Data
Developing a constitution for Europe / edited by Erik Oddvar Eriksen,
John Erik Fossum and Agustín José Menéndez
        p. cm
Includes bibliographical references and index.
  1. Law reform–European Union countries. 2. Constitutional
law–European Union countries. I. Eriksen, Erik Oddvar, 1955–
II. Fossum, John Erik. III. Menéndez, Agustín José.
   KJE976.D48 2004
   342.7302–dc22

                                                    2003020527

ISBN 0–415–32194–8 (hbk)
ISBN 0–415–37534–7 (pbk)

Contents

Tables

Contributors

Bruce Ackerman is Sterling Professor of Law and Political Science at Yale University. His publications include *Social Justice in the Liberal State* (1980), *We the People: Foundations* (1991), *We the People: Transformations* (1998), *The Stakeholder Society* (co-authored with Anne Alstott) (1999) and *Deliberation Day* (co-authored with James Fishkin) (2004).

Hauke Brunkhorst is Professor of Sociology at the University of Flensburg. Among his recent publications are *Demokratischer Experimentalismus – Politik in der komplexen Gesellschaft* (1998), *Globalisierung und Demokratie – Wirtschaft, Recht, Medien* (2000) and *Solidarität. Von der Bürgerfreundschaft zur globalen Rechtsgenossenschaft* (2002).

Carlos Closa is Professor of Political Science at the University of Zaragoza. Relevant publications include *Sistema Político de UE* (1997), *La Europeización del sistema político español* (editor) (2000), 'The Implicit Model of Constitution in the EU Constitutional Project', in E.O. Eriksen, J.E. Fossum and A.J. Menéndez (eds) *Constitution Making and Democratic Legitimacy* (2002), and the forthcoming *Spain and the European Union* (with Paul Heywood).

Erik Oddvar Eriksen is Professor of Political Science at ARENA, University of Oslo. Recent publications include *Kommunikativ ledelse* (1999), *Democracy in the European Union* (co-edited with John Erik Fossum) (2000), *Demokratiets sorte hull* (2001), *Understanding Habermas* (co-authored with Jarle Weigård) (2003) and *The Chartering of Europe* (co-edited with John Erik Fossum and Agustín José Menéndez) (2003).

Michelle Everson is Jean Monnet Lecturer in European Law at Birkbeck College, University of London. Her recent publications include 'Challenging the Bureaucratic Challenge' (with Christian Joerges), in E.O. Eriksen and J.E. Fossum (eds) *Democracy in the European Union* (2000), 'Adjudicating the Market', *European Law Journal*, Vol. 8, No. 1 (2002), ' "Subjects" or "Citizens of Erewhon"? Law and Non-Law in the Development of a "British Citizenship" ', *Citizenship Studies*, Vol. 7, No. 1 (2003), and 'Social Pluralism and the European Court of Justice: A Court between a Rock and a Hard Place', *Journal of Legislative Studies*, Vol. 8, No. 4 (2003).

John Erik Fossum is Senior Researcher at ARENA, University of Oslo, and Associate Professor at the University of Bergen. Publications include *Oil, the State, and Federalism* (1997), *Democracy in the European Union* (co-edited with Erik Oddvar Eriksen) (2000), 'The European Union in Search of an Identity', *European Journal of Political Theory*, Vol. 2, No. 3 (2003) and *The Chartering of Europe* (co-edited with Erik Oddvar Eriksen and Agustín José Menéndez) (2003).

Dieter Grimm is Professor of Public Law at the Humboldt University of Berlin. Among his publications are *Die Zukunft der Verfassung* (1991), *Zur Neuordnung der Europäischen Union. Die Regierungskonferenz 1996–97* (co-editor) (1997) and *Die Verfassung und die Politik. Einsprüche in Störfällen* (2001).

Jürgen Habermas is Professor Emeritus of Philosophy and Sociology at the University of Frankfurt. A brief selection of some of his books includes *The Theory of Communicative Action* (1981), *Moral Consciousness and Communicative Action* (1983), *The Philosophical Discourse of Modernity* (1985), *Postmetaphysical Thinking* (1988), *Justification and Application* (1991), *Between Facts and Norms* (1996), *The Inclusion of the Other* (1998), *Die postnationale Konstellation* (1998), *Glauben und Wissen* (2002) and *Zeit der Übergänge. Kleine Politische Schriften vol. 9* (2001).

Christian Joerges is Professor of European Economic Law at the European University Institute in Florence. He is co-editor of *Private Governance, Democratic Constitutionalism and Supranationalism* (1998), *European Committees: Social Regulation, Law and Politics* (1999), *Good Governance in Europe's Integrated Market* (2002), *Darker Legacies of Law in Europe: The Shadow of National Socialism and Fascism over Its Legal Traditions* (2003) and *Rechtsverfassungsrecht: Recht-Fertigungen zwischen Sozialtheorie und Privatrechtsdogmatik* (2003).

Massimo La Torre is Professor of Philosophy of Law at the Università di Catanzaro and at the Law School at the University of Hull. He has published several books and articles, including *Disavventure del Diritto Soggettivo: Una Vicenda Terica* (1996), *European Citizenship: An Institutional Challenge* (editor) (1998) and *Norme, Instituzioni, Valori: Per une Teoria Instituzionalistica del Diritto* (1999).

Paul Magnette is Professor of Political Science and Director of the Institut d'études européennes at the Université Libre de Bruxelles. Most recent publications include *La constitution de l'Europe* (editor) (2002) and *The Convention on the Future of Europe* (with Jo Shaw, Lars Hoffmann and Anna Verges) (2003).

Agustín José Menéndez is Ramón y Cajal Researcher at the Universidad de León. Recent publications include *Justifying Taxes: Some Elements of a General Theory of Democratic Tax Law* (2001) and *The Chartering of Europe* (co-edited with Erik Oddvar Eriksen and John Erik Fossum) (2003).

Christoph Möllers, Dr jur., is scientific assistant at the University of Heidelberg. He has published on German and European constitutional and administrative law. Recent publications include *Staat als Argument* (2000) and *Die Beendigung des Wertpapierhandels an der Frankfurter Wertpapierbörse* (with Hartmut Bauer) (2001).

Joseph H.H. Weiler is University Professor at New York University. He also serves as the Joseph Straus Professor of Law and European Union Jean Monnet Chair at NYU School of Law. Among his recent publications are *The Constitution of Europe, 'Do the New Clothes have an Emperor?' and Other Essays on European Integration* (1999), *Kompetenzen und Grundrechte* (with Bruno Simma and Markus C. Zöckler) (1999), *The EU, the WTO, and the NAFTA: Towards a Common Law of International Trade?* (2000) and *The European Court of Justice* (co-edited with Grainne de Búrca) (2001).

Acknowledgements

This book originates from research undertaken within the framework of the CIDEL project: Citizenship and Democratic Legitimacy in the European Union. Many of the contributors to the book are part of and affiliated with the project. CIDEL is a joint research project, with nine partners in six European countries. The project is co-ordinated by ARENA (at the University of Oslo) and is financed by the European Commission's Fifth Framework Programme. CIDEL is a multidisciplinary research project with around twenty researchers in the fields of political science, law, media research, and sociology. See http://www. arena.uio.no/cidel. Resultsfrom this project will be published in the series, Routledge Studies on Democratizing Europe, where this book is the first contribution.

This book would not have been published without the support of a large number of people and organizations. For financial support we would like to thank the Commission, the Norwegian Research Council and the University of Oslo. We as editors would in particular like to thank ARENA for providing such a stimulating environment for research on European integration. We would also like to thank Heidi Bagtazo and the editorial staff at Routledge for their support and their efficient handling of the manuscript. A final note of thanks goes to Geir Kværk for excellent technical editing of the manuscript.

Prologue

Hope and fear in constitutional law

Bruce Ackerman

Hope and fear, pride and humiliation – these great passions lie at the foundation of any constitutional order.

And in different combinations at different times. We must grasp these changing complexes if we hope to unlock the deeper dynamics at work, the larger challenges ahead, in constitutional construction.

Contrast the Philadelphia Convention of eighteenth-century America with the Brussels Convention of twenty-first-century Europe. The Philadelphians met in 1787 – at a moment just before the outbreak of the French Revolution. They were the last liberal constitutionalists to be entirely free of the fearsome images of the Reign of Terror that haunted their successors during the next two centuries.

For the Americans, it was England's Glorious Revolution that served as a more hopeful example. It assured them that revolutions were tricky, but manageable, affairs. The expulsion of the King in 1688 had led not to fearsome chaos but to the precedent-breaking creation of a Bill of Rights. Now that the Americans had expelled yet another English King, they took a good deal of Whiggish pride in pushing the Glorious Revolution to the next stage, reconstructing legitimate political authority on a grander scale.

A time-tested leadership gave further substance to this constitutionalism of hope. The previous decade of revolutionary struggle against England had provided the Americans with a cadre of leaders who had gained credibility throughout the continent – led by George Washington, who had self-consciously refused the temptations of military despotism for the sake of enlightened republicanism.

The elite's conduct of the revolution was not only a great source of popular pride, but it also served as a tremendous source of popular legitimacy when these same leaders proposed a constitution which would give further expression to their hopes for their 'more perfect Union'.

Things couldn't be more different as we contemplate the half-century preceding the proposal of a Constitution for Europe. If the first half-century of American Union was built on the foundations of hope and pride, European developments have been driven by fear and humiliation. The prelude for the Treaty of Rome was the disastrous destruction of World War II, not some triumphant collective act of liberation from imperial rule. By comparison with George Washington and Thomas Jefferson, not even Winston Churchill or Charles De Gaulle was a leader on a Continental scale, and, in any event, both failed to play a central role in blazing a path toward a new Continental order.

Nevertheless, the movement toward European Union has succeeded remarkably well. It seems that fear and humiliation can do as good a job as hope and pride in fueling the engine of political construction. This is old news, in a sense. Thomas Hobbes is the great political theorist of fear, and Carl Schmitt was his great twentieth-century pupil, emphasizing the role of a collective enemy in motivating the construction of political identity.

But their classic works need refinement in accounting for the present European situation. Schmitt turns out to be wrong in suggesting that political order requires the creation of an external enemy. A Schmittian fear of the Soviet Union may well account for NATO, but the European Community was generated by a different kind of anxiety. The Germans in particular, but the others as well, were afraid of their former selves, not some Schmittian Other. They were determined to make a decisive break with the populist nationalisms of their own past and thereby avoid the continuation of the European Civil War that crushed so many lives during the first half of the twentieth century.

A simple point, but one easily overlooked in standard treatments which emphasize the democratic deficit in the construction of the European Union. I don't deny that European elites have indeed occupied centre-stage over the past half-century – none of the accumulating set of Euro-treaties won a popular ratification comparable to that obtained in each of the thirteen American states at the Founding of the Constitution. Nevertheless, it would be wrong to ignore the deep fear and anxiety that served as the hidden popular legitimator of the on-going elite construction.

Most Europeans have never had the chance to vote at a referendum on the emerging structure of European government. But at the same time, they thoroughly appreciated how the ever-thickening web of European institutions made militaristic nationalism a thing of the past. For the generation that lived through the fears and humiliations of the 1940s and 1950s, this was no small matter, and it provided a deep foundation of popular support for the movement toward a more united Europe.

Perhaps a constitution based on fear is less noble than one based on hope – but as events have proved, it should not be despised. The pervasive fear of ordinary Europeans of a return to their humiliating past has served to legitimate a great constitutional achievement, entirely comparable to the construction of the United States of America.

But if this is true, it is a cause of concern for the future. The men and women who experienced the existential agonies of mid-century Europe are now moving inexorably to the grave. The rising generations are no longer eye-witnesses to the destruction of Berlin or London and they cannot share their predecessors' grim determination to avoid a repetition. The originating sources of fear and humiliation will no longer serve as a powerful engine propelling the European Union. For this project to endure or even prosper, other motivations must take its place.

And of course, there are other motivations. The first, most obviously, is economic self-interest. The common market has not only led to general enrichment, but it has given all European citizens valuable new rights to work within the larger economic sphere. The second are shared European values – in the Enlightenment, in the welfare state, in the rule of law. And the third is the evolution of social mores: Britons and Italians and Poles who are twenty-somethings share an increasingly common style of life – singing the same songs, eating the same foods, dancing the same social dance, more or less, in different languages.

These are formidable bonds, but the question remains whether, without more, they are enough to withstand the unknowable political challenges of the twenty-first century. Without the propelling force of fear and humiliation, will the Union withstand recurring populist appeals to renascent nationalism or the self-interested machinations of national elites?

Like most important empirical questions, this one is unanswerable through rigorous scientific techniques. But given the obvious dangers, it seems plausible to consider what, if anything, the new Constitution for Europe might do to respond to the problem. The American experience differs from the European in countless respects. But it does suggest that fear and humiliation are not the only engines of constitutional construction; it is also possible to appeal to the next generation's hope and pride in their emerging role as citizens of a new Union.

All Europeans have been citizens of the Union for some time now, and the new constitution reaffirms this status, guaranteeing a host of fundamental rights including the right to vote in parliamentary elections. But at present, this is a bare grant of legal status without much in the way of social significance. The Euro-citizen may get preferential treatment at customs when she returns from aeroplane trips to foreign parts. But this is hardly enough to generate hope and pride in their citizenship standing. How, then, to build up the social and political meaning of Union citizenship?

Here are a couple of suggestions. The first is a generalization of the recent 'baby bond' initiative of the Blair government. Under Gordon Brown's 2003 budget, all British children born since November 2002 will receive a government bond that pays them several thousand pounds when they reach the age of 18 (*Economist* 2003).

One of the intellectual sources of Brown's path-breaking proposal was *The Stakeholder Society*, published a few years ago by Anne Alstott and myself (Ackerman and Alstott 1999). The book argues for a sweeping reassessment of our present practices of family inheritance. Nobody chooses their mother and father, and it is wrong for a young adult's starting point in life to depend so heavily on the success of his or her parents. The right thing to do is to supplement the status quo with a new system of citizen inheritance. Our parents are hardly the only ones who have contributed to the present level of prosperity: all of us should inherit some wealth in our capacity as citizens in recognition of the contributions of our fellow citizens of all past generations. Blair's 'baby bond' gives practical substance to this fundamental principle of a just society.

And one that can serve as a model for Europe. The divergent histories of Member States only dramatize the moral arbitrariness of family inheritance.

Surely the Czechs have already paid heavily for the fact that their country was overrun by Russia after World War II. It is hardly their fault that they don't have very much to give to their children. Whatever was true in the past, the next generation of Britons and Czechs are now equally citizens of Europe. Granting each new child a 'Euro-bond', maturing upon early adulthood, not only gives new substance to a Continent-wide commitment to social justice; it will also serve as a key element in the construction of a constitution of hope. For the rising generation, the European Union will represent something more than a common market, or common ideals, or common mores. By providing each citizen with a financial head-start in life, the Euro-bond will serve to fill the motivational gap left by the demise of the constitution of fear.

I leave the details for another time. The key thing is to emphasize that a modest Euro-bond is well within the realm of political and economic feasibility. This isn't true of more ambitious proposals for creating a European-wide welfare state. Citizens of Britain or Germany have planned their entire lives around the particular benefits they have been promised by their particular welfare states. It would be a terrible breach of these social contracts to cut expected entitlements drastically so as to extend watered-down versions to nationals of other countries. In contrast, the baby-bond initiative provides an evolutionary supplement to existing national benefits, and one that can serve a distinctive token of common citizenship in a European Union committed to social justice.

More recently, I have been hard at work on a second proposal that can serve a similar constitutional function. This one builds on social science experiments developed by a friend of mine, James Fishkin, who is a professor of political science at Stanford. Over the past decade, he has developed a new kind of Deliberative Poll that he rightly sees as a quantum leap beyond the ordinary public opinion survey. The traditional poll merely asks respondents to provide 'top of the head' answers to a set of questions. Fishkin's exercise is more ambitious. He begins by selecting a representative sample from a national population, stratified by income, race and gender. After asking each respondent a set of questions raised by an election campaign, he invites them all to a central location to spend a couple of days deliberating on the issues. At the end of these discussions, he determines their impact by asking all participants the very same questions that appeared on their initial questionnaire.

The results often show big changes. For example, Fishkin conducted a Deliberative Poll in Britain just before the 1997 general election. His before-and-after questionnaire not only revealed large increases in the group's understanding of the underlying issues; it also found that that the percentage voting for the Liberal Democrats increased from 13 to 33 per cent. Fishkin has conducted about thirty similar experiments throughout the world. They demonstrate that ordinary people have an impressive capacity to participate constructively in political deliberation, regardless of their education levels.

We now propose to take the next step and use these experiments as the basis of a serious reform proposal. Our forthcoming book, *Deliberation Day*, argues for the creation of a new national holiday (Ackerman and Fishkin 2004). Everybody

takes a day off and is to attend a neighbourhood centre to hear a national television debate, and deliberate on the issues in small groups and with local political
leaders. Held two weeks before the election, the new holiday would serve as a
counterweight to sound-bite politics presently degrading our democratic life.
Our book explores both the philosophical foundations of our proposal and practical difficulties that it raises.

Like all new ideas, it will take a brave politician to bring Deliberation Day
into the real world. But I don't think the prospect is Utopian. For example, when
Britain ultimately holds its referendum on the Euro, it may well be in Tony
Blair's interest to give D-Day a try. After all, the case for the Euro can't be
persuasively made in the space of a sound-bite, and the new holiday provides
precisely the social context which would allow the government to make its case
for the Euro most persuasively.

But it is on the level of the European Union that D-Day has its greatest
attraction. If held two weeks before each parliamentary election, the new
holiday – call it Euro-Day – will serve as a crucial resource that allows ordinary
people to take the obligations of Euro-citizenship seriously. After confronting a
televised debate by competing Euro-leaders, they will have a precious opportunity to engage in neighbourhood discussions about the best path forward for the
Continent as a whole. Even if only a minority of people takes advantage of the
opportunity, Euro-Day would serve as a sociological anchor for a deeper and
wider discussion during the two-week run-up to the parliamentary elections.

This is not the place to take up the complex design issues raised by D-Day. It
is enough to take a step backward and consider how some clever combination of
Euro-bonds and Euro-Days might shape constitutional development over time.
Perhaps a quarter-century from now, young adults all over Europe will be stepping forward to claim their Euro-bonds as they set out in life and join their elders
in Euro-Day discussions on the political future of the Continent. Perhaps these
constructive affirmations of common citizenship will instill the civic pride and
hope that may propel the European Union beyond the limits reached by the
dynamics of fear and humiliation.

The point of such innovations is hardly to create a unitary Euro-citizenship
that will displace national loyalties. My aim instead is to encourage the construction of a more complex form of citizenship – in which one might become an
effective citizen of Europe, Britain and Wales at the same time. And what is
wrong with that?

Now is the time to raise this question, before it is overwhelmed by the coming
constitutional debate. The recent Constitutional Convention is indeed an
epochal event in the history of Europe, but it focused entirely upon issues of
significance to the political class: Should the President of the Council become an
important force in European affairs? What kind of Euro-wide majority should
be empowered to enact a law? And so forth.

These are important issues, but they should not distract us from the task of
creating new links between ordinary citizens and the Union as the older motivations wither and die. Perhaps it is too late to add this question to the current

round of constitutional debate; perhaps the Euro-bond and Euro-Day, or some better set of ideas, must await the next round of constitutional development.

Only one thing is clear: a Europe without committed citizens is a hollow shell that will be crushed in one or another of the unending crises that make up human history.

1 Introduction

A constitution in the making?

Erik Oddvar Eriksen, John Erik Fossum
and Agustín José Menéndez

> Convinced that, while remaining proud of their own national identities and
> history, the peoples of Europe are determined to transcend their ancient divisions
> and, united ever more closely, to forge a common destiny.
>
> (Preamble, CONV 850/03)

Introduction

The European Union, the Laeken Declaration asserted, is presently at a crossroads. It is faced with the imminent challenge of enlargement, so as to unify a
continent split by two World Wars and the Cold War. The institutional apparatus
deemed necessary for this was not put in place with the treaty amendments
introduced by the Treaty of Nice, signed in 2000. Further changes were needed.
The EU has thus embarked on another round of comprehensive reform, with
the result still undecided.

But this notion of crossroads has wider ramifications. It is evocative of a set of
deeper tensions pertaining to the transformation of the nation-state and the very
system of nation-states that make up the so-called 'Westphalian Order'. This order
elevated the principle of state sovereignty to the centre of politics, and raised
nationalism to the status as prime mode of allegiance. The Westphalian Order is
challenged through the dual processes of globalization and nation-state fragmentation. In Europe, a regional political order is being developed. The transformation
of the Westphalian Order has both conceptual and normative implications.

At the conceptual level it pertains to the relevance of the very vocabulary that
has been developed around the nation-state and that serves not only as a cognitive container, but also as point of reference for identity formation. The
adequacy of this vocabulary is being questioned through processes of globalization, Europeanization, internationalization, denationalization, regionalization,
devolution, multiculturalization, and so on. A gap has emerged between actual
developments and the conceptual tools that are used to depict these.

At the normative level the question is posed as to whether the principles,
values and modes of allegiance associated with the nation-state will remain
sustainable. In the global setting, there is a rising tension between the fundamental principles of state sovereignty and human rights. International law

contains both, but the institutional system in place clearly privileges state sovereignty. The EU, a post-national entity with a mixture of supranational, transnational and intergovernmental traits, is forged within this very tension of state sovereignty and human rights. This tension is also readily apparent in the Preamble to the Draft Treaty Establishing a Constitution for Europe, cited above, and permeates the entire integration process. What are the legitimating principles that the EU can and should draw on? Can it draw on the same as the nation-state? Or does it have to develop new ones?

In order to address this question we focus on constitution-making in Europe. The constitution designates the core principles of any given polity. It is also a vital intake to the assessment of the manner in which these normative ideals are thought embedded in institutional practice. These questions are pertinent now, not only for external reasons, but also because of the dynamic momentum built up by the EU itself.

A re-invigorated European Union

Since the early 1980s, the process of European integration has picked up new momentum. New members have been included, and new tasks have been added. The process of integration includes developments such as Economic and Monetary Union; increased cooperation within the fields of security and defence policy, justice and home affairs policy; and social policy. Other policy areas are also affected so that there are few, if any, domains that remain unaffected by the EU and completely within the remit of the Member States. The Union reaches deep into the Member States and affects citizens in a multitude of ways.

These changes influence, and at the same time reflect, the continued process of institution-building at the European level. This serves to 'Europeanize' the Member States. This political order breaks in important respects with the principles of classical international law. Increasingly the EU has developed into a political entity in its own right – with strong supranational traits and without any clear precedents. The EU has greatly contributed to the on-going process of convergence of national constitutional traditions, and it is widely acknowledged that the Union already possesses a *material constitution*.

Nevertheless, it is clear that the EU has developed into a political union without having received an explicit mandate by the people to do so. Its citizens have a wide range of rights, but these have been granted to them rather than demanded by them. The EU is widely critiqued for harbouring a *democratic deficit*. It is deficient with regard to what democratic legitimacy requires. The EU falls short not only in relation to the standards of *legitimate government* that it espouses, but also in relation to the standards for *efficient government*. The system in place, set up for six Member States, and found wanting then, has been made to function with fifteen members, and is now faced with the prospect of accommodating far more new members. Although this structure has been adapted to increased integration, this adaptation has not kept pace with its expanded size and scope.

Recent developments signal that the Union is now seeking to own up to this set of challenges. The EU is now for the first time in a direct and self-consciously acknowledged way involved in a *constitution-making* process. An important part of this was the Laeken decision (European Council 2001a) to establish a Convention on the Future of Europe – the so-called 'Constitutional Convention'.

The aim of this book is to address the challenge of forging a legitimate constitution for the European Union. First, does the EU *need* a constitution, and, if so, what is to be constituted? This question requires attention to fundamental principles, political-legal arrangements and sources of citizens' allegiance. The Charter of Fundamental Rights, solemnly proclaimed at the Nice Summit (2000), and the Laeken Convention on the Future of Europe, which produced a Draft Treaty Establishing a Constitution for Europe, provide us with essential elements to the question of forging a European democratic constitution.

Second, *can such a constitution be made*, and if so, will the EU be able to forge it? The question of a constitution must be considered in light of the type of entity that the EU is. Equally, recent developments that are conducive to further constitutionalization need to be considered. The Charter is important, as rights are essential ingredients in constitutions and because the Charter can be considered as a vital spur to further constitution-making. Equally important are the constitutional and legal traditions of Europe. How conducive are they to constitutionalizing the EU? Do they differ so as to produce conflicting impulses or do they cohere so as to serve as vital spurs?

The third set of queries revolve around *how* a constitution can (and should) be made. In particular, we address the role of the Convention on the Future of Europe in the constitution-making process, in terms of both process and product. How well did it handle the matters it addressed? What was the quality of the processes? Do the deliberation and negotiation processes in and around the Convention comply with the normative criteria for a constitution-making process?

In this introductory chapter we will provide a brief outline of the background for the constitution-making process, as well as give a short overview of how the contributions to the book help shed light on the questions posed above.

Does Europe need a constitution?

A growing number of scholars, especially legal ones, claim that the European Communities already have a constitution. This is not a constitution in the conventional sense, namely in the sense in which the term is usually understood in political theory; but rather what may be termed the *material constitution* of the European Communities. The contributions by Grimm, Habermas, Menéndez and Möllers remind us of an important three-fold distinction in the conceptualization of a democratic constitution:

(a) a *material* constitution that speaks to those social practices that are actually regarded as the basic norms of a given society;

(b) a *formal* constitution that refers to the set of legal norms that are contained in a single written document;

(c) a constitution in the *normative* sense based on certain 'ideal' standards, with particular emphasis on human rights and democratic procedures.

This means that a constitution proper not only has to be written and effective, but it also has to be connected to democratically enacted law, that is, it stems from the people and can be amended by them.

In their more than fifty years of existence, the Treaties which established the three original European Communities have been interpreted and applied as if they contained the basic constitutional materials of a new political community. The Paris Treaty of the European Coal and Steel Community (1951), the Rome Treaties of Euratom and the European Economic Community (1957) amount to the constitutive documents of the Union. They are its Founding Treaties. The European leaders, aided by European corporations and European citizens, and in particular by the rulings of the European Court of Justice and of national courts, have slowly but steadily given shape to the material constitution of the European Union. A basic set of norms have emerged that constitutes and determines the functioning of the European institutions and that establishes the basic rights that Europeans enjoy. This has been rendered possible by *three basic developments* with regard to how the Treaties are conceived.

First, the provisions of the Treaties have been considered as legally binding, and not as mere programmatic proclamations. This is the essence of what is technically referred to as *direct effect*, which positions laws enacted in Brussels as if they were enacted in national parliaments.[1]

Second, the institutional nexus foreseen in the Treaties has been considered as indicative of the will to create *a new political community*, hence, establishing a Community different from the Member States, even though it is compatible with the continuing existence of nation-states. The European Communities, as a new political community, was to ensure conflict-resolution, problem-solving and action coordination among Europeans. This required entrusting them with a certain set of competences. For instance, regulatory competences over the production and trade of coal and steel were needed from the very start. The integrative effect of the transfer of competences to the Communities could only be ensured if Community law was supreme in its field of competence. This, rather than the unqualified supremacy of Community law, is core to the 'principle of supremacy'.

Third is the choice to interpret both the provisions of the Treaties and the different norms produced by European institutions in the light of a very basic principle of Community law, namely the protection of fundamental rights. The interpretation draws on the common constitutional traditions of the Member States, and on international law – mainly but far from exclusively through the European Convention on Human Rights (ECHR). This testifies to the progressive affirmation of fundamental rights as part and parcel of Community law. Beyond the concrete affirmation of certain rights, including the elaboration, systematization and balancing of competing rights, the third development implies regarding Community law as a *constitutional legal order*, amenable to be integrated according to basic normative choices.

The claim, by a good number of scholars, that Europe already has a constitution, must be understood from such a perspective. The Court of Justice and national constitutional courts have developed the means to determine the contents of this material constitution of the Union out of the basic constitutional materials, that is, essentially the founding Treaties and the common national constitutional traditions.

But if this is so, is there then a need to draft a European constitution? This is a contentious issue, not only among politicians but also among scholars. Some analysts find that the existing material constitution might not only be enough, but might also be the best we can get (Maduro 2000). A formal constitution might even endanger the unique achievements of the process of European integration. The constitutional structure Europe has developed represents a unique structure, a non-state type of federal union. It reflects Europe's *Sonderweg* and is based on the principle of *constitutional tolerance* (Weiler 2001b: 52–3). Dieter Grimm maintains in his contribution – Chapter 5 – that since there is no European people there can be no European constitution.

Why, then, do so many Europeans favour the drafting of a constitution for the European Union? There is a good case for drawing up a European constitution. Jürgen Habermas (2000) notes that Europe embodies a distinctive form of solidarity connected to the welfare state. The nation-state can no longer be relied upon to protect this, due to denationalization and globalization. Currently, there are global structures of finance, production and trade that serve to weaken the boundaries of the nation-state. Globalization creates growing interdependence and escalation of risks that lead to and require transnational and supranational cooperation. To catch up with globalization, regional polities such as the EU are required; and a European constitution provides the best means of protecting Europe's distinctive form of solidarity in a globalizing world. But as he maintains in Chapter 2 of the present volume: 'the challenge before us is not to *invent* anything but to *conserve* the great democratic achievements of the European nation-state, beyond its limits'. This raises the larger issue of what to retain from the nation-state, and, further, whether the forging of a European constitution does imply the need to establish a European state, or whether the present structure can be reformed so as to accommodate such. Habermas also provides a set of specific recommendations for the type of European constitution that the Union can develop. In Chapter 6, Hauke Brunkhorst discusses the link between constitution and state. Can there be a constitution when there is no state? There is a main dividing line in the literature on the European constitution, and also in the contributions to this book, between those who argue that a constitution necessarily presupposes a state to be constituted (and most of the time, this means a nation-state) and those who do not see such a connection as necessary. That is whether a constitution requires a state – a hierarchical order with monopoly of power, but one that can be democratically controlled – or whether a constitution is compatible with a multi-level, multiple demoi polity. For the latter, democratic governance is possible without a government. But can there really be a constitution without a state, and what is at stake in such a case?[2]

Another set of reasons held up for a European constitution stem from the process of integration itself. It is important to remember that the process of constitution-making in the European Union will not unfold in the same manner as that which has characterized nation-state constitution-making. This is so for the simple reason that the European process is largely based on and draws on the fusion of national constitutional traditions. National constitution-making often refers to a *genuine beginning* of the national constitutional tradition – a big bang – whereas Community law cannot simply make reference to such a beginning, as it builds upon and furthers the national constitutional traditions. These traditions differ considerably.

But does a constitution really require a 'big bang', a founding moment? In Chapter 8, Christoph Möllers contrasts the revolutionary American–French constitutional tradition – which highlights the constitution as the order-forming politicization of the law, where the law is created by the people assembled in conventions – with the German–British common law tradition. With regard to the aforementioned three-fold distinction of constitution (formal, material and normative), the particular distinction between material and normative constitution brings the democratic principle to the fore. Democracy is the core requirement and intrinsic part of any set of legitimate constitutional standards. All proponents of a European constitution highlight the need for, and importance of, democracy.

The challenge of democracy

As noted above, the European Union is widely held to suffer from a democratic deficit. This is generally seen as due to the lack of European political parties, a weakly developed system of representative accountability, and the absence of a truly European public sphere. The assessment of the gravity of the democratic deficit hinges on:

(a)   the nature of the Union *qua polity*;
(b)   the *normative standards* that are applied to it and that it applies to itself; and
(c)   the nature of *citizens' demands* on the EU in terms of its democratic legitimacy.

The original design of the Communities was based on an *indirect* mode of legitimation. The *democratic* quality of the EU was derived from the democratic quality of the Member States, whereas the legitimacy of the EU was based on its performance. Over time, the EU emerged into a polity in its own right, however defined. It is no longer a mere derivative of the Member States; hence the indirect mode of legitimation is inadequate. The EU has not only become a polity, but has also affected and even transformed the Member States so much that the question of the legitimacy of the democratic Member State can no longer be seen as separate from, or independent of, the EU.

Today's EU is an entity with strong supranational features, as evidenced in the authoritative character of the legal structure, which is supported and enhanced in particular by the European Court of Justice. As already noted, in its rulings, it has long asserted the principles of supremacy and direct effect. The European Parliament, which is directly elected by the peoples of the Member States, is also supranational, and has recently increased its powers vis-à-vis the European Commission. The Commission is the executor of Union policies and is endowed with the right of initiative, which includes the right to issue legislative proposals. The particular non-hierarchical nature of supranationality that marks the EU is, among other things, a result of its peculiar 'separation of powers', which ensures the Member States a strong and consistent say in the decision-making processes of the EU, with no single Member State in a position to dominate the others.

In overall terms, the institutional structure of the EU embodies a complex mixture of supranational, transnational, intergovernmental and international elements. Whilst analysts differ on the precise definition and weighting of the elements, most agree that this structure is incomplete, in principled and substantive terms, due to its particular character *qua polity*, namely dynamism, openness and polycentricity (Preuss 1996: 138; see also Schmitter 2000).

Irrespective of the constitutional status of EU law, supranationality does mean that the same obligations are conferred upon all, that is, non-arbitrary norm enforcement. The citizens of Europe have achieved rights over and above their nation-states. The European Communities were established through three international treaties. They were formally regarded as classic international organizations. However, the very letter of the Treaties and the very shape of the original institutions indicate that the Communities were a design in tension.

Community law was moulded in the form of international law, but it was supplemented with traits of a cosmopolitan legal order. Whereas initially the decision-making process of the Communities closely resembled intergovernmentalism, it has over time been supplemented and supplanted with traits clearly reminiscent of a political community. In other words, it retains traits of the initial indirect and performance-based mode of legitimation, but combines these with clear traits of direct legitimation. The latter pertains to the way the citizens themselves are empowered through rights and called upon to authorize the laws and policies that affect them.

The integration process was long conducted by the political elites and cast in a technocratic language. It was widely seen as the game of bureaucrats, experts and politicians. Such an account, however, might be too simplistic. Whatever the ultimate personal motivations of Schuman or De Gasperi, Monnet or Spinelli, Adenauer or Delors, that is, whether they were guided by their personal interest, by their perception of the national or the European interest, by a conception of Europe as a future superpower, or by a notion of Europe as a kind of religious power, their visions did result in *an unprecedented entity*. The EU is not the result of a master plan cleverly crafted by a set of 'founding fathers' equipped with a clear blueprint for Europe. Rather, it can be seen as an outcome of different driving forces, of diverse motives, interests and concerns. The constitutional question, in terms of a normative and formal constitution, was left in abeyance by the founders.[3]

This dynamic of rapid integration without a concomitant broad-based process of reflection on what it amounts to in polity and legitimacy terms has come to an end. The strong popular opposition during the Maastricht ratification process (1992) has been interpreted as a cry for more democracy, openness and accountability. Subsequent reform efforts, notably the Amsterdam Treaty (1997) and the Nice Treaty (2000), have claimed to retain this commitment, albeit they have met with variable success.

Chartering Europe

A *constitutional moment* is not merely a process through which the constitution is made or amended, but also one in which it makes sense to say that *the people* has given itself a constitution. The European Union has a brief history of such attempts. The first one took place in the early 1950s, when a political union was considered a necessary counterpart to the project of constituting a Defence Community. A constitutional text was drafted by an *ad hoc* assembly (Griffiths 2001). The refusal of the French Parliament to ratify the draft treaty establishing the European Defence Community marked the fate of the very first and fledgling European 'constitutional moment'. The second one was the result of the first election of the European Parliament by universal suffrage in 1979. In the aftermath of the election, a group of the brand new representatives of the European people launched a new initiative to give the Communities a political constitution. The driving force of such an initiative was Altiero Spinelli. He had been an outstanding figure of resistance against fascism in Italy, was a major advocate of a federal Europe, and a member of the Commission in the 1970s. The initiative managed to mobilize the European Parliament, to convince the members that it should affirm itself as a *pouvoir constituant*. The Spinelli project was supported by a huge majority in the European Parliament, and also obtained support from some national parliaments. But the constitutional opening did not transform into a constitutional moment due to opposition from national governments. This was a constitutional moment *manqué*, even if the initiative played a major role in reactivating the process of European integration (Angelino 2003).

Some were prepared to consign the Charter of Fundamental Rights to that very same proverbial dustbin of history immediately after its proclamation. The process of drafting the Charter may, however, end up being the prelude to a successful constitutional moment. It was presented as a modest exercise of consolidation of the *acquis communautaire* on rights protection, but it has acquired importance well beyond that, as is discussed in several chapters in this book. The Cologne European Council of June 1999 resolved that a Charter of Fundamental Rights of the European Union should be established (European Council 1999). At the Tampere European Council, the 'masters of the Treaties' decided that this Charter should be drafted by a 'body' composed of representatives from national governments, national parliaments, the European Parliament and the Commission. This stands in marked contrast to processes based on intergovernmental conferences (IGCs), in which Treaty changes are the sole preserve of executive officials.[4] The strong presence of parliamentarians in the Charter Convention greatly added to the legitimacy of the undertaking.

This rather innovative 'body' was mandated to work in a transparent and participatory manner. The 'body', which had renamed itself 'Convention', a name with constitutional overtones, concluded its work in less than one year. The Convention almost unanimously adopted the Charter.[5] The resulting text is composed of fifty-four articles that spell out the civic, political and social rights of European citizens under Union law.

The Convention held open hearings and received written submissions (in total over a thousand). It might be a trifle optimistic to argue that the Convention contributed to the sparking of an authentically European-wide debate among the organizations of civil society, but it did try much harder to foster public debate than had previous IGCs. Its mobilizing effects should at no rate be over-estimated, but it certainly compared favourably with the intergovernmental approach that had preceded treaty changes before.

After the Charter Convention delivered the text, it was time for the 'masters of the Treaties' to decide what kind of status should be granted to the Charter. Before the Nice Summit of December 2000, they agreed that the final status of the Charter would not be clarified until the next IGC, scheduled for 2004.[6] The three main European institutions (the European Parliament, the Commission and the Council) confined themselves to solemnly proclaim the Charter on 7 December 2000.

The Charter Convention established a procedural precedent for constitution-making. Compared to the utter failure of the 2000 IGC, the relative success of the Charter Convention was striking. This triggered a reflection on the procedural qualities of IGCs and an enthusiastic endorsement of the Convention model. The inclusiveness, representativeness and transparency of the process were rightly associated with its capacity to produce a coherent result.

In relation to the requirements inherent in a normative conception of the constitution, however, insufficient attention was paid to the lack of a defined and democratic way of taking decisions. Conversely, the symbolic importance of reaffirming the basic political, civil and social rights that Europeans are said to acknowledge each other should not be underestimated.[7] A clear restatement of fundamental rights is, implicitly, an invitation to actually make use of such rights.

After its proclamation, the European Parliament, the Commission, some Advocate Generals of the Court of Justice, and even the European Court of Human Rights have made it clear that they will act as if the Charter were a binding document. This document helps render clear that the EU is not merely a free market project, but also a union of citizens built upon shared values and binding universal norms. Furthermore, the proposed Charter can be read as one of the most explicit statements – if not *the* most explicit statement – on the EU's commitment to direct legitimacy that has ever been produced. Many analysts also see it as having furthered the prospects for constitution-making in the European Union. Several of the chapters in this book discuss the need for a European Bill of Rights and the possible positive effects of such. In Chapter 4, Joseph Weiler provides a somewhat different account. He summarizes the arguments in favour of a Charter, but ends up on a cautionary note with regard to its possible constitutional implications.

A Constitutional Convention?

The Nice Treaty and the process of forging it are part of the general pattern of treaty-making in the EU. Those in charge of the integration process have consistently *failed* to engage in a debate on what are the fundamentals of the Union, and how they should be entrenched in institutional-constitutional terms. Nor have they provided a set of agreed-upon blueprints for how to think of the EU with regard to its legitimacy. They have voiced support for certain standards and principles, but these have only very recently been expressed in polity terms.[8]

The Charter Convention model has given inspiration to the body set up to prepare for the next round of reforms, the 2003 IGC. This body was labelled the Convention on the Future of Europe. It started its work in February 2002 and concluded it in June/July 2003. It is now widely depicted as *a Constitutional Convention*. Its membership was modelled on the Charter Convention. Its mandate was broader, its working method included working groups, and the applicant states had a number of representatives present, as active observers.

The Laeken Declaration did not explicitly commit the Convention to come up with a single coherent proposal. However, the semantics of constitution-making were clearly embedded in the choice of the procedure. The Convention also succeeded in forging agreement on a single constitutional proposal. That it was able to do so has influenced the IGC although at the time of writing what will come out of the IGC is still unsettled.

Why is the Convention's work and product likely to affect the eventual outcome of the IGC? The Convention was set up as a deliberative body, with a mandate, a time-frame and a cast of actors capable of discussing matters of principle and having opinions and views moulded and shaped over time; hence, institutionally speaking, it was equipped to handle the matter of forging a constitution. It was also composed of a majority of parliamentarians, many of whom wanted an EU with stronger representative institutions. Conversely, the IGC as an institution is composed of decision-makers who are compelled to produce final results within a very short time-frame. As the evidence has shown from countless IGCs, they have proven good at striking bargains on pragmatic issues. They are, however, far less well-equipped to handle matters of principle and of value, and how such relate to practice. In Chapters 11 and 12, respectively, Carlos Closa and Paul Magnette provide an overview of the Convention. Both assess its qualities as a deliberative body, and contrast it with IGCs.

The legitimacy of the Convention is not independent of its product. It did reach agreement, but the question is what kind of constitution this will be – a constitutional treaty or a European constitution? A constitutional treaty implies a draft proposal that relies on the existing institutional arrangement, including the ambiguous relationship between intergovernmentalism and supranationalism that permeates this. There is an intricate balance of institutional concerns in the structural make-up of the Union, as imperatives with regard to efficient problem-solving and policy integration are said to be put on a par with the imperative of preserving the autonomy and sovereignty of the Member States. At the same time the Convention sought to strengthen the European Parliament and make the Charter binding, both of which are steps in the direction of a proper constitution, in so far as the Charter qualifies as a constitutional bill of rights. In Chapter 13, John Erik Fossum assesses the Convention's work and its result in terms of whether its work bears the imprint of a constitutional treaty or a constitution proper.

This chapter and the book underline that the status of the constitution is all but independent of the process through which it was brought forth. Bruce Ackerman observes that a constitution-making process contains three phases, beginning with *a signalling phase*, where a movement earns the authority to establish a reform agenda under public scrutiny. This phase is succeeded by *a proposal phase*, in which alternatives are hammered out for constitutional choice; and a third phase, where proposals are to be ratified and subjected to *mobilized popular deliberation*. A constitution-making process may very well be successful in the first two phases only to experience that prior success catalyses 'a powerful backlash – in which a previously "silent majority" organizes in energetic defence of traditional constitutional prerogatives' (Ackerman 1991: 267).

The EU has not of yet, at least, managed to bring forth Ackerman's notion of constitutional moment. In fact, we might speculate whether the EU's complex and composite nature might not be particularly conducive to another type of constitution-making, that is, an ongoing self-reflective historical learning process, amounting to a *constitutional conversation*.

On constitutionalizing Europe

The first part of the book (Part I) deals with the question of why a constitution is required, and what possible arguments can be launched against such an endeavour. While Habermas and Eriksen argue for a constitution, Weiler and Grimm are sceptical and Brunkhorst warns against undemocratic constitution-making. In Chapter 2 Jürgen Habermas outlines the basic structure of a European constitution and compares it with the American one. He does not foresee a European constitution based on a collective identity symbolized by an empowered parliament, but opts for a federation of nation-states. In his constitutional set-up, the second chamber of government – 'the chamber of nations' – must have a stronger position than the directly elected parliament in order to secure equal protection and recognition of diversity. This is so because of the position and the legitimacy of the nation-states in Europe.

In Chapter 3, Erik Oddvar Eriksen assesses the constitution-making process with emphasis on incorporating the Charter of Fundamental Rights. Is the Charter a means to reduce the democratic deficit even if it does not fully comply with the notion of people-made law? The EU establishes *post-national rights*, including fundamental rights of a constitutional type. Eriksen analyses the connection between rights and democracy from a cosmopolitan perspective. The focus is on the contribution of fundamental rights to constitutionalism. In Europe, there is a constitution in the making, as the citizens have been assigned rights, but as they have not given themselves the rights explicitly, the validity of the rights may be of a dubious quality.

Joseph Weiler, in Chapter 4, warns against over-optimism and is careful in setting out the limitations and possible negative effects of a constitutionalized Charter of Rights. For one, he questions whether the Charter was really necessary, since Europeans already had rights entrenched and protected at the national and supranational levels. He further notes that the status of the Charter as a political declaration may be seen as another instance of 'Euro Double-speak'. What Europe really needs is a *human rights policy* 'to make rights real'. Finally, whilst human rights are a vital spur to integration, their capacity to foster differentiation, rather than assimilation, should also not be underestimated.

This part also deals with the question of what type of entity the EU is, and how conducive it is to constitutionalization. As noted above, Dieter Grimm maintains in Chapter 5 that since there is no European people, there can be no European constitution. The EU cannot be a federal state for the time being, as the 'constitution' can only be made by third parties, that is, the Member States; hence it can be nothing more than a *constitutional treaty*. The attempt to forge a conventional constitution in Europe might also fail to deliver what is more urgently needed, that is, genuine democratization.

In this section, different perspectives on the conception of a European constitution are provided. These also vary in terms of the desirability and even possibility of a European constitution. Hauke Brunkhorst, in Chapter 6, analyses the relationship between constitution and state. The EU's constitutional structure is evaluated according to three ideas of constitutionalism: the functionalist idea; the power-binding idea; and the power-establishing or revolutionary idea. It is found that the EU has a constitution both in functional and power-constraining terms. What is lacking, though, is the revolutionary idea of a democratic constitution made by the people, facilitated through *strong publics* (institutionalized discourse) and authorized through general public debate. It is not the conventions of an elite remote from the public, but only the citizens themselves who can turn the legally existing constitutional textbooks against the reality of European law.

The chapters in the second part of the book deal with the question of *how* a constitution can be made. Agustín Menéndez (Chapter 7) examines what constitution Europe needs, and the way it should be written. He distinguishes between the aforementioned three different conceptions of the constitution – *formal, material and normative* – and fleshes out their logical underpinnings and interconnections. Under modern conditions only a normative, that is, a democratic, constitution, based on human rights and the principle of popular sovereignty, can be deemed legitimate. This scheme is applied to the EU, which obviously has got a material constitution, while it lacks a constitution in the formal and democratic sense. The question is whether the Laeken process can establish such. Whether or not the EU can get a democratic constitution, however, does not solely depend on the intrinsic quality of the proposed clauses, but also on the nature and quality of the process – whether the people themselves are given the possibility of – and actually engage in – making and ratifying the constitution.

But there are different ways of making a constitution. Christoph Möllers (in Chapter 8) ventures into two of the different constitutional traditions of Europe: *the revolutionary French-American way* and *the German-British evolutionary* constitution-making. In the latter type, the constitution emerges from conventional sources and takes the role of power-shaping juridification of politics – from above. The former sees the constitution as a clear break with the past and it therefore must develop its own set of justifications. It relies on a clear theory of popular sovereignty and democratic legitimacy for this, whereas the latter sees the constitution in evolutionary terms, and as a means of constraining already established state power. Möllers argues that the European process embodies traits of both traditions and that this has implications for how it is assessed. As such, the Union is also faced with the fateful choice of determining the precise democratic status of the constitutional structure it is ultimately to endorse.

This is a theme picked up in Chapter 9. While Möllers addresses the historical traditions that are conducive to constitution-making in Europe, Massimo La Torre critically analyses an important theoretical basis for such an endeavour, namely the doctrine of *legal positivism*. He attacks such a realist conception of constitution-making for being un-democratic. Legal positivism is about the mere facticity of the founding principles of the legal order, and although it comes in different shapes, none of the variants grasps the normative core of modern constitutions, namely that they are based on principles safeguarding the individual. The chapter is a stern warning against state-made law. Only the people can make the law, and a constitution should be prior to a state; the permission to coerce stems from the citizens. But the constitutionalization of the EU has taken place without much popular input, of which fact the next chapter serves as an implicit reminder.

In Chapter 10, Christian Joerges and Michelle Everson trace the historical process of constitutionalizing Community law. They reconstruct the development as a *legal learning process*, and distinguish between three stages of legal renewal: from the EEC up to the Single European Act, which gave rise to a supranational body of law; via the Single European Act and the Maastricht Treaty, which highlighted social rights and the question of European democracy; to, finally, the Constitutional Convention as a new and mature phase of integration and constitutionalization. However, the development does not testify to a linear legal learning process as it is permeated by *governance reforms*, such as the Open Method of Coordination based on soft law. Courts are far from the only actors in the legal development of the EU.

In Part III, we ask *how* a constitution can and should be made. The contribution of the Convention on the Future of Europe to this process is assessed.

In Chapter 11, Carlos Closa assesses the Convention from the vantage-point of the 'constitutional moment'. The justification for such an inquiry emanates from the Convention's subtle transcending of its initial mandate. The Convention called upon itself to forge a draft constitution. Closa assesses the representative quality of the Convention. This is an important determinant of the legitimacy of the Convention's claim to have forged a text that the IGC should adopt without changes. Closa assesses the Convention from three angles: as an expert forum, as a diplomatic conference, and as a constituent assembly. He finds clear traits of the latter and that the Convention has altered the nature of the EU's constitutional politics, albeit the final answer awaits the conclusion of this process.

In Chapter 12, Paul Magnette focuses on the norms which governed the Convention's deliberations. The purpose of the chapter is to determine whether, why and the extent to which the Convention process differed from classical methods of intergovernmental negotiation in the EU. The IGC method is seen as harbouring a strong bargaining imprint. Magnette spells out the key tenets of the bargaining model and contrasts this with a deliberative model in order to examine whether the Convention can be properly deemed as a deliberative body, which would suggest a qualitatively different process. He finds that the creation of the Convention, and the way the members defined the rules governing their work, can be understood in deliberative terms. In overall process terms, the Convention's work was constrained by its operating under 'the shadow of the veto' imposed by the 2003/2004 IGC.

In Chapter 13, John Erik Fossum examines what the Convention's efforts at forging a constitutional and institutional framework have resulted in. Fossum presents two constitutional visions for the EU – *deep diversity* and *constitutional patriotism* – and assesses these in relation to the existing structure of the EU and the Convention's work and results. The result (the Convention's draft) is more than mere consolidation. If adopted, it will reflect a further step in the process of forging a viable political entity in Europe. The Convention has taken a number of decisions that appear to weaken the multiple constitutional *demoi* doctrine and that seem to move the EU closer to one based on constitutional patriotism. The Convention's very use of the terminology associated with constitution could be potentially significant as a rallying call to bring institutional reality in line with constitutional aspirations, although there is still a need to decide which constitutional aspirations should serve as the leitmotif.

Notes

1   See discussions in Chapters 3, 5 and 7.
2   See, among others, Mancini 1998; Weiler 1998; Diez-Picazo 2002; Eriksen and Fossum 2004.
3   Europe, notes Pascal Lamy, after the Maastricht popular upsets:

was built in a St Simonian way from the beginning, this was Monnet's approach. The people weren't ready to agree to integration, so you had to get on without telling them too much about what was happening. Now St Simonianism is finished. It can't work when you have to face democratic opinion.

(Lamy, cited in Ross 1995: 194)

4 Here parliaments in most cases only really enter at the ratification stage (in some cases the national electorates, through referenda, also enter then).
5 No final vote was held, but participants' accounts reveal that only two members of the Convention were against its adoption.
6 See the 'Declaration on the Future of Europe, annexed to the Treaty of Nice' (European Council 2000).
7 See, for example, Lenaerts and De Smijter 2001; Menéndez 2002; Eriksen *et al.* 2003.
8 In his May 2000 speech, Joschka Fischer spoke of the need to establish a European federation. For some of the academic responses to the debate see, for example, Joerges *et al.* 2000.

Part I

Why a constitution?

2 Why Europe needs a constitution

Jürgen Habermas

There is a remarkable contrast between the expectations and demands of those who pushed for European unification immediately after World War II, and those who contemplate the continuation of this project today – at the very least, a striking difference in rhetoric and ostensible aim. While the first-generation advocates of European integration did not hesitate to speak of the project they had in mind as a 'United States of Europe', evoking the example of the USA, current discussion has moved away from the model of a federal state, avoiding even the term 'federation' (Niess 2000). Larry Siedentop's recent book *Democracy in Europe* expresses a more cautious mood: as he puts it,

> a great constitutional debate need not involve a prior commitment to feder-alism as the most desirable outcome in Europe. It may reveal that Europe is in the process of inventing a new political form, something more than a confederation but less than a federation – an association of sovereign states which pool their sovereignty only in very restricted areas to varying degrees, an association which does not seek to have the coercive power to act directly on individuals in the fashion of nation states.
>
> (Siedentop 2000: 1)

Does this shift in climate reflect a sound realism, born of a learning process of over four decades, or is it rather the sign of a mood of hesitancy, if not outright defeatism?

Siedentop misses the mark when he complains of the lack of any profound or inspired *constitutional* debate on the fate of Europe, capable of seizing the imagi-nation of its peoples. For our situation today is not comparable to that of either the Federalists or the delegates to the Assemblée Nationale. At the end of the eighteenth century, in Philadelphia and Paris, the Founding Fathers and the French Revolutionaries were engaged in an extraordinary undertaking, without historical precedent. More than two hundred years later, we are not merely heirs to a long-established practice of constitution-making; in a sense, the constitu-tional question does not provide the key to the main problem we have to solve. For the challenge before us is not to *invent* anything but to *conserve* the great demo-cratic achievements of the European nation-state, beyond its own limits. These achievements include not only formal guarantees of civil rights, but levels of social welfare, education and leisure that are the precondition both of an effective private autonomy and of democratic citizenship. The contemporary 'substantification' of law means that constitutional debates over the future of Europe are now increasingly the province of highly specialized discourses among economists, sociologists and political scientists, rather than the domain of constitutional lawyers and political philosophers. On the other hand, we should not underestimate the symbolic weight of the sheer fact that a constitutional debate is now publicly under way. As a political collectivity, Europe cannot take hold in the consciousness of its citizens simply in the shape of a common currency. The intergovernmental arrangement at Maastricht lacks that power of symbolic crystallization which only a political act of foundation can give.

An ever-closer Union?

Let us then start from the question: why should we pursue the project of an 'ever-closer Union' any further at all? Recent calls from Rau, Schroeder and Fischer – the German President, Chancellor and Foreign Minister – to move ahead with a European constitution have met sceptical reactions in Great Britain, France and most of the other Member States. But even if we were to accept this as an urgent and desirable project, a second and more troubling question arises: would the European Union in its present state meet the most fundamental preconditions for acquiring the constitutional shape of any kind of federation – that is, a community of nation-states that itself assumes some qualities of a state?

Why should we pursue the project of a Constitution for Europe? Let me address this question from two angles: (i) immediate political goals, and (ii) dilemmas stemming from virtually irreversible decisions of the past. If we consider the first, it is clear that while the original political aims of European integration have lost much of their relevance, they have since been replaced by an even more ambitious political agenda. The first generation of dedicated Euro-federalists set the process in train after World War II with two immediate purposes in mind: to put an end to the bloody history of warfare between European nations, and to contain the potentially threatening power of a recovering post-fascist Germany. Though everybody believes that the first goal has already been achieved, the relevance of peace-keeping issues survives in a different context. In the course of the Kosovo war, its participants became aware of subtle yet important differences in the way that the US and UK, on the one hand, and the Continental nations of Europe on the other, justified this humanitarian intervention – the former resorting to maxims of traditional power politics, the latter appealing to more principled reasons for transforming classical international law into some sort of cosmopolitan order. This is a difference that exemplifies the rationale for developing a European Union capable of speaking with one voice in matters of foreign and security policy, and bringing a stronger influence of its own to bear on NATO operations and UN decisions. Recent attempts by Persson, Solana and Patten to mediate between North and South Korea offer the first sign of a more serious intention by the EU to engage in global affairs.

The second goal, the containment of a potentially dangerous Germany, may have lost its salience with the growing stability of democratic institutions and spread of liberal outlooks in the Federal Republic, even if the unification of the country has revived fears of some return to the self-assertive traditions of the German Reich. I need not pursue this question here, since neither of the two original motives for integration could be regarded as a sufficient justification for pushing the European project any further. The 'Carolingian' background of the founding fathers – Schuman, De Gasperi, Adenauer – with its explicit appeal to the Christian West, has vanished.

Of course, there was always a third strand in European integration – the straightforward economic argument that a unified Europe was the surest path to growth and welfare. Since the Coal and Steel Community of 1951, and the subsequent formation of Euratom and the European Economic Community of 1958, more and more countries have become gradually integrated through the free exchange of people, goods, services and capital between them – a process now completed by the single market and single currency. The European Union frames an ever denser network of trade relations, 'foreign' direct investment, financial transactions, and so forth. Alongside the US and Japan, Europe has gained a rather strong position within the so-called Triad. Thus the rational expectation of mutual benefits within Europe and of differential competitive advantages on world markets could, to date, provide a legitimation 'through outcomes' for an ever-closer Union. But even making allowances for the consciousness-raising impact of the Euro, which will soon become a unifying symbol in everyday life across the Continent, it seems clear that henceforward economic achievements can at best stabilize the status quo. Economic expectations alone can hardly mobilize political support for the much riskier and more far-reaching project of a *political union* – one that deserved the name.

Beyond a 'mere market'

This further goal requires the legitimation of shared values (Fossum 2000). There is always a trade-off between the efficiency and legitimacy of an administration. But great political innovations, such as an unprecedented design for a state of nation-states, demand political mobilization for normative goals. Constitution-making has hitherto been a response to situations of crisis. Where is such a challenge, we might ask, in today's rather wealthy and peaceful societies of Western Europe? In Central and Eastern Europe, by contrast, transitional societies striving for inclusion and recognition within the Union do face a peculiar crisis of rapid modernization – but their response to it has been a pronounced return to the nation-state, without much enthusiasm for a transfer of parts of their recently regained national sovereignty to Brussels. The current lack of motivation for political union, in either zone, makes the insufficiency of bare economic calculations all the more obvious. Economic justifications must at the very least be combined with ideas of a different kind – let us say, an interest in and affective attachment to a particular ethos: in other words, the attraction of a specific way of life. During the third quarter of the past century, Eric Hobsbawm's 'Golden Age', the citizens of Western Europe were fortunate enough to develop a distinctive form of life based on, but not exhausted by, a glistening material infrastructure. Today, against perceived threats from globalization, they are prepared to defend the core of a welfare state that is the backbone of a society still oriented towards social, political and cultural inclusion. This is the orientation that is capable of embedding economic arguments for an ever-closer Union into a much broader vision. Of course, rapid economic growth was the basis for a welfare state that provided the framework for the regeneration of postwar European societies. But the most important outcome of this regeneration has been the production of ways of life that have allowed the wealth and national diversity of a multi-secular culture to become attractively renewed.

The economic advantages of European unification are valid as arguments for further construction of the EU only if they can appeal to a cultural power of attraction extending far beyond material gains alone. Threats to this form of life, and the desire to preserve it, are spurs to a vision of Europe capable of responding inventively to current challenges. In his magnificent speech of 28 May 2001, the French Prime Minister spoke of this 'European way of life' as the content of a political project:

> Till recently the efforts of the Union were concentrated on the creation of monetary and economic union. [...] But today we need a broader perspective if Europe is not to decay into a mere market, sodden by globalization. For Europe is much more than a market. It stands for a model of society that has grown historically [...] .[1]

Globalization and social solidarity

Economic globalization, whether we interpret it as no more than an intensification of long-range trends or as an abrupt shift towards a new transnational configuration of capitalism, shares with all processes of accelerated modernization some disquieting features. Rapid structural change distributes social costs more unequally, and increases status gaps between winners and losers, generally inflicting heavier burdens in the short run, and greater benefits only in the long term (Vobruba 2000). The last wave of economic globalization did not stem from any inherent evolution of the system; it was the product in large measure of successive GATT rounds – that is, of conscious political action. Democratic governments should therefore also have the chance, at least in principle, to counter the undesired social consequences of globalization by complementary social and infrastructural policies. Such policies have to cope with the needs of two different groups.

Their purpose must be to bridge the time-gap for short-run losers by investments in human capital and temporal transfers, and to offer permanent compensation to long-run losers in – for example – the form of a basic income scheme or negative income tax. Since neither group is any longer in a strong veto position, the implementation of such designs is a difficult task. For the decision on whether or not to maintain an appropriate level of *general* social welfare largely depends on the degree of support for notions of distributive justice. But normative orientations move majorities of voters only to the extent that they can make a straightforward appeal to 'strong' traditions inscribed in established political cultures. In Western Europe, or at any rate its Continental nations, this assumption is not quite unfounded. Here the political tradition of the workers' movement, the salience of Christian social doctrines and even a certain normative core of social liberalism still provide a formative background for social solidarity. In their public self-representations, Social and Christian Democratic parties in particular support inclusive systems of social security and a substantive conception of citizenship, which stresses what John Rawls calls 'the fair value' of equally distributed rights. In terms of a comparative cultural analysis, we might speak of the unique European combination of public collectivisms and private individualism. As Göran Therborn remarks:

> the European road to and through modernity has also left a certain legacy of social norms, reflecting European experiences of class and gender. [...] Collective bargaining, trade unions, public social services, the rights of women and children are all held more legitimate in Europe than in the rest of the contemporary world. They are expressed in social documents of the EU and of the Council of Europe.
>
> (Therborn 2001: 85)

But if we grant this assumption, there remains the question of why national governments should not be in a better position to pursue countervailing policies more effectively than a heavy-handed EU bureaucracy. At issue here is the extent to which intensified global competition affects the scope of action of national governments. In a recent book I argued that there has been a shift towards a 'post-national' constellation (Habermas 2000). Some counter-considerations have been adduced since then (Grande and Risse 2000). No linear relation exists, it is observed, between economic globalization and the decreasing autonomy of the national state; nor is there always an inverse relation between levels of social welfare and employment. Independently of growing global pressures from without, the state has anyway had to learn to play a less dominant role *within national arenas*, in its interactions with powerful social agents (Esser 1999). National governments may be compelled to lower taxes on capital under the pressure of international competition, but they still seem to enjoy a range of options in policy areas that have an immediate impact on interdependent rates of unemployment and levels of social welfare (Scharpf 2000).

Normative appeals

Such arguments do not undermine, however, the general thesis that national governments, whatever their internal profiles, are increasingly entangled in transnational networks, and thereby become ever more dependent on *asymmetrically negotiated* outcomes. Whatever social policies they choose, they must adapt to constraints imposed by de-regulated markets – in particular, global financial markets. That means lower taxes and fiscal limits which compel them to accept increasing inequalities in the distribution of the gross national product.[2] The question therefore is: can any of our small or medium, *entangled and accommodating* nation-states preserve a separate capacity to escape enforced assimilation to the social model now imposed by the predominant global economic regime? This model is informed by an anthropological image of 'man' as rational chooser and entrepreneur, exploiting his or her own labour-power; by a moral view of society that accepts growing cleavages and exclusions; and by a political doctrine that trades a shrinking scope of democracy for freedoms of the market. These are the building blocks of a neo-liberal vision that does not sit well with the kind of normative self-understanding so far prevalent across Europe as a whole.

This diagnosis suggests a normatively loaded, perhaps a 'social democratic', reading of the economic justification for the European project. It might be objected that any such partisan view must divide the political spectrum along ideological lines. But in the absence of a stronger motivation, this may be necessary to mobilize public debate. As a strategy, it is innocent in so far as its success would at best be a procedural outcome – the creation of a more encompassing political framework. A European constitution would enhance the capacity of the Member States of the Union to act jointly, without prejudicing the particular course and content of what policies it might adopt. It would constitute a necessary, not a sufficient condition for the kind of policies some of us are inclined to advocate. To the extent that European nations seek a certain re-regulation of the global economy, to counterbalance its undesired economic, social and cultural consequences, they have a reason for building a stronger Union with greater international influence. Mario Telò and Paul Magnette express the hope that

> Europe will develop an open regionalism that strikes an innovative balance between protectionism and free trade, social regulation and openness. The European Union is now being challenged to develop a better balance between deregulation and re-regulation than national rules have been able to achieve. [...] The Union may be seen as a laboratory in which Europeans are striving to implement the values of justice and solidarity in the context of an increasing global economy.
>
> (Telò and Magnette 2001: 85)

With a view to the future of a highly stratified world society, we Europeans have a legitimate interest in getting our voice heard in an international concert that is at present dominated by a vision quite different from ours.

This would be a way of giving a normative appeal to the European project for those who take a critical view of the impact of economic globalization on nation-states. But even neo-liberals opposed to political goals of this kind must heed other considerations. For further reasons to move European integration forward lie in the uneasy effects of previous decisions that are now irreversible. There is first the need for a reform of EU institutions imposed by the contradiction between the limited capacity of the European Council to reach agreements among diverging Member States, and the political decision to admit several new and even less homogeneous members. The enlargement of the EU will increase the complexity of interests in need of coordination, which cannot be achieved without further integration or 'deepening' of the Union. The EU has set schedules for enlargement that put it under a self-imposed pressure for reform, but reform remains in a deadlock that the Treaty of Nice has not resolved. To date the problem of enlargement has failed to act as a lever for the solution of the more severe *structural* problems that emerge (i) from an asymmetry between a rather dense horizontal integration through markets and the rather loose vertical integration of competing national governments, and (ii) from a corresponding deficit in the democratic legitimation of EU decisions.

Positive coordination

So far, national governments have retained most of their competencies for cultural, economic and social policies, while they have transferred their monetary sovereignty to an independent and supposedly non-political institution, the European Central Bank. They have thereby renounced an important means of state intervention. As monetary union completes the process of economic integration, the need for harmonization of major public policies increases. National governments, resting as they do on different schemes of taxation, social policy regimes, neo-corporatist arrangements, remain entrenched in distinct legal and political traditions. They therefore tend to respond differently to the same stimuli, and the interactive effects of their disparate policies can produce mutually counterproductive backlashes. (The uncoordinated reactions of neighbouring governments to protests against the sudden rise in oil prices in 2000 provide a harmless case in point.) National governments still compete with one another in pursuit of the most promising adaptation of their welfare regimes to fiscal constraints imposed by the 'evaluation' of global financial markets. At the same time they face the challenge to agree on minimal social standards – steps in the direction of a 'social union', as envisaged by Delors, to promote a European-wide convergence in levels of provision and benefit.

Yet these discrepancies between an advanced economic and a retarded political integration could be overcome by the construction of higher-order political agencies, capable of 'catching up' with the pressures of de-regulated markets. From this perspective, the European project can be seen as a common attempt by the national governments to recover in Brussels something of the capacity for intervention that they have lost at home. This is at any rate the view of Lionel Jospin, who has called for common economic management of the Euro-zone, and for the long-run harmonization of corporation taxes within it. Such a move would also meet another well-known problem. The so-called 'democratic deficit' of European authorities, in particular of the Commission, is a source of growing dissatisfaction within the broader population – not only of the smaller states like Ireland or Denmark, or countries that have temporarily rejected entry into the Union like Norway or Switzerland. So far, the Commission has mainly pushed market-enhancement policies that require only 'negative coordination', which means that national governments are expected to refrain from doing things. Beyond this threshold, the present kind of indirect legitimation through national governments is no longer sufficient.

Regulatory policies with a widely perceived *redistributive impact* would require 'positive coordination' on both the output side – that is, implementation – and the input side – that is, legitimation – of a quite different kind. At present, legitimacy flows more or less through the channels of democratic institutions and procedures within each nation-state. This level of legitimation is appropriate for intergovernmental negotiations and treaties. But it falls short of what is needed for the kind of supranational and transnational decision-making that has long since developed within the institutional framework of the Union and its huge network of committees. It is estimated that European directives already affect up to 70 per cent of the regulations of national agencies. But they lack any serious exposure to a timely and careful public opinion or will-formation in those national arenas that are today alone accessible to holders of a European passport.

The opacity of decision-making processes at the European level, and the lack of opportunity for any participation in them, cause mutual distrust among citizens. Claus Offe has described the issues that stir fears within, and arouse rivalries between, different nations – concerns over fiscal redistribution, over immigration from and investment flows to other states, over the social and economic consequences of intensified competition between countries with different levels of productivity, and so forth. Though himself a sceptical observer, he suggests 'state-building' as the solution – a European state-building which does not reproduce the template of the nation-state – and remarks that

> the agency that will eventually realize a regime of 'organized civility' governing the entire European space [...] will have to conform to two criteria that all European states have now come to take as the standards of acceptable political rule: legitimacy and efficacy.

> (Offe 2000: 13)

Civic nations

So much for the reasons why we should support and promote the project of a European constitution in the first place. But does Europe in its present shape meet the conditions necessary for the realization of such a design – that is: for the establishment, not simply of a confederation, but a federation of nation-states? We may address first the familiar objections of the Eurosceptics, and then deal more specifically with some of the prerequisites for a Union that would assume at least some qualities of a state.

Eurosceptics reject a shift in the basis of legitimation of the Union from international treaties to a European constitution with the argument, 'there is as yet no European people' (see Böckenförde 1997; see also Grimm, Chapter 5 in this book). According to this view, what is missing is the very subject of a constituent process, the collective singular of 'a people' capable of defining itself as a democratic nation. I have criticized this 'no-demos' thesis on both conceptual and empirical grounds (Habermas 1998: 129–54). A nation of citizens must not be confused with a community of fate shaped by common descent, language and history. This confusion fails to capture the voluntaristic character of a civic nation, the collective identity of which exists neither independent of nor prior to the democratic process from which it springs. Such a civic, as opposed to ethnic, conception of 'the nation' reflects both the actual historical trajectory of the European nation-states and the fact that democratic citizenship establishes an abstract, legally mediated solidarity between strangers.

Historically, national consciousness as the first modern form of social integration was fostered by new forms of communication, the development of which was indeed *facilitated* by the stabilizing contexts of traditional communities. The fact that modern democracy and the nation-state have developed in tandem, however, does not indicate a priority of the latter over the former. It rather reveals a *circular process* in the course of which democracy and the nation-state stabilized each other. Both have jointly produced the striking innovation of a civic solidarity that provides the cement of national societies. National consciousness emerged as much from the mass communication of formally educated readers as from the mobilization of enfranchised voters and drafted soldiers. It has been shaped as much by the intellectual construction of national histories as by the discourse of competing parties, struggling for political power.

There are two lessons to be learnt from the history of the European nation-states. If the emergence of national consciousness involved a painful process of abstraction, leading from local and dynastic identities to national and democratic ones, why, firstly, should this generation of a highly artificial kind of civic solidarity – a 'solidarity among strangers' – be doomed to come to a final halt just at the borders of our classical nation-states? And secondly: the artificial conditions in which national consciousness came into existence recall the empirical circumstances necessary for an extension of that process of identity formation beyond national boundaries. These are: the emergence of a European civil society; the construction of a European-wide public sphere; and the shaping of a political culture that can be shared by all European citizens.

A catalytic constitution

These functional prerequisites of a democratically constituted European Union project points of convergence between rather complex processes. We should not forget, however, that this convergence in turn depends on the catalytic effect of a constitution. This would have to begin with a referendum, arousing a Europe-wide debate – the making of such a constitution representing in itself a unique opportunity of transnational communication, with the potential for a self-fulfilling prophecy. Europe has to apply to itself, as a whole, 'the logic of the circular creation of state and society that shaped the modern history of European countries' (Offe 2000: 13).

A European constitution would not only make manifest the shift in powers that has already taken place. It would also release and foster further shifts. Once the European Union had gained financial autonomy, the Commission had assumed the functions of a government and the Council had become something like a second chamber, the European Parliament would attract more attention for the better-staged and more visible exercise of competencies which are already remarkable. Full budgetary powers would not be necessary in the begin-ning. The focus of politics would move to some extent from national capitals to the European centres – not just through the activities of lobbyists and business organizations, which have quite a strong presence in Brussels already, but through those of political parties, labour unions, civic or cultural associations, public interest groups, social movements and 'pressure from the street' – protests no longer merely by farmers or truck-drivers, but arising from the initiatives of citizens at large. Relevant interests formed along lines of political ideology, economic sector, occupational position, social class, religion, ethnicity and gender would moreover fuse *across national* boundaries (Schmitter 1996). The perceived transnational overlap of parallel interests would give rise to cross-boundary networks and a properly European party system, displacing territorial by functional principles of organization.

Creating a public sphere

There will be no remedy for the legitimation deficit, however, without a European-wide public sphere – a network that gives citizens of all Member States an equal opportunity to take part in an encompassing process of focused political communi-cation. Democratic legitimation requires mutual contact between, on the one hand, institutionalized deliberation and decision-making within parliaments, courts and administrative bodies and, on the other, an inclusive process of informal mass communication. The function of the communicational infrastructure of a demo-cratic public sphere is to turn relevant societal problems into topics of concern, and to allow the general public to relate, at the same time, to the same topics, by taking an affirmative or negative stand on news and opinions. Over time, these implicit attitudes coagulate to constitute public opinion, even though most citizens do not send public messages beyond voting or non-voting. So far, however, the necessary infrastructure for a wide-ranging generation of diverse public opinions exists only within the confines of nation-states.

A European-wide public sphere must not be imagined as the projection of a familiar design from the national onto the European level. It will rather emerge from the mutual opening of existing national universes to one another, yielding to an interpenetration of mutually translated national communications. There is no need for a stratified public communication, each layer of which would correspond, one by one, to a different 'floor' of the multilevel political system. The agenda of European institutions will be included in each of a plurality of national publics, if these are inter-related in the right way.

The pressing question 'Can the European Union become a sphere of publics?'[3] is often answered from a supranational rather than a transnational perspective. If we look for monolingual (usually English-speaking) media with multinational audiences penetrating national borders we find a business elite reading the *Financial Times* and the *Economist,* or a political elite reading the *International Herald Tribune* with a digest of the *Frankfurter Allgemeine Zeitung* – which means: nothing specifically European. This is not a promising model for the audiovisual communications of a general public, even for cross-boundary communication via print media. In the audio-visual sector, the bilingual, French–German television channel Arte is already more plausible, though still aimed at a notionally supranational public. A real advance would be for national media to cover the substance of relevant controversies in the other countries, so that all the national public opinions converged on the same range of contributions to the same set of issues, regardless of their origin. This is what happens temporarily – if only for a few days – before and after the summits of the European Council, when the heads of the Member States come together and deal with issues of equal perceived relevance for citizens across Europe. The fact that these multiple, horizontal flows of communication have to pass through the filters of translation does not reduce their essential significance.

Within the present Union of fifteen members there are thirteen different, officially recognized languages. This constitutes at first glance an embarrassing obstacle to the formation of a shared polity for all. The official multilingualism of EU institutions is necessary for the mutual recognition of the equal worth and integrity of all national cultures. However, under the veil of this legal guarantee it becomes all the easier to use English as a working language at face-to-face level, wherever the parties lack another common idiom (Kraus 2000a, 2000b). This is in fact what now happens anyway, in ever wider circles. Small countries like the Netherlands, Denmark, Norway or Sweden provide good examples of the capacity of formal education in schools to spread English as a second 'first' language, across their whole populations.[4]

Sharing a political culture

The generation of a European public opinion depends on the vital inputs of actors within a European civil society. At the same time, a European-wide public sphere needs to be embedded in a political culture shared by all. This widely perceived requirement has stimulated a troubled discourse among intellectuals, since it has been difficult to separate the question 'What is Europe?' from the fact that the achievements of European culture – which did not, in fact, seriously reflect upon its own nature and origin until the eighteenth or nineteenth centuries – have been diffused across the globe (den Boer 1998). The main religion in Europe, Christianity, obeyed its missionary imperative and expanded all over the world. The global spread of modern science and technology, of Roman law and the Napoleonic Code, of human rights, democracy and the nation-state started from Europe as well. Let me therefore mention two more specific experiences of our countries that resonate still in the rather remarkable responses they have evoked. For Europe has, more than any other culture, faced and overcome structural conflicts, sharp confrontations and lasting tensions, in the social as well as in the temporal dimension.

In the social dimension, modern Europe has developed institutional arrangements for the productive resolution of intellectual, social and political conflicts. In the course of painful, if not fatal, struggles, it has learnt how to cope with deep cleavages, schisms and rivalries between secular and ecclesiastical powers, city and countryside, faith and knowledge, and how to get along with endemic conflicts between militant religious confessions and belligerent states. In the temporal dimension, modern Europe has institutionalized a comprehensive spectrum of competing conservative, liberal and socialist interpretations of capitalist modernization, in an ideological system of political parties. In the course of a heroic intellectual appropriation of a rich Jewish and Greek, Roman and Christian heritage, Europe has thus learnt a sensitive attitude and a balanced response, both to the deplorable losses incurred by the disintegration of a traditional past and to the promise of future benefits from the 'creative destruction' of present productivity.

These are dispositions that act as a spur to critical reflection on our own blind-spots, and to a de-centring of selective perspectives. They are not in contradiction with the well-taken – and only too deserved – critique of our aggressive colonial and Eurocratic past; the critique of Eurocentrism itself emerges from a continuing self-criticism. The secularization of the egalitarian and individualist universalism that informs our normative self-understanding is not the least among the achievements of modern Europe.

The fact that the death penalty is still practised elsewhere – even in the United States – reminds us of some specific features of our heritage:

> The Council of Europe with the European Convention of Human Rights, and its European Social Charter, have transformed Europe into an area of human rights, more specific and more binding than in any other area of the world. [...] The clear and general European support for International Crimes Tribunal, again in contrast to US fears, is also in the same line.
>
> (Therborn 2001: 49ff.)

What forms the common core of a European identity is the character of the painful learning process it has gone through, as much as its results. It is the lasting memory of nationalist excess and moral abyss that lends to our present commitments the quality of a peculiar achievement. This historical background should ease the transition to a post-national democracy based on the mutual recognition of the differences between strong and proud national cultures. Neither 'assimilation' nor 'coexistence' – in the sense of a pale *modus vivendi* – is an appropriate term for our history of learning how to construct new and ever more sophisticated forms of a 'solidarity among strangers'. Today, moreover, the European nation-states are being brought together by the challenges which they all face equally. All are in the process of becoming countries of immigration and multicultural societies. All are exposed to an economic and cultural globalization that awakes memories of a shared history of conflict and reconciliation – and of a comparatively low threshold of tolerance towards exclusion.

This new awareness of what Europeans have in common has found an admirable expression in the EU Charter of Basic Rights. The members of the 'Convention', as it is called, reached agreement on this document within a remarkably short space of time. Even though the European Council in Nice only 'proclaimed' and did not adopt in binding fashion its catalogue of basic rights, the Charter will exert a decisive influence on the European Court of Justice. Thus far the Court has been primarily concerned with the implications of the 'four freedoms' of market participation – free movement of persons, goods, services and capital. The Charter goes beyond this limited view, articulating a social vision of the European project (Däubler 2000). It also shows what Europeans link together normatively. Responding to recent developments in biotechnology, Article 3 specifies each person's right to his or her physical and mental integrity, and prohibits any practice of positive eugenics or the reproductive cloning of human organisms.

Designing a framework

Taking it as a premise that a European constitution is both feasible and desirable, let me finish with a few remarks on some problems to do with its design. Joschka Fischer has outlined the challenge we face – how to find the right combination of a 'Europe of nation-states' with a 'Europe of citizens' (Fischer 2000). He has also mentioned some more or less conventional alternatives for strengthening the European Parliament, establishing an effective and legitimate executive, and creating a democratically accountable Court of Justice.[5] These proposals do not exhaust the range of imaginative options, but Fischer rightly focuses on the core problem of a federation of nation-states that need to preserve their integrity by occupying a much more influential position than the constituent elements of a federal state normally do.[6] The intergovernmental element of negotiation between former nation-states will remain strong. Compared with the presidential regime of the USA, a European Union of nation-states would have to display the following general features:

- a Parliament that would resemble the Congress in some respects (a similar division of powers and, compared with the European parliamentary systems, relatively weak political parties);

- a legislative 'chamber of nations' that would have more competencies than the American Senate, and a Commission that would be much less powerful than the White House (thus splitting the classical functions of a strong Presidency between the two);
- a European Court that would be as influential as the Supreme Court for similar reasons (the regulatory complexity of an enlarged and socially diversified Union would require detailed interpretation of a principled constitution, cutting short the jungle of existing treaties).[7]

In this context a few remarks may be in place.

1   The political substance of a European constitution would consist of a definite answer to the issue of the territorial boundaries of the Union, and a not-too-definite answer to the question of how competences are to be distributed between federal and national institutions. It is important to settle soon the thorny problem of which countries will finally belong to, and which are to be excluded from, the Union; the determination of frontiers is compatible with a 'variable geometry' that would facilitate the process. For the time being, we might differentiate between a centre and a periphery, depending on the pace and degree of integration. The issue of a 'Europe of different speeds' touches on the problem of a provisional regulation of competences which leaves some room for experiments.

   The embattled delimitation of what is to be reserved for executive authorities, what is up for co-legislation and what remains in the competence of national legislatures must certainly be settled in broad outline from the beginning. But this part of the organizational nucleus of the constitution should be kept open for revisions at fixed dates, so that we can learn from unanticipated consequences within a stable framework. Such a temporalization of essential clauses squares with the idea of a democratic constitution as an ever more exhaustive realization of a system of basic rights under changing historical circumstances.[8]

2   'Subsidiarity' is the functional principle that meets the needs of the diverse and territorially distinct units of a federation. But the wider the differences – in size of territory and population, economic weight and level of development, political power and cultural form of life or collective identity – between these constituent units, the greater the danger that majority decisions at the higher instances will violate the principles of equal protection and mutual recognition of diversity. Structural minorities limit the range of valid majority decisions. In such situations, legitimacy can only be secured on the condition that some areas are reserved for consensual negotiations. As we know from countries like Switzerland or the Netherlands, however, consensual procedures suffer from a lack of transparency. Here European-wide referenda would give citizens broader opportunities and more effective means to participate in the shaping of policies (Grande 1996, 2000).

3   Some minor suggestions are worth consideration. It would help to overcome the legitimation deficit, and to strengthen the connections between the federal legislature and national arenas, either if certain members of the European Parliament at the same time held seats in their respective national parliaments, or if the largely neglected Conference of European Affairs Committee (which has met twice a year since 1989) could reanimate horizontal debate between national parliaments and so help to prompt a re-parliamentarization of European politics (Blichner 2000). Are there alternative modes of legitimation too? The approach labelled 'comitology' attributes legitimating merits to the deliberative politics of the great number of committees working in support of the Commission (Joerges and Everson 2000). But here there is a deficit on the output as well as input side, since federal legislation is implemented only through national, regional and local authorities. To meet this problem, Ingo Pernice has suggested transforming the present Committee of Regions into a chamber that would give sub-national state actors a stronger influence on EU policies, and thereby facilitate the enforcement of European law on the ground (Pernice 1999).[9]

The politics of unification

For European unification to move forward, however, there still remains a vacant space which would have to be filled by the political will of competent actors. The overwhelming majority of the population that is currently resistant or hesitant can only be won for Europe if the project is extricated from the pallid abstraction of technocratic administrative discourse: in other words, if it is politicized. Intellectuals have not picked up this ball. Still less have politicians wanted to burn their fingers with such an unpopular topic. The fillip given to a constitutional debate by Fischer's speech at Humboldt University (Fischer 2000 – see above; see also Joerges *et al.* 2000), prompting Chirac and Prodi, Rau and Schroeder to react with their own suggestions, is all the more noteworthy. But it is Jospin who has pointed out that no reform of procedures and institutions can succeed before the content of the political project behind it becomes clearer.

The markedly unilateral orientation of the Bush Administration can be regarded as an opportunity for the EU to define a more distinctive foreign and security policy towards the conflicts in the Middle East and the Balkans, and relations with Russia and China. Differences that are coming more into the open in environmental, military and juridical fields contribute to a silent strengthening of European identity. Still more important is the question of what role Europe wishes to play in the Security Council and, above all, in world economic institutions. Contrasting justifications of humanitarian intervention, not to speak of basic economic outlooks, divide the founder states of the EU from Great Britain and Scandinavia. But it is better to bring these smouldering conflicts out into the open than to let the EU splinter over dilemmas that remain unresolved. In any case, a Europe of two or three speeds is preferable to one that breaks up or crumbles away.

In his speech of 28 May 2001, Jospin gave an unmistakeable hint as to what the 'mechanism for strengthened cooperation' agreed at Nice might mean:

> Naturally it could be applied to the coordination of economic policy in the Euro-zone, but also in fields like health and military procurements. With this kind of cooperation, a group of states that has always been indispensable could once again give new impetus to the construction of Europe.

A sober calculation of interests might well have led the French and German governments to seize the initiative again. The *International Herald Tribune* (12 June 2001) dryly commented: 'In the last resort, the French will be prepared to pay a certain price for Berlin not becoming the capital of Europe.' In line with the policies of Genscher and Fischer, Germans would be well advised to agree. Since diplomacy is at an impasse, open political controversy over the direction in which the EU should develop can only be of benefit. The constitutional–legal dispute between 'federalists' and 'sovereignists' masks a substantive dispute between those like Jospin, who regard harmonization of important national policies as urgent, and those like Schroeder, who would like a façade of tailormade central institutions deprived of all significant fiscal powers. All sides, however, can agree that delimitation of the competences of federal, national and regional levels is the core political issue to be settled by any European constitution.

Notes

This chapter was originally published in *New Left Review*, 11, 2001: 5–26.

1 Speech to the Foreign Press Association, Paris, 28 May 2001.
2 For Germany, see Hauser and Becker 1999.
3 This is the title of an informative empirical analysis by Philip Schlesinger and Deirdre Kevin (2000).
4 Kraus (2000b) cites a poll finding that even a majority of the German-speaking Swiss prefer English to the two other national languages for communication across linguistic borders.
5 Fischer offers an option between the models of the US Senate and the German Bundestag for the second chamber, and a choice between two constructions, one developed from the European Council of Ministers, and the other resembling the present Council, but with a directly elected president, for the executive.
6 In this respect Article 3 of the new Swiss Constitution is interesting, in that it applies the principle of subsidiarity to yield a rather strong position to the constitutive units: 'The cantons are sovereign, so long as their sovereignty suffers no restriction from the federal constitution; they exercise all rights that are not transferred to the confederation.'
7 See the study for a reorganization of the treaties: European University Institute 2000a, available, with companion texts, at:
   www.iue.it/RSCAS/Research/Institutions/ EuropeanTreaties.shtml.
8 See my argument in Habermas 1996, ch. 9.
9 For another conception, see Rousseau 2000.

3   The EU and the right to self-government

Erik Oddvar Eriksen

> The people are the only legitimate fountain of power, and it is from them that the constitutional charter, under which several branches of government hold their power, is derived.
>
> (Federalist Papers, No. 49 [Madison])[1]

The EU is in the midst of a constitution-making process, namely in a process of specifying the rights and obligations of the citizens of the Union. There are long traditions of rights entrenchment to build on and there are well-developed systems with legal personalities and adjudicatory machinery. The initiative taken to incorporate a Charter of Fundamental Rights into the new Treaty of the EU indicates that a new order is underway. At the December 2000 Summit in Nice the Charter was solemnly proclaimed. The eventual incorporation into the Treaties has been postponed until 2004.

The Charter is a step in the process of constitutionalizing the EU. It is a constitution-making vehicle (Eriksen *et al.* 2003). This process of constitutional-ization is no doubt driven forward by the particular developments within the EU pertaining to closer integration, and given impetus by the particularly vexing challenge of enlargement. The development interacts with and reinforces the European Court of Justice's own embrace of constitutional principles and prac-tices from the constitutional arrangements of the Member States. This process was taken a firm step forward by establishing the Convention on the Future of Europe (2002), which deemed itself a constitutional convention. It was originally initiated by Declaration 23 annexed to the Nice Treaty and put into motion by the Laeken Declaration (2001). A proposal for a Constitutional Treaty was submitted to the Council on 20 June 2003, in which the Charter of Fundamental Rights is incorporated as Part Two.

The Convention on the Future of Europe was spurred by the Charter Convention, which it largely duplicated in terms of its composition: it was made up of a majority of parliamentarians. Its deliberations were public, and so were the relevant documents.[2] It organized links to civil society organizations and was open to inputs and submissions from civil society actors. However, the conven-tion did not really comply with democratic criteria, as it was not mandated by the people through a popular vote nor are its proposals as of yet subjected to a genuine public debate. Thus there is a 'constitution-making process' going on and citizens have been assigned rights but they have not given these rights to themselves. Moreover, owing to the establishment of the internal market, citizens have already obtained a whole range of rights. For example, as employees in foreign countries they have the rights to the same kind of social security rights as native residents. Citizens can now sue their own government if it does not comply with Community law. The EU establishes *post-national rights*, including fundamental rights of a constitutional kind. But as its citizens have not given themselves these rights, what kind of validity can they possibly possess?

Judge-made law is undemocratic. A proper constitution should not, according to democratic criteria, be made unless it has been mandated by the people and been subjected to public debate and ratified through proper legislative processes subjected to judicial review. In this chapter I assess the constitution-making process with emphasis on the incorporated Charter of Fundamental Rights. Is the Charter a means to reduce the democratic deficit even if it resonates badly with the idea of people-made law? What is the connection between rights and democracy in a cosmopolitan perspective?

I proceed by outlining the democratic problem of the Union, before addressing the Charter and its politico-legal implications – in section three. The question is why a constitutionalized bill of rights is needed to bolster post-national democracy. Rights require democratic enactment in order to be legitimate. I therefore, in the fourth section of this chapter, delineate the basic democratic assessment criteria: congruence and accountability. In the fifth section, before concluding the chapter, I address the internal relationship between rights and democracy in a post-national order.

The democratic deficit

The EU is a mix of intergovernmental, supranational and transnational elements. It is a construction that is demanding both in descriptive and normative terms. It is a complex network of institutions for regulating common affairs, but it is not unitary and self-contained as a political unit. It is an entity with strong supranational elements, as evidenced in the supranational character of the legal structure, which is supported and enhanced in particular by the European Court of Justice (ECJ). As I will return to, it has in its rulings long asserted the principles of supremacy and direct effect. Those principles have informed the actual operations of the EU and its legal development. Based on the Treaties, the ECJ has been a firm interpreter and developer of Community law. Over time, Community law has developed into a pseudo-constitutional system based on a set of fundamental principles. It has emerged into a body of law which is autonomous of, separate from and superior to Member State law. The integration process is based on non-arbitrary norm-enforcement in which the same obligations are conferred upon all. This has unifying consequences as law is a medium for stabilizing behavioural expectations. It connects non-compliance with foreseeable sanctions and subjects all to the same norms and obligations. But the law is not made in a very democratic manner, as *the Council of Ministers*, which is the most powerful EU institution, is made up of representatives from the Member States. It legislates on behalf of the Union (together with the European Parliament) and enjoys near exclusive executive competences within pillars II (common foreign and security policy) and III (justice and home affairs). It is the co-legislator (with the European Parliament) in pillar I (European Communities) and decides some things by unanimity and some by qualified majority vote. It has a rotating presidency lasting for six months. *The European Council* is arguably the most important of the EU's five major institutions as it convenes heads of state and the government for short summit meetings. It meets at least twice a year with Commission representatives present.

In contrast to the intergovernmental Council, *the European Parliament* is a supranational institution. It is directly elected by the citizens of the Member States but has not until recently had much legislative power. Nor has it had much authority to hold the executive accountable. However, the Treaty of Amsterdam (1997) increased its role, as did the Maastricht Treaty (1992). The Parliament's powers vis-à-vis the European Commission have been enhanced. The system now resembles the structure of well-known federal states with two legislative chambers where a single Council for legislative affairs is the equivalent of a Senate or Bundesrat, and the Parliament a Congress (or the House of Commons). However, as there are now seven different procedures for the European Parliament's participation in Council decisions, there is a great need for simplification of procedures, and of the Union's institutions. Analysts and decision-makers recognize also the need for clarifying the competencies and the powers of the institutions. The Nice Treaty (2000) added complexity by approving a qualified majority system which privileged the larger states. It was imposed in order to safeguard their ability to block decisions in an enlarged Union. Once again an IGC failed to make necessary decisions. The really hard decisions were postponed.

The European Commission has executive functions – within pillar I – and is endowed with the right of initiative, which includes the right to issue legislative proposals. In addition, there are hundreds of committees, which were originally established to control delegation of powers from the Council to the Commission. They are involved in the process of shaping and adopting statutory acts within the confines of the delegated authority of the Commission. Initially it covered such areas as agriculture, trade and customs policies. It now also comprises amongst others research and development, environmental affairs and telecommunications.

Such a system blurs the constitutional distinction between legislative and executive powers, between politics and administration. It is not democratically accountable, and control by the European Parliament is a recurring theme. Consequently, even if the institutional make-up of the Union resembles the separation of powers, akin to the separation of power in a nation-state, there are profound differences and problems. Hence, the so-called *democratic deficit*, which is due to the lack of a truly European public sphere, inadequate entrenchment of citizens' rights, executive dominance, judicial activism, lack of Europeanized political parties, weak representation and representativeness of the system. In the indirectly elected Council, common affairs are conducted according to diplomatic and intergovernmental bargaining modes of decision-making, behind closed doors, while the Parliament lacks power, is remote and has low voter turnout. In the areas in which it does co-decide legislation, it does not have the right of initiative and does not even have the last legislative word.[3]

To summarize, the democratic problems of the Union are due to the following deficiencies:

- European citizens do not have proper rights, nor do they have the ability, to make the laws that affect them.
- The final legislative power lays with the Council of Ministers, a body whose democratic representativeness is clearly inadequate, in that the ministers are accountable to their state only and not to all of Europe's citizens.
- The European Parliament is a representative body, but one with circumscribed legislative powers and prerogatives.
- There are also no truly European wide political parties that in organizational terms reach down into the national arenas.
- The EU's 'constitution' is not based on a coherent and consistent set of democratic principles, and the procedures for constitutional change are democratically deficient in that each Member State is left with a veto.

Consequently democratic reforms are called for. One should, however, recall that the EU itself for a long time now has committed itself to the norms of the democratic *Rechtsstaat*. The Maastricht Treaty represented the most important single change here in that it laid down the basic principles for democracy in the Union. These principles were further amplified in the Amsterdam Treaty, in terms of democracy, freedom, the rule of law, social policy, solidarity and cohesion. The terms indicate that the evaluative standards, as expressed in official submissions to the process, have become more explicitly linked to democratic legitimacy. There is thus not only a gap between democratic principles and actual practice, but also a gap between the self-proclaimed aims and principles of the Treaties and the actual situation in the Union. Is the proposed Charter of Fundamental Rights a means to close this gap? Several measures are required in order to mend the democratic deficit of the Union. The question is whether a Charter in the form of a constitutionalized bill of rights enhances the democratic quality of the system.

Chartering Europe

All articles on the rights of EU citizens in the Treaty of the Union have now been collected in one document of 54 articles, inspired by the Convention for the Protection of Human Rights and Fundamental Freedoms, also known as the European Convention on Human Rights (ECHR), by the Social Charters adopted by the Council of Europe, by the common constitutional traditions of the Member States and by the Community and case law of the ECJ.

A citizens' based polity

The Charter adds to the fundamental rights of Union citizens by expressing the principles of humanism and democracy in the preamble. The Charter contains provisions on civil, political, social and economic rights. Put together, these are intended to ensure the dignity of the person, to safeguard his or her essential freedoms, to provide a European citizenship, to ensure equality, to foster solidarity, and to establish justice. The numbers of rights that are listed are comprehensive. They range from classical civil rights to social and economic rights. In addition to provisions which most charters and bills of rights hold, and which pertain to such clauses as the right to life, security and dignity, there are numerous clauses that seek to respond directly to contemporary issues and challenges. For instance, there are clauses on protection of personal data (Article 8), freedom of research (Article 13), protection of cultural diversity (Article 22), protection of children (Article 24), right to collective bargaining (Article 28) and protection of the environment (Article 37). The Charter prohibits eugenic practices, the trafficking of human bodies and body parts, the reproductive cloning of the human organism, and it forbids the death penalty. The latter is a forceful reminder of the disasters that originally initiated the EU, and symbolizes its ethical distinctiveness and value base. The rights in the Charter are of a diverse nature, and it is not always clear what they actually stand for.[4] In the final section of the preamble a distinction between 'rights, freedoms and principles' is drawn which is hard to uphold. Some are pure rights which are legally binding of the powers, others are principles or policy clauses, and the Charter also contains precepts that designate responsibilities with no connection to rights at all. This may be confusing (cf. Llorente 2003: 420). In the categorization of the Charter's rights, Menéndez (2003b: 184) distinguishes between fundamental *rights proper*, *ordinary rights* and *policy clauses*.

Despite ambiguities, the Charter marks the *EU as a polity* with extended domains of competencies, and as an entity in need of legal constraints. The EU is consequently not merely conceived of as an instrument for solving the problems of the Member States or as a common market. This is consistent with the fact that the Union clearly has moved beyond an intergovernmental organization, which is evidenced in the supranational character of the legal structure. The case law of the ECJ rendered explicit the latent principles of the doctrines of Supremacy (1964) and Direct effect (1962, 1974). The former doctrine states that, in case of disputes between a national norm and an EC legal norm, the national norm must give way; and the latter doctrine says that under certain conditions EC norms (Treaty law and secondary legislation) confer rights on citizens that must be protected in national courts.[5]

> Direct effect implies supremacy, but the latter has wider significance, since all Community law, irrespective of its direct applicability, is supreme over national law, constitutional law included.
>
> (Baquero Cruz 2002: 94)

Although their precise status in relation to national constitutional orders remains unclear, due to legal disagreement over the actual primacy of Community law,[6] there is a hierarchy of legal sources placing Community law above national law. In the draft of the new constitution of June 2003, the following wording has been agreed upon:

> Article 1–10: Union Law

> 1.   The constitution, and law adopted by the Union's Institutions in exercising competences conferred on it, shall have primacy over the law of the Member States.

> 2.   Member States shall take all appropriate measures, general or particular, to ensure fulfillment of the obligations flowing from the Constitution or resulting from the Union Institutions' acts.
>
> (CONV 850/03)

Even though the Member States are the contracting partners so that a new 'constitution' has to be accepted by an IGC, the EU is increasingly taking the shape of a polity in its own right. In many regards the EU is a political entity performing many of the functions of the nation-state. The Commission, the European Parliament and the ECJ form a new supranational power-wielding regime with far-reaching consequences for the ordinary man and woman in Europe. The EU allocates resources throughout Europe; it affects the distributive pattern and shifts the balance of goods and burdens between states, regions and groups. Its law-making affects the interests and values of European citizens and the identities of the Member States, but the power of the Union is not balanced by a proper set of enforceable citizens' rights:

> The Treaties lack a catalogue of fundamental rights bringing the relations between the Community and the natural and legal persons subject to it under the guiding principles of freedom and equality.
>
> (Grimm, Chapter 5 below)

The interests and values of citizens are not properly protected by the system in place; they need to be safeguarded by a system of entrenched rights.

Direct legitimacy

The Charter denotes the EU as an entity built upon the individual, his or her freedom and well-being, with rights that should not be outweighed by collective welfare claims or national concerns. The citizens of Europe have now, in principle, achieved rights over and above their resident states. Further, the proposed Charter can be read as one of the most explicit statements, if not *the* most explicit statement, on the EU's commitment to direct legitimacy that has ever been produced in the EU. The institutions and rights provided to citizens by the EU in themselves are to provide the necessary basis for legitimate government. It speaks to the claim that the EU is a full-blown polity.

> Protection of fundamental rights is a founding principle of the Union and an indispensable prerequisite for legitimacy.
>
> (European Council 1999)

As mentioned in the introduction, in reality the Charter is a clear manifestation of the EU as a political entity and not a market. The four market freedoms are merely listed as policy goals in the preamble, whereas there are a wide range of social rights listed as fundamental and ordinary rights in the body of the text. However, the Charter is not without defects. As I will return to, it does not have any direct effect with regard to the established institutional structure. Further, the Charter only applies to the actions of the EU institutions and the Member States' authorities when implementing Community law. It is not designed to replace other forms of fundamental rights protection. Article 51 (Section 2) states that the Charter does 'not establish any new power or task for the Community or the Union, or modify powers and tasks defined by the Treaties'. Section 1 states that the Charter will only be made to apply to the 'institutions and bodies of the Union' and only to the Member States 'when they are implementing Union law'. Formally it is not binding, even though it is written *as if* 'it were a binding legal text', following a proposal made by member Cisneros and endorsed by President Herzog.[7]

Even though the Charter is not as yet legally binding, '[i]n practice, [...] the legal effect of the solemn proclamation of the Charter of Fundamental Rights of the European Union will tend to be similar to that of its insertion into the Treaties on which the Union is founded' (Lenaerts and De Smitjer 2001: 298–9). The Charter reflects the well-established rights – and value-basis of the Community. The Charter 'is a legally enforceable text which underlines the importance of the rule of law in the EU and it is the ultimate proof of the focal role that EU citizens have come to play in the European integration process' (*ibid.* 300). Moreover, since it codifies existing positive law, in one sense it may be seen as already binding. It has also increased its legal bite over a short period of time as the Court of first Instance has invoked the Charter as legal authority in several judgments (cf. Menéndez 2002: 474). It has been referred to by institutional actors like the European Ombudsman and the Commission, and some Advocates-General have also pointed to the quality of the processes drafting the Charter as a special source of justification:

> I know that the Charter is not legally binding, but it is worthwhile referring to it given that it constitutes the expression, at the highest level, of a democrati- cally established political consensus on what must today be considered as the catalogue of fundamental rights guaranteed by the Community legal order.[8]

However, the European Constitutional Convention reached an agreement on 13 June 2003 that it should be incorporated in full in the future constitution of the

EU. It did not reopen the text.[9] The Charter is, however ambivalently reflective of a rights-based constitutional patriotism (Fossum 2003b: 336). It is an answer to the problem of the potential intrusive power of the EU. The Charter has merits from a normative point of view, but why did it come about? By what reasons was it sustained?

Predictability and security

The Charter enhances the *legal certainty* of the citizens of Europe as everybody can claim protection for the same interests and concerns. The principle of legal certainty is only secured in a limited sense at the Community level, however. The citizen cannot be sure what rights he or she really is entitled to. Not all the Member States, for example, have ratified all the ECHR's subsequent protocols and the ECJ has no clear and incontestable foundation on which to base its rulings. A bill of rights enhances consistent rights enforcement in the EU area. This is especially important in the pluralistic constitutional setting of the EU. As these often reflect particular traditions and customs, they potentially give rise to conflicting court rulings.

> The rights regime of the European Union is inconsistent in terms of content as well as variable in terms of implementation and levels of enforce-ment between Member States.
>
> (Duff 2000: 4–5)

The founding treaties of the European Community contained no reference to fundamental rights. However, as integration deepened, and as the Community came to have more far-reaching effects on the daily lives of citizens, the need for explicit mention of fundamental rights was realized. The European Court of Justice (ECJ) developed this idea[10] as the Community is not bound by the ECHR in the same way as the subscribing Member States. The EU is not itself a signatory to the Convention. It has been argued by many over the years that the power of the legislative and administrative bodies of the Community needs to be constrained by a set of fundamental rights, in the same way as constitutions and the ECHR constrain the authorities of the Member States. The problem was attended by the IGC leading to the Maastricht Treaty (TEU), and in what is now Article 6(2) of the Amsterdam Treaty, recognition of the concept of fundamental rights is enshrined. By this clause the EU is obliged to respect the rights guaranteed by the ECHR and deriving from the constitutional traditions of the Member States. However, the text is rather weak and imprecise. The EU Committee of the British House of Lords urged for a legally binding charter based on the ECJ as the legal authority, because '[w]ithin the framework established by the Maastricht and Amsterdam Treaties, there is greater scope than before for EU actions and policies to impinge on individual rights and freedoms' (House of Lords 2000).

Another source of the initiative of making a charter of fundamental rights is the argument that the EU, which is 'a staunch defender of human rights externally

[…] lacks a fully-fledged human rights policy' (Alston and Weiler 1999: 4).[11] A constitutionalized bill of rights provides the EU with the legal competence required to carry on being a firm promoter of human rights worldwide. It is difficult to be a champion of cosmopolitan law and urge others to institutionalize human rights when one is not prepared to do so oneself. When basic institutions are lacking in the EU with regard to human rights, it is difficult to lead by example. The ensuing document is intended to do something to remedy this deficiency. The Charter substantiates the rights mentioned in Article 6(2) of the Treaty on European Union (TEU) by spelling out the specific obligations of the institutions.

A bill of rights, even one that is not more than the codification of existing law, decreases the room for discretion of the ECJ and national courts when dealing with EC law of fundamental rights. The need for legal certainty has been accentuated by the recent development towards an actual Justice and Home Affairs policy of the EU. It is in policy fields such as migration law, border control, police cooperation, and so on, that the rights of citizens are most often threatened.[12]

A political document

Although, as Joseph Weiler contends in his contribution to this volume (Chapter 4), the Charter was not made by a specifically designated constitutional convention and thus lacks legitimacy, it is *a public document* that was made by political actors – 46 out of 66 voting members, and 26 out of 39 from the candidate countries. The deliberations were relatively open and inclusive (de Schutter 2003; Schönlau 2003). The decision to frame a Charter of Fundamental Rights was taken at the Cologne European Council (3–4 June 1999). In October 1999, at the Tampere European Council, it was decided to establish a 62-member Convention (headed by the former German President, Roman Herzog) to draft a Charter of Fundamental Rights of the European Union.[13] This is the first time that the European Parliament was represented in the same manner as the Member State governments and the national parliaments in a process of a constitutional nature.

The process resembled a constitutional one, and this new regime moves the system of human rights beyond the present one which is dominated by the courts. The Charter was made by the representatives of the citizens of the Member States. It was openly deliberated by representatives of national governments and national parliaments, the Commission and the European Parliament, and has also received inputs from non-governmental organizations.[14] To some extent it was also subjected to public debate.[15] The Charter was politically decided and so implies a *democratization of human rights politics*. From the Charter onwards, fundamental rights have not been merely judge-made. Even though the Charter was not made directly by the people or by a constitutional convention, it was made by representatives of the people and is important in order to curb the impression of, and also the actual power of, judge-made law in the EU. Democratic legitimacy is also the reason for the European Council's decision in Cologne:

> Protection of fundamental rights is a founding principle of the Union and an indispensable prerequisite for her legitimacy. [...] There appears to be a need [...] to establish a Charter of fundamental rights in order to make their over-riding importance and relevance more visible to the Union's citizens.
>
> (European Council 1999)

In general, a constitution containing a bill of rights increases transparency and comprehensibility for ordinary citizens and makes existing law liable to public scrutiny. It enhances the possibility of public reflection and democratic delibera-tion. Furthermore, as it is merely consolidating already existing rights, and as its provisions are based on the common European constitutional traditions, the burden of legitimation may be rather modest, as Menéndez contends in Chapter 7 of the present book. But a constitution requires legitimation. What are the basic democratic assessment criteria?

Congruence and accountability

Constitutions protect citizens' freedom by entrenching a host of individual rights and stating that basic rights should not be altered by simple majority vote. They are a means not only to curb the stupidity and maliciousness of popular rule, but also to institutionalize and regulate it properly.

Rights and democracy

Rights entrenchment enhances the predictability and legal security of citizens. The Charter process represents a very important development in the constitu-tionalization of the EU, viz., in forging a constitution that limits the powers of the Union. Constitutions guarantee civil and political rights, they regulate the activity of political bodies by stating rules for elections, representation and deci-sion-making, and they generally establish areas of competence, terms and qualifications. Bills of rights empower judges to protect liberty and hinder democracy by means of majority vote from crushing individual rights (Brennan 1989: 432). In this perspective the Charter is, however, found wanting. It is weakly developed with regard to citizenship rights, as a person must be a citizen of a Member State to qualify as a citizen of the Union, and also with regard to political rights. The onus is on human rights, which undoubtedly has been strengthened. The Charter has not introduced 'any concrete policy changes nor altered anything significant within the existing legal, political and constitutional framework' (de Búrca 2001: 129).

The Charter is not only limited in substantive terms, with regard to institutional reforms, but also in procedural terms. Direct participation in legislative processes is required for the system to be deemed democratic, for the people to give themselves the laws they are to obey by, and the rights they need for protecting their values and interests. The need for participatory rights and further democratization of the EU can be supported by an additional argument: in situations where rights collide, a correct interpretation of the situation is needed to choose the appropriate norm. Only the hearing of all affected parties can provide an adequately informed basis for resolving hard questions. This is so because what is right or good for *A* in one context, may be wrong or bad for *B* in another context. Rights need to be interpreted and adapted to the task environment – they need to be contextualized. Human rights, which can be correct by abstract moral standards, by the rational will of autonomous persons, require democratic legitimation and public deliberation to be correctly implemented (cf. Brunkhorst 1999; Michelmann 1999). According to the discourse theory of democracy a common action norm is legitimate only when it has been accepted in a free, open, inclusive and rational debate, that is, where all affected parties can be effectively heard.[16] Thus proper rights protection calls for adequate legislative procedures.

Democracy is a *principle* specifying what it means to get political results right. Only by adhering to democratic procedures can power holders justify their decisions; only by employing these procedures can collective goals be achieved legitimately; and only through legal procedures can laws be changed and new laws enacted correctly. Accordingly, to be legitimate, a constitution-making process should comply with the criteria of congruence and accountability.

The hub of rights

Constitutional democracy designates a system of procedural rules with a normative content. It specifies not only who is authorized to make collective decisions through what procedures, but also what it takes to justify them to the people who are bound by them, namely the citizenry. The normative principles of the democratic constitutional state can be pinned down to two basic legitimating criteria: *congruence* and *accountability*. By congruence is meant the basic democratic principle that those affected by decisions should also be responsible for them: it pertains to the need for egalitarian procedures of decision-making. This is an approximation: too little congruence will lead to lack of legitimacy as too few are participating, while too much is held to reduce efficiency in large polities because the larger the number of actors that are to have a say, the longer it takes to reach a common position. In real-world democracies, there has to be a proper balancing between legitimacy and efficiency.

Participatory rights are the focal point of rights, and the core element of congruence. Political rights are *the right of rights* (Arendt 1986). They have a special position amongst rights as they constitute the nucleus of citizenship: the member of a state owes allegiance to a government and is entitled to protection from it. Only such rights empower the citizen to affect the conditions for his/her role in society. Civil and social rights, for their part, do not actually extend beyond the private dimension, in that their contribution is to secure the individual's position as a private actor. It is, however, fair to say that such rights secure the legal and material basis necessary for the realization of political rights and are thus justified.[17] But in principle, these may also coexist with paternalistic and authoritarian political conditions in a society. Only political rights of participation are of an irreducibly collective nature, as they involve citizens in processes of opinion and will formation above and beyond their own private reality. Moreover, they are not (primary) goods to be distributed: they can only be had by being used; they require the citizens themselves to act.

Entrenching such rights renders clear that citizens are capable of regulating their common affairs through law and can give themselves a constitution. Rights, then, should not be conceived of as merely protective rights against an intrusive government but as instruments for *ensuring equality and freedom in the realization of the idea of the sovereignty of the people*. As an objective legal structure, rights impose on the state the duty to protect citizens so that they may make use of equally distributed rights to govern themselves. Rights are not only for protecting the negative freedom of private persons but also for ensuring peaceful coexistence and coordination of action plans by means of law. Consequently, one should understand rights not as weapons in the hands of private actors, or as merely protective rights against an invasive government, but as basically cooperative entities mutually assigned to, and by, the citizens themselves. The nexus of rights is internally related to the political autonomy of citizens (Habermas 1996: 274). In democracies, rights are not only justified by moral principles, but also in fact authored (*ex ante*) or at least subscribed to (*ex post*) by citizens themselves. However, the mutual recognition of rights is not only a logical, but also a practical prerequisite for democratic constitution-making. This is because it makes clear that the law is a means for justice.

Law represents a coercive order that connects non-compliance with sanctions, but as it confers upon all the same rights and obligations, it is at the same time a medium for peaceful conflict-resolution. It subjects power-wielding bodies to principles of correct conduct and is hence a resource for justice. It authorizes and also limits the use of political and administrative power. Law is the legitimate organization of power (Kelsen 1944: 7). It is not merely an instrument of power, or a matter of will. While *power* represents the executive authority and is a means of organizing efficient realization of goals, the law prevents the power apparatus of the state from programming itself. Law prevents a situation in which the power holders define what is right. It prevents the power from authorizing itself: it prevents might becoming right. Hence political power is institutionalized by way of law; it is only through law that political bodies can claim authority, and it is through legal procedures that the use of power can be justified and checked. Law is Janus-faced: it is the word and the sword of the sovereign but it also claims to be correct or right, and is therefore, in democracies, internally related to the approval of the people.

Hence, the salience of *accountability*, which is the second assessment criterion. It designates that decision-makers can be held responsible by the citizenry and that, in the last resort, it is possible to dismiss incompetent rulers. The significance of accountability as an assessment criterion is due to the fact that representative democracy 'is not a system in which the community governs itself, but a system in which public policies and decisions are made subject to the verdict of the people' (Manin 1997: 192). A range of rights and institutions in modern democracies exist to ensure this: open and free communication, free elections and public scrutiny all aim to make sure that the representative acts in the true interests of those represented. 'In genuine representation, the representative must eventually be held to account so that he will be responsive to the needs and claims of his constituents, to the obligations implicit in his position' (Pitkin 1972: 57).

On the one hand, accountability highlights the importance of elections and representative institutions that stand for or act for citizens; on the other hand, elections are 'merely one of many possible devices for keeping alive popular acceptance and belief' (Pitkin 1972: 108). A plethora of bodies exist towards which decision-making bodies must justify their decisions.

> Political accountability is not to be confined to electoral accountability but extends also to a continual process of giving account to an informed and active civic society.
>
> (Harlow 2002: 12)

Whether or not accountability is effective eventually depends on the actual sanctioning power in the hands of citizens, whether they really are empowered to throw 'the rascals' out of office whenever necessary. In concrete terms there is thus, with regard to control, a distinction to be drawn between *delegate control*, in which citizens mandate the representatives *ex ante*, and *control through sanction*, in which citizens endorse or rebuke the representatives' actions *ex post*.

Democratic requirements

Congruence and accountability are the basic criteria for checking the democratic quality of political decision-making bodies; they are the criteria for assessing democratic legitimacy. Thus, in order for a regime to be legitimate, it must, at a minimum, be organized in such a way that the public realm is open to free access, that governmental positions are open to all, that those who govern are appointed by election at regular intervals, and that the decision-making power is independent of social and economic interests. However, this is insufficient when considering the complexity of modern politics, which today is radically increased because of devolution downwards as well as upwards: delegation of power both down the chain of governance to local municipalities, professions and service-producing agencies, and upwards to international and supranational bodies, in particular the EU. Citizens' interests are affected by processes of denationalization, globalization and multiculturalism in ways and by bodies which are difficult to hold responsible via the ballot box. *Denationalization*, which is a less demanding concept than globalization, denotes the relative increase of cross-national transactions (compared to national exchanges) and the extension of social spaces beyond national control (Zürn 1999: 7). There is no longer an overlap between decision-making participants and affected parties. Denationalization shatters the two symmetries necessary for effective participation: first between citizens and decision-makers that 'they are to hold to account, and secondly between the "output" (decisions, policies and so on) of decision-makers and their constituents' (Held 1995: 16). Without *input congruence*, participation in making the decisions that affect one, there can be no self-determination; and without *output congruence*, without overlap between the polity and the territory it controls, 'the *spatial congruence* of political regulations with socially integrated areas', there can be no effective participation (Zürn 1999: 8).

However, owing to the integration processes in Europe, there is a multilayered structure of governance in which the national level is merely one. There is not one single *demos* that can claim exclusive authority, and one on which the political authority can be based. There are multiple and overlapping *demoi* based on different political authorities and with their own norms of accountability and congruence. The existing institutional multiplicity in a multi-level system of governance suggests that a mix of processes and procedures is relevant for an assessment of the democratic quality of governance today.

From what has been said, a political order, to be democratic, has to comply with criteria beyond the legal accountability and electoral representativeness that constitute the nation-state model of democracy. The deliberative notion of democratic legitimacy, which hinges on public accountability, non-coercion and non-exclusion, provides us with a far-reaching set of criteria. Democratic legitimacy is ultimately seen to consist in approval of decisions in a free debate (constrained and mediated by rights). This theory, then, is equipped also to assess from a democratic point of view decentralized subnational and transnational institutions of governance as well as supranational polities. On the one hand, the question is to subject decision-makers to a certain degree of accountability and responsibility. On the other hand, the question is about the possibilities for participation in collective opinion and will formation in order for people to reflectively and effectively influence decision-making in governmental bodies. The latter – congruence – calls attention to participation rights, namely elections, referenda, direct representation and possibilities of voice and popular protest in general with regard to policy-making that has consequences for citizens' interests and values.

According to these criteria, we see that there is a long way to go for the European system of governance to be fully democratic. Those affected do not exert very much influence on the laws and institutions they are influenced by. But what is equally obvious is that a democratic system of governance can only be designed through a set of individual rights. With the Charter in place, the EU is taking one step forward in making law enforceable without having recourse to a well-developed common identity like that of nation-states. The recent reform processes show that EU institutions are increasingly committing themselves to a *post-national mode of legitimation*. This means that the EU itself has to provide the necessary basis for congruence and accountability. There is no well-developed collective identity to appeal to, comparable to nationhood, no collective macro-subject encapsulating *la volonté générale* in the making, but the bare bones of cognitive rational rights and democratic principles. Hence the importance of constitutional arrangements and the positivization of human rights as identity-shaping mechanisms. But how do we know that a constitution or a bill of rights is legitimate? What is the relationship between rights and democracy?

Constitution and/or democracy?

Rights are needed to bolster post-national democracy. But what is the precise connection between rights and popular rule? Why is a bill of rights really needed for democracy to prevail?

Constitutional authorship

Constitutions assign competences, positions and powers. They specify fundamental procedural conditions for democratic legislation: constitutions contain rules for creating norms, for making statutory law as well as for amending the constitution. A constitution is enabling; it is not merely prohibitive (Holmes 1995: 161ff.). As a rule, a written constitution, which cannot be amended by simple majority vote, contains checks and balances, horizontal and vertical separation of powers, overrepresentation of small jurisdictions, judicial review and delegation clauses, and so on. Although constitutions make democratic politics possible, they are not self-sufficient – they cannot by themselves provide the basis of legitimacy as judges are bound by the principle of legality. In a legal system, only a norm can ground the validity of another norm (Kelsen 1970). There is a hierarchy of norms and the law itself cannot ground its own legitimacy. Judges decide what is legal and illegal, but cannot themselves establish the distinction. It is the legislators – citizens or their representatives – who give the laws, and furnish the judicial system with the norms they are to act upon.

The Kelsian *Grundnorm*, stating that the constitution is binding (which is the most basic norm making possible the derivation of other norms), cannot on its own ground the legitimacy of constitutions. The legitimacy of the basic norm springs from some extra-constitutional power. The idea of *We the people* amounts to the required *deus ex machina*. This is what constitutes the legitimating and unifying premise of the constitution.[18] It is only the people, or those authorized by 'the people', who can lay down the law and make it binding on every part, as the *pouvoir constituant*, the constitutive power, necessarily lies with the people. In the Republican tradition, the legitimating power is seen to emanate from the free will of the people, a union of free associates; or as Rousseau (1762) framed it, from the discovery of *la volonté générale*, which subjects all particular interests to the higher-level interest of all. Kant mediates this idea with the concept of individual rights, the right to freedom, which can only be made possible by a state granting everybody the same rights. In the Kantian perspective the coerciveness of the law is intrinsically linked to the ideal of equal liberties for all (Kant 1785). A constitution is also a system of rights that constitutes the legal medium, and hence is authorized to enforce norms. It is a means for compelling compliance but it cannot itself establish the required legitimacy. The authority of the law stems from the fact that it is made by the people and hence claims to be just or in the public interest, and that it is made binding on every part to the same degree and amount. The *legitimacy of the laws*, then, paradoxically also stems from the very fact that they are *obligatory and coercive*.

The right to self-government

Constitutional arrangements not only enable but also require and warrant popular participation in the law-making process. That is, they enable and warrant *government by the people*. The idea of constitutions or the rule of law should be interpreted as a way to explicate the meaning of democratic self-legislation. The democratic principle entrenched in modern constitutions refers to the manner in which citizens are involved in public deliberations, collective decision-making and law-making through a set of rights and procedures that range from freedom of speech and assembly to eligibility and voting rights. These political rights, and their attendant institutions and procedures, are to secure the *public autonomy* of the individual. They ensure that the addressees of the law can also participate in the making of the law.

The legitimacy of a constitution-making process in which fundamental rights are positivized hinges on the actual involvement of the people in collective opinion- and will-formation processes in the informal fora for public communication of the civil society, as well as the quality of the deliberation and decision-making processes in the institutionalized parliamentary and executive nexus. In this perspective, the constitution establishes procedures for the exercise of the right to self-government. The law is not only justified because it is in accordance with constitutional procedures; it must also reflect the collective opinion- and will-formation processes that precede the legislation. It is not legitimized exclusively by clauses carried by the legislator (Maus 1989: 208).

A constitution should be seen, then, not as a fixed set of rules, but rather as a principle for how to conduct common affairs with the means of law. As such the idea of a constitution refers more to a set of ideal rules about which one can negotiate and deliberate, but ones that cannot be done away with totally in so far as one lives within and wants to continue living within a law-based society. They are constitutive for the game of law and politics as such. Constitutional rules can be compared to *the rules of grammar*, and

> should not be thought of as hindrances or chains. Grammatical principles do not merely restrain the speaker [...]. Far from simply handcuffing people, linguistic rules allow interlocutors to do many things they would not otherwise have been able to do or even have thought of doing.
>
> (Holmes 1995: 131)

From this perspective, constitutions not only distribute competences, positions and powers; they also establish a framework for government without any specific goal, but with an infinite number of possibilities (Elkin 1993: 125). Constitutions specify fundamental procedural conditions for democratic legislation, and must therefore be interpreted as abstract structures of legal principles, which may be specified in various ways according to empirical circumstances.

Substance or procedure?

To repeat, democracy is internally related to rights. Therefore there is a democratic argument for entrenching a bill of rights in a European constitution. The idea of democracy can only be explained by the concept of rights, which entails the positivization of human rights and other values and goals. The political process is governed by rights, and positive law equips rights holders with resources that can be used against the incumbents of power. The problem is that the rights of the citizens in the EU are not made by citizens themselves (cf. Brunkhorst 2002b: 218ff.). It is only the political process that can render them legitimate. This links in with a theoretical problem of discourse theory on how to square the circle between constitutionalism and democracy, between the principle of a legally constrained government and the principle of self-government.

In discourse theory, individual rights – basic rights – are conceived of as taking priority over and restricting collective will-formation, at the same time as they are to be justified in a free discussion. The recognition of basic rights is both the presupposition and the product of democratic discourses (Wellmer 1998: 270). Basic rights are 'answers that meet the demands of political communication among strangers and ground the presumption that outcomes are rationally acceptable' (Habermas 2001: 771). But rights are *reasonably contestable*. This is due to the indeterminacy of moral reasons, the prevalence of normative disagreements, the fallibility of claims, the revisability of moral stands, and the fact that norms are prone to collide. How can we know that rights are 'right'? How do we know that (or when) rights are justified?

Human rights, which lend justification to basic rights, are moral categories justified by the free will of autonomous persons, but they owe their political legitimacy to a democratic process of enactment. Because they raise different validity claims, the one is not reducible to the other. While human rights can be justified with reference to universal moral claims and humanity as such, democracy refers to procedurally achieved agreements within territorially circumscribed polities. In principle, the opposition between democracy and constitution is a false one because democracy itself 'cannot prescribe the procedures for testing whether the conditions for the procedures it does prescribe are met' (Dworkin 1996: 33). Democracy and constitution mutually presuppose each other, but actually there is a tension between the two as democracy so far has been achieved only at the level of the nation-state, while moral claims, and hence human rights, transgress every border and constricted territory. On the other hand, the universal, moral elements are built into modern constitutions as far as they have incorporated human rights. Constitutions with bills of rights contain universal elements that refer to a larger community of citizens, to humanity as such.

Human rights are *supra-positive* but claim universal validity. They stem from the convictions and rational insights of moral self-legislative human beings but they can only be made binding for all members of a polity through a constitutionalizing process. This can also be given a normative twist: unless affected parties have had their say, we cannot know whether they have been understood, interpreted and implemented correctly. It is their political enactment through the intervention of political authorities whose legitimacy is recognized, and who possess capacity to ensure compliance, that transforms human rights into valid basic, constitutional rights, namely, rights that are enacted and can be invoked before courts and whose violation by anyone can be redressed by courts.

A bill of rights, which establishes the boundaries of the polity, draws on substantial moral categories as its legitimating source. A constitutional convention and a political ratification process transform this into a legally binding document. However, if it is the procedure that legitimizes rights, what, then, legitimizes the procedure? If it is rights that justify the procedure, what justifies the rights? Circular argumentation crops up here, because rights that are to ensure the process must be justified procedurally. But the procedure rests on rights, which must again be justified, and so on, and so on (Michelman 1997: 162f.). *Infinite regress* arises between procedure and rights, between democracy and constitution, that there is, a procedurally unaccounted for substantial rest. It is, for example, not possible to argue for everyone's right to participate in a debate without going back on some substantial, normative and non-procedural argument, such as people's freedom, equality and dignity as postulated by natural law. There is a substantial rest – a moral element or a concept of justice unaccounted for – also in the discourse theory of law, which initially claims to have gotten rid of all natural law elements and is procedural all the way down: whether laws are right depend solely on the quality of the process (Alexy 1996; Habermas 1996; Apel 1998).

The democratic procedure, for its part, cannot guarantee a correct result. Perfect procedural justice is impossible (Rawls 1971: 198). This is so because even in a just procedure one has to deal with cognitively limited and socially constrained actors and fallible processes of deliberation. Hence *the burden of judgement*: even reasonable actors may after a rational discussion remain at odds with each other (Rawls 1993b: 54ff.). Moreover, legal texts are *irreducibly open-textured* and cause indeterminate results (Hart 1961: 128). The net upshot is that the processes that confer legitimacy on the laws cannot ensure correctness:

> A truly democratic process is itself inescapably a legally conditioned and constituted process. It is constituted, for example, by laws regarding political representation and elections, civil associations, families, freedom of speech, property, access to media, and so on. Thus, in order to confer legitimacy on a set of laws issuing from an actual set of discursive institutions and practices in a country, those institutions and practices would themselves have to be legally constituted in the right way. [...] The problem is that whether they do or not may itself at any time become a matter of contentious but reasonable disagreement [...].
>
> (Michelman 1998: 91)

To identify the law without recourse to morality or substance seems impossible. But when we cannot be sure whether these substantial elements are correct, how can we know that a constitution is legitimate?

The legitimacy of the constitution

There is a serious problem in determining the legitimacy of the constitution, and the stated problem of infinite regress of legitimating sources pops up again in the theories that try to do away with it. The regress cannot be ended unless an agreed upon substantial standard has been invoked, according to Michelman (1999: 52). But such a standard subverts self-government (Post 1995). This problem does not disappear in so far as elements that are of a substantial and moral kind are needed for ensuring a correct process, such as constitutional essentials. But we cannot know whether these are correct unless there is a democratic process of their assessment and enactment. This process does not necessarily generate a correct result, as mentioned. But even though legitimacy by consent may thus be immoral (Raz 1998: 163), there is no other manner in which to cash in the idea of democratic constitution-making than through popular approval.

The legitimacy of the constitution rests on the recognition of political authority, but the authority cannot rest on that of its makers, because no one 'can have authority over future generations' (Raz 1998: 164). How can earlier generations legitimately bind later ones? This is the big question in the norma-tive battle over the validity of a constitution, and one that in the last resort comes down to the problem of substance and procedure.

The tension is resolved, according to Habermas, once the constitution is conceived in generational terms: even though people are constrained by the constitution authored by their forefathers, the present understanding and the full use of the constitution depend on the agency of the present generation. As a self-correcting learning process,

> [t]he allegedly paradoxical relation between democracy and the rule of law resolves itself in the dimension of historical time, provided one conceives of the constitution as a project that makes the founding act into an ongoing process of constitution-making that continues across generations.
>
> (Habermas 2001: 768)

The constitution is a *cross-generational learning process* – a self-reflective, self-reinforcing spiral-like historical learning process. This should not be taken to imply a complete overhaul and change of a constitution, that a new one is made by every new gener-ation – a perpetual constitutional revolution – but merely that the reasons for its justification change and should be subjected to a public test.

> The same law can be valid for a variety of reasons, and these may change without the law changing.
>
> (Raz 1998:169)

However, this solution is dependent on the inherent normative quality of the constitution. It depends on the quality of substantive norms as it is the basic legal structure itself that allows for the possibility of revision and ongoing interpretation of the founding act. It is its democratic character, the way it enables a rational basic law interpretation, that has the right warranting effect (Michelman 1999: 57). Put differently, it is the degree to which the constitution ensures equal worth and respect for every person, free and equal access to unrestricted public discourse, a broad and equitable political franchise, and so on, that makes possible a constitutional learning process and a rational interpretation of basic law, that is, judging whether or not it is just, whether it is in everyone's equal interest or is equally good for all. Thus, it is not a fully procedural solution.

A bill of rights and a constitution do not settle once and for all the question pertaining to the basic rules of society. In a democratic society based on the rule of law, citizens are conscious (or should be) of the incompleteness and fallibility of institutionalized rules. At least at critical moments, citizens become reflexively aware of the imperfectness of the entrenched rules and procedures. This normative ideal is reflected in the constitutional model outlined by Bruce Ackerman. He sees constitutional politics as happening at over-heated and rare historical moments where it interrupts the normal political process and shifts it in another direction. *A constitutional moment* is not merely a process through which the constitution is made or amended, but one in which it makes sense to say that *the people* has given itself a constitution. That is when *We the people*[19] are called upon, when 'a broad movement of transformative opinion has [...] earned the authority to set major aspects of the political agenda' (Ackerman 1998: 409). We can speak of a constitutional moment when the citizens are mobilized to lay down the law as equally binding on every part of society.

> During periods of constitutional politics, the higher lawmaking system encourages an engaged citizenry to focus on fundamental issues and determine whether any proposed solution deserves its considered support.
>
> (Ackerman 1998: 6)

However, 'constitutional moments must come to an end'; they must result in a written text or be aborted. There are ample historical examples that such moments do not necessarily 'need ripen into a new constituational solution' (Ackerman 1998: 346, 409). The European Union already has a brief history of such attempts, with the draft for a Constitutional Treaty (of June 2003), emanating from the Convention on the Future of Europe (2002), as the most far-reaching and promising example, as is discussed in the last part of this volume.

Constitutionalizing post-national democracy

With the recent reform processes and the Charter in place, the EU is taking one step forward in making law enforceable without having recourse to a well-developed common identity. It so to say reconstitutes itself on a new basis. As the EU is not a state, nor remotely a nation-state, it has to find another basis than agreement on substantial values – shared commonality and allegiance, nationhood or collective consciousness – for the actual legitimation of rights. It has to rely on the bare bones of cognitive rational principles of sovereignty and citizenship. Democracy and human rights refer to the core basis of legitimacy of nation-states and are the only viable normative resource basis for a post-national political order. For the first time in human history, we are now witnessing the development of a democratic system that is not based on a conception of a culturally homogenized people, or brought about through war or brute force, but one that has emerged through voluntary cooperation, negotiation and deliberation. As other resource bases are lacking, the Union can only build on the two legitimating entities, human rights and democracy. It is the inclusive procedures constituted by the rights of the citizens to participate and hold to account that bear the burden of legitimation. In such a complex and pluralist setting, one plainly cannot base interventions on what Europe is or what it is to be a European, as a collective identity is lacking, or at least is contested. Identification with common concerns is rather to be shaped and struggled for through public and institutionalized processes of political communication. To put it simply: it has to be created. The lack of pre-political identification with the emerging political community can be compensated for by a public debate that forms catalytic functions of enlarged citizenship, solidarity and plural identities (Kleger 1998: 144f.).

Such identification is, however, also needed for more expedient reasons as the common market is exhausted as a resource for further integration. With the internal market and monetary union more or less in place, the Union needs a clearer understanding of what it is and what it aspires to. The pending enlargement to the East and South, the establishment of a common foreign and security policy, and, not least, the question of social measures at the EU level pose new kinds of problems of cooperation. The questions raised in these policy areas are difficult to handle within the established economic, free-trade frame of reference for the politics of the Union, as they affect the very basis for cooperation. They require a notion of the collective enterprise, that is, a conception of the entity's foundation, mission or vision beyond that of a free market.

The constitutional development of the EU may be a solution to this problem as far as it will have an identity-shaping effect. Establishing the convention and a proposal for a European constitution is an important way to foster such, because they revolve on the basic rules for action coordination and intercultural coexistence and contribute to root such rules in the civic culture European-wide. But how far this will lead depends on a European public sphere that still remains in latency.

Conclusion

In order to meet the challenge of *efficiency*, to face up to new exigencies and to solve problems rationally, nation-states increasingly have to establish and partake in international and transnational structures of governance. This, however, is detrimental to democratic *legitimacy* as democracy is confined to the territory of the nation-state. In a 'globalized', denationalized world, the requirements of legitimacy and of efficiency, of input and output congruence, no longer coincide.

Those who can be kept accountable have little control over the factors affecting people's lives, and those who have the decisive power are beyond democratic reach. In Europe the EU testifies to political initiatives building up supranational political institutions, and has shown a remarkable and unprecedented capacity to take on new collective measures and deepen integration. But it is a process that may sap parliamentary sovereignty at the state level, and supranational rights enforcement does not in itself alleviate this problem. At the present level of institutionalization, as long as there is no such thing as a cosmopolitan democracy, there is a tension between popular sovereignty and human rights as the former is only institutionalized at the level of the nation-state. In the international arena, human rights politics are not democratically enacted. This is the background for the need for democratic procedures over and above the nation-state.

There has for some time now been a process of rights entrenchment in the EU, which has come close to a constitutionalizing one. From a cosmopolitan point of view, such rights are important as they contribute to establish democratically controlled institutions at a regional level to cope with global problems. State and world citizenship form a continuum as people increasingly are affected by supranational powers. The EU can usefully be conceived of as an *intermediate institution* for grappling with exigencies connected to globalization, and thus is an interesting experiment in post-national regulation. By this, international law is pushed beyond the limitations of the Charter of the United Nations, which on its behalf prohibits violence, and thus aggression, against other states, but forbids the intervention in the internal affairs of a state (Article 2.7). The EU has clearly progressed beyond this initial stage of a purely voluntary association. It is not merely an intergovernmental organization, or an economic arrangement, but is an entity with strong supranational elements equipped with executive power. This is evidenced in the supranational character of the legal structure, which is supported and enhanced in particular by the European Court of Justice. National law gives way to Community law within the competence of the Communities. This increases the need for safeguarding the rights and interests of citizens and of the Member States. Hence, the need for a politically sanctioned constitution entailing a charter of fundamental rights and a catalogue of competencies.

The EU Charter is a very important contribution to a constitutionalization of the EU. It helped bring about the Convention on the Future of Europe. Further, the Charter enhances the legal certainty of citizens, clarifies the Union's basis of identity and legitimacy and, consequently, reduces the democratic deficit even though it is weak with regard to protecting citizens' public autonomy. The Charter Convention and the Laeken Convention might not have had a popular mandate. But the Charter consolidates, and therefore derives legitimacy from, the authorized character of the common constitutional traditions. Moreover, as most of the decision-makers are parliamentarians, it fares better in democratic terms than is the case with treaty-making at IGCs. From a democratic point of view, law made through open deliberation by representatives is better than that based on judicial activism or made through closed-door intergovernmental bargaining. However, even though democracy is internally related to rights as there is no democracy without the protection of the fundamental rights of the individual, it is only through a democratic process of enactment that we can know which rights are right, and how they should be delineated. It takes democracy to justify rights, and citizenship requires membership and participation in the very structures that affect individual interests. In Europe, state power is being domesticated by supranational law, and the only basis of legitimacy for this law is the constitutional developments in Europe that emerged in the wake of the French Revolution, and which for more than two hundred years now have contributed massively to the stabilization of nation-states. In this tradition constitutions are seen as arrangements for respecting the equality and the autonomy of the individual in the realization of the idea of popular self-government.

Notes

1 Madison, Hamilton and Jay 1788.
2 They can be accessed from the Convention website. See http://european-convention.eu.int/. See also the discussion in the last part of this volume.
3 On this see further Dieter Grimm's contribution to this volume (Chapter 5) and Eriksen *et al.* 2003: 22–3.
4 For an extensive comment, see Meyer 2003.
5 Van Gend, Case 26/62 (1963), ECR: 1. Case Costa 6/64 (1964), ECR: 585.
6 This is evidenced, for instance, in rulings on the constitutionality of the Maastricht Treaty by the German Constitutional Court and the Danish High Court, both of which refused to grant EU law *Kompetenz-Kompetenz*.
7 See CHARTE 4105/00 (Convention on the Charter, 2000). See also Eckhout 2000: 98.
8 Advocate-General Mischo in Joined Cases C-20/00 and C-64/00, Booker Aquaculture Ltd. Cited from Brand 2002: 401–2.
9 Except for a change, on a British initiative, in the preamble saying that the ECJ must pay 'due regard' to an interpretative text underlining that the Charter does not create new rights.
10 The leading Case is Internationale, 11/70 (1970), ECR 1125.
11 And further, 'the Union can only achieve the leadership role to which it aspires through the example it sets' (Alston and Weiler 1999: 5).
12 In its first report on human rights, the EU Committee of the House of Lords emphasized that 'the Community has no criminal jurisdiction, no police, no criminal courts, no prisons', and that a number of ECHR provisions would thus be largely inapplicable within the Community. While it remains the case that the Community has no explicit powers in these areas, important changes have taken place:

> There is provision under Title VI of the TEU, for closer operational co-operation between police and customs officials, also involving Europol, in the prevention and combating of crime. While such co-operation remains essentially intergovernmental there is greater involvement of Community institutions and a greater choice of legally binding instruments.
>
> (House of Lords 2000)

13 The Convention consisted of (a) representatives of the Head of State or Government of the Member States, (b) one representative of the President of the European Commission, (c) 16 members of the European Parliament, and (d) 30 members of the Member State Parliaments (two from each of the Member States). It was led by a Praesidium of five.

14 The process is unique in the EU. There are reports of processes of 'a genuine dialogue' within the Convention which led to change of positions over time. See Schönlau 2003: 131.
15 The drafting of the Charter took place in an open manner, in contrast to the IGC-2000 process, which was mainly conducted behind closed doors. The Convention consulted with other organizations and conducted open hearings to representatives from civil society. Hundreds of NGOs submitted briefs to the Convention on different aspects of the Charter. It received more than 1,000 documents from more than 200 different sources. These briefs can be accessed on the Internet: http://db.consilium.eu.int/df/default.asp?lang=en.
16 'Only those statutes may claim legitimacy that can meet with the assent of all citizens in a discursive process of legislation that in turn has been legally constituted' (Habermas 1996: 110).
17 This is not to say that they cannot be justified on other grounds. Cf. Eriksen 2003: 367ff.
18 'Reflecting the will of the citizens and States of Europe to build a common future, this Constitution establishes the European Union, on which the Member States confer competences to attain objectives they have in common', Article I–1: Establishment of the Union, CONV 797/03.
19 'We the people of the United States [...] do ordain and establish this Constitution for the United States of America', US Constitution Preamble.

4 Human rights, constitutionalism and integration

Iconography and fetishism

Joseph H.H. Weiler

Introduction: Mirror, mirror on the wall – who is the most beautiful of all?

The advent of the Charter of Fundamental Rights of the European Union is one of the factors which is feeding the renewed debate about a constitution for Europe. For many, the Charter is the first, important element in a would-be European constitution. It is appropriate that fundamental rights (German preference) or human rights (French preference) should be at the centre of such constitutional discussion. But it is also appropriate that one does not allow the normative complexity of the trinity of human rights, constitutionalism and integration to be obscured by our enthusiasms for all three. This essay is meant, thus, to highlight some of the darker aspects of the ongoing debate.

There is an undeniable celebratory tone to our human rights discourse. We brandish human rights, with considerable justification, as one of the important achievements of our civilization. We hail our commitment to human rights and their embedment in our legal systems among the signal and mature proofs of Europe's response to, and overcoming of, its inglorious recent past in World War II. We consider human rights, alongside democracy, as a foundational value of our political order, something it is even worth fighting for. The recent 'adoption' of the EU Charter (however ambiguous its formal status in the EU legal order) is a final apotheosis of this discourse. Human rights have undoubtedly achieved an iconographical position in European culture. And though we distance ourselves, with disdain, from the more vulgar expressions of American end-of-history triumphalism which gushed forth with the fall of the Soviet empire, that very disdain cannot but conceal Europe's sense of its cultural superiority and hence its own brand of self-satisfaction and triumphalism. We raise the mirror of human rights, as evidenced by both national and transnational instruments before our collective face, and smile with satisfaction: Yes, WE are the most beautiful of all. But, as we know, the Mirror, if only we look carefully, does not hide our warts, blemishes and, at times, downright ugliness. At the least, it returns a more nuanced picture to the self-admiring gaze.

The following are three central features in the debate on human rights, constitutionalism and integration.

First, human rights are part of a broader discourse of, and commitment to, constitutions and constitutionalism, often to the thick, hard version of constitutions and constitutionalism found in, say, the German and Italian legal orders, which embody the notion of constitution as a higher law. Such developments are noticeable even in countries such as Denmark, Belgium, France and others which had a softer version of constitutionalism and a long tradition of scepticism towards American-style judicial empowerment. For its part, the EU already has a very robust version of constitutionalism and the EU Charter is, as noted, perceived by many as the first element in a would-be European Union formalization of that brand of constitutionalism.

Concomitantly, human rights also signify the ever-increasing acceptance of (and resignation to) the central role of courts and judges in public discourse. Courts are most audacious in asserting their power when they garb themselves in the mantle of guardians of the human rights guaranteed by constitutional documents. They are, too, most successful in mobilizing support for and legitimating their power in the context of human rights. Europe adds an interesting nuance to this phenomenon too. First, one should not forget this little element of self-serving and self-interest as the European Court of Justice rushes to embrace the Charter into its jurisprudence, a Charter which pointedly was not made part of the European legal order by those whose political and democratic legitimacy is much higher than that of the European Court. Second, whilst there has always been a specific critique of the so-called 'activism' of the European Court of Justice, one that is perhaps currently even increasing, and it has even been couched, from time to time, in the language which objects to a *gouvernance des juges*, a more careful look at such criticism usually discovers that it issues from a nationalist sentiment worried more about the loss of national sovereignty to Europe than of popular or parliamentary power to judges. If the European Court were 'activist' in the opposite direction, namely slashing European Union power (and make no mistake, this too would be a form of judicial activism), you would find the same critics celebrating the European Court of Justice. In other words, most of the critique is not of judicial empowerment as such, but of the content which it embraces. Significantly, when national courts, in acts of *national judicial empowerment*, claiming to protect *nationally defined human rights*, strike out at the European Court of Justice (and there have been quite a few such expressions in recent years), they are celebrated as protecting national values and identity and sovereignty. Few seem to protest that it is the judiciary, often in ways constitutionally shielded from parliamentary challenge, which is deciding fundamental issues which define the relationship of a Member State to the Union.

Second, beyond constitutionalism and its concomitant commitment to, or acceptance of, courts and judges as such, there is in the discourse of human rights a great faith in the *judicial protection* of human rights. We may call this the Habeas Corpus syndrome. The point I wish to make is simple enough: increasingly, the measurement of the efficacy of these documents, of their very reality as meaningful legal instruments, is in their invocability by individuals and their enforcement, at the instance of individuals, against public authority by courts. It is the writ of Habeas Corpus which solidified its position in legal history. In today's world, documents and declarations which do not have such a quality are oft derided as 'hortatory', aspirational, embryonic, all awaiting realization of their potential by arriving at the promised lands of individual invocability and judicial enforceability.

Finally, human rights have become an important part of European integration and European identity discourse. This debate takes place at two levels. The first is the bland affirmation of human rights as being part of a common patrimony, et cetera, et cetera, good stuff for politicians to drone on about, something akin to Beethoven's Ninth or the European Flag. But there is a more serious dimension to this prattle. As the polity grows, as the ability of national mechanisms and instruments to provide democratic legitimacy to European norms is increasingly understood as partial and often formal rather than real, the necessity of democratizing decision-making at the European level becomes ever more pressing. Such democratization requires, in its turn, the emergence of a polity with social commitments, allegiances and ties which is a *conditio sine qua non* for the discipline of majoritarian decision-making. No *demos*, no democracy. Europe rightly shies away from an ethnic, religious or any other thick form of organic self-understanding and political identity. The only normatively acceptable construct is to conceive the polity as a community of values, much in the original spirit (though not practice) of post-Revolution France and the United States. When one grasps for a content for such a community of values, the commitment to human rights becomes the most ready currency. Here are values around which, surely, Europeans can coalesce (and celebrate).

There is much truth and much value to our polities in our commitment to constitutional orders which celebrate democracy, human rights and the rule of law; in the seriousness with which we take this commitment as evidenced by our willingness to make human rights a veritable legal instrument, often of superior normative value, opposable by individuals against public authorities and adjudicated and enforced by our courts; and in our placing human rights, alongside markets and economic prosperity, as defining the values of our emerging European polity. But there are, too, shades, nuances, warts and downright ugly aspects to this picture which are also worth bearing.

Constitutional patriotism: the last refuge of the scoundrel?

Why is it that we give such importance to the constitutional integrity of our legal orders? Why is it that, despite the fact that the European Union has a functional legal order, there are strong voices which would like to root it in a formal constitutional document? Why is it that we talk of crisis when national and European constitutionalisms conflict, not least in the area of human rights?

There is, of course, no one answer to this question. But any answer would, I believe, have to include at least a shade of the following.

We consider the integrity of our *national* constitutional orders not simply as a matter that is important to the good functioning of government and an orderly distribution of political power, but also as one of moral commitment and identity. Our national constitutions are perceived by us as doing more than simply structuring the respective powers of government and the relationships between public authority and individuals or between the state and other agents. Our constitutions are said to encapsulate fundamental values of the polity, and this, in turn, is said to be a reflection of our collective identity as a people, as a nation, as a state, as a Community, as a Union. When we are proud and attached to our constitutions, we are so for these very reasons. They are about restricting power, not enlarging it; they protect fundamental rights of the individual; and they define a collective identity which does not make us feel queasy the way some forms of ethnic identity might. Thus, in the endless and tiresome debates about the European Union constitutional order, national courts have become in the last decade far more aggressive in their constitutional self-understanding. The case law is well known. National courts are no longer at the vanguard of the 'new European legal order', bringing the rule of law to transnational relations, and empowering, through EC law, individuals *vis-à-vis* Member State authority. Instead they stand at the gate and defend national constitutions against illicit encroachment from Brussels and Luxembourg. They have received a sympathetic hearing, since they are perceived as protecting fundamental human rights as well as protecting national identity. To protect national sovereignty is *passé*; to protect national identity by insisting on constitutional specificity is *à la mode*.

On this reading, modern liberal constitutions are, indeed, about limiting the power of government *vis-à-vis* the individual; they also articulate fundamental human rights in the best neo-Kantian tradition; and they reflect a notion of collective identity as a community of values which is far less threatening than more organic definitions of collective identity. They are a reflection of our better part.

But, like the moon, like much which is good in life, there is here a dark side too.

It is, first, worth listening carefully to the rhetoric of the constitutional discourse. Even when voiced by the greatest humanists, the military overtones are present. We have been invited to develop a *patriotism* around our modern, liberal, constitutions. The constitutional patriot is invited to *defend* the constitution. In some states we have agencies designed to protect the constitution whose very name is similar to our border defences. In other countries, we are invited to *swear allegiance* to the constitution. In a constitutional democracy we have a doctrine of a *fighting* democracy, whereby democratic hospitality is not extended to those who would destroy constitutional democracy itself. To be a good constitutional liberal, it would seem from this idiom, is to be a constitutional nationalist, and, it turns out, the constitutional stakes are not only about values and limitations of power but also about its opposite: the power which lurks underneath such values.

Very few constitutionalists and practically no modern constitutional court will make an *overt* appeal to natural law. Thus the formal normative authority of the constitutions around which our patriotism must form and which we must defend is, from a legal point of view, mostly positivist. This means that it is as deep or shallow as the last constitutional amendment: in some countries, like Switzerland or Germany, not a particularly onerous political process. Consequently, vesting so much in the constitutional integrity of the Member State is an astonishing feat of self-celebration and self-aggrandizement, of bestowing on ourselves, in our capacity of constituent power, a breathtaking normative authority. Just think of the near sacred nature we give today to the constitutions adopted by societies – great segments of which were morally corrupted – of the World War II generation in, say, Germany, Italy and elsewhere.

A similar doubt should dampen somewhat any enthusiasm towards the new constitutional posture of national courts which hold themselves out as defending the core constitutional values of their polity, indeed its very identity. The limitation of power imposed on the political branches of government is, as has been widely noticed, accompanied by a huge dose of judicial self-empowerment and no small measure of sanctimonious moralizing. Human rights often provoke the most strident rhetoric by courts. Yet constitutional texts in our different polities, especially when it comes to human rights, are remarkably similar. Defending the constitutional identity of the state and its core values turns out in many cases to be a defence of some hermeneutic foible adopted by five judges voting against four. The banana saga, which has taxed the European Court of Justice, the German Constitutional Court, the Appellate Body of the World Trade Organization and endless lawyers and academics, is the perfect symbol of this farce.

Finally, there is also an exquisite irony in a constitutional ethos which, while appropriately suspicious of older notions of organic and ethnic identity, at the very same time implicitly celebrates a supposed unique moral identity, wisdom and, yes, superiority, of the authors of the constitution, the people, the constitutional *demos*, when it wears the hat of constituent power and, naturally, of those who interpret it.

It was Samuel Johnson who suggested that patriotism was the last refuge of the scoundrel. Dr Johnson was, of course, only partly right. Patriotism can also be noble. But it is an aphorism worth remembering when we celebrate constitutional patriotism, mostly embodied in human rights, national or transnational.

The Charter and the judicial protection of fundamental human rights

The European Charter is with us and we should make the best of it. But it is still worth asking whether Europe really needed it. Will it actually enhance the protection of fundamental human rights in the Union? European citizens and residents do not, after all suffer from a deficit of judicial protection of human rights. Their human rights in most Member States are protected by their constitution and by their constitutional court or other courts. As an additional safety net they are protected by the European Convention on Human Rights and the Strasbourg organs. In the Community, they receive judicial protection from the European Court of Justice using as its source the same Convention and the constitutional traditions common to the Member States.

So why a new Charter at all?

Most important in the eyes of the Charter promoters was the issue of perception and identity. Ever since Maastricht, the political legitimacy of the European construct had been a live issue; the advent of European Monetary Union with its barely accountable European Central Bank added fuel to a perception of a Europe concerned more with markets than with people. It may be true that the European Court guarantees legal protection against human rights abuses, but who is aware of this?

A Charter, its supporters said, would render visible and prominent that which until now was known only to dusty lawyers. Additionally, the Charter, as an important symbol, would counterbalance the Euro and become part of the iconography of European integration and contribute both to the identity of and identification with Europe.

Has this been borne out? Time will tell, but for now the Charter is a classical European story, akin to the concept of European citizenship heralded with great triumph at Maastricht: An exercise characterized by high-falutin rhetoric by all and sundry and a simultaneous conspicuous failure to take decisive steps to integrate it into the legal order of the Union. We have become so habituated to this kind of Euro double-speak, that we fail to notice.

Lawyers will point out with great excitement that the Court is already making reference to the Charter and that it may become 'incorporated' in the legal order by judicial activity. I am not at all sure whether this is a positive development, from either a pragmatic or a normative perspective. I wonder if a stony silence by the Court or a defiant refusal to take note of the Charter would not, pragmatically, provide greater impetus to eventual political action. I also wonder, as indicated above, whether it is proper for the Court to go very far with judicial incorporation of the Charter given the fact that it was, let us not mince words, constitutionally rejected as an integral part of the Union legal order. One cannot chant odes to democracy and constitutionalism and then flout them when it does not suit one's human rights agenda.

Clarity was a second justification often invoked to justify the exercise. The current system of looking to the common constitutional traditions and to the European Convention on Human Rights (ECHR) as a source for the rights protected in the Union is, it is argued, unsatisfactory and should be replaced by a formal document listing such rights. But would clarity actually be added? Examine the text. It is, appropriately, drafted in the magisterial language characteristic of our constitutional traditions: 'Human Dignity is Inviolable', and so on. There are many things that could be said for this tradition, but clarity is not one of them. When it comes to the contours of the rights included in the Charter, I do not believe that it adds much clarity to what exactly is protected and what is not.

Note, however, that by drafting a list and perhaps one day fully incorporating it into the legal order, we will have jettisoned, at least in part, one of the truly original features of the pre-Charter constitutional architecture in the field of human rights – the ability to use the legal system of each of the Member States as an organic and living laboratory of human rights protection which then, case by case, can be adapted and adopted for the needs of the Union by the European Court in dialogue with its national counterparts. The Charter may not thwart that process, but it runs the risk of inducing a more inward-looking jurisprudence and chilling the constitutional dialogue.

Drafting a new Charter, it was said, would give the chance of introducing much needed innovation to our constitutional norms, which were shaped by ageing constitutions and international treaties. Issues such as bio-technology, genetic engineering, privacy in the age of the internet, sexual identity and, most importantly, political rights empowering the individual could be dealt with afresh, placing the Charter at the avant-garde of European constitutionalism.

I leave it to the reader to judge whether the Charter has introduced such innovation. In some instances the language used by the Charter risks 'deconstitutionalization' of certain rights. The formula quite frequently used of rights 'guaranteed in accordance with the national laws governing the exercise of these rights' may turn out to do considerable damage to constitutional protection of human rights. Whilst it is a formula one finds in constitutional orders of the Member States and international treaties, and whilst it is possible to develop a jurisprudence which separates the existence of a right from its exercise, in the particular circumstances of the Community, it will be very difficult ever to challenge constitutionally a Community (let alone a Member State) measure which replicated the existing law in this or that Member State. This may turn out to be a very regressive development for the protection of human rights.

Another regressive scenario is one under which there will be great pressure on the Court to reject any progressive interpretations of various formulae found in the Charter if this turns out to have been rejected by the Convention which drafted the Charter. For example, a proposal to introduce to the Charter 'the right for everyone to have a nationality' was rejected during the drafting process. It will be difficult for the Court to articulate such a right. Likewise, Genetic Integrity was dropped from Article 3 on the Integrity of the Person. This too might have subsequent interpretative consequences. Many more examples can be found. In general it will be much harder for the Court to crystallize a Community right when such was considered and rejected by a political constituent assembly. In some areas the Charter actually cuts down on protection now offered in the legal order of the Community. Article 51(1) actually reduces the categories of Member State acts which would be subject to European scrutiny, and Article 53 at least raises problematic issues on the supremacy of Community law in this area.

But most troubling of all is the fact that the Charter exercise served as a subterfuge, an alibi, for not doing that which is truly necessary if the purpose was truly to enhance the protection of fundamental rights in the Union rather than talk about enhancing such protection.

The real problem of the Community is the absence of a *human rights policy*, with everything this entails: a Commissioner, a Directorate General, a budget and a horizontal action plan for making effective those rights already granted by the Treaties and judicially protected by the various levels of European Courts.

Much of the human rights story, and its abuse, takes place far from the august halls of courts. Most of those whose rights are violated have neither knowledge nor means to seek judicial vindication. The Union does not need more rights on its lists, or more lists of rights. What are mostly needed are programmes and agencies to make rights real, not simply negative interdictions which courts can enforce.

The best way to drive the point home is to think of competition policy. Imagine our Community with an Article 81 and 82 interdicting Restrictive Practices and Abuse of Dominant Position, but not having a Commissioner and a Competitive Directorate-General to monitor, investigate, regulate and prosecute violations. The interdiction against competition violations would be seriously compromised. But that is exactly the situation with human rights. For the most part the appropriate norms are in place. If violations were to reach the Court, the judicial reaction would be equally appropriate. But would there be any chance effectively to combat Anti-Trust violations without a DG4? Do we have any chance in the human rights field without a similar institutional set-up?

One reason we do not have a policy is because the Court, in its wisdom, erroneously in my view, announced in Opinion 2/94 that protection of human rights is not one of the policy objectives of the Community and thus cannot be a subject for a proactive policy.

Far more important than any Charter for the effective vindication of human rights would have been a simple Treaty amendment which would have made active protection of human rights within the sphere of application of Community law one of the policies of the Community alongside other policies and objectives in Article 3 and a commitment expeditiously to take all measures to give teeth to such a policy.[1] Not only was such a step not taken, but Article 51(2) made absolute that such a development would be even more difficult to take in the future.

Human rights and integration

As mentioned above, the classical vision regards a commitment to fundamental human rights as a unifying 'universal' ideal, one of the core values around which the peoples of Europe may coalesce in a shared patrimony. When the European Court held itself out as the guarantor of fundamental human rights in the field of Community law, was it not merely giving judicial expression (and teeth!) to a common heritage rather than contending with cultural diversity? The answer to this question is 'Yes, but ...'

Beyond a certain core, reflected in Europe by the European Convention on Human Rights, the specific definition of fundamental human rights often differs from polity to polity. Even in a relatively homogeneous cultural zone such as Western Europe, these differences might reflect fundamental societal choices and form an important part in the different identities of polities and societies. They are often that part of social identity about which people care a great deal. Often people might consider that these values, as an expression of their specific identity, should be respected against any unifying encroachment. Given that the rights are considered fundamental, so would be the differences among them. When the Court has to choose this or that variant of a right 'for Europe', it is making, implicitly, a choice about the cultural identity of Europe. The stakes, thus, are high. They are even higher if we consider that many would consider that the *autonomy* of different societies (certainly nation-states) to make these identity choices is as important as the choice actually made, and that this autonomy should be protected by boundaries as fundamental as the rights themselves. In essence, the exercise of European judicial protection of human rights inevitably manifests the inbuilt dilemma of a multi-nation and multi-cultural polity – that of reconciling the vindication of universal fundamental rights with the vindication of national autonomy guarded by fundamental boundaries.

It is worth exploring in greater detail the manifestation and contours of this problem in the context of European integration since this problem challenges the classical view which regards human rights as a net integration value.

Modern liberal states, taking their cue principally from a Franco-American rather than British democratic tradition, increasingly acknowledge a 'higher law' – typically a constitution, and, in more recent times, international treaties – which binds even the legislature of the state. In an increasing number of modern democracies the higher law is backed up by courts and a system of judicial review which give it, so to speak, teeth. Within this constitutional ethos, judicial protection of fundamental human rights has a central place. Subjecting the democratically elected legislature to a court and the norms of a 'higher law' of fundamental human rights, despite the counter-majoritarian image, is regarded increasingly as a complementary foundation of democratic governance.

Whence this strong appeal of human rights? I think it has to do with two roots. The first of these regards fundamental rights (and liberties) as an expression of a vision of humanity which vests the deepest values in the individual, and which, hence, may not be compromised by anyone.

The other root for the great appeal of rights and part of the justification, even if counter-majoritarian, looks to them as an instrument for the promotion of the value *per se* of putting constraints on power. Modern democracy emerges, after all, also as a rejection of absolutism – and absolutism is not the prerogative of kings and emperors.

Similar sentiments inform the great appeal of fundamental boundaries in non-unitary systems such as federal states and the European Union. I use the term 'fundamental boundaries' as a metaphor for the principle of enumerated powers or limited competences which are designed to guarantee that in certain areas communities (rather than individuals) should be free to make their own social choices without interference from above. If you wish, if fundamental rights are about the autonomy and self-determination of the individual, fundamental boundaries are about the autonomy and self-determination of communities.

At first blush it would seem that these two basic principles need not clash at all. There could be, it would seem, a neat, tidy way to situate fundamental rights and fundamental boundaries within the constitutional architecture of Europe.

For example, one set of norms and institutions – national-constitutional and/or transnational – would take care of human rights: ensuring that no public authority at any level of governance would violate the basic autonomy and liberty of the individual. Another set of norms – national-constitutional and/or transnational – would take care of boundaries: ensuring that transnational governance would not encroach on fundamental societal choices of, principally, states.

The adoption of the European Convention of Human Rights by the Member States of the Council of Europe is a reflection of this tidy arrangement: the High Contracting Powers of the Convention retain their full prerogatives as sovereign states. State boundaries constitute thus fundamental boundaries *par excellence* which guarantee full autonomy of their respective national societies. The one self-limiting exception concerns the core fundamental human rights given expression in the ECHR which may not be transgressed in any of these societies. Thus, the universalism of human rights and the particularism of fundamental boundaries may rest together like the wolf and sheep.

You will note, however, that I used the term 'core fundamental human rights' in drawing this idyll. The neat arrangement which the ECHR may be said to represent can only work in relation to a core which gives expression to those 'rights', or to those 'levels of protection', which are said to be universal, transcending any legitimate cultural or political difference among different societies in, at least, the universe of Europe. The ECHR is premised on this understanding.

Crucially, the ECHR does not exhaust the spectrum of human rights. By its own self-understanding, whereas the ECHR provides the 'minimum standard' of protection 'below' which no state may fall, the High Contracting Parties are free, perhaps even encouraged, to offer 'higher' standards of protection to individuals. Indeed, part of the uniqueness of states, part of what differentiates them from each other, may be the very way they give protection beyond the core universal standard.

Thus, the commitment to, and the acceptance of, the ECHR as a universal, culturally transcendent core of human rights is, surely, an expression of a very important aspect of the political culture of a state which brings it together with other states and societies. When this is backed up by submission to transnational machinery of enforcement, the commitment is all the more expressive.

But, I would argue, the differences in the protection of human rights in these societies within the large band which exists beyond the universal core is no less an important aspect of the political culture and identity of societies. Human rights thus constitute both a source of and an index for cross-national differentiation and not only cross-national assimilation.

There is no dramatic conclusion to this final consideration. It is simply meant as a sobering reminder when we reflect on the import of the various instruments of human rights. In the process of integration, human rights becomes the perfect vehicle both for our celebration and hopes and for our hesitations and fears.

Note

1   For a full-fledged discussion of the need and content of such a policy, see Alston and Weiler 1999.

5 Treaty or constitution?

The legal basis of the European Union after Maastricht

Dieter Grimm

The legal form of the Community as a topic for reform

The Intergovernmental Conferences that have assessed and developed the Treaty of Maastricht have had to deal with matters of content, but also with the form of the legal basis on which the European Union rests. To date this basis has consisted of a number of international treaties among sovereign states. Yet the object of these treaties is precisely the transfer of sovereign rights to the supranational Community that was created by the states. So far this has not resulted in a new superstate in which the contracting parties exist only as constituent sub-states. Conversely, the EU does not resemble traditional international institutions, in which Member States agree to restrictions on the exercise of their sovereign rights without ceding them. Because the European Union – or, to be more precise, the European Community as its central pillar – possesses sovereign rights which are exercised with direct effect in the Member States, it breaches the dated dualism of states and international organizations and transforms itself into an intermediary polity that is both unprecedented and that lacks – even now – an adequate terminology.

This odd intermediate position rubs off onto the legal foundation. The broader the sphere of Community competencies became and the more intensively it was perceived by the Community organs, the more questionable it became whether the foundation in international law was sufficient to legitimize European sovereign power or whether the Community required the kind of legitimacy that states enjoyed. This question attracted public resonance only in the aftermath of the Maastricht Treaty, even though the European Parliament had first raised it in the mid-1980s. The discussion that ensued revealed the extent to which European integration had escaped public consciousness and had lost support among the populace. The reason for this chasm was quickly identified as a European democracy deficit whose removal, alongside the necessary reforms relating to the spatial enlargement of the Union, was to be the focus of the reform debates. The request to replace the international treaties with a constitution that is familiar to the Member States plays a key role. More plausible than the treaty agreement, the constitution is to bring the

EU closer to the citizens of the Member States and, above all, accord it the same legitimacy-conferring power that emanates from state constitutions.

It has, of course, become customary for European legal scholars to speak of the international treaty agreement as the constitution of the European Community, and the European Court of Justice, too, presumes that the Community possesses a constitution in the form of the treaties. However, if European legal scholars' assumption were right, the call to substitute the legal foundation would be void from the outset. In that case one could certainly talk about improving it, but hardly about creating it. Consequently, clarification is needed whether the treaties meet the demands that are associated with the idea of a constitution, or whether, and in what respects, they fall short of the demands. Then the question can be addressed whether a constitution – be it a newly created or a reformed one – would be able to meet raised expectations of democratic legitimacy. Finally, the response to the previous question will have repercussions on the present reform discussion about the basis of legitimacy, the institutional order and the division of competencies in the Union. I have discussed the first two points in detail elsewhere (Grimm 1995), and will reiterate most of them below. The response to the third question is offered here for the first time.

Treaty or constitution?

Constitution

The concept of constitution

When a Constitution for Europe is talked about today, what is meant is a basic legal order for the polity of the sort that emerged in the late eighteenth century in the wake of two successful revolutions in North America and France, and which has since spread steadily and now almost reaches worldwide. Constitutions in this sense had not existed before the eighteenth century. Instead, the concept had been used to refer to several features of a country, with legal institutions only one among many others. In contrast, the creation of a constitution in the normative sense owes much to the coming together of two circumstances. First, once religious patterns of legitimacy had faded, political rule was only deemed justified if it was supported by the consensus of the governed. Second, having experienced absolutism in either monarchical or parliamentary form, the governed were no longer prepared to grant an unconditional political mandate but only one tailored to specific goals and limited to certain means and forms. When the ancestral rule in both countries was brought down by revolutionary means, these aspirations inevitably had to result in the modern constitution.

The reason for this is that this programme found its own mode of realization in the law. The historical consensus of society about the form and the objectives of its political unit could only gain bindingness and durability through law. The limitation of the political mandate and the adequate organization of the system of government (*Herrschaftsapparat*) was no less dependent on law. Yet, since its positivization in early modern times, the law had itself become the product of state decision-making. Under these circumstances, the objective of legalizing state power could only be achieved by splitting positive law into two different groups of norms: one on the institution and exercise of state power, and the other on the conduct and relations of the individual. Both groups of norms then had to be hierarchically ranked and assigned to different sources. The norms in the first group have their origin in the sovereign and bind the state's power, and since they are to bind state power, they necessarily take primacy over the norms in the second group enacted by that power. The constituent source of state rule is not exposed to the arbitrary will of the governors. The second group of norms follows from state power and claims bindingness only if it satisfies the requirements of the first group.

The constitution has become the common term for the first group of norms. As the source of legitimacy and guideline for the exercise of authority, it refers to state power not only in some respects in the sense of qualifying authority (as was the case in pre-constitutional times), but in all respects and constitutive of authority. The claim to comprehensive validity must certainly not be confused with the total legalization of politics. Total legalization is neither desirable nor possible. The task of politics consists in the production of a just social order under changing circumstances. Total legalization of politics would render the discharge of such a basic task impossible. That would instead confine politics to the implementation of norms and thus ultimately reduce it to administration. A society so organized would render itself incapable of adaptation or even survival. The claim to comprehensive validity means only that no extra-constitutional holders or expressions of public power will be tolerated. By contrast, the constitution can regulate neither the input to the national policy-forming process nor its outcome in full. It is a basic order confined to laying down the goals and framework for politics, and otherwise left open to be fleshed out politically.

The constitution is not tied down to particular contents. Yet some typical features follow from its function of legalizing rule. Constitutions usually lay down the principle of legitimacy for political rule and the basic conditions of legitimacy of its exercise. This is done in the so-called 'state structure' or 'state objectives'. Then, all constitutions contain provisions as to the institution and exercise of state power: organizational and procedural rules guaranteeing the handling of public power in conformity with certain principles and intended to avert abuses of state power, usually adopting the rule of law and the separation of powers for the purpose. Again, the constitution regularly sets limits to the state's power of coercion, on the one hand, and to individual freedom and social autonomy, on the other. This is the object of fundamental rights. The combination of all three elements is admittedly not conceptually necessary to a constitution. But a document that does not acknowledge any kind of legal bindingness or excepting major bearers of governmental functions or expressions of public power from regulatory intervention would no longer be termed a constitution, but would be a case of semi- or sham constitutionalism.

Though in nature a complex of legal norms, the constitution is not exhausted in its legal validity. On the basis of its legal effect, it is instead an important factor for social integration. By fixing a society's basic consensus as to the principles of its coexistence and the settlement of its disputes, it links holders of different convictions and interests, enables them to settle their differences peacefully and facilitates the acceptance of defeats. By separating lastingly valid principles of action from decisions necessary in the short term, it gives the political process a structure that agents and the public can take as a guide, guarantees stability in change, and frees politics from continual debate over goals and procedures for forming a unity that would overstrain it given the standing need for and complex objects of decision. The constitution does all this, not by itself, but by drawing on social prerequisites that it can itself no longer guarantee. But for what it actually does there is at present no equivalent. Without a constitution, the situations it is designed to overcome would recur.

According to the above, a constitution as it is understood here has the following characteristics: it is a system of legal norms (1) that refers to state power and deals with its institution and exercise (2). Legitimate state power originates from the constitution; therefore it must be distinguished from the power that it creates – *pouvoir constitutes* – and must derive from the constituent power – *pouvoir constituent* – that lies with the people (3). The constitution claims comprehensive validity (4), in the sense that it conclusively determines the competence of bearers and expressions of public powers to govern. There is no space for proprietors of public power outside the constitution. Content-wise it regulates public authorities only within the terms of the basic framework (5). It sets targets and limits. It does not prescribe particular outcomes, but instead leaves a space for political creativity. The constitution *qua* foundation and limit of the competence to govern sits above the legal measures produced by the organs of the state and takes priority in the case of conflict (6). Finally, it is not exposed to the arbitrary will of the governors as it is the logically prior condition for the action of the organs of state (7).

The constitutional nature of the Treaties

On this basis the question of a European constitution can now be given a better answer. The problem here is the possibility of disconnecting the constitution from the state. Historically, the former related to the latter, and derived its significance from the legalization of state power. While the European Union consists of states, it is not itself a state. For all the uncertainty over how to characterize it and how it should develop in the future, this remains unquestioned. Yet this statement would constitute an answer to the constitutional question only if sovereign powers rested with the state alone. This is certainly true of the past. States could of course enter into international obligations or join international organizations, but international obligations or decisions by international organizations took on domestic validity only on the basis of a national incorporating act. The establishment of the European Union has changed this. It has been endowed by the Member States with sovereign rights (*Hoheitsrechte*), which it now exercises on their behalf but with the same effect, in particular with direct domestic effect. Though not itself a state, it wields sovereign powers such that only states traditionally had.

The sovereign powers which the European Union exercises within the Member States are, however, not governed by their constitutional law, though the national constitutions regulate the conditions upon which the Member States may transfer sovereign rights to the Community. Once they are transferred, their subsequent exercise by the Community bodies is no longer subject to national law. Nor could it be otherwise. A supranational organization to which Member States transferred sovereign powers for their common exercise would immediately fall apart if every member could subject the exercise to its own national legal regime. It admittedly remains a moot point whether domestic validity of Community legal acts falls under the – nationally verifiable – reservation that it stays within the limits of the treaty powers and does not clash with supreme national constitutional principles. But national constitutional law cannot claim to apply to the institutions of the Communities. Each system has its own sources and its own validity conditions. This does not mean that they can never conflict. But in that case it is national law that – in principle – must give way, not Community law.

A question then arises which did not come up before the creation of the unprecedented entity that the European Community is – because of the congruence of state and legal order. Does the need for legalization that was met by the constitution refer to the form of government, namely the state, or rather to the means of government, namely sovereign power? Once the question is put in this way, the answer is no longer hard to find. The state is bound by law because, and in so far as, it exercises public power. That power contains the danger and the potential for abuse that are supposed to be restrained by the national constitution. What needs legalization once the state's monopoly of power goes and it shares its authority with non-state bearers is, then, sovereign power, irrespective of whether it lies with the state or with a supranational entity. If the historical achievement of the constitutional state, the legalization of power, is to be maintained, then logically we also need to legally bind the public power wielded by the European Community as the branch of the European Union empowered for sovereign action. Otherwise, partial absolutism would impend in the Member States where European public power intervened.

To be sure, the legal binding of the public power exercised by the European Community is not missing. The Community, owing to the lack of a pre-existing social substrate that could unify it, exists only as a legal community. The law it is bound by in making its legal acts is what is known as primary Community law. It is to be found in the treaties that the Member States have concluded to establish and advance the Community. At present the version that applies is the one resulting from the Treaties of Maastricht, Amsterdam and Nice. This law constitutes the Community, sets its objectives, establishes its institutions, assigns their powers, and orders their procedures. These are all areas dealt with at national level in the national constitutions. The question is whether primary Community law can on that ground itself be called a constitution, as assumed by European legal scholars, or whether the specific form of legal binding of power contained in a constitution remains restricted to the state. A proper answer to such a question can only result from a proper comparison between the Treaties and the constitution. Here the same features can be taken as a basis that has already been worked out for the constitution.

The object of the legal norms contained in the Treaties is, as with Member States' constitutions, public power. This is transferred by the Treaties to the Community at the same time as they regulate it organizationally and substantially. That too is done by way of a basic order, even though it contains more in some ways and less in others than national constitutions usually do. The Treaties lack a catalogue of fundamental rights bringing the relations between the Community and the natural and legal persons subject to it under the guiding principles of freedom and equality. This position is in no way changed by the newly adopted but unelaborated respect for human rights and fundamental freedoms. By contrast, they are much more exhaustive and detailed on objectives and organizational and procedural rules than are national constitutions. Neither of these points, however, deprives the Treaties of their character as a basic order. Fundamental rights are a usual but not indispensable component of constitutions, and wealth of detail in no way changes the fact that the Treaties form the basis and the framework of the numerous acts through which the Community produces, applies or implements secondary law.

Primary Community law also claims comprehensive validity. Who may act bindingly for the Community and what conditions have to be complied with thereby are exhaustively regulated in the Treaties. There is no European public power outside the Treaties, and no manifestation of such power that cannot be traced back to them. Compared with states, however, the powers reach less far. While states claim potential omni-competence, here the principle of limited individual empowerment applies. The Treaties thus do not have the full contents of a constitution. On the other hand, national constitutions' totality shrinks in proportion to the transfer of sovereign powers to the Community, though admittedly without this being made explicit in the text, as is the case in federal constitutions. Primary Community law also claims primacy over the legal acts enacted by the Community – secondary Community law. It lays down the conditions for the latter to have validity. After all, the Community organs have no power to alter the law they are subject to. Primary Community law can be amended only by the Member States, to which it owes its existence, by treaty.

Today, constitutions are certainly no longer usually brought in or amended by treaty. But in the nineteenth century treaty-based constitutions could be found, both through state mergers or out of revolutionary pressure on kings, who did not necessarily fully abandon their pre-constitutional legitimacy while partially recognizing popular sovereignty. Even in these cases, however, amending the constitution was a matter not for treaties but for constitutional decisions, even if several agencies had to be brought to agree. On the other hand, it is inherent in a constitution in the full sense of the term that it goes back to an act taken by or at least attributed to the people, in which they attribute political capacity to themselves. There is no such source for primary Community law. It goes back not to a European people but to the individual Member States, and remains dependent on them even after its entry into force. While nations give themselves a constitution, the European Union is given a constitution by third parties. It consequently does not have the power of disposal of its own constitution. The 'masters of the Treaties', as it is sometimes put, are still the Member States, who have not been, as it were, absorbed into the Union.

Democracy

The so-called 'democratic deficit'

This comparison enables us to state that the Treaties have various functions in relation to the European Union's public power that in the domestic context would be served by national constitutions. To the extent that constitutions are concerned with legalizing political rule, the Treaties leave nothing to be desired. Fundamental requirements of modern constitutionalism are thus met in the Community. This gives the justification for the position that European legal science has taken on the constitutional question. The Treaties are not, however, a constitution in the full sense of the term. The difference lies in the reference to the will of the Member States rather than to the people of the Union. Many European lawyers gloss over this. The European public power is not one that derives from the people, but one mediated through states. Since the Treaties have not an internal but an external reference point, they are also not the expression of a society's self-determination as to the form and objectives of this political unity. In so far as the constitutions are concerned with the legitimacy of rule by those subject to it, the Treaties fall short of the constitutional mark. This provides a justification for the position that has dominated European political discourse on the constitutional question.

This intermediate status is also reflected in the shape of the basic order. Institutionally, the European Union does not follow the state model, but has developed a pattern of its own, marked by its supranationality. The guiding, rule-giving body is the Council, made up of representatives from the Member State governments. The most important Community decisions thus lie in the hands of agents who have their reference point, as far as legitimacy and responsibility go, not in the Union, but in the Member States. The Community interest finds its organizational locus, by contrast, primarily in the Commission. From it comes the initiative for Council decisions; it sees to their execution and can, if need be, with help from the European Court of Justice, assert Community law against the Member States. Community interests are also represented by the European Parliament now that its members are no longer nominated from national parliaments but directly elected by Union citizens. Yet it does not, as in Member States, form the centre of democratic mediation but remains, even after its advance from a merely consultative to a co-decisional role, essentially restricted to the role of a veto player.

This institutional arrangement is increasingly criticized because it can no longer meet the requirements of democracy stemming from the degree of integration now reached. In fact the Community could at the beginning live well enough on national democracies. Not only was the Council, the central decisional body, made up of representatives of Member State governments, but, moreover, its decision-making rule was unanimity, and the volume of decisions was comparatively slight. Nowadays, the number of decisions to be taken has grown considerably in both numbers and areas. Moreover, because of such an increased volume, the Council has delegated a number of decision-making powers to the Commission, and those that it has reserved for itself are often no longer subject to the unanimity requirement. But this opens up a democracy gap: the democracy principle is valid for the Member States, whose own capacities for decision are, however, dwindling; decision-making powers are accruing to the European Community, but the principle of democracy is only weakly developed there. This leads to a growing need for European policy to have democratic legitimacy of its own, one not derived from Member State governments.

The remedy is mostly sought in the Parliament, the only Community institution endowed with direct democratic legitimacy through European-wide elections. The European dimension is, however, only brought out in the simultaneousness of what are national elections. They take place according to national electoral law, national parties compete for seats in the European Parliament; domestic issues dominate the voters' decision; electoral reporting takes place within the national context. That is why a European electoral law is included in the catalogue of demands that is to boost the European Parliament. The principal aim is to give Parliament those powers that people's representative bodies usually have: legislative powers, budgetary powers, the forming of and the checking on government. This sort of extension of powers would of course affect the other institutions, especially the Council, which would be pushed from its central position embracing both legislative and executive functions. On these conceptions it would change into a second legislative chamber, where nations would be represented, while the Commission would move up to government. Some would like to round off this institutional structure with the election of a European president.

This construction is obviously inspired by the national constitutional state, and in that case it would certainly seem appropriate to clothe it in constitutional garb. This would do more than just take account of the demand, widespread since Maastricht, for a more transparent and comprehensible basic order for the European Union. A constitution that added all those missing elements to the Treaties would additionally relate the Union more closely to the people and thus close that legitimacy gap that the treaty-based construction has left in its wake. One could now do without indirect democratic legitimacy through national governments and their parliamentary back-up (*Rückbindung*), which, moreover, fails when a Member State is outvoted in the Council. The Council would no longer have to bear the burden of legitimacy and could focus on the protection of Member State interests (as a whole and not individually) by providing a counterweight to the centralizing and unifying tendencies of the Union. It is, however, tacitly assumed that the transfer of state patterns of legitimacy to the European Union would have the desired democratic effect. Precisely that premise is not self-evident and requires closer examination.

Democracies are characterized by legitimating political rule consensually, and not transcendentally, traditionally or through elites. State power derives from the people and is exercised on their behalf by special agencies which in turn are answerable to the people for such exercise. The people are certainly not some community whose unity and will are pre-given, just needing to be given expression through the state bodies. They are instead permeated by divergences of opinions and interests, out of which negotiation or majority decision in the political process must first create unity, which can of course change. The key problem of this sort of system, in which possession and exercise of state power are separated, is mediation between people and institutions, and the biggest danger comes from the latter's tendency to become independent. The constitutional solution to this problem lay in the periodic election of a representative body in which the various social interests were present and strove for compromise, to be embodied in laws by which the state's executive was bound. On top of this came the constitutional guarantee of free communication, without which the elections could not work.

Democracy ought not, however, to be equated with parliamentarianism. Admittedly, it is hard to conceive of democracy in large states with a continual need for decisions without a freely elected parliament. But the parliamentary process does not by itself guarantee democratic structures. On the one hand, the voters' individual preferences are no longer adequately expressed in the highly generalized electoral option between vaguely defined parties. The individual is instead thrown back on additional civic organizations and channels of influence in order to assert his or her views and interests. On the other hand, a party-recruited parliament cannot adequately reflect and process the multiplicity of social views and interests. The parliamentary process instead builds on a social process of interest mediation and conflict control that partly eases the burden on parliamentary decision-making and partly patterns it. The links between the individual, social associations and the state bodies are chiefly maintained by the media, which create the public needed for any general opinion-forming and democratic participation at all.

It is, accordingly, a 'statist shortcut' to assume that the mediation of opinion and interests, policy formation and decision-making, the assurance of stability and legitimacy that produce social cohesion are brought about by state organs alone. These are instead dependent on the manifold mediatory structures within society which, while they relate to the state institutions, are neither guaranteed by them, nor able to be replaced by them. This is why the success of democratic constitutions depends not just on the intrinsic excellence of their regulations, but equally on the external conditions for their effectiveness. This also applies to the central institution of democratic states, the parliament. The democratic nature of a political system is attested to not so much by the existence of elected parliaments, something which is today guaranteed almost everywhere, as by pluralism, internal representativity, freedom and capacity for compromise of the intermediate area of parties, associations, citizens' movements and media. Where a parliament does not rest on such a structure which guarantees constant interaction between the people and the state, democratic substance is lacking even if democratic forms are present.

Requirements of European democracy

It is well known that the mediation processes essential to democracy are not running satisfactorily even at the national level, partly because of the growing self-absorption of the political parties, partly because of asymmetries in interest representation, partly because of deficits in communications systems, which are often oriented more to economic imperatives than to opinion formation. At the European level, though, even the prerequisites are largely lacking. Mediatory structures have hardly even been formed yet. There is no Europeanized party system, just European groups in the Strasbourg parliament, and, apart from that, loose cooperation among programmatically related parties. This does not bring any integration of the European population, even at the moment of European elections. Nor have European associations or citizens' movements arisen, even though cooperation among national associations is further advanced than with parties. A search for European media, whether print or broadcast, would be completely fruitless. This makes the European Union fall short not just of ideal conceptions of a model democracy but even of the already deficient situation in Member States.

The prerequisites cannot simply be created. It can admittedly be expected that advancing parliamentarization of the European Union would also enhance the pressure to Europeanize the party system. A similar development could be expected with interest groups. It can certainly be assumed that there would be Europeanization at the level of leaderships and officials, while the levels of membership, because of lesser communicatory competences, would continue to be defined nationally. The distance between elite and rank and file, which, in view of the professionalization of politics, is already a problem for democracy nationally, would accordingly increase still further in a European context. In addition, the degree of emergent oligarchy would depend on party positions. Parties representing lower-class interests would suffer from even greater internal distance here than those tending to represent higher strata, and a similar gap could be expected between associations representing the interests of mass memberships and of anonymous enterprises. New social movements and especially *ad hoc* initiatives, which are increasing their importance at national level, would, by contrast, be largely barred from the European level.

Prospects for Europeanization of the communications system are absolutely non-existent. A Europeanized communications system ought not to be confused with increased reporting on European topics in the national media. These are directed at a national public and remain attached to national viewpoints and communication habits. Accordingly, they cannot create any European public or establish any European discourse. Europeanization in the communications sector would, by contrast, mean that there would be newspapers and periodicals, radio and television programmes offered and demanded in a European market, and this would create a nation-transcending communicative context. But such a market would presuppose a public with language skills enabling it to utilize European media. That would be the case either if every journalist could use his or her own language and still be sure of being generally understood, or else – more realistically – if some European lingua franca were to place itself (like Latin in the past) alongside the mother tongues without being confined to an educated stratum. The European Union is a long way away from that.

Here, then, is the biggest obstacle to Europeanization of the political substructure, on which the functioning of a democratic system and the performance of a parliament depend: language. Communication is bound up with language and linguistically mediated experience and interpretation of the world. Information and participation as basic conditions of democratic existence are mediated through language. In the European Union there are now eleven languages, none of which covers a majority of the population. Even English and French are each foreign languages to over 80 per cent of the Union population. Even though these two languages predominate in the Community institutions and foreign-language competence in the younger generation is increasing, this does not change the fact that the large majority of Community citizens can communicate only in their own mother tongue, and thus remain cut off from direct understanding or communication in any European-wide communication. This is not just a private loss. Citizens are instead 'participatively restricted' (Lepsius 1993: 255) and therefore disadvantaged in the European opinion-forming and interest-mediation process, which suffers much more than any national one from remoteness from its base.

The importance of the language factor for the possibility of European democracy is often underestimated, partly because a concept of democracy that is confined to the area of organized opinion-formation predominates, so that the language skills of the functional elites, or even a large-scale translation system, are taken as sufficient; partly because of a failure to perceive the democracy's dependence on the opportunity to communicate. Pointing to multilingual states like Switzerland, Belgium or Finland, or multinational countries of immigration like the US, does not refute this. The above-mentioned European countries have between five and ten million inhabitants with two or three languages; the European Union has 370 million who speak eleven languages. The difference is not merely quantitative. It is certainly more important that a country like Switzerland had formed a national identity well before constitutionalization and relates its multilingual political discourse to it. The US, with some 250 million inhabitants, certainly comes closer to the European Union and similarly brings together people of many nationalities. By contrast with Europe, these have, however, abandoned their nation-state-based cohesion and accepted a new political homeland with a majority language and country-wide communications.

The absence of a European communication system, owing chiefly to language diversity, has the consequence that for the foreseeable future there will be neither a European public nor a European political discourse. Public discourse instead remains for the time being bound by national frontiers, while the European sphere will remain dominated by professional and interest discourse conducted remotely from the public. European decisional processes are accordingly not under public observation in the same way as national ones. The European level of politics lacks a matching public. The feedback to European officials and representatives is therefore only weakly developed, while national politicians orient themselves even in the case of Council decisions to their national publics, because effective sanctions can come only from them. These circumstances give professional and technical viewpoints, particularly of an economic nature, excessive weight in European politics, while the social conse-quences and side-effects are not properly taken into account. This shortcoming cannot be remedied, even by growing national attention to European policy themes, since the European dimension is just what is lacking here.

If this is true, the conclusion may be drawn that full parliamentarization of the European Union on the model of the national constitutional state will aggra-vate rather than solve the problem. On the one hand, it would loosen the Union's ties back to the Member States, since the European Parliament is by its construction not a federal organ but a central one. Strengthening it would be at the expense of the Council and therefore inevitably have centralizing effects. On the other hand, the weakened ties back to the Member States would not be compensated by any increased ties back to the Union population. The European Parliament does not meet with any European mediatory structure in being; still less does it constitute a European popular representative body, since there is as of yet no European people. This is not an argument against any expansion of parliament's powers. That might even enhance participation opportunities in the Union, provide greater transparency and create a counterweight to the domi-nance of technical and economic viewpoints. Its objective ought not, however, to be full parliamentarization according to the national model, since political deci-sions would otherwise be shifted to a level which cannot ensure democratic accountability.

The suspicion that this assessment is based on the premise that democracy is possible only on the basis of a homogeneous *Volksgemeinschaft* (ethnic community) is, after all, unjustified. The requirements for democracy are here developed not out of the people, but out of the society that wants to constitute itself as a polit-ical unit. It is true that this requires a collective identity, if there is a will to resolve conflicts without resort to violence, to accept majority rule and practise solidarity. But this identity by no means needs to be rooted in ethnic origin; it might have other bases. All that is necessary is for the society to have formed an awareness of belonging together that can support majority decisions and soli-darity efforts, and for it to have the capacity to communicate about its goals and problems discursively. What obstructs democracy is accordingly not the lack of cohesion of Union citizens as a people, but their weakly developed collective identity and low capacity for transnational discourse. This certainly means that the European democratic deficit is structurally determined. It can therefore not be removed by institutional reforms in the short term. The achievement of the democratic constitutional state can for the time being be adequately realized only within the national framework.

Treaty reform

Structure and tasks of society

Converting the European Union into a federal state can in these circumstances not be an immediately desirable goal. The reason is, to be sure, not that the political form of the nation-state ought to be preserved for its own sake. The entitlement of political units to exist cannot be assessed without considering what problems they are expected to solve. In this respect the nation-state, understood as a political unit that regulates its internal affairs autonomously, is something whose time is past. A large part of the problems needing political treatment can no longer be effectively solved in the narrow state framework of the European countries. This finding creates the pressure for supranational integration. If this is none the less not to be pushed as far as a European state, that is because it could not meet the democratic requirements of the present. Its level of legitimacy would be lower than a nation-state's, also lessening its capacity to solve problems, something that has not just technical but also legitimatory prerequisites. The need is instead to retain the special nature of the European Union as a supranational arrangement, and to build on this special nature; not to copy national patterns.

This is significant for the organizational structure as well as for the power structure of the Community. In relation to the institutions, the present functions of Council and Commission should essentially be kept. If the Union is an association of independent states for the achievement of certain tasks and for the communitarization of certain policy areas, then the decisions of the Union must retain their ties back to the democratic and functionally more agile Member States. That can, however, only be assured if the Council, being the organ in which the Member States are represented, keeps its central place in the institutional structure and if its function-transcending competences are not curtailed. It is here that the supranationality of the Community is expressed. The transformation of the Council into a second, nation-based chamber of the European Parliament would be incompatible with it. Because it functions like a hinge (*Scharnierfunktion*), it would also seem impossible to scale down the Council by not guaranteeing one seat to every Member State. The reforms of the mode of operation of the Council, made necessary after the accession to the Union of Austria, Finland and Sweden, have to take place below this threshold. Specific voting quotas (*Abstimmungsquoren*) do not follow from the supranationality of the Community, so far as they deal with treaty amendments.

If the Council keeps its present position, it follows that the Commission cannot transform itself into a government of the Union. It must keep on being an initiating and implementing organ. That said, it is not obligatory in a thus constituted Commission for every Member State to be represented at all times. The incoming accession of ten new Member States will result in the breaching of the limits beyond which the institution is incapable of being effective. Even now the size of the Commission means that related tasks are imprudently separated to match the internal division of departments. Whether this problem can be solved by some states agreeing to a common member of the Commission or a rotation, or if a hierarchy is introduced within the Commission (as is particularly the case with the British government), it lies beneath the threshold which is of interest here and which is determined by the supranationality of the Community. In contrast, the office of the President of the Union would reflect a degree of unity that cannot be attained in the foreseeable future. Thus, the Union does not need to be represented by one single person. Such an office would lack precisely the kind of internal legitimacy that can only derive from a European identity.

If the Council keeps its central position for the time being, the consequence for the European Parliament is that it cannot advance to become the central legitimacy-conferring organ of the Union. Conversely it should not be concluded that an association of states that is not yet a state itself does not require parliamentary legitimacy for its decisions. Unlike traditional international organizations, the European Community through its organs applies law with direct domestic effect. National parliaments are not sufficiently able to influence outcomes. It is accordingly indispensable to compensate the lack of national parliamentary control at the Community level. The absence of the European Parliament would imply the lack of a forum for criticism and control independently of the government that appraised Community law projects from a European rather than a national perspective. The absence of the European Parliament would also take away a level of transparency that enables public participation in the debate. On the other hand, the task of the Council of Ministers, which is dependent on the negotiation (*Aushandlung*) of national interests, is obstructed by publicity. The absence of the European Parliament would finally mean that expert discourse (*Fachdiskurs*) would lack the necessary political counterweight, and that the departmental projects would not have sufficient control of their external consequential costs and side-effects.

The European Parliament is thus credited with everything but a marginal position. It is not to be doubted that it requires weighty decision-making powers if it is to fulfil its function. It could not perform that function effectively in the role it was initially given of a mere consultative organ. European law-making requires parliamentary co-decision. The supranationality of the Community is not opposed to an expansion of parliamentary powers. The Community-specific boundary line is only drawn in the case where the parliamentary power would go beyond co-decision. So long as Parliament lacks the social substructure that would elevate it to a European peoples' representative body, decisions have to be tied back to the democratic processes of the Member States. That would cease to be the case if Parliament were entitled to override the Council. Thus, the parliamentary powers cannot be stretched beyond cooperation on an equal footing with the Council. Absolute equality, however, would evoke the danger of blockages, which, to the extent that nineteenth-century constitutionalism in Germany can teach lessons, would ideally require mechanisms of resolution. But one cannot turn to Parliament for help.

As regards the division of competences, the supranationality of the Community prescribes that the Member States must keep sufficient political substance for their own decisions. This is currently not secured by the Treaties. Since they do not distribute the responsibilities between Community and Member State according to subjects, as is the case in federal states, but rather commit the Community to a goal (the common market) and determine the authority to regulate according to targets, all policy areas come under one potential Community caveat. Since the Community can only exercise its regulatory powers in the interests of the market, economic issues are more compelling and threaten to dominate over other areas that are not primarily economic issues. The right of Member States to continue to regulate all non-border-transcending issues according to their own ideas is not a sufficient counterweight. Rather, they too get caught in the maelstrom of Community law, for they would otherwise be liable to reverse discrimination. The Council can also not be relied on to pull the brakes on the desire to protect national areas of responsibility, because the European level is often used to avoid national responsibility or circumvent internal restrictions or resistances.

The danger of exhausting (*Auszehrung*) the national political level was recognized during the negotiations of Maastricht. From the two possible routes of providing a remedy, subject boundaries in the form of positive or negative competence catalogues, or functional boundaries in the form of a general directive on distribution, the Maastricht Treaty opted for the second route and introduced the subsidiarity principle to limit the competences of the Community. Without further elucidation the principle is too vague to be used as a benchmark in case of doubts about competency. Even the European Court of Justice does not consider it to be a justiciable norm on the basis of which it could make legally based, as opposed to politically motivated, decisions. The subsidiarity principle thus relies on precision in its contents and procedural supporting measures. It should also not be applied in a forward-looking manner but must make allowance for the control of earlier decisions. The *acquis communautaire* does not provide an absolute limit. This, of course, does not exclude an expansion of Union powers. Following Scharpf (1993) and the reasons he enumerates, I would expect that expansion to be in the area of foreign and security policy rather than in domestic policy areas.

Legal foundation of the Community

The answer to the constitutional question follows from the fact that a European federal state is, because of its (likely) weak democracy, not a short-term desirable goal. Here, though, a distinction between the external form of the constitution and its internal ground of validity seems useful. In so far as the call for a consti-tution is only about the constitutionalization of the existing legal bases of the European Union, so that their objectives and structures become more trans-parent for Union citizens, this can be achieved by separating those constitutional features that are typically embodied in national constitutions from the numerous specific regulations that have additionally found their way into the Treaties. The external form of the 'core treaty' thus created would now be brought into line with a constitution. Yet this would neither imply an internal change of the treaty character, nor would the other treaty features lose their status as primary Community law. The same is true of the institutional reforms that will become necessary, as the organizational structure and the decision-making procedures are in danger of reaching the limits of their performance after the impending enlargement of the European Union. They can be satisfied through treaty amendment without them having to be transformed into a constitution based on the nation-state model.

In so far as the call 'from treaty to constitution' is aimed at adding those elements to the Treaties that continue to separate them from a constitution in the full sense of the term, this would result in the transformation of the European Union into a state. This is not clear to many who, because they are sympathetic to constitutions or in the interest of democracy, call for a European constitution. The missing elements consist of popular legitimation of the legal norms that constitute the Union, and the implicit self-determination of the Union citizens over form and content of their political unit. But a constitution would also change the basis of legitimacy of the European Union. No longer would the Member States determine, through their national constitutional provisions of democratic will formation, the form and direction of the European Union. The basic decisions would rather be taken by the people of the Union (*Unionsvolk*), or in their name. It would be the constitutional fount, so to speak, of the Union. This would still be the case were the Member States to participate in the creation and in the amending of the constitution. They would do so not as 'masters of the treaties' but, rather, similar to what is the case with the German Bundesrat, as an organ of a self-determining Union.

With it, constitutive elements of the current basic order would be abandoned at the same time. The principle of limited individual empowerment of the Community through the Member States would break down. Even if, as is the case with the German Constitution, the Community continued to possess only explicitly transferred powers, whilst the presumption of competence lay with the Member States, it would not change the fact that this distribution of powers would be determined by the constitutional power of the Union, or of Union bodies thus empowered, and not by national constitutional powers, which means, accordingly, that the distribution of powers could be changed indepen-dently of the unanimous will of the Member States. With a constitution in the full sense of the term, the Union would gain competence-competence. Likewise, the primacy of Community law over national law would be the result no longer of the Member States' orders issued in the treaties, but of the constitutional precept in the Community constitution. The Community would in principle be able to provide itself with constitutional powers instead of having to live off the allocation of powers by the Member States. These attributes are foreign to a union of states (*Statenverbund*). They characterize the state.

Since such a state, however, does not possess the intermediary structures on which the democratic process thrives, the Community after its full constitutionalization would be a largely self-supporting organization, further removed from its basis than before. Whilst there is no unilateral dependent relationship between social structures and political institutions, institutional reforms can foster social developments. Under the existing conditions long periods of development have to be anticipated. Institutional advances must, for this reason, not be overstretched. This is particularly the case with constitutions. The proper legal foundation for an association of states is the treaty. It possesses all the properties that provide for the legal bindingness of Community powers, whilst leaving the fundamental decisions about the Community to the Member States, where they can be controlled democratically. A European constitution could not bridge the existing gulf and would, therefore, not be able to live up to expectations. The legitimacy it conveyed would be a sham legitimacy. At the end of the day, the constitution remains bound to the state, and those who call for a European one should know exactly what they would be setting in motion.

This is of importance principally for primary Community law. If the treaty is not only the historical form of its materialization, but continues, by its nature, to be an agreement between states, then amendments and additions are also reliant on the treaty form. Review of the basic order of the Community, as contained in the Treaties, is thus a matter that can occur neither at the Community level nor through majority decisions of the treaty partners. Rather, in addition, treaty amendments continue to require a unanimous vote by the Member States in the Council and, moreover, must be ratified in accordance with national constitutions. It is, of course, possible for the European Parliament to participate in the treaty revision process. But as a pure Community organ that is independent of the Member States, it cannot take precedence over the lack of unanimity in the Council, or a Member State's failure to ratify. Not in form but in substance does the principle of enumerated competences in Article 235 of the Treaty of European Community (TEC) come close to a treaty amendment. It would be worth considering discarding the provision and relegating additional powers to the treaty amendment process.

Clinging to the treaty as the basis of legitimacy for the Union also has consequences for the jurisprudence of the European Court of Justice. It is entitled to interpret and apply primary Community law but is not competent to change it in the process. Treaty changes that the Member States have not consented to, or measures that are based on such amendments, are not legally binding in the Member States. That is the essence of the *Maastricht* decision of the Federal Constitutional Court.[1] Yet it is extraordinarily difficult within the realm of interpretation to make a sharp distinction between the adaptation of primary Community law to changed circumstances regarding its realization, or its development in the light of new circumstances, on the one hand, and treaty amendment, on the other hand. The jurisdiction of the European Court of Justice is thus an opening for the creeping constitutionalization of the Treaties, and Weiler (1991: esp. 2413) has not unreasonably characterized its activity as 'constitutionalization' of primary law. If one does not want to allow the Member States to double-check those treaty inter- pretations they consider tantamount to a treaty amendment, then at least awareness should be sharpened as to the narrower limits of interpretation of a treaty- interpreting court of a supranational community compared ro the constitution- interpreting court of the Member States.

The current plans for reform (1996)[2]

If one projects these reflections onto the draft constitution that the Committee on Institutional Affairs of the European Parliament presented on 10 February 1994 (European Parliament 1994), as well as onto the report of the '*Reflexionsgruppe zur Regierungskonferenz 1996*' of 5 December 1995 (European Council 1995a, 1995b), then both differ considerably, particularly on what concerns the legal nature of the European basic order. While the reflection group deals with the development of the treaties without changing its nature, the Parliamentary draft transcends the boundary between treaty and constitution. This is not only expressed in the name but also pervades the contents. The Union's basis of legitimacy is no longer the unanimous will of the Member States but the sovereignty of the people: '*All power of the Union derives from the citizens*' (Art. 1(1)). Accordingly the entry into force of the constitution does not require unanimity among Member States. A majority of the Member States that corresponds to four-fifths of the citizens suffices (Art. 47). Once it is enacted, the constitution detaches itself completely from the will of the Member States and passes over to the self-determination of the Union. Constitutional amendments are no longer the result of treaty agreement of the Member States and ratification in their Parliaments but of the process of law- making by the Union organs (Art. 31(1)).

Although the Parliamentary draft retains the basic principle that the Union has only those powers that the constitution expressly grants (Art. 8(1)), such a transfer will in future be an instance of internal empowerment through constitu- tional law, and not an external empowerment through treaty agreement. Even the ability of self-empowerment, which, according to Art. 235 TEC, requires unanimity in the Council, is relegated to the process of institutional law-making and the majority principle (Art. 9, Art. 31(1)). Moreover, the Union has the right to create through law additional institutions or agencies with legal personality (Art. 13(3)). Although the existing institutional order largely remains in place, the Council loses importance. In the legislative arena, Council and Parliament are ranked on an equal level, while the executive functions of the Council are reduced (Arts 15, 16, 18). Unanimous Council decisions are only designated for a transitional period before being phased out (Art. 20). In financial respects the draft constitution also separates the Union from its dependency on the Member States and places it, albeit somewhat unclearly, on its own footing (Art. 40).

From quite a different perspective, the reflection group is guided by the aim of increasing the legitimacy of the Union in the eyes of citizens, as well as providing it both with an institutional order that is tailored to future enlargement, and with an increased capacity for external action. Whilst it strives for a 'simpler treaty', it does not move away from the basic structure of the treaty. Amendments to primary law will continue to require unanimity in the Council and ratification through national parliaments. The institutional balance will also be kept. The Council is to keep its position as 'the highest expression of the Union's political will' and 'highest instance of decision-making'. There is no unanimous agreement regarding the transition to the majority principle and its application to extra-treaty matters. Parliamentary powers should be simplified but not expanded considerably. Some Members want to involve the national parliaments in order to make the subsidiarity principle more effective. The principle of subsidiarity is not, however, to be supplemented with a catalogue of competences. Although the interim report still speaks of a 'quasi-constitutional process', the treaty revision stops short of a constitution in the full sense of the term and thus does not transform *sub silentio* the supranational Community into a federal state.

Notes

This chapter was originally published as 'Vertrag oder Verfassung: Die Rechtsgrundlage der Europäischen Union im Reformprozess Maastricht ii', in D. Grimm *et al.* (eds) *Zur Neuordnung der Europäischen Union. Die Regierungskonferenz 1996–97*, Baden-Baden: Nomos, 1997. It was translated by Jo Eric Murkens.

1   BVerfG 1993; English translation in *Common Market Law Reports*, Vol. 57, No. 1 (1994).
2   Note that this chapter was originally published in 1997.

6 A polity without a state?

European constitutionalism between
evolution and revolution

Hauke Brunkhorst

Three ideas of constitutionalism

Europe still has a constitution without a state. Since the 1960s, legal scholars and
the judges of higher European and national courts have stressed – although
applying different constitutional concepts – the constitutional quality of parts of
European law.[1] The European Treaties seem to include all the essential elements
of a constitution:

- basic rights – including political rights and even affirmative action (Art. 13,
  141 TEC) and a variety of social rights (Bogdandy 1999: 26);
- an organizational (or procedural) element (*Organisationsrecht*): procedural
  norms, norms dealing with the order of institutions, competences, and so on;
- a clear distinction between primary law, which is on the higher level, and
  secondary law, which is governed by the rules of primary law.

After Maastricht and Amsterdam, the treaties of the many European communities constitute one, and only one, European Community. Before Amsterdam, there
were a variety of treaties and the same variety of communities; after Amsterdam,
there were a variety of treaties but only one community (Bogdandy 1999: 10, 32f.,
38ff.). Visible to every European citizen is the unity of Europe in our passports,
which are first those of the European Community, and then of the Member State.
Europe today is a supranational political union with a single – yet expandable and
expanding – territory, and a single citizenship (Ipsen 1987: § 181, 8, 41, 50, 53–4;
Bogdandy 1999: 10, 13, 25, 32f.). Yet here we are confronted with an initial
problem, which seems to be one of the specific problems of this new and unique
type of political union. If the European Union (EU) is *one* community with a
plurality of treaties, then the Schengen Convention refers to a different territory
than the treaties of Maastricht (TEU) and Amsterdam (TEC). Norway, for instance,
belongs to the territory inside the EU's external borders as defined by Schengen,
but it is not a Member State of the EU.[2] The Norwegians have no European passport, but they do have European borders and, incidentally, European law without
being citizens of the EU. They are addressees of European law with a *status negativus*
but without *status activus* (Jellinek 1979: 82).

Today, most of the legislation of all Member States (and even of non-Member States like Norway) stems from the legal bodies of the Union (Zürn 1996: 11; Bogdandy 1999: 3 [note 121]).[3] In cases of conflict, European law prevails over national law, including posterior parliamentary legislation and constitutional norms (Ipsen 1987: RN 32; Alter and Meunier-Aitsahalia 1994; Classen 1994: 240f.; Heintzen 1994: 574ff., 585ff.; Alter 1996; Joerges 1996c: 78ff.; 1996d: 230; Kaufmann 1997a: esp. 522, 526f., 534; Alter 1998: 121; Augustin 2000: 253; Grimm 2001a: 229f.; Classen 2001: xivf.; Scharpf 2002: 76). Though the discussion here has not come to an end, and the European Court of Justice (ECJ) has a much stricter interpretation of the issue of European law supremacy than some of the national supreme courts, even the German Constitutional Court (Bundesverfassungsgericht) has given up its claim to be the ultimate interpreter of basic rights concerning German citizens and German territory.[4] After the – up to a point – revolutionary Treaty of Amsterdam, there exists a European *unity* of civic rights, of budget, of political action, of organizations, an internal and external legal personality, an order of legal steps (*Stufenbau des Rechts*), and the ECJ claims the so-called 'competence-competence' (*Kompetenz-Kompetenz*) for its judgments, and in all matters concerning the interpretation of European law (Ipsen 1987: RN 9, 13; Oeter 1995: 687; Bogdandy 1999: 38ff..; Schwarze 2000: 464f.; Eriksen 2001: 9; Brunkhorst 2002a: 531f.).

From a *functionalist* point of view, there is no doubt that the European Union, which is neither a state nor a state in the making, has a constitution. Its legal and political systems are structurally coupled, thus satisfying the functionalist criterion of a constitution that is modern – and not only a *politeia* or any universal concept or a system of norms that submits law to political power, or, vice versa, political power to the judges – is the *structural coupling of the legal and the political system* (Luhmann 1990; 1993: 440ff.; 1997: 92ff.; Neves 2000: 80ff.). This is the *first* – evolutionary – idea of a constitution. European primary law stabilizes the borders that separate the legal from the political system, and secures the reciprocal independency of both systems. Yet the point here is that structural coupling fulfils this function of separating two autonomous social systems by organizing the reciprocal dependencies that connect both social systems systematically. Independence here grows both through and together with the growth of reciprocal dependency.[5] A constitution understood in a functionalist way specifies (1) regulative or procedural norms, and (2) constitutive or enabling norms. The *enabling* norms allow the permanent political change of law, on the one hand (political legislation), and the autonomous interpretation of law by courts, on the other (judicial reinterpretation of political action). The *procedural* norms have the function of legalizing political intervention in the legal system. Legalized political intervention causes a permanent irritation of the legal system by changing political will formation. Yet procedural norms also regulate the judicial review of political decisions and actions, and this causes permanent irritation of the political system. Because their independence is guaranteed by the constitution, both systems can influence each other, and learn from each other through *reciprocal* irritation. There is no doubt that Europe has a constitution in the functionalist meaning of that term. What we have may be called a 'treaty', or it may be called a 'constitution', but in any case we are in the middle of an ongoing *constitutional evolution*.

Usually the structural coupling of law and politics presupposes the implementation of democratic elections, the separation of powers, the formation of political parties and associations, and the effective guarantee of egalitarian basic rights (Neves 2000: 83ff.). But from a mere functionalist point of view this *must* not be the case. The very idea of systems theory is that there exists nothing in the world which has no functional equivalent. Therefore – again from a functionalist point of view – one can imagine constitutional regimes which are modern but which are not democratic or egalitarian: for instance, what John Rawls (1993a) called 'well-ordered hierarchical societies'.[6] As an *evolutionary* advance (Luhmann 1990), the structural coupling of law and politics is not at the same time a *revolutionary* advance (Brunkhorst 2003).

What the *constitutional revolution* (be it factual, as in the American and French cases of the late eighteenth century; be it counterfactual, as in the case of the German Basic Constitutional Code from 1948 [*Grundgesetz*]) adds to the *social evolution* of constitutionalism (as in the cases of Britain and Germany in the nineteenth century, the EU or functionally differentiated global systems today) is more than illusions of feasibility, and celebratory explanations ('*Machbarkeitsillusionen*', '*Gesänge und feierliche Erklärungen*'), as Luhmann once put it ironically (Luhmann 1990: 176, 180, 184). From the *revolutionary* or – more generally – *normative* point of view of the citizens of a polity or – more generally – of those who are affected by binding decisions, constitutions are systems of egalitarian legal norms that enable democratic politics (Jesch 1961; Habermas 1992; Maus 1992; Brunkhorst 2002b: Chs 1, 3; Möllers 2003a: 56). It is thus not clear that Europe has a fully fledged constitution in the normative meaning of a system of rights and organizational (or procedural) norms that enable democratic politics. There exists, as we have seen, egalitarian rights (TEU Art. 6 Para. 1, 2; TEC Art. 2, 12, 13, 17–22, Art. 144, 255, Para. 3, Title III; and *de lege feranda* the Charter of Basic Rights) and a strong commitment to democracy on the European level (TEU Art. 6, Para. 1, 4; TEC Art. 19, 22). The Treaties (as well as the blueprint of the new 'Constitution for Europe') prescribe a system of double legitimation by states *and* peoples or citizens. The legal subjects of the European Union 'are not only the Member States but their citizens as well' (Heintzen 1994: 570; see further Augustin 2000: 225). The European Parliament today is no longer only a parliament of 'an ever closer union among the peoples of Europe' (TEU, Art. 1, Para. 2), but is also the parliament of a single people or the European citizens, and this notion of a 'people' includes in principle all addressees of European law.[7] Henceforth, as a set of legal documents, the European Treaties are a constitution not only in a functionalist (or evolutionary) way, but also in a normative way.

But here we have to draw a further distinction. In the light of the tradition of a 'rule of law' regime that limits political power and domination, Europe has a *normative* constitution. Referring to this (British or German) tradition, a constitution is defined basically as a 'legalization of state power' (Grimm 2001a: 229:

'*Verrechtlichung der Staatsgewalt*'). This is the *second* – power-binding – idea of a constitution. But this is not the meaning of a fully fledged *revolutionary* constitution, which belongs historically to the tradition of the French and American Revolutions of the eighteenth century (Möllers 2003a: 4ff.). Such a constitution is a foundation of political power ('*herrschaftsbegründend*'). A normative constitution that binds state power can be heteronomous in the sense that it has been imposed on the people; they may accept it or not (for instance, the German Constitution of 1871). Differing from this second case, a normative constitution which is revolutionary is – like the German Constitution of 1918 – a constitution that goes back to the constituting will of the people (*pouvoir constituant*) (Siéyes 1981: 117–95). The basic constitutional question here is not – as Hannah Arendt once nicely put it – how state power can be 'limited', but how the power of a citizenship (or a people) can be 'established' (Arendt 1974: 191, 193). Here we have the *third* – power-establishing – idea of a constitution, which I – following Arendt – will call revolutionary, be it the outcome of an actual revolution or not.[8]

Such a revolutionary constitution presupposes the existence of a *strong public*, and I define a strong public here as the normatively effective, constitutional coupling of moral influence and political or administrative power: in other words, the constitutional coupling of convincing *discussions* – the very source of moral influence – and *binding decisions* – the very source of political power. In a fully fledged constitutional regime the moral influence of a public is enabled by:

1   a working system of *basic rights*.

They have to guarantee the inclusion of everybody's *voice*. This degree of normatively egalitarian constitutionalism is enough to constitute a *weak* public. But for the formation of a *strong* public, discussions and moral influence regularly have to be transformed into binding decisions and administrative power. This can be done only by means of:

2   a working system of egalitarian organizational and procedural *norms* (universal suffrage, general elections, popular votes, political parties, egalitarian representation, etc).

These norms have to guarantee the inclusion of everybody's *vote*. Together with the social condition of any public influence, which relies on:

3   the communicative use of mass-media of dissemination and the formation of associations of civil society,

a revolutionary constitution constitutes, and is reinforced by, a strong public. Such a strong public does not presuppose any homogeneity of culture or language, and can be designed with a variety of different cultures and languages, but it presupposes that there exists a working egalitarian procedure to transform public discussions into binding decisions.[9] There is some reasonable doubt whether Europe today has, or tomorrow – after the ratification of the new Constitution for Europe – will have, a democratically appropriate revolutionary constitution.

Constitutional evolution in Europe: planned and unplanned change

The existing European constitution is a constitution in permanent, deliberative making: a 'constitution-in-the-making' (*Wandelverfassung*: Ipsen – Ipsen 1983: 32; Schuppert 2000: 246). This European constitution-in-the-making has a latent and a manifest aspect. European constitutionalism on the side of social *latency* is mere evolutionary development, whereas on the side of *manifest* politics it is a deliberatively planned process, the *making* of a constitution. In the evolutionary process, the national and the European legal professionals, together with the new class of European bureaucrats, lobbyists, councillors, agents and politicians, play a major part. Case-studies made by, for example, Karen Alter or Susanne Schmidt have shown especially that legal dogmas from European Court decisions of the 1960s, such as those of European law *supremacy* or *direct effect*, and the growing constitutional power of the Court and the Commission are the effect of a silent evolutionary process.[10]

During the 1960s the power of the European Court of Justice (ECJ) was weak, whilst some major European states like France were critical of deeper integration in some areas. Precisely at that time, however, national courts started to apply more and more European norms. After some experiences with the rejection of their judgments by the highest national courts, they found it more convenient to back their decisions with legal expertise from the ECJ.[11] The effect was that the higher national courts usually no longer dared to cancel a decision of a lower court that was backed by ECJ jurisprudence, and since the 1980s the courts of last instance have anyway had to refer to the binding advice of the ECJ.[12] So by a great number of single court decisions, European law was progressively affirmed as superior over national law and a new level of European legal integration – security of expectations (Luhmann 1987: 99, 105; 1993: 126, 131f., 152) through the national application of European law – was evolutionarily *selected*, and *re-stabilized* through the functional differentiation of an autonomous legal system on the supranational level of the EU (Alter 1996). The new centre of this system is allocated in the courts (Luhmann 1993: 321). The same type of evolutionary process was observable in the politics of liberalizing European telecommunications or electricity energy markets in the 1980s. Here the European Commission's legislative power grew to a new level, and the Commission – usually backed by the now stronger ECJ – became the first guardian of the Treaties (Schmidt 1988; see, further, Scharpf 1999). Another example of the silent evolution of European constitutional institutions is the politics of re-regulating the common market, which was conducted by European legislative bodies during the 1980s and 1990s. Re-regulating politics were 'largely unforeseen by the European Treaties', and they functioned as a necessary compensation of the negative side-effects of de-regulating national markets which were foreseen by the Treaties (Everson 1999: 282ff.; Eriksen 2001: 7). In any case the centre of the now re-stabilized autonomous political system of Europe is not – as in the constitutional design of the nation-state – the Parliament, but the executive bodies (Commission, Council). Here we have a clear case of *gubernative Rechtsetzung* (governmental legislation) (Bogdandy 2000a). But this is different from the case of the nation-state, where governmental legislation still can be described as most important but *additional* to parliamentary legislation and *under control* of the parliament. With supranational organizations like the EU, governmental legislation is mostly out of parliamentary control, and replaces most parliamentary legislation (Bogdandy 2000a: 91).

On the other hand, there are the great decisions of consensual treaty change which are taken by the European Council like Maastricht, Amsterdam or Nice, and there are also major political and economic problems, which are usually solved by the leaders of state governments operating in a system of permanent cooperation. Here planned changes, backed by great power, are the rule, and political action is located on the intergovernmental level – driven primarily by national economic interests. Whereas unplanned evolution is more on the side of *supranational* institutions, deliberative intervention and planned change – as Moravcsik has shown – are the domain of *intergovernmental* consent.[13]

But planned or unplanned, voluntary or involuntary, latent or manifest, constitutional social change in Europe has an asymmetrical structure. In spite of a lot of social welfare efforts, social embedding politics, new regulatory institutions, equality politics, affirmative action, environmental politics, and so on, most social change in the Union is directed towards *negative integration* (Scharpf 1999: 43ff.; 2002: 76f.). Positive integration through social welfare politics, distributive justice, and so on, needs a system of domestic resources based on individual European taxes. This is already foreseen in the Treaties, and it seems to be feasible *in principle*, especially if it comes to taxes whose loss on the national level is partly due to the enforcement of the common market. These are primarily taxes on savings and incomes and corporation taxes (Menéndez 2003a). But even the Constitutional Convention did not dare to put this on the agenda. This is only partly due to a (not very democratically established) economic theory of neo-liberalism which still provides the background philosophy for the convergence and deficit criteria of the Union, and the politics of its completely independent Central Bank (Guéhenno 1996).

More important here is the fact that the 'European constitution-in-the-making' (*Wandelverfassung*) as a whole is the product of an evolutionary process without revolutionary backing, or any functional equivalent for a revolutionary constitution that constitutes a new political and social regime by the will of the people. In particular, the most powerful institutions of supranational government, the Central Bank, the Commission, the Court, have – contrary to their national equivalents – no direct democratic legitimation at all, and to change their legal competencies requires unanimous consent and not only qualified majorities, as in the case of national constitutional change (Scharpf 2002: 75f.).

Without direct democratic backing, these institutions are powerful when it comes to negative integration, which is completely backed by the intergovernmental consensus of the Treaties. Yet positive integration (taxes, redistributive politics, European welfare, etc.) lacks even the indirect democratic backing of intergovernmentalism. This – in my view – is the main difference that separates the existing (and coming) constitution of the EU from the formation of the US constitutional regime in the eighteenth and twentieth centuries, or from the 'mega-constitutional politics' of Canada, which in a lot of other aspects, as Fossum (2003a) has shown, is more comparable with the European constitutional system than the United States. Whereas a lot of pressure for all the major changes within the 1982 constitutional regime of Canada stemmed from *below*, from citizens' appeals and movements, from civil society, all important constitutional change in the EU – including the Constitutional Convention – has come from *above*, the product of a more or less closed elitist politics, which is the politics of a ruling elite of governmental, administrative and legal professional agents and agencies. When it comes to the US, the instructive comparison with the early US system of taxation, undertaken by Menéndez (2003a: 35ff.), is convincing in regard to the close relation between taxation and democratic representation, but a major difference remains. It is much easier to call for the democratization of an externally imposed, and undemocratic but existing, system of taxes, than to call first for a new tax base of all public expenditure, and then for representation (Menéndez 2003a: 50).

The democratic deficit of supranationalism

The so-called 'democratic deficit' of the Union is based on its social structure. The great winners of the Union are the new ruling class of governmental leaders, administrative agencies and legal and scientific professionals. States conduct themselves as one single, internally united actor, only in legal terms. The idea of an indivisible subject underpins the fiction of states as masters of the treaty. The legal fiction of sovereign states presumes that governments and all internationally acting national actors can be controlled by their national parliaments and by their peoples. But this is more or less a pure fiction, and, at the very least, an ideology to keep the politically ruling class in power (Wolf 2000). If it comes to the question of winners and losers, of social class interest and political power, we have to draw distinctions between the nation and the government, between national interest and that of the so-called 'political class', between those who are actually in power, and those who are more or less disempowered but should be in power, provided we take the constitutional norms seriously.

A democratic regime that takes the egalitarian norms of the constitution seriously needs *transparency* of decision-making and a *short* chain of legitimacy (Oeter 1995: 695f., 699ff.; Krajewsky 2001: 167ff., 176f.; Oeter 2002: 49). The paradigmatic cases of fully fledged democracy, therefore, are all *constitutional regimes of direct or parliamentary democracy* (see Table 6.1, box 1).

Table 6.1 Decision-making processes and chains of legitimacy

DECISION-MAKING	*Transparent*	*Non-transparent*
CHAIN OF LEGITIMACY		
Short	1 direct or parliamentary democracy	3 delegative democracy/populist regimes
Long	2 democratic intergovernmentalism	4 trans-/supranational organizations

In the second case of a *long* chain of legitimacy and *transparent* decision-making, we are concerned with *democratic intergovernmentalism*. This case is problematic from a democratic standpoint because of the *long* chain of legitimacy. One example may be NATO – if we look at it from the point of view of its basic idea (see Table 6.1, box 2).[14] Another example could be the branches of intergovernmental regimes (Council of Ministers and Prime Ministers) within the EU. But here we have to take into account the fact that only the first consent to the Treaties had sufficient democratic backing, because all subsequent changes could be implemented only with the consent of all other member states (Scharpf 2002: 74, note 15).

The third case is that of a regime with a *short* chain of legitimacy and a decision-making procedure which is *non-transparent*. This actually is the case with populist regimes, or what O'Donnell (1994) has called in a more specific way *delegative democracies*. Here we have for example a directly elected president, but there is neither sufficient (legal) access of the public, nor sufficient (legal) control by the people or their direct representatives over those who are really in power. Therefore most of the Latin-American (or the Russian) presidential regimes are omnipotent when it comes to decision-making, but impotent when it comes to the implementation of their advanced legal programmes (O'Donnell 1994: 55ff.). Even if in such a regime the system of public communication and civil society (newspapers, television, NGOs, protest movements, etc.) works well, there are – for example – no charges brought against those who are responsible for criminal acts of state power. This was the case with the Brazilian 'street kids' or the anti-corruption campaigns in most Latin American states: 'Cases of corruption are reported daily in the mass media but very little juridical investigation takes place' (de Souza Santos 1999: 59) (Table 6.1, box 3).

In this last case we have no democracy at all, and this is the case of *non-transparency* combined with *long* chains of legitimacy, which is true for all transnational or supranational organizations today, like the UN, WTO or EU. They are, if we regard matters pessimistically, *post*-democratic (Guéhenno 1994), or, if we regard matters optimistically, *pre*-democratic regimes – on the road to a 'third democratic transformation' that comes after the ancient *polis* and the modern nation-state (Dahl 1989) (Table 6.1, box 4). These regimes are regimes of *hegemonic law* (Brunkhorst 2002b: 171ff.). They are in favour of the social class structure described at the beginning of this paragraph because they tend to become – as Max Weber once suggested with reference to the German Imperial State (*Kaiserreich*) – a 'system of organized irresponsibility' ('*System organisierter Verantwortungslosigkeit*') (Weber 1921: 126ff.).[15]

So it seems clear that in a political order that has long chains of legitimacy and highly non-transparent processes of decision-making, as is the case with the EU, this structure is good only to keep those groups and organizations of the united European nation-states in power who *are* actually in power. The thesis of the states as sovereign masters of the treaties is so far nothing other than an ideology. Keeping the states masters of the treaties actually weakens democracy, internal and external to state borders. The united political class of state executives needs only *output* legitimation, an efficient but not very democratic Europe. *Input* legitimation therefore is only in the interests of the present losers in the unification process: the parliaments, the unions, the peoples. Fritz Scharpf's important question: 'Europe – effective *or* democratic?' (1999b), has a realistic background in the fragmented and socially differentiated power structure of Europe which is usually neglected in the political and scientific discourse.

Deliberative democracy

Is deliberative democracy a way out of the democratic deficit of supranationalism?[16] It depends. In relation to the EU, the idea of deliberation allows, first of all, a conceptually, as well as empirically, reasonable distinction to be drawn between supranational and intergovernmental modes of decision-making. Whereas intergovernmental decision-making is the effect of power-backed *bargaining* processes, supranational decision-making (Commission, Court and Parliament) has become more and more a matter of *arguing*, backed by convincing reasons, primarily in the European Commission's Committees (Joerges and Vos 1999).[17] For some scientific observers, comitology has become the realization of communicative rationality on earth. There is something true in that, because expert deliberation is essential for democratic legitimation in complex societies. Every specialized discourse is internally linked with democracy in the specific sense that the cognitive value, truth and validity of all expert judgements (of the scientific or the legal system) presupposes that *all* objecting voices have to be heard or taken into account – at least counterfactually. This is the basic idea of Peirce, Dewey, Habermas, Apel or Putnam. Consequently John Dewey, or today Hilary Putnam, suggests that the growth of democratic communication is a necessary condition for the solution of social, political, economic and even technical problems, and 'a requirement for experimental inquiry in *any* area' (Putnam 1991a: 64; see also Dewey 1984; Kloppenberg 2000; Putnam 1991b: 217). Here starts the fabulous success of deliberative democracy in the present discourse on national, European and global political institutions

But insight turns into blindness if we identify deliberation with democracy, because there is no democracy at all without egalitarian procedures of decision-making. We must therefore distinguish sharply between *deliberation* and *decision*. Democratic self-determination needs more than a right to express yourself (Möllers 2002). If democracy is rule by discussion, then it is not only discussion but also ruling; and if ruling is not organized by egalitarian procedures, then there is no democracy at all. The paradigm cases of deliberation are those of scientific or juridical discourse. The paradigm cases of democratic decision-making are those of the parliamentary debate or the public debate which leads to egalitarian votes and elections, hence binding decisions. These are linked to, but not backed by, argumentative consent (or reasonable dissent), as is the case with court decisions (judgments) or scientific assertions. The highly specialized deliberation of professionals is linked to democracy only in the material fact-based (*sachlich*) sense that a true *problem-solving discourse* has to take into account all possible perspectives concerned, all possible objections, criticism, proposals, and if it comes to the application of law, all interests and even needs which are affected by a legal decision (Günther 1988). EC Committees have to deliberate about the BSE crisis, technical standards, the health of consumers and all further relevant issues. In all these cases, as well as in court decisions, a broad spectrum of NGOs, legal and scientific experts, party-members, lobbyists, minority groups, women's groups, ages, outsiders, and so on, are very important to keep committees or courts open for new, neglected or silenced voices. But deliberations which have to be *materially inclusive* in respect of all the facts need not be *socially inclusive*, like parliamentary decisions, popular elections or voting. The deliberative supranationalism of EC Committees (or the ECJ) is not, and – if it wants to preserve its problem-solving capacity – cannot be, socially inclusive. Therefore, deliberative supranationalism is not, and cannot be, a normatively appropriate equivalent or alternative to democratic legitimation and pluralistic representation. There is no hope for mending the representative deficit of supranational organizations only through deliberation (Everson 1999: 292, 296f., 298). Deliberative democracy, administrative action closer to the citizens (*bürgernahe Verwaltung*), a 'cooperative state', and so on:

- 'cannot guarantee that *each* member of the society is only represented *once*,' and
- 'does not guarantee that *all* members of the society are *actually* represented' (Krajewsky 2001: 185f).

If materially inclusive factual deliberation goes together with non-democratic or democratically insufficient, hence socially exclusive, representation, nothing (and not the best Habermasian discursive rules) can guarantee that deliberation does not fall back into an ideology which only disguises particular social class interests. It is here that *legal formalism* comes in:

The fact that deliberation is just and civic now is no guarantee that it will always be so, and some measure of formal legal intervention may nonetheless be required to ensure that the deliberative process does not fall prey to powerful and organized interests.

(Everson 1999: 306)[18]

The usual scientific discourse does not require much legal formalism, because specialized scientific argumentation does not change the world by itself. *Problem-solving procedures* need only open doors to 'let all noises in' (John Cage), because there could be an unheard voice (Jürgen Habermas). But *decision-making procedures* require some more compulsory means of guaranteeing legal equality.[19] If the search for scientific and technical insight is directly related to the implementation and interpretation of law's binding decisions, then the (Deweyite) scientific 'culture of dynamism' must be replaced by a 'culture of formalism' (Koskenniemi 2001: 494ff.). Legal formalism is the only guarantee that the voices of weak, silenced and poor citizens will be taken into account, even in cases where the good will of those who have strong, elaborated and rich voices turns into the bad will of their particular interests.

Nothing other than legal formalism prevents material fact-based, inclusive deliberation from producing social class biases. This is so because:

Deliberative models are often favoured by the deliberative class – primarily professors who are, naturally, empowered by any process which privileges that which they have and which legitimates, even aggrandizes, their status and actual or pretended *modus operandi*, and in which the model for ideal government is a well-conducted seminar.

(Weiler 1999a: 348)

A social class bias – be it the class of university professors, jurists, politicians, higher officials, ecology activists or industrial leaders – seems to be unavoidable if democratic deliberation goes together with undemocratic representation. If the weak public of deliberative bodies – the so-called 'auditive democracy' (Eriksen and Fossum 2002: 420) – does replace the strong public of representative political bodies, then we are approaching the case of an 'unconstitutional role of a constitutional body' (Eriksen and Fossum 2003). The finality of the Union then will no longer be democratic, but at best 'good governance', enlightened absolutism and firm policing (*'gute Polizey'*).

State sovereignty, popular sovereignty and the internal contradiction of European constitutionalism

Since Maastricht and Amsterdam at the latest, the European Treaty constitutional system has no longer been legitimated by the intergovernmental treaties alone, but *firstly* by the ever more closely integrated (plurality of) peoples of Europe, and *secondly* by Union citizens as a whole, who are a *single European people in the making*.[20] European citizenship is backed by the principle of European (and not Member State) democracy, which is acknowledged explicitly in Art. 6, Para. 1 of the TEU, and in the system of citizens' rights in part two of the TEC, and backed by the increasing (but still too weak) power of the European Parliament. Therefore the seccession of one or even all Member States is legally bound to the participation of the Union citizens or Union people: they have to be asked (Brunkhorst 2002a: 534ff.). The Union now has a 'double legitimation' (Classen 1994: 259f.). Yet the *intergovernmental* track of legitimation is formally democratic but materially undemocratic, because it combines lack of transparency with long chains of legitimacy. And the other track, the *supranational* track of legitimacy, is insufficiently democratically institutionalized, from a formal point of view as well as from a substantial point of view.

The old idea of *state sovereignty*, which is deeply rooted in German constitutional discourse of the nineteenth century (Oeter 1995; Schönberger 1997; Möllers 2001b), is presupposed only by the intergovernmental track of legitimation. But this legal fiction is – firstly – deeply relativized by the inclusive principle of a democratic people. In the constitutions of the Member States the meaning of 'people' is procedural and not substantial, and this idea goes back to the constitutional revolutions of the eighteenth century in France and America (Maus 1994: 602ff.; Hofmann 1995: 17). The procedural meaning of 'people' includes the idea that those who are the addressees of law should be the authors of law (Habermas 1992; Oeter 1999: 38, 50ff.; Augustin 2000: 370ff., 397, 400, 402f.; Brunkhorst 2002b: 102ff., 226ff.). Because borders concern always both sides of a border line, secondly, the will of both sides – if we follow the principle of democracy – has to be taken into account in all questions concerning state borders and the 'external effects' of national legislation (Joerges and Vos 1999). Moreover, thirdly, the legal fiction of state sovereignty is relativized, for example, by Art. 24, Para. 1 of the German Constitution (*'Der Bund kann durch Gesetz Hoheitsrechte auf zwischenstaatliche Einrichtungen übertragen'*)[21] (see Oeter 1995). Fourthly, and at the very least, state sovereignty today is relativized by the reciprocal interpenetration of European and national law, which mediates and even assimilates the law of all states of the Union and abolishes the nineteenth-century fiction of impermeable states (Bogdandy 1999: 27f.; in general: Langer 1994: 17ff.; Maus 2001; Brunkhorst 2002b: 146ff.).

Contrary to the notion of state sovereignty, the notion of *popular sovereignty* must be strictly separated from the former (see Oeter 1995: 671f., 675f.; Walker 1998: 359f.; Brunkhorst 2002b: 96ff.; see further Walker 2001). The clear-cut distinction between autonomous legal self-determination (*Selbstbestimmung*) and heteronomous determination by another's alien will (*Fremdbestimmung*) therefore no longer implies the distinction between statehood and its absence.[22] Popular sovereignty only means that those who are affected by binding legal decisions have to be included as free and equal members in the procedures of producing these decisions. Popular sovereignty has no substantial meaning at all and aims only at the completely constructive formation of a common will from case to case (see, e.g., Kelsen 1921: 6ff., 60f., 84f.; Habermas 1992; Maus 1992; Oeter 1999; Lepsius 2000: 390ff.; Brunkhorst 2002b). Therefore the non-substantial notion of popular sovereignty is not only prior to all concepts of substantial communities or states, but it can also be separated from states and any particular community. Explicated in this way, the legal idea of popular sovereignty is presupposed by the second, the supranational, track of democratic legitimation of European law.

There is a clear tension between these two tracks of legitimation. On the one hand, the *organizational* norms of the present treaty-based constitution (and the blueprint of the new constitution as well) are clearly in favour of the hegemonic dominance of the executive branches of the intergovernmental and the supranational European institutions (Council and Commission). On the other hand, there are the *rights* of the European citizens, and the explicit acknowledgement of the principle of democracy on the level of the Union, reinforced by a still as-if-valid Charter of Rights (which is part of the blueprint of the constitution).[23] The rights of European citizens speak in favour of a European popular sovereignty which is the sovereignty of the people in the singular *or* the (more and more closely united) plurality of peoples of the Union. The *egalitarian rights* of European citizens clearly contradict the *non-egalitarian*, hegemonically disturbed *organizational and procedural structure* of decision-making in the Union. The democratic deficit of Europe relies on the fact that the citizens of Europe have rights, but have not given these rights to themselves:

> But you could create rights and afford judicial remedies to slaves. The ability to go to court to enjoy a right bestowed on you by the pleasure of others does not emancipate you, does not make you a citizen. Long before women and Jews were made citizens they enjoyed direct effect.
>
> (Weiler 1997: 503)

Yet the rule of law without public autonomy is not well-ordered freedom but, at the end of the day, well-ordered and convenient slavery. The history of the elitist integration of Europe is a paradigm case of *legalization without democratic politics*, effected by the political elites, backed and legitimated by the freestanding authority of the courts which apply and interpret European law. It resembles in this respect the old German Reich of 1871. At best, it limits political power, but does not establish it by the will of the people.

A unique evolutionary advance

The European Union is not a state and – as far as we can see – is not on an evolutionary track to statehood. *Étatism* is misleading anyway. The argument of the famous Maastricht ruling of the German Constitutional Court that the Union is neither a federal state (*Bundesstaat*) nor a federation of states (*Staatenbund*), but something in between, an association of states (*Staatenverbund*), goes in the wrong direction. The word 'state' (*Staat*) is what all these variants of concepts have in common. But the Union is a unique political entity which is not only a post-national, but also a post-statist entity. Any constitution of Europe therefore has to be a *constitution without a state*.

There exists no federal force or authority (*Bundeszwang*), no federal army, police, jail, and all the other cruel means of state power (Bogdandy 1999: 33). The Union is an independent union of nation-states which are just as independent as the Union itself (Bogdandy 1999: 13). Without its own monopoly of power, and without any material means of coercion to correct recalcitrant or insubordinate Member States, the Union works quite well as a legal and political community. European law is implemented everywhere in Europe, applied by national courts, concretized by national parliaments which have no legal alternative, and which cannot reject any European directive. European law meanwhile affects *any* area of national life (Grimm 1997: 26). Henceforth what in social evolutionary terms is most innovative about the European Union is a completely *new division of powers*. This new division of powers is that between, on the one hand, a non-statist and supranational legal and political order, and, on the other hand, a still statist monopoly of power, and a statist dominance over most social welfare concerns (Alter 1996: 458ff.).[24] Reduced to the important function of the old police state (*Polizey-Staat*) of the seventeenth century, the state has found an evolutionary niche in the storms of globalization. The new division of powers enables constitutions to function without a state. But these new constitutional regimes need strong and democratic nation-states for the implementation and enforcement of supranational law. This condition is fulfilled by the European Union but not – for example – by its Latin-American sister MERCOSUR, and not by other transnational or supranational organizations like the United Nations or the World Trade Organization, which have a basic constitutional structure (in part) similar to the EU (Brunkhorst 2002c).

There seems to exist only one historical prototype, and this is a *confederation* (*Bund*) of states. Historical examples are the North American Confederation from 1778/81 to 1788, or the *Deutsche Bund* from 1815 to 1866 (Schmitt 1989: 363ff.).[25] Here we have a similar division of powers as in Europe today. In some respects, these cases can now be described as 'preadaptive advances' of an evolutionary new type of social system like the EU, UN, WTO, and so on (Luhmann 1997: 392f., 501, 512f.). As Carl Schmitt suggested in the last chapter of his *Verfassungslehre* of 1928, the unity of a confederation must not rely on the (substantial) unity of a nation, but can rely as well on the family resemblance of political principles like democracy, human rights, international law among others (Schmitt 1989: 376). Schmitt correctly observed that in a working confederation the question of state sovereignty has to be kept open as long as the confederation exists (Schmitt 1989: 373; Oeter 1995: 674). Further, the Member States can no longer be described as impermeable 'legal persons' (as in the theories of Laband, Jellinek or Triepel) (Schmitt 1989: 371, 378, 381, 383).[26]

Yet a political body like the EU is not a confederation of states only. The whole Schmittian idea of a confederation or *Bund* of states suffers from being fixed to Jellinek's concept of a state as a legal and empirical subject, and henceforth falls short when it comes to the new evolutionary formation of supranational organizations with a double legitimation like the EU. The European Union is, as we have seen, a confederation of states *and* peoples

(Bogdandy 1999: 13). It is exactly here that the Schmittian concept of a confederation or *Bund* ends. Only as a confederation of citizens or *Bürgerbund* is the Union a 'constitutional association' (Bogdandy 1999: 13). With the notion of a European confederation of its own citizens (*Bürgerbund*), the democratic moment comes into play, which is of no import in Carl Schmitt's work on constitutional doctrine (the *Verfassungslehre*): if a confederation is not only a confederation of states but also equally based on its own, autonomous citizenship, then only the notion of procedural and intersubjective *popular* sovereignty comes into play. In such a confederation of states and citizens, the question of state sovereignty has to be kept open, but not the question of popular sovereignty. The latter can be ascribed to any process of will-formation which allows all subjects of law equal access to binding decisions. As differentiated from state sovereignty, popular sovereignty is – as we have seen – always already organized, procedural, coordinated and divided (see especially Oeter 1995: 671f., 675f.). The metaphysical question of a divine-like last decision is here dissolved into a circular process of revisable decisions which has to be held open for new and better arguments. Yet this constitutional and legislative power of the people(s) allows only as much state sovereignty, delegated legislation, administrative organization, and so on, as the constitution itself declares (Arndt 1963: 25, cited from Möllers 2001b: 422). Only popular sovereignty, therefore, fits the double structure of a confederation of states *and* citizens.

The coming constitution – a revolutionary perspective?

If there is any democracy in Europe, and if it is not less democratic than the former nation-states, it will be a democracy within *and* without the nation-state, and it must be more than national democracy *plus* deliberative supranationalism. Otherwise the non-democratic structures of the Union in concert with globalization will destroy what is left of the democratic nation-state. Europeans have something to lose in the process of Europeanization. Even if there is no way back, we still can *look* back to the democratic nation-state and generalize its democratic idea, abstract it from the state and re-specify it for European and global contexts. A democratically 'too modest constitutionalization could be proved retrospectively to be an evolutionary step towards the autonomy of the European technocracy' (Hofmann 2000: 205).

When it comes to the question of the coming European constitution, there seems to be no need for any European monopoly of power, because the new division of powers does work. The coming constitution of Europe 'only' has to democratize the European body of political and legal organizations and to give impulses to revitalize democracy on the level of states and regions. There exist a lot of good ideas, concerning:

* new forms of direct, veto-based democracy, giving more democratic power to the regions (Abromeit 2002);

- the unification of national parliaments, cooperating together with the supranational European Parliament in major decisions which would give much more weight to and public interest in national *and* European parliaments;[27]
- suggestions to end European 'green-room' politics by different versions of transparent two-chamber systems combined with a much stronger role for the European Parliament (Oeter 2002: 43ff.).

Only the latter suggestions have some chance of being partly realized during the present process of reconstitutionalizing Europe.

In the end there is only one structural problem that stands against the constitutionalization of European democracy, and that is the existing power structure. All the more or less convincing suggestions to democratize Europe are like 'long green-table games', since the 'ultimate instruments of control do not rest with the people but with the decision-makers' (Eriksen 2001: 8). The new European ruling class will allow democratization only if the pressure from below becomes stronger. In the end, it is not the *conventions* of an elite remote from the public but only the *citizens themselves* who can turn the legally already existing democratic constitutional textbooks *against* the marked lack of democratic legitimation in the real performance of European law. Legal textbooks, and especially constitutional texts, are not only words. They do not follow the particular interests of those who have invented them, with the intention of furnishing their undemocratic power with a convenient ideology. Constitutions which are positive law are part of what Hegel once called *objective spirit*. Therefore, they 'can strike back' (Müller 1997: 56).

Maybe in this respect the peace demonstrations across all European countries from 15 February onwards in 2003 were the beginning or the first sign of a social movement that could mobilize the power used to enforce a new, citizen-based European constitution. What was so amazing here was that, for the first time, the citizens of Europe *as* Europeans stood up as a *decentred, network-regulated unit* against the united, but in this question deeply divided, political leadership of the European governments. For the emergence of a European public which could enforce the constitutional process from below, the anti-war protest on and after 15 February might have been even more significant than the somewhat clandestine Constitutional Convention.

Here for the first time European citizens formed a common will on the streets, which was backed by a constitution-breaking majority. The protest of the European citizens was not only against Blair and Aznar, and for Chirac and Schroeder, and for a single European voice in basic issues of foreign policy; it also made everyone aware that the *representation* of the common will of European citizens in the organic bodies of the EU is completely insufficient. And this is since 1776 and 1789 the basic question directly addressed to the constitution: the question of equal representation. It was once: 'No taxation without representation!', or more politically, as in Paris: 'The Third Estate *is* the nation.' It is now: 'No democratic interventionism without representation!' Seen this way, the demonstrations of 15 February were not so much for a small 'Core Europe' (*Kerneuropa*) as for European democracy and a rule- and power-founding constitution of Europe.

Acknowledgements

I have to thank my colleague Geoff Parker from the English Department of Flensburg University, who did a wonderful (full-time) job in correcting my German English. For important (juridical) hints and advice, I am very grateful to Christina Hoss and Andreas Fischer-Lescano. Also very helpful were the discussions of an earlier version of this chapter with the people from ARENA, on 4 March 2003 in Oslo.

Notes

1 BVerfGE 22, 293 (296); ECJ RS. 294/ 83 Les verts/ Europäisches Parlament, 1986, 1357 (1365); Grimm 1997: 9; 2001a: 215f. (note 1), 229f.; see further: Weiler 1991: 2407; Augustin 2000: 249, 274 (note 248); Schwarze 2000: 464f.; for critical remarks on the German translation of *charte constitutionelle* in the 'les Verts – Decision' of the European Court of Justice as 'Verfassungsurkunde' see Möllers 2003a, quoted from the copy: 37.
2 Where not specified as the Treaty of Maastricht, I use 'EU' or 'European Union' as the name of the whole community.
3 In France already by 1992, 53 per cent of all legal acts had a European background.
4 BVerfGE 2 BvL 1/97, 6 June 2000; see Scharpf 2002: 76.
5 This – as a sociological insight – goes back to Durkheim (1893) (see especially the foreword of Luhmann); see further: Di Fabio 1991.
6 One can here argue that non-democratic constitutional regimes are only in a 'nominalist' or 'symbolic' (see Löwenstein 1997; Neves 1998) and not in a 'normatively' effective way *constitutional* regimes (as Neves argues in Neves 1992; see also Neves 2000: 84). But this, I guess, means to smuggle some normative arguments into systems theory.
7 Oeter 1995: 682f; Augustin 2000: 377 (people in the making), further: 108ff., 370ff., on the very concept of a (heterogeneous) people: 310f., 336ff., 345, 347f., 375f., 387, 390, 397, 402f.; on the addressee concept of a heterogeneous people, see further: Oeter 1999: 50, 53.
8 Möllers in the quoted manuscript draws a similar distinction between evolutionary and revolutionary ideas of a constitution, but does not restrict the term 'evolution' to the process of 'structural coupling'. For a more restricted idea of a revolutionary constitution which binds constitution to sacrifice (and hence to a substantial notion of 'collective identity'), and therefore rejects the idea of a European constitution, see Haltern 2003a. On Arendt's idea of a revolution: Wellmer 1999: 125–56.
9 See now for a strong criticism of Grimm's and others' *single language* thesis: Hanschmann 2003; see further: Oeter 2002: 55.
10 Alter 1996: 458ff; Schmidt 1998; for the legal foundations, see Ipsen 1987: RN 16, 58–61 (on 'supremacy' and 'direct effect').
11 Based on Art. 234 TEC.
12 See, e.g., BVerfGE 73, 339ff.
13 Moravcsik 1998: 3ff., 18, 84 ('Wheat, not nuclear weapons or French grandeur, was the vital interest that fundamentally motivated de Gaulle's European policy'), 150, 317.
14 Meyer 1997: 110; Tomuschat 1997: 114. Owing to its democratic control by national parliaments, NATO was not very useful to support a war of aggression during the Iraq-crisis in February 2003.
15 For an application to the EU: Oeter 1995: 696, 699.
16 See Bohman 1996; Bohman and Rehg 1997; Cohen and Sabel 1997; for a critical perspective, see Schmalz-Bruns 1999; van Aaken 2002.

17 For the distinction between arguing and bargaining see Elster 1991; for an application to supranationalism: Krajewsky 2001: 177.
18 In the same direction with regard to citizens' participation in governmental legislation: Bogdandy 2000a: 86.
19 For the distinction between these two types of procedural rationality, see Habermas 1990: 125f.
20 Augustin 2000: 108ff., 377, 393; Fossum 2001: 15 (with reference to the 'Charter'); 2003a: 9, 26 (with the interference: 'Citizens as rights bearers cannot be content with a system of constitution making in which the heads of government negotiate among themselves').
21 'The Federation may by a law transfer sovereign powers to international organizations' (official translation).
22 This is the thesis of Grimm (2003) ('Within the basic legal order, then, runs the line of the state between foreign (*Fremd*) determination and self-determination'). For earlier statements in the same direction, see Grimm 2001a: 250ff.; 2001b: 265, 270.
23 On this 'as if' character, see Fossum 2001.
24 Alter 1996: 458ff; see further Poscher 2003: 6:

> The nation-states accept the supremacy of Community law. They also accept that the European Court of Justice's jurisprudence is superior to that of national courts, including constitutional courts. However, conferring powers of enforcement to the Community is not in sight, neither in normative nor in factual terms.

25 For a new description of the EU as a confederation: Schönberger 2003; for a comparison of the EU with North American confederalism, see Menéndez 2003a: 35ff.
26 For the idea of an impermeable state subject, see Triepel 1899: 111.
27 See, e.g. the very convincing suggestions of Grözinger (2004).

Part II
Can it be made?

7 Three conceptions of the European constitution

Agustín José Menéndez

Systems of law for [...] a multitude of human beings [...] which, because they affect each one another, need a rightful condition under a will uniting them, a constitution.

(Immanuel Kant 1798: 455)

Introduction

This chapter aims at clarifying whether and in which sense the Laeken process[1] can make a constitutional difference for the European Union. If a text with some constitutional reference in its name ('Constitution for the European Union', 'Constitutional Treaty of the European Union') is to be approved at the end of the process, in what relevant sense could we say that the Union has got a constitution? Will this imply that the Union has become a more legitimate polity? Would this mean that something has been finally done to mend its democratic deficit?

Answering such questions requires an analysis of the present constitutional shape of the Union. Analytical clarity is highly needed. This can be partially brought about by means of distinguishing, as I do in the opening section, between the formal, the material and the normative conceptions of the constitution.[2] The three conceptions are analytically complementary, although it is also argued that, at the end of the day, the normative conception of the constitution is *the* supreme one. On such a basis, an account of the present constitutional state of the European legal order is put forward in the following section; it is considered whether the Union has a constitution in the material, formal and normative senses. The conclusion is that the Union does not have such a thing as a *complete formal constitution*, and that the Union does not have a democratic constitution, that is, a democratic constitution in a relevant sense. This is so despite the fact that we can make reference to a basic set of legal materials which are interpreted by courts as the *material constitution* of Community law, both in a structural and in a substantial sense. This, and nothing else, is what is meant when it is said that the European Communities have a constitution.[3] Having said that, consider the different rationales for writing a European constitution. Finally, the conclusions aim at clarifying the extent to which the Laeken process can be expected to result in the affirmation of a European constitution in a normative sense. It is argued that the Laeken process is best understood as an attempt at laying the ground for an eventual democratic constitution for Europe, which could only result from the actual exercise of popular sovereignty by European citizens and not as a constitution-making process in a normative sense.

The different conceptions of the constitution: formal, material and normative

The concept 'constitution' is used in many different (sometimes even contradictory) ways in political and legal discourses. Such a usage is not peculiar to this particular concept, but one could argue that is characteristic of all political terms, the definition of which is part and parcel of political struggles (Stevenson 1938; Alexy 1993: 138; and Santiago Nino 1989: 15; for the constitution, see Sartori 1964: fn 5). The plurality of conceptualizations of the term 'constitution' is rather problematic when we enter a constitution-making process. This is so because the different conceptions of the constitution lead to very different interpretations of the procedure and the agenda of constitution-making, and also to different preferences concerning the outcome of constitutional deliberation. Such assessment applies with special intensity to an eventual European constitution-making process. While it is increasingly evident that the constitutional traditions of the Member States of the European Union uphold a common set of values,[4] there are differences within the national constitutional traditions concerning the conception of the constitution (including the adequate process through which a constitution is written) (see Fioravanti 1996: 25–53; 2001; Fioravanti and Mannoni 2001; see also Möllers, Chapter 8 in this book). On the one hand, some constitutional traditions, specially the British one, are rather at odds with the idea of an overt process of constitution-making. The constitution tends to be regarded as the outcome of a long evolutionary process. On the other hand, most continental traditions endorse explicitly the idea of a positivized constitution, or, what is the same, a constitution the value of which is necessarily associated with the fact that it has been intentionally decided. If only for these reasons, a basic, even if incomplete, conceptual clarification of what we mean by a constitution, and what we intend by making or amending *our* constitution, is essential for the success of any constitutional debate, and especially for the success of the European constitutional debate.

The formal conception of the constitution

The formal constitution can be defined as the set of legal norms contained in a document (or compilation of documents) that is referred as the constitution in social practice.

The idea of a formal constitution is intrinsically modern. Modernity came hand in hand with the identification of law with written law.[5] Liberal revolutions in continental Europe further tied the concept of law to the idea of systematic bodies of legislation (the *Code Civil* being the archetypical example of such association; see, among others: Van Caenegem 2001: 1ff.). Within this *enlightened* tradition, both in continental Europe (see, for example: Hespanha 1999: 201ff.; see also Fioravanti 2001: fn 8; and Van Caenegem 1995), and in the United States,[6] arose the association of *the* constitution with *one single* document.

The formal conception stresses three basic features: the written character of the document; the singularity of the constitution; and the relevance of the social practice that refers to the document as *the constitution*. Firstly, there must be a physical object which can be referred as the constitution, be it a piece of paper, parchment or some other material. Secondly, the formalistic understanding of the constitution goes hand in hand with a monogamic relationship between a document identified as the constitution and the constitution of a given political community. This is closely associated, as Kelsen noted,[7] with the fact that the formal conception of the constitution brings about legal certainty.[8] Thirdly, the formal conception of the constitution presupposes also a widespread social practice that identifies the document with the constitution of the given society. Therefore, the formal understanding of the constitution has a clear sociological slant, to the extent that 'social practice' is essential in determining which text is to be labelled as the constitution.

The material conception of the constitution

The material constitution can be defined as the *norms of social interaction* that are regarded as basic norms according to social practice. Legal scholars tend to refer to the material constitution in a more narrow sense, namely as the norms that can be considered as *basic norms of the legal order* of a given community according to the social practice of the legal actors of the said community.

As it is the case with the formal conception of the constitution, the material understanding refers to social practice within the relevant society. But instead of considering relevant the social practice that labels something as *the constitution*, it focuses on what social actors regard as the *basic norms* of the given society. Thus, it considers social practice in a wider sense in order to determine which are the basic rules that structure the society and/or its legal order.

It must be noticed that the concept of the material constitution emerges either in the absence of a formal constitution or in opposition to the concept of a formal constitution. In the first sense, the concept has been crucial to British legal and political academics. Social practice in the United Kingdom converged around the premise that there was not such a thing as a formal constitution in Great Britain.[9] But when legal and political scholarship became a respectable academic enterprise in the nineteenth century, British legal scholars reconstructed the *living constitution* in order to give form and content to the disciplines of administrative and constitutional law.[10] In the second sense, the material conception of the constitution has proved to be a major critical tool. Such a critical edge can be used for different political purposes, ranging from the undermining (see Mortati 1998; a critical comment in La Torre 2003) to the vindication (Lassalle 1862) of formal democratic constitutions.

The legal understanding of the material constitution is but a specialized variant of the material understanding of the constitution. The main peculiarity of the legal version is that the relevant social practices are those of legal actors (or scholars) themselves, and not the practices of society at large.[11] Within the legal understanding, we can distinguish two different sub-conceptions of the material constitution.

Firstly, some authors emphasize the *structural elements* of such a constitution (the structural material constitution). Thus, Hans Kelsen offers a characteristically legal twist to the material conception of the constitution by defining the constitution as '[t]hose rules which regulate the creation of general legal norms, in particular of the statutes' (Kelsen 1992: 124, fn. 13). He assumes that such rules are identified by legal scholars. Informed by a different conceptual framework, H.L. Hart came to a similar point. The Oxonian philosopher defined law as the union of primary and secondary rules. Among the latter, he included the rule of recognition, which determines the feature or features that are taken as a conclusive affirmative indication that a given norm is part of the legal order.[12] The structural material constitution is closely associated to the idea of an *autonomous* legal system, that is, a system that decides for itself which norms are part or are not part of the legal system.[13]

Secondly, some other legal scholars stress the *substantial elements* of the material constitution (substantial material constitution). This is especially so in those states where courts review the constitutionality of statutes. In those legal systems, legal scholars tend to identify the material constitution with the substantive contents that are mandated or prohibited by the constitution, or, what is the same, with the *canon of constitutionality*.[14]

The normative conception of the constitution

The normative constitution is composed of those norms that are characterized by certain properties which are normatively relevant.

The basic insight underlying the normative conception of the constitution is to be found in Article 16 of the Declaration of the Rights of Man and of the Citizen of 1789: 'Any society in which the protection of rights is not guaranteed and the separation of powers is not established has no constitution.'

According to the said article, the constitution is not something to be determined by mere reference to social practice. 'Ideal' standards (in the sense of counterfactual) play a major role. No matter what the vast majority of the people say, a society in which rights are not protected and the powers of the state are not separated has no constitution. This emancipation from facts is the key element in the normative conception of the constitution. The concrete 'ideal' standards to be considered vary with different normative conceptions of the constitution. There could be as many normative conceptions of the constitution as there are normative theories, that is, theories about what is *right*. But one can distinguish between two main families of normative conceptions along the usual procedural/substantial divide. A *substantive normative* conception of the constitution will point to the intrinsic normative qualities of constitutional norms. Therefore, the relevant normative properties will be related to a substantial conception of the good. Neo-liberal (or, more exactly, what is called in Italian *liberist*) conceptions of the constitution consider as constitutional the basic norms protecting the right to private autonomy. A standard example of such a substantial normative conception of the constitution is that put forward by Epstein (1995). Similarly, it is very conceivable that some argue in favour of an ethical understanding of the constitution, in which the constitution is required to reflect the positive morality of the given political community. In its turn, a *procedural normative* conception of the constitution will refer to the qualities of the process through which the norms were agreed upon. That is, all norms approved through a given process will be defined as constitutional. Democratic conceptions of the constitution could be said to be standard examples of procedural conceptions of the constitution. But also conceptions which consider constitutional the norms produced by wise legislators, for example, will qualify as procedural. It goes without saying that the procedural/substantive conception points to basic types. All conceptions of the constitution combine procedural and substantive elements, only they put more or less emphasis on one or the other.

Among the different normative conceptions of the constitution, special attention should be paid to the *deliberative democratic* conception. It will take a considerable amount of time and space to fully justify this claim. It will suffice here to state that no other conception of the constitution comes so close to the self-understanding of the common constitutional traditions of the Member States of the Union, which affirms that the constitution should reflect the will of the people. This results in demanding standards applicable to the constitution-making process, as we will see in a moment. Such standards also have an indirect role to play in assessing the most fundamental substantive contents of any constitution, that is, the most basic fundamental rights.

The deliberative democratic conception of the constitution defines as constitutional those norms that meet the highest standards of democratic legitimacy, those norms that were elaborated through demanding processes of deliberation and decision-making in which most citizens actually exerted their political autonomy. As is well known, the democratic principle of political legitimacy requires that all those affected by common action norms should have the right to participate in the deliberation and decision-making of the said norms (Habermas 1996: 110). Thus, the democratic principle is clearly associated to the idea of the formation of the common political will in a way which is respectful of the autonomy of all citizens (Habermas 1996: 84ff.). This democratic intuition seems at odds with the basic implication of the affirmation of constitutional norms, namely the existence of mandated and required contents of common action norms. While the democratic principle seems to affirm the free formation of the common will, constitutionalism requires enforcing certain contents even against the common will.

But this apparent conflict is revealed as illusory. There are very good democratic reasons for distinguishing between the constitution and ordinary laws. In fact, such a distinction is essential in order to justify a sense of authorship of the laws on the side of citizens. That is, in itself, key to any justification of the obligation to obey the laws of any democratic political community.

To demonstrate this, it is convenient to proceed in five steps.

Firstly, social integration in modern societies cannot be achieved without having resort to law.[15] This implies that the discourse principle (Habermas 1986: 107, fn. 27) must be further specified into the democratic principle, which states that all those affected by common action norms should have the right to have a say in the deliberation and decision-making of the said norms. Common legal norms are thus identified with *statutes*.

Secondly, a literal understanding of the principle will not only protect the *public autonomy* of citizens, but it will also demand the effective exercise of such political autonomy. A considerable degree of civic virtue will be required (Pettit 1997; Viroli 2002; Maynor 2003). But this implies tilting the balance between public and private autonomy too much in favour of the latter, something that creates the risk of overly confining the scope of private autonomy (Ackerman 1991: 11, 28). This is the main reason that explains why the democratic principle is further specified into the *principle of democratic legality*,[16] which affirms that the representatives of all those affected by statutes should have the right to have a say in the deliberation and decision-making of statutes. This allows the establishment of a process of law-making which does not require a permanent political mobilization of citizens.

Thirdly, we must consider that representation, even if understood as democratic representation, presents considerable risks. Any chain of representation, even if short and transparent, creates the conditions under which the representatives can act contrary to the will of those whom they represent. This explains the main reason why the principle of legality must be further spelled out. We should distinguish, at the very least, between the constitution and ordinary statutes. Constitutional norms will be those legal norms that meet the highest standards of democratic legitimacy, those norms that were elaborated through demanding processes of deliberation and decision-making in which most citizens actually exerted their political autonomy. Ordinary legal norms (statutes) will meet the minimum democratic requirements, but they would be better regarded as provisionally legitimate because they are not as intensively legitimate as constitutional norms.[17] Their legitimacy will only be complete if they are in compliance with the constitutional norms established in the higher (i.e. constitutional) track of democratic law-making.

Fourthly, the democratic principle presupposes a political community in which all citizens want to acknowledge and respect the equal political rights of other citizens. Such rights represent the basic substantive values which constitute democracy. Even if such rights can only be properly realized through their positive affirmation by the law, their validity is not dependent on their being endorsed by the democratic process.[18] They point to a *thin substance* (Estlund 1993, 1998) which is the core of any democratic constitution. This thin substance is the most important part of the constitution. It does not contradict the democratic principle, but underpins it: it is its very essence.

Finally, the remaining contents of any positive constitution must be seen as reflecting basic *ethical choices* of a given political community. The legitimacy of such choices constraining the ordinary legislature stems from the fact that such contents have been established through constitutional law-making processes, which ensure a stronger democratic legitimacy than ordinary legislative procedures.[19]

The key elements are summarized in Table 7.1.

Table 7.1   The identification of constitutional norms according to each conception of the constitution

Conception	How do we know whether a legal norm is a constitutional norm?
Formal	It is contained in a document (or a compilation of documents) which is designed as 'the constitution' according to social practice within the given society
Material	*Sociological*: It is a norm considered as forming part of the basic structure of society according to social practice within the given society
	Legal variant: It is a norm considered as forming part of the basic structure of the legal order according to the social practice of legal scholars
Normative	It presents certain normative properties
	Democratic variant: The norm overcomes the highest standard of democratic legitimacy (it is possible to say, in a meaningful way, that most of its addressees can see themselves as authors of the norm)

The relationships between the different conceptions of the constitution

In the previous section, analytical clarification of the concept 'constitution' has been offered by means of establishing three different subsections or components of the aggregate term 'constitution': the formal, the material and the normative. These three conceptions are not competing; neither are they unrelated to each other.

Firstly, as indicated, the three conceptions, when seen together, capture the sum total of meaning attributed to the constitution in legal and political debate. The purpose of singling out and distinguishing among three such conceptions is analytical and helps clarify the nature of the debate. They should be seen not as alternative conceptions of a single concept, but as complementary conceptions that spell out different ways in which the term 'constitution' is used in a relevant sense.[20] Additionally, the three-fold distinction allows us to determine the sense in which a given political community has or does not have a constitution.

Secondly, the normative relevance of the different conceptions is strikingly different. In normative terms, the most relevant question, if not the only relevant question, is whether we can talk of a constitution in a normative sense. The affirmation that a legal system has a formal or a material constitution does not have any *direct* normative relevance. The fact that social practice points to a given document as the constitution, or that we can reconstruct the material constitution of a given political community, does not say much about the crucial question as to whether the concrete political community actually has a constitution in a normatively relevant sense.

Does the European Union already have a constitution? If so, in what sense?

The present debate on the European constitution revolves very much around the question of whether the European Union already has a constitution (or not). On the one hand, several different actors have referred to the Communities as already having a constitution. The German Constitutional Court already spoke in such a vein in 1967,[21] while the European Court of Justice started to do so in the 1980s.[22] Scholars have anticipated and echoed this claim. The lack of a proper European constitution is sometimes said to be an essential part of the legitimacy deficit of Union.[23] Instead of the congeries of treaties and secondary norms, it is argued that what is needed is a true constitution for the Union (Mancini 1998; Habermas, Chapter 2 in this book).

In this section, the three-fold distinction between the formal, the material and the normative constitution is used in order to interpret those claims, and to determine whether they are contradictory (as is not infrequently assumed) or simply refer to different conceptions of the constitution (as will be argued here).

Does the European Union have a material constitution?

The European Union already has a material constitution. We can make reference to the basic set of legal materials which are interpreted by European courts as the material constitution of the Community legal order. In that sense, the European constitution is not an empirical fact, but 'a particular understanding that is the result of a decision to adopt a particular point of view' (Richmond 2000: 97). This is true both in a structural and substantial sense of the material constitution.

European law is an autonomous legal order. As will be shown below, scholars disagree on whether it was so from its very inception, or whether autonomy resulted from the acceptance of the doctrine of supremacy of Community law affirmed by the European Court of Justice in the mid-1960s. But they agree that the European legal order is, as it stands now, an autonomous legal order.

Moreover, the European Court of Justice has repeatedly affirmed that there are certain substantive contents prohibited or mandated by Community law. As a result, such contents must be seen as the benchmark of constitutionality of both secondary Community legislation and national legislation implementing Community law, or claiming an exception from Community law.

The structural material constitution

The three founding Treaties of the European Communities were, formally speaking, international treaties. However, one could argue that they established the Community legal order as autonomous, separate and distinct from national legal orders. Thus, from the very inception of the Communities, it was correct to reconstruct a material constitution (both in a structural and a substantial sense) from the text of the Treaties themselves.

It is true that the Treaties aimed at *functional* integration of the Member States, but it is equally true that they were conceived of as a stepping stone in a wider process of regional integration in Europe. Five supportive arguments can be put forward. Firstly, many relevant documents, such as the Schuman Declaration and the preambles of the Treaty of Paris and the Treaty of Rome, explicitly affirm that the Communities were seen as means to reach a wider and explicitly political end.[24] Secondly, the history of European integration indicates the persistence of a political end that is furthered through different means which are selected depending on the context and open possibilities at each time. For example, a good many of the promoters of the failed European Defence Community were also supportive of the European Economic Community and European Atomic Community.[25] Thirdly, we have the comments of contemporary observers, not yet 'distorted' by knowledge of what would happen later (see, among others, Haas 1961: especially 36; and Kitzinger 1960: especially 24). They further support the characterization of the Treaties as containing the basic elements of the material constitution of the Communities. Fourthly, the political ambitions of the Communities are reflected in the Treaties. Even if there is no open rupture with the 'template' of international public law (cf. De Witte 1986), there are a good number of Treaty provisions that support the autonomy of the Community legal order. Not only is the institutional structure of the Communities much further developed than that of standard international organizations (in that respect, the establishment of a Court of Justice with compulsory jurisdiction is clear), but also the system of sources of law foreseen in the Treaties goes well beyond the standard paradigm of international law as it stood in the 1950s. Fifthly, the Treaties state the basic principle of equality of Community residents (the principle of non-discrimination on the basis of nationality [Art. 6 TEC]). The principle of supremacy of Community law can be seen as a further specification of the principle of equality. This is so because only if Community law is *supreme* can we be sure that European residents will be equal before the law within the scope of application of Community law.

However, a good number of scholars remain sceptical of the argument that the Treaties already laid down a material constitution of the Communities.[26] Such scholars doubt that the Treaties could be read as establishing a legal order distinct from public international law. But most scholars are ready to accept that even if the Treaties did not lay the foundations of a European material constitution, the latter acceptance of key decisions of the European Court of Justice by national political and legal actors would have brought about the constitutionalization of Community law at the latest in the 1970s. In two sweeping decisions, the famous *Van Gend en Loos* and *Costa* judgments,[27] the European Court of Justice argued that Community law should be regarded as a legal order *of its own*, which should not be conceptualized following the lines of either national or international public law. As is well known, the cases established the doctrines of *direct effect* of Treaty provisions and the *supremacy* of Community over national norms. Both presupposed the affirmation of Community law as an autonomous legal order. Thus, they must be interpreted as claiming that the European legal order is structured around its own material (structural) constitution. Such an affirmation implied, at a more basic level, the claim that the Community legal order had a material constitution of its own, while the doctrines of direct effect (of Treaty provisions) and supremacy of Community law must be seen as the main elements of the structural material constitution of the Communities. The combined claim of autonomy and the intended avoidance of any specific reference to the template of public international law or national law allowed the Court itself to undertake the further refinement of the secondary rules of the Community legal order, that is, of its *material constitution*. Such cases implied not only a *legalization* of the Treaties, but also their *constitutionalization*, once the doctrines of supremacy and direct effect of Treaty provisions were accepted by national constitutional courts (Alter 2001).

The substantial constitution: the benchmark of constitutionality

The European Court of Justice has slowly but steadily rendered clear that it regards certain norms of Community law as binding on the Community and the national legislatures. Therefore, such norms are interpreted as establishing mandated or prohibited contents for European legislatures within the field of application of Community law. Those are, mainly, the four economic freedoms and free competition, and fundamental rights.

THE FOUR ECONOMIC FREEDOMS AND FREE COMPETITION

There is little doubt that the *free movement of goods*, as established in Article 28 TEC (ex Article 30), stands in a privileged position among the substantive principles of the European material constitution. A leading scholar has claimed that the leading cases on the free movement of goods can be considered as standing only next to *Van Gend en Loos* and *Costa* in terms of constitutional importance (Weiler 1999b: 354; but see Bogdandy 2001b: 881). The substantial constitution of the Communities further includes the other three fundamental economic free-doms, namely the free movement of workers, the free provision of services and the free movement of capitals.[28] To this, we should add the basic provisions on competition law, including those in ex Articles 85 and 86 TEC.

The Treaty provisions on the basic order of the economy of the Union have been the core of the benchmark of constitutionality of the Court of Justice, something rather unsurprising given the basic goal of the Rome Treaty, namely the creation of a common market among Member States (Weiler 1999b: 359, fn. 57; Baquero Cruz 2002). Leaving aside the value assessment of such an effort (Galtung 1973, 1975), what is relevant is that the analysis supports the same basic conclusion that has been put forward here, namely that the basic economic freedoms enshrined in the Treaties are an essential part of the Community's material constitution.

FUNDAMENTAL RIGHTS AS A GENERAL PRINCIPLE OF COMMUNITY LAW

Next to the four economic freedoms, fundamental rights and liberties have become an integral part of the substantial constitution of the European Union.

The original text of the Treaties contained scattered references to funda-mental rights. The relevant provisions were Article 6 TEC (non-discrimination on the basis of nationality) and Article 119 TEC (equal pay for equal work of men and women). It was the Court which affirmed a general principle of protec-tion of fundamental rights as part of the unwritten law of the Communities.[29]

Since then, the Court has specified the fundamental rights protected by Community law case by case (Lenaerts and Van Nuffel 1999: 548ff.). The solemn proclamation of the Charter of Fundamental Rights can be interpreted as further evidence of the increasing salience of fundamental rights within the parameter of constitutionality of Union law. At any rate, the Charter constitutes the best evidence available of the catalogue of rights and freedoms that are considered as fundamental, and, therefore, as part of the said parameter of constitutionality (Menéndez 2002).

A major issue in the coming years will be the relationship between the two main elements of the substantive material constitution of the Communities approach. The progressive affirmation of fundamental rights has slowly and steadily led to the reappraisal of economic freedoms as specific contents of more abstract fundamental rights. This is related to the progressive weighing and balancing of economic freedoms against fundamental rights, and especially, collective goods and social rights (de Schutter 2001; Menéndez 2003b; Moral Soriano 2003).

Does the European Union have a formal constitution?

The European Union does not have a *formal constitution*. There is no single docu-ment, or compilation of documents, which social practice refers to as *the constitution of the European Union.* Firstly, the claims that the European Union does not have a constitution and that it should give itself one are considered plausible in political discourse. If there was a well-established social practice of referring to a document as the European constitution, such a claim would not be plausible. Secondly, there is not even a consolidated practice among jurists and legal practitioners of referring to one single 'consolidated text' as the constitution. It could be possible to compile into one single document all the relevant legal texts incorporating the *material constitution*; and allegedly this is what the Robert Schuman Centre of the European University Institute has already done (European University Institute 2000b). However, such a compilation fails to be endorsed by a widespread social practice of pointing to such a document as the constitution.

Having said that, it must be added that the solemn proclamation of the Charter of Fundamental Rights of the European Union can be interpreted as a first step in the formal constitutionalization of the Union. If it can be shown that the Charter is legally valid (Menéndez 2003b), it must be seen as a first fragment of a written constitution of the European Union. The legal validity of the Charter is not obvious, given that it has not (yet) been formally incorporated into the Treaties. But its legal validity can be based on two grounds. Firstly, and more weakly, it gives positive and concrete form to the four universal values that Community law claims to endorse, namely dignity, freedom, equality and solidarity.[30] Secondly, it consolidates the common constitutional traditions on the protection of fundamental rights. The Charter is, at the very least, an authoritative restatement of the common constitutional traditions.

Does the European Union have a normative constitution?

The answer to this question depends on the conception of the normative constitution which is advocated. From a deliberative democratic sense, the Union does not have a constitution. Firstly, it does not have a complete written constitution, which is a basic precondition from a deliberative democratic perspective. In the absence of a written constitution, citizens could not know which norms they are the authors of. Secondly, it is difficult to argue that the material constitution of the Union has been endorsed in a meaningful sense by European citizens. European citizens have never been asked formally to approve the concrete substantive norms that are part and parcel of the material constitution (with the exception of fundamental rights, as argued below). This is the deepest root of the *democratic deficit* of the European Union. Under such circumstances, one of the two basic goals of a constitution-making process for Europe should be to foster the formation of a coherent common will of Europeans supporting the future European constitutional text.[31]

One caveat should be made. To the extent that it is accepted that the Charter of Fundamental Rights is a fragment of the written constitution of the European Union (as argued above), it is convenient to consider whether the Charter can be said to be democratically legitimate.

Some leading commentators have pointed to the lack of democratic legitimacy of the Charter-making process (Weiler 2002 and Chapter 4 in this book). The claim is that, despite its positive innovations, the Charter Convention was not as democratically legitimated as would be proper of a *constitutional assembly*. The members of the Convention had not been *directly* elected by the people and they lacked a *direct mandate* concerning the contents they should favour as representatives. All this is very correct. However, two further factors must be taken into account. Firstly, it must be considered that the Charter Convention did not aim at writing anew the catalogue of fundamental rights of European citizens. The democratic legitimacy required for consolidating the already existing fundamental rights provisions in Community law must be different from that of actually writing a catalogue of rights without the authoritative limit provided by positive law. In that sense, the low but relevant degree of representativeness of the members of the Charter Convention, and the transparency of the Charter process, might be sufficient. Secondly, the fact that fundamental rights provisions in Community law are based on the *common constitutional traditions*, and that such common constitutional traditions are perceived as democratically legitimate, means that the burden of legitimacy is considerable lightened, to the extent that it can be argued that national catalogues of rights are legitimate from a democratic standpoint. If that is so, the democratic legitimacy of the Charter will stem not so much from the Charter process, but from its condition of restatement of the common national constitutional traditions.

Some interim conclusions

In this section it has been shown that the European Union *already* has a material constitution, both in a structural and a substantial sense, but it cannot be said to have a formal constitution or a normative constitution, at least according to deliberative democratic standards.

This allows us to draw one first conclusion, namely that a good deal of the apparently contradictory statements in the public debate on the European constitution are not as contradictory as they seem to be. When somebody claims that the European Union already has a constitution, they tend to mean that it has a material constitution, both in a structural and in a substantial sense. This does not contradict the claim that the Union does not have, and therefore needs, a *democratic constitution*. This is so because the existence of a material constitution does not entail democratic legitimacy.

A second conclusion that can be drawn is that an eventual democratic constitution of the Union will not *constitute* the Union anew, but will reconstitute it along democratic lines. This is so for two reasons. Firstly, the constitution of the Union will coexist with the different national constitutions. Most Member States of the Union are already constitutional states. The constitutionalization of the Union has proceeded as a 'fusion' of established constitutional traditions (Fioravanti 2001: fn. 85; Habermas 2001: fn. 43), which in themselves are a precious democratic *patrimoine* (as brilliantly argued by Brunkhorst, Chapter 6 in this book; Pizzorusso 2002). This process has been eased by the universalistic drive of constitutionalism, and by the common ethical underpinnings of constitutionalism in the Member States of the Union. Secondly, constitution-making will proceed within the constitutional framework (even if open to be changed by the constituting power) provided by the structural and substantial material constitution of the Union.

Some rationales for a European constitution

The three-fold distinction between different conceptions of the constitution can also be of some use in order to determine the different specific rationales for a European constitution (see Table 7.2).

The case for a written European constitution is related to the basic value of the constitutional form. Thus, a formal constitution will help clarify the basic rules of the European legal order. This is a value usually associated with the

Table 7.2 Some rationales for a European constitution

Conception of the constitution	Rationales
Formal	*Readability:* Allowing for a democratic use of constituent power
	Legal security: Rendering clear which are the common action norms that we should comply with
Material	*Hierarchy of sources of law:* Normatively sound theory of the sources of law
	Politicization of the Union: Reconsidering the balance between the goals of the Union
Normative (deliberative democratic)	*Constitutional democratization:* Democratizing the EU through an unconventional constitutional process that manages to form a coherent common will of Europeans
	Constitutional democratization: Drafting new rules of Treaty amendment which are democratically sensitive
	Legal democratization: Reviewing ordinary law-making processes to render them more democratic

words 'transparency', 'visibility' and 'legal security' in usual parlance. In itself, a written constitution will render clearer to citizens which are the basic structuring rules of the European constitutional order, and, thus, which are the common action norms that are expected to guide their action. This will also render it easier to determine whether they should feel obliged to comply with Community law. Moreover, the *formal value* of the constitution stands in a close relationship to the democratic use of the constituent power. A clear definition of which are the *present* constitutional rules is a basic precondition for a meaningful exercise of the constituent power by citizens on any future occasion. This might be especially relevant in a federal type of political community such as the European Union.

The case for drafting a European constitution in compliance with democratic standards of legitimacy is three-fold. Firstly, the process of drafting such a constitution could be unconventionally[32] democratic in itself. The advocates of the constitution could structure their own agenda of political mobilization in order to render clear that a wide majority of citizens are in favour of the European constitution. Bruce Ackerman (1991), in his analysis of unconventional constitutional moments, points to such possibilities. Secondly, the constitution could be one that defines the process of constitutional amendment in such a way that it could be meaningfully said that any amendment will meet the highest democratic standards of legitimacy. Thirdly, the constitution could be one that enhances the democratic standards that guide or inform the process of ordinary legislation. Even if ordinary statutes cannot be expected to meet the same degree of legitimacy as the constitution,[33] they should be supported by the ordinary common will of citizens, something which could only be guaranteed by a proper design of the process of law-making.

The Little Europe of the Coal and Steel Community could derive a more than sufficient legitimacy credit from Europeans' diffuse support for some kind of integrationist project and, in an indirect and mediated way, from the political legitimacy of the Member States. But once Community norms started to have a clear and evident impact on the daily lives of European citizens, diffuse and indirect sources of legitimacy ceased to be enough.[34] When seen in such a light, it can be said that the democratic deficit of the Union is two-fold. Firstly, the Union's material constitution has neither been subject to a democratic constitution-making process of elaboration (as have the most recent national constitutions), nor been democratically endorsed by democratic consistent majorities.[35] The European material constitution is open to be amended only through the amendment of what formally keeps on being international treaties. The constitutional legitimacy of Treaty reforms is indirect, and it is based on the 'incorporation' mechanism characteristic of international law, in open contradiction with the logic of democratic constitution-making.[36] On the other hand, the actual legislative procedures of the Communities are based on the double indirect legitimacy of the norms, given that the influence of direct representatives in deliberation and decision-making upon such norms is mediated by members of the executive.

The case for amending the material constitution is thus two-fold. Firstly, there is a case for introducing a *normatively* sound description of the *sources* of

Community law. There are good democratic reasons not only to amend the process through which secondary legislation is made, but also to establish a proper hierarchy of norms, in compliance with a constitutional principle of legality. Secondly, there is a case for reconsidering the balance between the different goals pursued by the Union. The proper balance between economic and social goals should be reconsidered in the light of the openly political character of the Union.

Conclusion

In this chapter, it has been argued that the debate on the European constitution requires some previous conceptual clarification. A three-fold conceptualization has been proposed by means of distinguishing between the formal, the material and the normative conceptions of the constitution (in the latter case, special attention was paid to the deliberative democratic variant of such a conception). Equipped with such analytical distinctions, we can interpret the apparently contradictory claims of the present European constitutional debate as supportive of the following diagnosis. The Union already has a constitution in a material sense, while it lacks a constitution in a formal and in a democratic sense. Furthermore, the three-fold distinction allowed us to distinguish between different concurrent rationales for entering into a constitution-making process in Europe.

Under such premises, it can finally be said that the Laeken process can contribute to the constitutionalization of the Union in a democratic sense. Its different steps can contribute to initiate a democratic debate on the European constitution, and an eventual Constitutional Treaty or Constitution could render clearer which is the material constitution of the Union. At the same time, it is not very likely that the Laeken process will result in a *democratic* constitution of the Union. The Laeken Convention, despite its positive structural and procedural features, cannot be said to be a proper constitutional assembly. Its members have not been *directly* elected by European citizens, and, consequently, their actions have no relation to a thorough electoral debate on citizens' preferences on the shape and contours of the European constitution. If, as is very likely, the Constitutional Treaty has to be ratified by all Member States before it enters into force, it will be hard to call the Treaty both a constitution, and a democratic constitution. Moreover, the Draft Text proposed by the Convention has not established a proper distinction between constitutional and non-constitutional contents, as all four parts are given the same formal status. This is likely to result in an over constitutionalization. A too thick constitution cannot but be a straitjacket on democratic decision-making.

In a provocative manner, I am tempted to conclude by claiming that the first commandment of the democrat is not to take the name of the constitution in vain. What is to be referred as the constitution is not a purely semantic question, but one based on the normative value of the concept – a value that stands for the strong evocative power of the term. It will be a pity to frustrate expectations by presenting an *octroyée* constitution as a substitute of a democratic constitution.

Europe needs a democratic constitution, not a new *Statuto Albertino*. If we are not writing a democratic constitution democratically, but merely laying the ground for it, we should have the courage to acknowledge it openly.

Notes

1 As has already been made clear in the Introduction, by the Laeken process is understood the whole procedure of reform of the primary law of the Union stemming from the Laeken Declaration: the wide-ranging public debate, the Convention, the national debates, the Intergovernmental Conference and the national ratifying debates.

2 One could say that the concept of constitution is thus to be defined at the crossroads of critical normative theory and the *common constitutional traditions of the Member States*, to use a well-known expression of the European Court of Justice. This strategy seems to be not very dissimilar from the one suggested by Sartori (1964: 858).

3 See references in note 25.

4 This is rendered clear by the development of the concept of 'common constitutional traditions' in the case law of the European Court of Justice, especially as regards the protection of fundamental rights in Union law. The solemnly proclaimed Charter of Fundamental Rights of the European Union renders this even more explicit.

5 Hart (1961: 95) associates modernity and legality, but one could argue that premodern law might have been unwritten, or only partially written, and still it was founded on a social practice which regarded as *authoritative* certain sources of law.

6 The United States Constitution of 1787 became in time the 'archetypical' constitution. The Federalists supported both a written constitution and adherence to the *common law*. The latter was not an obvious choice, as the reasons in favour of a constitution would also support a thorough codification of ordinary law. However, Federalists preferred to avoid such an exercise as they feared that this might undermine the protection of vested property rights. It would be not fully inaccurate to claim that Shays' rebellion was causally more effective in convincing pro-federalists than the Federalist Papers. See Beard 1913: 52ff. See also Kramnick 1987: 137–8.

7 Kelsen 1945: 124: '[A] solemn document, a set of legal norms that may be changed only under the observation of special prescriptions, the purpose of which is to render the change of these norms more difficult.'

8 Such certainty is not infrequently reinforced by the provision of specific procedures to produce a new document which should be labelled as the constitution. However, such special procedures are based on normative reasons which require rendering the constitution *special* vis-à-vis ordinary laws. The same normative reasons explain that the formal conception of the constitution tends to be associated with a punctual characterization of the constitution-making process. There is a point or a reduced number of points in time in which the text of the constitution is solemnly ratified and proclaimed as such a constitutional text. Only in such a way is it possible to preserve the legal certainty stemming from the specific *constitutional form*.

9 But see MacCormick 1978. See the judgment on *John MacDonald MacCormick* vs *Lord Advocate*, 1953 S.C. 396 (Court of Session). The background to the case is explained in an extremely entertaining way by MacCormick 1950.

10 A similar kind of motivation can be found in the Germanic area, where the process of codification of private law was unsuccessful until the very end of the nineteenth century, something which fostered the dogmatic reconstruction of the law, the elaboration of legal concepts. This is what underlies Christoph Möllers' characterization of German and British conceptions of the constitution as the formalization of already existing norms, as opposed to the French and American models, in which the

constitution establishes a new political order by political fiat. (See Möllers, Chapter 8 in this book.) But perhaps one should clearly differentiate between the conception of the constitution in political culture and the conception of the constitution in legal dogmatics. In Germany, the latter, and not the former, is rather close to the British conception of the constitution.

11 In the Kelsenian move, this is what allows legal theory to remain pure, uncontaminated by social, political and ideological motives. Kelsen 1992: 7. See also Hart 1961: 114–15, fn. 10.

12 The other secondary rules in Hart's model are (1) *the rules of change*, which determine the processes through which primary norms are altered, and (2) the *rules of adjudication*, which empower given institutions or individuals to make authoritative determinations of the question whether, on a particular occasion, a primary rule has been broken. See Hart 1961: 95–7, fn. 10.

13 It is one thing for a legal system to be autonomous, and another for it to be closed. A post-positivist conception of law cannot accept the claim that legal systems are closed to general practical reasoning. See Alexy 2002a.

14 The substantial character of the substantial understanding of the material constitution fosters a further consideration of the constitution from a normative standpoint, and thus renders clear the need for considering the *normative* conception of the constitution.

15 Habermas 1996: 460. A good deal of the literature on the obligation to obey the law (and, more generally, on political obligation) does not pay sufficient attention to the central role played by law in social integration. The basic endorsement of autonomy leaves us with no option but to have resort to law in our social and political interaction. This does not mean that there is any intrinsic legitimacy proper of the form of law, but that we cannot opt out from law. A related argument is in Habermas 1986: 179. See, in a different but related sense, Martin 1993.

16 The principle of legality also requires that the actions of the administration be supported on democratic statutes. The administration is to be 'programmed' by democratic law. But here I am emphasizing the democratic, representative aspect of legality.

17 One could refer to further refinements of the principle of legality: the phenomenon of decree laws or legislative decrees constitutes an example of how the democratic principle needs to be implemented differently in order to preserve itself; other modalities of the principle of legality, which have only been partially acknowledged by legal theory, correspond to budgetary laws, to labour laws; and in many democratic states one finds specificities associated with national minorities or special territories, such as islands.

18 See Michelman 1998: 64–98, especially 91: 'A "truly democratic" process is itself inescapably a legally conditioned and constituted process.'

19 Some choices are rendered legitimate by the requirement of *substantive coherence*. It is open to be decided whether certain ethical choices are to be constitutionalized or not. But once certain choices are constitutionalized, then others might be also constitutionalized to render the first ethical choice a morally acceptable one. I claim that this is the case with the right to private property and strongly progressive taxation. See Menéndez 2001: 151ff., fn. 30.

20 Different normative conceptions of the constitutions stand in a relation of competition. They present themselves as the *correct* normative conception, to the exclusion of other conceptions.

21 See 22 BVerfGE 293 at 296. The European Communities were said to have a constitution of their own laid down in the Treaties. Referred to by Zuleeg 1997. See also Richmond 2000: 86.

22 See Case 294/83, *Parti écologiste 'Les Verts'* v *European Parliament* (1986), ECR 1357, paragraph 23. This move had already been advocated back in 1955 by Advocate

General Lagrange, who in case 8/55 argued that the Treaty of the European Coal and Steel Community should be regarded as 'the Charter of the Community from the material point of view [...] even though concluded in the form of a Treaty'. This is supported by many scholars. See, among others, Cassese 1991 and Weiler 1999c.

23 The discussion on the democratic deficit ('legitimacy gap') was sparked by the remarkable pamphlet by Marquand (1979). The effective direct election of the Parliament resulted in the second constitutional proposal in the history of the Communities, the Spinelli project (European Parliament 1984).

24 See the Schuman Declaration and the Preamble to the European Economic Community Treaty.

25 See Simpson 2001 on the *dramatis personae* behind the European Convention and the Communities; Griffiths 2001 on the continuity between the effort in support of Defence and Political Union and the Economic Community. Marjolin 1986 is extremely instructive.

26 See, for example, Eleftheriadis 1998: 259. Eleftheriadis neglects the fact that the German Constitutional Court (who, on p. 260, he considers as representative of the German constitutional theory tradition, which has 'traditionally pursued a rigorous commitment to the idea of constitutional law as a determinate body of rules and principles') referred to the Treaties as a 'constitution' in the late 1960s, before the *Solange I* judgment.

27 Case 26/62 *Van Gend en Loos* (1963), ECR 1, and Case 6/64 *Costa* (1964), ECR 585.

28 A propos the free movement of capital, Directive 88/361, for the implementation of the free movement of capital, combined with the new drafting of Article 52 TEC introduced by the Treaty of Maastricht, implied a change of the parameter of constitutionality in that respect.

29 *Stauder* (Case 29/69, 1969, ECR 419) and *Internationale* (Case 11/70, 1970, ECR 1125).

30 See the preamble of the Charter: 'Conscious of its spiritual and moral heritage, the Union is founded on the indivisible, universal values of human dignity, freedom, equality and solidarity.'

31 The other main objective would be that the constitutional norms themselves would be such as to enhance the democratic participation of European citizens in the deliberation and decision-making on ordinary common action norms. See section below: 'Some Rationales for a European Constitution'.

32 Of course, constitution-making can be conventionally democratic, if a process of constitution-making has already been established which properly tests the existence of a coherent common will in favour of the amendment of the constitution. But such a process has not been established in Europe. Under such circumstances, the *democratization* of constitution-making can only happen *unconventionally*.

33 See section above: 'The Normative Conception of the Constitution'.

34 One could argue that such clear and direct impact can be traced back at the very least to the completion of the Customs Union in 1969, which is not by coincidence the same year of the first judgment in which the European Court of Justice acknowledged the unwritten general principle of fundamental rights protection as part and parcel of Community law.

35 As Bruce Ackerman argues the Federal Constitution in the US was. See Ackerman 1991: 32ff., fn. 74.

36 Treaty reform, as is argued below, is a process that has been characterized by a scarce feeding back of public spheres debates, and which ultimately revolves around a binomic decision. One could argue that the absolute democratic quality of the process of Treaty reform has remained stable since the founding of the Communities. However, the democratic relevance of the issues contained in Treaty amendments has become transformed. The loss of bite of national regulatory power implicit in the reinterpretation of the economic communities in the Single European Act or the

Treaty of Maastricht had far superior implications than the transfer of sovereignty and national regulatory power in the Paris and Rome Treaties. Thus, the match between the democratic relevance of the issues at stake and the democratic quality of the amendment procedures has increased, not decreased. Keeping the same Treaty amendment procedure has rendered the democratic deficit *worse*.

8   The politics of law and the law of politics

Two constitutional traditions in Europe

Christoph Möllers

Constitution: meaning and institution

The following considerations will present two different historical meanings of the concept of constitution and some of its institutional implications for the present discussion. But why is an historical reconstruction of this term of any use for the actual constitutional debate in Europe? An answer to this question can be given easily: historical considerations are relevant for this debate just because the debate claims to be a *constitutional* debate. There are many good reasons to believe that the European integration presents a unique development, that the Treaties of Rome created an entirely new type of public organization, and that this organization is, therefore, not approachable with traditional categories. This would mean that the next step of the European integration taken by the next amendment of the Treaties could be analysed without any further reference to traditional categories like constitution. But on a descriptive level there already seem to be too many elements of the European integration that remind the observer of traditional constitutional orders. On a normative level there is a strong desire to deliver certain institutional virtues to the European integration that are connected with the idea of a constitution. In such a context we also have to take into account an historical perspective to understand what we mean by these references. In a philosopher's words: 'Grasping a concept is mastering the use of a word – and uses of words are a paradigm of the sort of thing that must be understood historically' (Brandom 2000: 27).

But the ubiquitous use of constitutional traditions remains too often implicit. If any meaningful contemporary use of the term cannot ensue without an historical-systematic investigation,[1] this is particularly important in a jurisprudential context which is always particularly oriented towards the past (Kirste 1998: 352f.; Ost 1999: 43f.), and it may be especially helpful for the European discourse, which has to reinsure itself with concern to the meaning of traditional legal notions.

A jurisprudential confrontation with the term 'constitution' must, on the one hand, study the usage of the term and, on the other hand, check for its conclusiveness, i.e. work ahead with regard to the history of the concept and analyse it theoretically. The first part of this project will be pursued in the following sketch.[2] The conceptual analysis will be supplemented by a concluding remark about the specifically jurisprudential contribution of a European constitutional discourse.

Two types of constitution

In order to enable a more precise usage of the category, without committing ourselves to a certain definition prematurely, two constitutional traditions can be categorized. This categorization allows for a more selective usage of a concept that is sometimes deployed too indiscriminately. The chosen distinction[3] is based upon the difference between law and politics: the first, French–American type of constitution created a specific democratic stock of traditions which is – this was shown in 1989 – still relevant. Its great theme is the democratic politicization of law-making through the foundation of a new system of government. An older form of constitutionalism conversely stresses the juridification of an already existing governmental system. This tradition can be found – with many differences between the individual cases – in Germany and Britain, for example. As will be shown, both constitutional traditions are necessary for a European constitutional theory.

To found a new order: constitution as politicization of law

What are the common characteristics of the constitutional idea that arose at the end of the eighteenth century from the American and French Revolutions? Two basic features can be systematically extracted.[4]

Foundation of a new political order

The new constitutions founded a new order. They did not just limit an already existing authority (Arendt 1963: 183f.; Böckenförde 1991: 42–3; Preuss 1994: 19–20). This point – probably not accidentally often overlooked in the German discussion – has implications for the theory of the liberal constitutional state that can hardly be overrated: in the organization of revolutionary constitutions, every form of the exercise of public power requires an immanent form of justification defined by the constitution. The constitution determines the form and the content of the sovereign power and, in doing so, terminates the previous political order: it founds a discontinuity, a rupture that finds its institutional correspondence in France in the Revolution and in the United States in the Revolutionary War. With this, constitution becomes an *exclusive* concept: it is striking that certain forms of order are now no longer labelled as faulty or wrong constitutions; rather, their claim to be constitutions at all is denied.[5]

The concept of the democratic *pouvoir constituant* can be affiliated with the foundation of a new order; the former, however, hardly plays a role in the American tradition (Sieyès 1789: 124–5). The idea of a *pouvoir constituant* designates, for one, the subject of founding a new order, namely the people, and it guarantees, for another, that the process of constitution-making can be transformed into a perpetual form, based on the introduction of certain institutions (Böckenförde 1991: 100) – in France, through the institution of the general law that is also responsible for the definition of subjective rights (Carré de Malberg 1984). This perpetuation is guaranteed by procedures, not by specific purposes of sovereign power. Because the basis of sovereignty is self-determination, sovereignty becomes an unfinished end in itself (Kelsen 1925: 39–40). The constitution's substance is limited to procedures of legitimation and the naming of utopias ('Life, Liberty and the Pursuit of Happiness').

The tradition's egalitarian concern for the individual (democratic equality) also follows from its founding character (Henkin 1994: 214f.). Only this, at least in theory, enables a radical break from the authoritarian status quo. Because the constitution should not be orientated towards already existing authority structures, it must make individual freedom its systematic reference point. The addressees of the constitution are those who are individually subjected to the new authority without any interference from other intermediate corporations.[6] As a result, this does not necessarily mean a lower-level or less intrusive governmental presence than before: both the French Revolution and the founding of the United States may have more likely led to an increase in public power, and the time before and after the Revolution in France may be portrayed as an administrative continuum.[7] However, the constitution organizes, establishes and justifies these interventions through the invention of citizenship, through the right to vote and through civil rights. The constitution founds a new form of sovereignty that is limited from the start by the rights of the individual. It does not organize an already existing sovereignty.

Normativity, supremacy and the written form of the constitution

The normative claim of this constitutional tradition is implied in its founding character (Preuss 1994: 20–1). The constitutional revolution eliminates the recognition of the status quo as a legitimate point. As a result, traditions lose their justifying value[8] and must be replaced by 'new democratic traditions' that are specific to the constitution. This disengagement from the past is, at the same time, a disengagement from previously existing political practice and, therefore, an intensification of the difference between political practice and the normative demands of the constitution: the pre-constitutional inventory of privileges must be forgotten.[9] In doing so, the constitution opens up a horizon for the future that, along with the perpetuation of the democratic *pouvoir constituant*, also works towards the perpetuation of changes (Preuss 1994: 24f.; Ost 1999: 175f.).

Beginning in the United States, this emphatic normativity developed into the legal concept of the constitution as the supreme law (Wahl 1981: 493f.). The establishment of supremacy is successful under certain institutional premises: besides an interpretable constitutional text, it also requires institutions of review that are specific to the constitution – constitutional courts.[10] The example of

France shows, on the other hand, that a revolutionary constitutional tradition can also develop over a long period of time without this sort of pronounced constitutional supremacy.

Not only the political-utopian content but also the legal supremacy of the constitution is favoured through its written form (Stourzh 1977: 218f.; Preuss 1994: 21–2; Finer 1997: 1503f.). The documentation of the constitutional content creates a decisive effect of formalization. This is the practical condition to consistently refer to the constitutional norms and its claim for the future: the objectification of the constitution in one text makes the constitution an autonomous piece of sense and the reference to its content again and again open for new interpretation. This creates its specific political normativity. Similar to a piece of art, its object character enables it to portray potential oppositions to 'social reality'. The objectification of the constitution in a text calls forth its symbolization (Corwin 1936: 1072–3). The function of the written form is not necessarily the fixation of a certain content because the textual understanding obviously changes quite considerably over time and this change is by no means undesirable.[11] However, the documentation of the constitution helps ensure that its political-utopian demand becomes less dependent on political practice. But the written form also has meaning for the supremacy of the constitution: if constitutional changes are tied to changes in the constitutional text, then this increases the constitutional distance from specific day-to-day political problems and emphasizes its demand for supremacy.

Result

The revolutionary constitutional tradition demands a comprehensive democratic politicization of law-making. The discontinuity that is at least feigned through the revolutionary foundation of constitutional law justifies the necessity to focus the production of law on a single democratic reference point, in which all citizens must be able to participate as free and equal individuals. This must be guaranteed for traditional pre-revolutionary law, at least to the extent that it is possible to change it in a democratic process. The central meaning of democratic law (*loi, Gesetz*) for the democratic state results from this. The availability of democratic proceedings alone justifies the legal system and can even – as strived for in the figure of the *pouvoir constituant* of the people – legitimize its abolition in favour of another system.

To shape the powers: constitution as juridification of politics

The profile of the revolutionary constitutional idea becomes clearer when contrasted with another constitutional tradition that strives towards not founding a new political order, but the legalization or juridification of the already existing one. In the European constitutional tradition Britain and Germany can be named as examples of this tradition – of course with weighty differences in detail.[12]

Limiting powers by legalization of government

Since the time of early constitutionalism, the Germany version has aimed not at founding a new democratic order, but rather at limiting the already existing governmental system, which was conceptually identified at first with the person of the king and later with the legal personality of the state.[13] The constitutions 'do not constitute a new polity; rather, they represent a system of limitations to the sovereign power' (Brandt 1968: 46). A structurally similar constitutional understanding arose in Britain in a completely different historical context.[14] Here, the idea of the constitution was also not used to found a new order. The gradual juridification of the legitimate power apparatus also functioned as the 'constitution'.

The original constitutional situation in the United States was the existence of a representative body, a parliament, without an administration.[15] It was just the opposite in Germany and Britain: a representative body with gradually increasing importance was allocated to the already existing monarchy (Schönberger 1997: 56f., 148f.). The king's 'original' power was to be put in its place through the constitution.[16] This starting point has always been the common denominator in two important traditions: the German *Rechtsstaat* and the British rule of law.[17] Therefore, it is no coincidence that neither constitutional tradition, unlike those in France (Rousseau 1762: I, 7, II) and the United States (Madison *et al.* 1788: no. 51), has developed a democratic theory within its constitutional system. In Germany the constitution as a power-limiting institution lacked a principle of justification, a legitimizing process. Until 1918 the legitimacy of government remained merely a background topic for German public jurisprudence, which not accidentally called itself *Staatsrecht* instead of constitutional law. In Britain, on the other hand, the established legitimacy of the traditional theory of sovereignty was successfully united with a modernization of institutions. Parliamentarism was the result. The question of legitimacy was practically solved as a matter of parliamentary deliberation.[18]

The old fear of unrestrained tyranny is closely connected to this idea of limitation of power. However, for a modern variation of power-limiting constitutional theory, it is important to see that limitation of power does not weaken public institutions, but just legalizes them. This shaping of political power through juridification in no way leads necessarily to a decrease of its influence, but, rather, is more likely to increase it,[19] just as the modern constitutional state may have an infinitely more precise control over its citizens than an absolutist ruler. The juridification of the power apparatus may improve organizational rationality (Reinhard 1999: 291f.) raising executive powers. For this reason, the constitutional tradition developed here will be called a power-shaping – not a power-limiting – tradition in the following.

Restricted normativity of the constitution

Lacking a revolutionary rupture, the normative demand of the power-shaping constitutional tradition remained limited. Starting in imperial Germany, the attempt to integrate social reality into the concept of constitution – by theorists like Carl Schmitt and Rudolf Smend – has been regularly made (Korioth 1990:

282f.). Influential terms like *Verfassungswirklichkeit* (Lassalle 1862), *Verfassungswandel* (e.g. Hsü 1932), *Materielle Verfassung* (Smend 1928) or constitution as *politische Grundentscheidung* (Schmitt 1927: 23f.) are witnesses to this tradition which are still in use.[20] The lack of experience with a revolutionary change in government as well as the doubts concerning the ability of legal forms to grasp social reality as a 'whole' are reflected in these notions. The constitution is not the text or the norm; the constitution *is* the total condition of society. At the same time, the fact that the concept of constitution should integrate the 'whole society' made this concept more and more synonymous with that of the 'state' – a development that became obvious in the German discussion, at the latest, during the Weimar Republic. State and constitution developed into integral, but interchangeable categories (Möllers 2001a: 141f.). At this point, the allegedly compelling correlation between state and constitution arises, which has become of such central importance for the discussion of European constitutionalism in Germany.

In Britain, normative contents also remained limited but in quite another way (Vorländer 1999: 34–5). The development appears less in the dogma of parliamentary sovereignty[21] and the modest juridification of constitutional supremacy; this phenomenon also finds itself imposed upon institutional development in France. It appears more clearly in the absence of a constitutional text (Dicey 1959: 4f.; Löwenstein 1967: 43f.) and in the corresponding identification of the constitution with a certain inventory of tradition (Maitland 1908: 526f.) that is continuously to be developed. Constitution *is* an evolutionary process of political practice. Therefore, in both traditions the constitution does not raise a normative demand for absoluteness with respect to the existing political system. As a result, the constitutional concept in both traditions assumes an evolutionary rather than revolutionary form over time.

Result

Accordingly, the power-shaping constitutional tradition – unlike the order-founding tradition – does not require a concept of democracy. Rather, its central theme is limiting a pre-democratic sovereignty through legal form. In connection to this, a special function is assigned to the courts not only in the German but also in the British tradition. As legal protection in Germany compensated for the lack of democratization (Jesch 1961: 24f.), so did and does jurisdiction in Britain guarantee that the sovereign is obligated to certain standards of justice that especially originate from the tradition of common law[22] and represent a specific form of constitutionalization without constitutional text. With this, constitution describes, in both traditions, the result of a process of juridification, not a process of politicization.

The traditions correlated: constitution as coupling of politics and law

The ideal-typical acumination of the two constitutional traditions allows a more exact description of their relationship with one another and of their applicability to European integration. Order-founding and power-shaping constitutional traditions do not principally contradict one another; moreover, both traditions can be constantly recognized in the member-state constitutional systems of the present. However, on the one hand, the aspect of democratic freedom to create a political order and, on the other hand, the legal formality of the political process can unfold in antagonistic directions. Such contradictions have been known to constitutional theory for a long time, and – e.g. in the question of the democratic legitimacy of constitutional courts[23] – they have occupied academic discussion until today. However, the attempt is not infrequently made to dissolve this antagonism in favour of one of the two traditions. In this way, the perception of constitutional law's 'political character', the influential constitutional theory which has prevailed since its origin in the Weimar Republic, questions constitutional normativity in political contexts.[24] Conversely, the current academic debate on 'constitutionalization' seems to prefer juridification over politicization.

The supposition behind such approaches – that democratization and juridification would necessarily interfere at the expense of the other – underlies the thesis of a zero-sum game between democratic politics and legal form. In contrast, one may point out that western legal systems have long been familiar with the antagonism of two forms of law, one driven by politics and one that arose autonomously, and that this dualism may have a necessity of its own (Hofmann 1998: 40f.).

On a theoretical level the necessary correlation between both constitutional traditions can be described by quite a diversity of theories and terminologies – for instance as the structural coupling of politics and law (Luhmann 1990: 193f., 204f.; 1993: 468f.), as the deliberative circle of law and democracy (Habermas 1992: 167f.; Gerstenberg 1997: 27f.), or simply as the juridification of democratic-parliamentary law-making (Kelsen 1925: 234) – so that both constitutional traditions can be understood as having equal rights. Finally, this also allows for the hypothesis that legal form and democratic law-making can reciprocally strengthen each other.[25] In contrast, abatements in the juridification of the political process lead to deficits that can be portrayed as both malfunctions and deficits in legitimacy. For example, political 'considerations' in court decisions question the legitimacy of the political system that exerts influence and the legitimacy of the legal system that submits itself to such an influence. A too extensive constitutional adjudication can, on the other hand, lead to an over-juridification of political processes which overuses constitutional textual claims to legitimacy. This diminishes the normative power of the constitution and, at the same time, questions the ability of a political system of self-government to function.

In order to apply both constitutional traditions to European integration, the question is not, therefore, which of the two is the 'better' tradition.[26] More accurately, on the European level one observes both new forms of political law-making processes with specific claims to a legitimacy of their own, and intensive forms of legalization of the originally intergovernmental political process. The European Parliament can be named as an example of the first phenomenon, and procedural standards, developed by the European Court of Justice (ECJ), are an example of the second trend.

If the coupling of politics and law through constitutions is not about a zero-sum game, as shown, then there are many reasons to believe that European institutions lack not only structures of democratic law-making but also suitable forms of juridification. In this way, the Council's arcane legislative techniques neither have legal form nor are they democratic. In so far as we are dealing with a double deficit in the democratic foundation of the order and in its legal form, then the distinction between an order-founding and a power-shaping constitutional concept can present a possibility for analysing the European *status constitutionis* that connects the question of whether Europe 'has' or 'should have' a constitution. This also allows for a more exact reconstruction of the normative cost/benefit balance of a Europeanization of the constitutional idea. In this, some phenomena can be traced back to the one, some to the other constitutional tradition. At the same time, these traditions should, however, also submit a critical scale against which European integration is to be measured.

Three constitutional assessment standards for European institutions

Three categories derived from these constitutional traditions could be specified and applied as a critical measure for the European institutions:[27]

1   The idea of *equal rights of political participation* as the normative implication of the first, revolutionary tradition and as an institutional key element of a future European democratic process. This egalitarian standard is both the most obvious and the most difficult to be realized for a European legal order. It is mainly directed towards the European legislative process and in particular to the role of the European Parliament. Formally, it would be necessary to apply strictly egalitarian standards to the election of the Parliament and to give the right to fully participate in all legislative decisions and to initiate them. The Parliament had to become the representation of all European citizens and not (as it is regulated in Art. 189 TEC) the representation of the separate peoples of the Member States. But this formal solution would only be a start. It is one of the most amazing features of western democracies that an egalitarian electoral process leads to a more or less stabilized bilateral political conflict. If democracies generally function as the combination of a procedural consensus and a substantial conflict (Mouffe 2002: 90–4), it is the organization of this conflict on the European level that remains problematic.

2   The idea of an incremental *constitutionalization* as the normative implication of the second, evolutionary tradition. This is the constitutional feature the European integration comes closest to. The central role of the ECJ as the creator of a jurisprudence of principles and subjective rights and the emergence of standards of administrative due process are prime elements of this constitutional model. But there are still many lacunae in this process. Problems emerge in particular within the complicated administrative system

of the EU in which judicial review is impeded by the cooperative structures between Member State and Commission and between Member State and Member State. But in general the many layers of European basic rights that have come into existence underline a strong commitment to a law-oriented constitutional tradition – and represent the positive side of a lack of democratic commitment.

3   Finally, the idea of a *constitution* as a *political document* that claims to be the supreme law for all the institutions of the European Union. This idea can be traced back to both constitutional traditions, and diverse phenomena can be analysed with its help. On the formal side the codification of a single constitutional treaty in a single readable political document without annexes, declarations, and so on, etc. would be an important step in this direction. But to guarantee a substantive supremacy, it is crucial to regulate the diversity of intergovernmental decision-making processes in the European Union. The increased influence of the European Council (Art. 4 TEU), which simultaneously has the function of an informal body of coordination, a legislator and a constitution-maker, is incompatible with the idea of constitutional supremacy. Different standards of review of the ECJ towards Community and Member State Acts are another possible object of scrutiny.

The contribution of jurisprudence to constitutional theory

The two constitutional traditions reconstructed here assign different tasks to academic jurisprudence. Evolutionary processes of constitutionalization allow jurisprudence to become an important legal source by the establishment of principles and systematic arguments. On the other hand, the influence of the discipline is limited not only through revolutionary incidents but also through the activity of the democratic legislator – jurisprudence's restrained 'positivist' self-image is the methodical correlate here. This correlation explains the importance of jurisprudential law-making and philosophically inspired arguments, which are increasingly prevalent in international and supranational regulatory contexts (Möllers 2001b: 43–50). This affinity is, certainly, just another formulation for a democratic deficit because legal expertise – like every other expertise – lacks a mandate for legitimate law-making. Against this background, jurisprudence must be careful not to privilege certain constitutional concepts only because they could strengthen its own institutional role. Concretely, this means that the recommendation for the problem of coupling politics and law on the level of the European Union cannot simply be 'law'. Many aspects speak much more to the fact that the Union has hit the 'limits of informal constitutional development' (Peters 2001: 478), which presents itself, above all, as a phenomenon of juridification without corresponding democratic procedures.

Besides the danger of privileging certain forms of constitutionalization, jurisprudence also faces the danger of a lack of temporal distance from the European constitutional project. This results from interventions in primary law that are comparatively frequent and intense and from the multiplicity of official proposals for a European constitution.[28] It may be of particular urgency for jurisprudence, necessarily equipped with a retrospective and an historical perspective, to reconstruct longer and more basic tendencies within current developments. Inevitably, every use of the concept of constitution on the European level feeds on the pathos transferred to it in the history of nation-states (Haltern 2003b). Thus, the question in what way this pathos is deserved and can exist requires theoretical confirmation or critique.

The negotiations about the European constitution in the Convention[29] for the preparation of the 2004 Intergovernmental Conference only indirectly concern this level of discussion. The structure of the Convention remains, in the end, normatively irrelevant. Historically we know that constitutional conventions have almost never lived up to the democratic and deliberative qualities which became key elements of the constitutions they created.[30] We also know that this original defect had little relevance for the constitutional practice or for its political acceptance. Therefore an investigation of the decision-making processes inside the Convention may be of great historical interest. Such an investigation may also help to interpret its result. But it cannnot give us any normative instruments with which to evaluate this result. Of real importance are the design of the ratification procedure and the participation mechanisms contained in a future constitution. The designation of such a document as 'constitution' is, then, an occasion not only for elation but also for further investigation. In this, there must always be a reminder, of a central task of the constitutionalism of the western tradition: making democratic politics possible through law.

Notes

1 For an interesting argument in this direction that refers to many legal categories, see Derrida 2001.
2 For the elaboration and application of this analysis in the context of the legal institutions of the European integration, see another piece by the author (Möllers 2003b).
3 On these two traditions, see Vorländer 1999: 15; Brunkhorst 2002b: 84f.
4 Stourzh 1977: 294–5. For a concise history of the concept, see Ball and Hanson 1989: 50.
5 Art. 16 Declaration of the Rights of Man: 'Any society in which rights are not guaranteed, nor the scope of power determined, has no Constitution.' For the American tradition, see the quote in Wood 1969: 267: 'All countries have some form of government, but few, or perhaps none, have truly a constitution.'
6 The clearest expression is the prohibition of corporations in the Loi Le Chapelier.
7 For France: de Tocqueville 1851, and the analysis in Furet 1978: 209f.
8 The classical critique is Burke 1774: 181f.
9 Sewell (1994: 109) talks of a 'rhetoric of amnesia' in Sieyès.
10 For this interrelation with a view on the United States, see Luhmann 1990.
11 In *McCulloch* v. *Maryland* 4 Wheaton 316 (1819), John Marshall's much quoted statement: 'In considering this question, then, we must never forget that it is a constitution we are expounding,' exactly refers to this fact.
12 To underline the different approach to parliament, see Fraenkel 1991; and to the notion of the state, see Schönberger 1999.
13 For Germany: Boldt 1975: 25f; Böckenförde 1991: 33f.

14 The origins are analysed in Pocock 1957: 46f.
15 The making of the Federal Administration by congress is described in: Elkins and McKitrick 1993: 50f.
16 On the British rule of law, see Dicey 1959: 183f.; Löwenstein 1967: 74f. For a comparison with the United States, see Lepsius 1997: 207f.
17 For a German reception of the British rule of law, see Gneist 1879.
18 Burke 1790: 45–6. For a distinction between this concept of deliberation and a genuine democratic theory, see: Bessette 1994: 40f.
19 For a critique of the conjecture that separated powers and judicial control could minimize statal power, see Luhmann 1988: 48f.; Foucault 1997: 21f.
20 A comparative critique with an eye to Anglo-American traditions is Hennis 1968: 24f.
21 For a canonized description, see Dicey 1959: 37f. More moderate for contemporary circumstances is Barendt 1998: 86f.
22 Allan 1993: 136f. For an historical perspective, see Asch 1997.
23 For the so called 'counter-majoritarian' difficulty, see Thayer 1893; Bickel 1962.
24 This is clear in Schmitt's construction of a contradiction between rule of law and democracy: Schmitt 1927: 125–6.
25 For this connection, see Möllers 2001a: 178f.
26 Stolleis (1995: 295) remarks that the inclusion in European constitutional discourse of constitutional history before 1789 does not necessarily imply its re-feudalization.
27 This is attempted in Möllers 2003b: 29–54.
28 See the outlines for European constitutions of the European Parliament (1984; 1994).
29 http://european-convention.eu.int/default.asp?lang=DE
30 For an historical account of democratic deficiences of most constitutional conventions, see von Beyme 1968; Elster 1998b.

9   *Wille zur Verfassung*, or the constitutional state in Europe

Massimo La Torre

Introduction

In this chapter, I will consider and criticize the implicit normative implications that the 'classical' positivistic conceptions of law have for our understanding of constitutionalism. By 'classical' positivistic conceptions of law, I refer to the most outstanding positivist legal theories of the nineteenth and early twentieth century, the kind of Austin, Gerber, Laband, Jellinek or Santi Romano. Such authors played a major role in the theoretical development of law in Europe, especially in *public law*. Their thought can still be said to have a considerable influence on the way in which law is conceived and analysed in Europe. A critical scrutiny of the central tenets of their theories is thus quite pertinent at the very time at which a constitution is being written for the European Union.[1] This is so because the way in which law is conceptualized has a major feedback on the critical standards applied to constitution-making processes and to their outcomes, that is, the actual rights and values it positivizes. Therefore, what *conception of European law* is sustained has a direct impact on how the European *constitution-making process* and the eventual European constitution are/will be assessed.

The argument which I develop in this chapter assumes a basic contrast between two conceptions of the constitution in general, and of the European constitution in particular, which for the sake of clarity can be named *democratic* and *realist*.[2] A *democratic* conception of the constitution regards the constitution as the most legitimate expression of the will of the people. As such, it is not only closely associated with the revolutionary ideals of the French Revolution, but also contains a set of demanding critical standards that the constitution-making process and the constitution as an end-product will have to comply with, in order to be regarded as legitimate.[3] At a minimum, a European constitution *proper* presupposes active citizen participation in its forging, and significant citizen endorsement (through the expression of their will in debates and elections). Moreover, the idea of a democratic constitution is closely associated with citizens' mutual acknowledgement of their fundamental rights, as entrenched in the constitution. The democratic credo, whereby citizens are the ultimate source of political legitimacy, not only renders the association between the state and the constitution contingent, but is also critical of the *state*, in the sense of being *the* monopolist of violence.

In contrast, a *realist* conception of the constitution regards the constitution as a mere set of founding standards of the legal order, with no explicit reference to *critical* standards of legitimacy applicable to the process through which constitutional provisions are established, or to the substance of such provisions (thus, with no reference to democratic sanction). In fact, the standards embraced by the realist conception tend to be purely sociological, not critical or counterfactual. To the realist, the constitution is not the creation of the will of the people, but a *grounding context* which sets limits on the popular will, that is, on ordinary statutes, be they enacted at the European or at the national level. In other words, the constitution deactivates the *pouvoir constituant* as a public and 'constructed' space and bows before social power. Thus, force remains the ultimate foundation of the legal order, which for that reason is closely associated with the traditional understanding of the state. As a consequence, the writing of a constitution is to be regarded either as not necessary or as a prelude to the forging of a state, which in the European case would lead to a necessary tension between the Union as a state, on the one hand, and the Member States, on the other.

With such a contrast in mind, I proceed to a reconstruction of the leading classical elaborations of European legal positivism. My two points are that classical legal positivists have rarely discussed the option of a democratic versus a realistic conception of the constitution, and they have implicitly tended to favour the latter. First, the conception of the constitution which ends up being advocated has tended to stem from the most basic assumptions of public law dogmatics, and not from an open and critical analysis of the different conceptions of the constitution. The simultaneous affirmation of the man-made (positive) character of law, and the scientific aspirations of legal dogmatics have pushed positivists into conceiving of the constitution in quite peculiar ways. Second, such conceptions have tended to come closer to a *realistic* understanding of the constitution, as described in the first section of this chapter. This is demonstrated in the second section, where the implicit normative assumptions about the constitution are rendered explicit through an assessment of some of the key positivist legal scholars. This analysis renders visible the 'unholy alliance' (so to speak) of positivism and undemocratic conceptions of the constitution. Such an alliance explains the tendency to misrepresent the goals of the constitution-making process, and the repeated failures to assess properly the eventual outcome of constitutional processes, that is, constitutions in a substantive sense.

But the analysis will be incomplete if it does not consider the features of contemporary European constitutionalism, as developed after World War II (see the third section of this chapter). This supplementary analysis provides some insights into how to rescue the major theoretical and normative contributions of European legal positivism without falling prey to its pitfalls. The traumatic experiences of the thirties and forties fostered a reconsideration of classical legal positivism. In theoretical terms, this prompted a thorough reformulation of positivistic legal theories, something which is sometimes expressed by means of labelling the most recent legal positivistic theories as post-positivistic, in contrast with classical legal positivistic ones. In legal terms, it led to the enactment of constitutions such as the Italian one of 1948, or the German one of 1949, which explicitly grounded their legitimacy on their condition of expression of the will of the people. Such constitutional understanding partially explains the progressive affirmation of democratic standards in European Union law, through the influence of the *common constitutional traditions* of the Member States. In the conclusion, it is further argued that the writing of a Constitution for the European Union must be based rather on post-positivistic than on classical legal positivistic doctrines. There are worrying signs of a revival of classical legal positivistic doctrines at the European level, something which would be extremely damaging from the perspective of democracy, both at the European and at the national level.

The hidden normativity of classical legal positivism

It is not an easy task to provide a clear and short definition of legal positivism. This is so to the extent that legal positivism is a perennial source both of reassurance and of controversy. Disagreement stems from the existence of a very qualified competitor and challenger, namely natural law doctrines.[4] For our present purposes, what it is here referred to as classical legal positivism can be defined by reference to three main features. First, 'positivism' claims that law is 'posited', man-made, 'artificial', and hence can be remade. This stands in marked contrast to natural law, whose change is not equally at the disposal of human beings.

Second, the idea of 'artificiality' is connected with that of a specific form of man-made law, the one produced by the state. The law of the legal positivist is the law of a special historical political formation, the modern state. Such a positivist obsession is so strong and permanent as to mark a continuity of attitudes over the last two centuries. Such continuity characterizes another strange idea, which again is related to the view of the law as mere state law. The addressees of legal rules – according to such diverse scholars as Hans Kelsen, Alf Ross, Karl Olivecrona, H.L.A. Hart and, most recently, a number of post-Hartian jurisprudents – are only judges and *state* officials. Law is only addressed to, and concerned with, law officers, and that renders it, literally, an autonomous social order.[5]

Third, positivism claims that law is also, and primarily, a *fact*. The notion that law is a fact is what gives it its validity and legal force. This is clearly illustrated by the 'normative force of the factual' as noted by Georg Jellinek, or by the centrality given to effectiveness in Hans Kelsen's 'pure theory'.[6] This tendency is related to the unattainable objective of offering legal studies a noble and 'hard' epistemology, and of presenting it as a sort of 'empirical science' (Burdeau *et al.* 1997: 36).

Having said that, it does not take much to realize the tensions between the main tenets of classical legal positivism. The assumed centrality of 'facts', and the claim to build law (legal doctrine) as a kind of empirical science, do not obviously fit with the view of law as 'man-made', and therefore as conventional, changeable and unstable. Scientific facts cannot be unstable and highly contingent, as laws are. This tension leads to a rather peculiar characterization of law, and, by implication, of the constitution as the central piece of the legal order. Positivists tend to be tempted to attribute to law the same ontological status as nature (one could even talk of the same ontological 'density'). This can be done by means of equating the laws of nature with the laws of the state. As a consequence, the constitution tends to be distinguished from politics, and from political fights and agreements, since it must be stable, objective and permanent in order to be studied scientifically. This is so because *hard sciences* (in the classical positivistic, and today rather contested, understanding, even in the natural sciences) can only be so if they have a stable and objective object, which permits the scientist to observe regularities, and predict.

The surreptitious implication of the *affirmation of legal positivism as a science* is that constitutions can no longer be conceived of as political creatures, nor can they be considered as man-made agreements. To the contrary, constitutions are conceived of according to the pre-modern meaning of political order. They become an 'essence'. Quite paradoxically, the constitution loses its sense of a 'formal' asset and acquires that of a 'material constitution', that is, the 'nature' of the state. This is very odd given the legal positivists' accentuation of form. But easing the inner tension of positivism requires equating the constitution with the 'material constitution' of the state (Burdeau *et al.* 1997: 44–5). The concepts of 'constitutional' or 'representative' state, 'constitutional monarchy' or 'constitution of a free people' are disregarded in favour of the apparently more scientific reference to 'state law'.

Such a move is far from devoid of consequences, two of which cannot be ignored. First, the 'scientific' definition of the constitution supports both anti-liberal doctrines which reject the political role of the constitution as an act of self-determination, and historical conceptions of the constitution which deny the creative capacity of the common will. To put it briefly, it is Burke's, not Paine's, view which the legal positivist takes as his or her own at the end of the day. Scientific virtue is thus acquired at the price of implicitly and silently endorsing the realistic, not the democratic, conception of the constitution. The central insights of constitutionalism, namely the limitation of state powers through the recognition of fundamental rights and the separation of powers, become incompatible with legal positivism, except as some kind of 'noble lie', or as an accidental ethical decision. Constitutional provisions become a kind of a morality without legal consequences, or, more paradoxically, an act of self-limitation by the sovereign through which the sovereign paradoxically retains its dignity and its ultimate power. Second, the term 'constitution' is deprived of normative discriminating power. Any state will be given the dignity of being 'constitutional', whoever the author and whatever the contents of the constitution. The notion of constitution becomes an empty one, which could be applied to any state or body politic.

So, what is the relationship between classical legal positivism and the idea of a constitution? First, the proclaimed scientific approach to law favours legal analyses of the constitution which are mainly, if not exclusively, descriptive. As a consequence, constitutions are not given a high normative status. Constitutional law is seen as *weak* law, deprived of the force to resist changes decided by the ordinary legislature. Second, the seemingly neutral state-centred definition of law forces the characterization of constitutions either as 'positive morality' (something non-legal) or as ordinary law. Accordingly, the notion of (legal) state, *Rechtsstaat*, takes the upper hand. Constitutionalism henceforth becomes fundamentally equivalent to 'legalism' or to the 'rule of law', and the latter is defined as a 'self-limitation' of state sovereignty, as a series of disciplinary or administrative procedures internal to the state machinery. It might be recalled here that 'rule of law' (*Rechtsstaat*) in classical German public law means paradigmatically administrative jurisdiction. Third, and in consequence, the notions of democracy (as government of the people by the people), constitution in a strong sense (as an act of self-institution) and fundamental rights (as individual entitlements independent of legislation) are banished from the province of public law. Fundamental rights are suggestively replaced by 'public subjective rights', actionable not before ordinary judges, but exclusively in front of administrative courts. Such *subjektive öffentliche Rechte* are often conceptualized as *Reflexrechte*, a reflex of legislative supremacy. It must be added that this development was fuelled by the political reaction against the French Revolution, characterized as the harbinger of anarchy, chaos and subversion. Human rights were characterized as 'nonsense upon stilts' (in the words of Jeremy Bentham), while catalogues of civic freedoms were said to be no more than 'anarchical fallacies'.

Democratic constitutionalism is widely rejected within *classical* legal positivist doctrines, because it is seen as a formidable threat to monarchical regimes (the only really appropriate body to express the idea of 'political superiority').

Positivistic alternatives to democratic constitutionalism

As an alternative to democratic constitutionalism, three main strategies have tended to be elaborated: (i) liberal, (ii) legalist and (iii) traditionalist.

For the liberal strategy (adopted mainly in post-revolutionary France), a constitution means a monarchy limited through a charter formally conceded (*octroyée*) by the king to the people, by means of which the king promises to limit his own prerogatives and to safeguard and respect a few civil and political rights. Government (*Gubernaculum*) and *jurisdictio* (law concerning individual entitlements and private agreements) are here kept separate through some form of parliamentary control.

In the legalist strategy there is no need for an explicit constitutional charter. The procedural form given to state acts – with the conceptual configuration of the state as a collective legal subject – is seen as sufficient. In the best case some sort of jurisdiction internal to the executive power is envisaged.

Communitarians or traditionalists conceive of the constitution as an historical *Verfassung*, and are opposed to the liberal rights-based conception of a formal *Konstitution* – an opposition which we find explicitly expressed in Hegel's legal philosophy. This strategy is also characteristic of political romanticism. However, we are usually confronted with two versions of such an approach, a moderate and a radical. The moderate envisions a constitution as a collective practice which nevertheless makes room for some individual rights and some degree of parliamentary control, such as would be the case with the British Constitution. Burke's proposals could perhaps be ascribed to this moderate model. In the radical view, constitution (*Verfassung*) is a deeper communitarian practice, based on organic and corporative institutions (*Stände*), and on monarchical prerogatives intended to work as a unifying and crowning instance of social hierarchies. Stahl's *Rechtsphilosophie* could be a good example of a theory that defends this latter view.

Things are turned a trifle more complex by the tendency of some authors to combine the idea of state sovereignty with the revolutionary idea of the constitution as an act of self-institution. Despite the triumph of classical legal positivism in the nineteenth century, a *latent link* between positivism and constitutionalism remained. We may eventually come to reinterpret legal positivism as the general theory of law that is most congruent with modern (democratic) constitutionalism (see the third section of this chapter). But in the nineteenth century and the early part of the twentieth century, the idea of the constitution as an act of self-institution tended to be conceived of in existential terms, that is, as an act of self-affirmation by the people, albeit not in discursive terms as the outcome of a process compliant with the requirements of discursive public interaction. *Decision*, not *deliberation*, is to be the essential content of the founding, constitutional moment. *Auctoritas, non veritas, facit legem* (authority, not truth, makes the law) was the motto that was most cherished and repeated by legal positivists. Therefore, the *latent link* between legal positivism and modern constitutionalism was based on a romantic conception of a constitution, or, more specifically, on the idea of an existential, not a deliberative, general will. This leads to the conclusion that no democracy would be possible without a strong *demos* (a thick cultural and national unity that is, in the end, an *ethnos*).

The purpose of the next section is to substantiate the claim made here by means of a reconstruction of the theories of some of the outstanding representatives of classical legal positivism. Attention will be paid to John Austin's analytical jurisprudence (first sub-section), to mainstream German public law in the nineteenth century (second sub-section), and to the attempts to transcend legal positivism in the twentieth century (third sub-section).

Constitutionalism in classical legal positivism

John Austin's analytical jurisprudence

In all his works, but especially in his famous *The Province of Jurisprudence Determined*, John Austin pursued a basic positivistic aim, namely to draw a sharp line between law and morality. This separation aim led him to associate law and force very closely. For the British legal theorist, a true law is a command and a command only, that is, an intimation of a wish to do, or forbear from acting, backed by the threat of a sanction. Therefore, the distinction between law and morality is not based on the distinction between 'is' and 'ought', or on their respective epistemological qualities, but rather on the fact that only law derives from political superiors, from the *sovereign's final will*. Consequently, law is depicted as a *command supported by a menace*. Laws without sanctions are not considered 'proper' laws. Accordingly there are only 'duties', not rights, said differently, rights are paraphrases of duties and judges are mainly thought of as officials subordinate to the political superior's will and expression of wish.

The consequences of such an approach are far from negligible and take Austin away from a democratic conception of law and politics. First, political society is defined as a hierarchical order (Austin 1954: 196). Political society is in essence seen as a fractured body, in short, a *class society*, a society of 'superiors' and 'inferiors' (p. 216). Political equality, democracy, government of the people by the people, is, as mentioned, 'nonsense upon stilts', to use again the expression which Bentham, Austin's tutor, used in order to downplay human rights. This is so to the extent that political superiority is a good which cannot be redistributed according to liberal or egalitarian criteria (p. 216). Only *the few* can have full political competence, since by nature human beings do not have equal wisdom and talents. This is the reason why every political society, every state, 'every supreme government is a *monarchy* [...] or an *aristocracy*' (p. 218, my italics). No true democracy is conceivable within such a positivist jurisprudential framework. Second, proper constitutionalism is equally inconceivable, to the point of being regarded as an absurdity, a logical contradiction (p. 254). In fact, 'sovereign or supreme power is incapable of legal limitation, whether it resides in an individual or in a number of individuals' (p. 223). Separation of powers is 'too palpably false' (p. 235). Thus, the constitution and the constitutional laws are not true laws, but mere *positive morality* (p. 259). Third, Austin's theory leads to a utilitarian downgrading of freedom. Political liberty cannot be an end in itself, since it is merely 'a mean to that furtherance of the common weal, which is the only ultimate object of good or beneficent sovereignty' (p. 270). And political liberty at the end of the day is only appeal to duty and obedience, in that it 'is coupled with a legal right to it: and, consequently, political liberty is fostered by that very political restraint from which the devotees of the ideal liberty are so fearfully and blindly averse' (p. 271). In short, wherever one turns around in the precinct of a political society, one can only be confronted with power ('might'), duty ('subjection to an impending menace'), with constraints, and with inequality of natural talents and social conditions. Not much is thus left of constitutionalism or democracy, one might add.

Mainstream German public law in the twentieth century

Similar observations stem from a close analysis of the works of the founding fathers of Continental public law, the lot of Friedrich Carl von Gerber, Paul Laband and Georg Jellinek.

The history of German modern public law might be said to begin with a bold statement made by Gerber: 'State authority is will power by a subject conceived as an ethical organism' (Gerber 1880: 19). This implies the extension to the domain of public law of the 'will dogma' theory (*Willensdogma*), which was first elaborated in order to reconstruct and interpret contract law. This extension to the domain of public law is far from neutral in legal and political terms.

First, the state is conceived as *individual subject* endowed with a will of its own. Such a will, far from being equivalent to private 'autonomy', is now characterized as 'state power' (*Staatsgewalt*). Second, 'state power' finds its holder not in the king as such, but rather in the state itself, conceived as a corporation, a *legal person*. As a consequence, the reality of the state is no longer circumscribed to the person of the king. It is now claimed that the state really exists as an entity based on the people, and not merely as a necessary presupposition, a mythical body or a fiction. Third, the state is said to have *a will of its own*, which is not the outcome of a legal or theological construction (as it is, for instance, in the medieval doctrine of the king's two bodies), but is said to be affirmed in the spirit of the people (the *Volksgeist*, in Gerber's classical formulation). Fourth, state power is closely associated with dominion (*Herrschaft*) (Gerber 1880: 21). This implies that the entirety of the people is subject to the state will as *domination*. Fifth, the state should be *sovereign* in order to be faithful to the spirit of the people, which, as was indicated, constitutes the state's foundation. State sovereignty entails that 'state power' should not be subject to a power external and superior to itself. In that sense, sovereignty has little to do with the actual rights or prerogatives of the king (Gerber 1880: 22).

The *Willensdogma* doctrine thus marks a paradigm shift in German doctrine, as it gives rise to a boldly impersonal view of the state, in the sense of being detached from the very person and the rights of the king. One could further add that such 'impersonalization' necessarily leads to the affirmation of the king as a mere 'organ' of the state.[7]

The problem here, as in any imperativistic doctrine, is how to reconcile the affirmation of political will as domination and command with the acknowledgement of *limits* to power, which is something intrinsic to the idea of law and legal order. What we are interested in observing is that the *Willensdogma* clearly rules out that the constitution could be the answer to such a puzzle. In its view, the constitution is nothing else than a document describing and cursorily organizing the organs of the state. It cannot be seen as a constraint on the actual action of state agencies. To put it differently, a constitution is not a rule controlling state activity; it is rather the *normality* – so to speak – of such an activity. The solution to the tension between power and legal limits is to be found elsewhere, namely in the doctrine of state purposes. It is the reference to state purposes that establishes limits to the action of state agencies: 'State power is no absolute will power. It should only serve state purposes and exist solely for them' (Gerber 1880: 31). It must be added that such state purposes are culturally determined, they are determined by the 'spirit of the people', the (in)famous *Volksgeist*.

Laband and Jellinek pursued Gerber's paradoxical dogmatic construction further. They were partly motivated by the historical and social circumstances under which they found themselves. The tension between the affirmation of the power of the state and its limits became even more acute after the foundation of the Second Reich. The underlying concern of legal dogmatics at the time was the tension between the sovereignty of the State and its federal structure. To put it differently, the key question was how the Reich could be at the same time a sovereign *and* a federal state. The puzzle stemmed from the fact that the states that made up the Reich did not disappear. To the contrary, they preserved their ancient status. How can states keep on being sovereign, at the same time as they form a new, and fully sovereign, Reich? It was in response to such a concern that Laband and Jellinek elaborated the doctrine of state self-limitation. The theory of state self-limitation was based on a clear-cut distinction between (i) *sovereignty* (*Souveränität*) and (ii) *sovereign rights* (*Herrschaftsrechte*). On the one hand, the idea of sovereignty, or, better, full or absolute sovereignty, was clearly affirmed. In Paul Laband's most famous treatise, *Das Staatsrecht des Deutschen Reiches*, we read that:

> [t]here is no dimidiated, divided, diminished, dependent, relative sovereignty, but only either sovereignty or not sovereignty. Nevertheless, an entity which does not have any sovereignty features, and therefore is subject to a superior legal power in some respect, can in spite of this hold sovereign rights on free human beings and their groupings, thus be a state power.
>
> (Laband 1911: 73)

On the other hand, Jellinek, in his famous monograph *Gesetz und Verordnung*, affirmed that sovereignty was to be conceptualized as a negative attribute, as the fact that the state as a legal (collective) personality does not suffer any (legal) limitation. The key additional affirmation was that sovereignty was actually compatible with different sets of concrete powers and competences of the state (Jellinek 1887: 200). The different sets result from acts of *self-limitation* of the state, by means of which a detailed picture was formed of the ends to which state action would be directed. This results in the affirmation of sovereign powers and competences, which are constrained by the law; it is thus the law that formalizes the *self-limitation* of the powers of the state. This can be expressed differently by means of saying that the puzzle is solved by means of distinguishing between *actual* and *potential* sovereignty (Jellinek 1887: 200). In short, sovereignty means the possibility of exercising all conceivable legal powers, but sovereignty is not necessarily equivalent to the sum of concrete valid legal powers. This conceptual stipulation thus makes it possible to have both a federal state holding full sovereignty and subordinate federate entities that can still be given state dignity and prerogatives. States could continue to be sovereign while the exercise of their sovereignty was transferred to the Reich.

Even if the main concern which motivated Laband's and Jellinek's dogmatic elaborations was the tension between sovereignty and federalism, the resulting doctrine of self-limitation had wide implications for the conceptualization of the state as a 'constitutional' order, at least in the narrow sense of a 'legal' state. As just indicated, a state in this perspective was 'legal' by an act of self-limitation.

But if the state could limit itself, the constitution was not the founding and limiting act of the state; the constitution was necessarily external or previous to the state. Constitutions were said to possess neither a specific legal function, nor a specific legal efficacy. They were either equated with the 'material constitution' and with ordinary legislation, or with a programmatic (if not rhetorical) declaration without direct legal effect. The 'real' constitution, which was related to the factual mode of state functioning, was thus said to change through the mere exercise of state power (Jellinek 1906: 34).

We are not very far from Lassalle's famous, critical and somewhat cynical view of a constitution as the concrete power relations within a given community. The only relevant difference, perhaps, is that while Lassalle conceives of constitutions as relational entities emerging from social conflict, Jellinek's view is more faithful to the idea that connects an organic compact sovereignty with a constitution as its 'deep grammar'. This renders possible the decoupling of constitutional change from law (Jellinek 1906: 3). In a way, the constitution becomes a matter of course: any state has a constitution, and therefore is a 'constitutional' state.

Twentieth-century positivism

Nineteenth-century legal positivism can be characterized as a sort of hybrid of two rough materials: on the one side, the legal form, rule or norm (*normativity*); on the other side, the social and political context; power-relations (*facticity*). Once these two poles are assumed in their pure form, they reveal the very deep tensions at the core of legal positivism. On the one hand, *facticity* radicalized leads to a positivism of social facts, which is very well represented by institutionalist and realist doctrines. On the other hand, normativity radicalized results in the 'pure theory of law', which confines law to rules and the relations between rules.

The pluralistic turn of sovereignty: Santi Romano

Gerber, Laband and Jellinek were central figures in the development of public law dogmatics in Germany. Owing to the central position of German legal culture in Europe, their influence extended all over the Continent. Santi Romano could be said to have been, perhaps together with Orlando, their counterpart in Italy. As such, he can only be characterized as the leading author of a legal tradition with a far from minor influence in the development of European legal dogmatics. One of the major theoretical contributions of Romano was to show that the formalistic liberal State, characterized by its minimum set of competences and societal footing, was no longer functional to the emerging mass society. In a series of articles written before World War I, Romano foresaw the forthcoming crisis of the liberal state and tried to elaborate on how the state should be reformed. The Italian publicist advocated the explicit recognition of the *materiality and purposiveness* of law, which had been obscured, even hidden, by nineteenth-century positivist doctrines. For our present purposes, it is important to notice that he reaffirmed at the very same time the notion of political power which was usually assumed by positivistic doctrines. This is because Romano's drive for the materialization of law was not based on a counterfactual, normative conception of law, but on an *ethical* conception of law (as a kind of positive morality). This explains why, in his view, state prerogatives should prevail over legal provisions. The affirmation of the *pluralistic* character of law, of a plurality of legal orders, is instrumental to this. Moreover, Romano characterized the political order as merely one social order among many, without rank-ordering or listing them in order of preference. It is quite revealing that one such social order was the mafia. Consequently, Romano's pluralism served to dignify forms of corporatism and hierarchical social distinction. It thus goes without saying that Romano's state theory has obvious, even if implicit, normative consequences. A central one is that the constitution is characterized as the unitary principle intrinsic to any single legal order, and not as the supreme or master rule of the legal system:

> We use the expression 'constitutional law' or the equivalent 'constitution' to designate that part of every institution, that is, of every legal order, which is its essential structure and which is the basis of all its parts. [...] In short: constitutional law, or a constitution, is the state supreme order.
>
> (Romano 1933: 9)

To put it in negative terms, constitutionalism is not equated with a special set of laws (an 'institution'), and constitutional status does not denote any special character or trait of a norm. A further consequence is that every state has, and cannot but have, its own constitutional law: 'The state by definition is a legal order [...] and one cannot therefore conceive of it in any of its forms outside the law' (Romano 1933: 10). All state expressions are legal acts. In such a configuration of state activities, there is no room for a specific 'constitutional moment' or for a review of the constitutionality of legislative acts.

The logical turn of the material constitution: Stahl and Kelsen

A further central reference is that of Friedrich Julius Stahl's philosophy of law. In his work, we are confronted with the idea of constitution as the articulation and differentiation of human society, whereby the state comes to existence as an 'institution': 'Organization (*Gliederung*) of human community whereby the state exists as an institution (*Anstalt*)' (Stahl 1878: 205). Here the essential words are *Gliederung* and *Anstalt*. According to Stahl, a constitution is only possible if a community is structured in organic units which are ranked 'spontaneously' (i.e. without the intervention of public authority) along a hierarchical scale. Thus, the constitution is something connected not to an (open-ended or unspecific) form of political order, but to a special form, that is, one endowed with stability and a hierarchical ordering. The constitution is connected to an 'institution' (*Anstalt*). Central to Stahl's conception of the constitution is the idea of *hierarchy*, both in a social sense – as a structuring principle of society as a whole – and in a political sense. This is the overarching criterion that rules the relationship between government and citizens. The two notions, *Gliederung* and *Anstalt*, converge into one, which presides over Stahl's view of a constitution: hierarchy. This is a principle of society as a whole, as well as for the political as the overarching criterion in the relationship between government and citizens. While democratic constitutionalism implicitly or explicitly affirms the equal civic competence of citizens, thus opening the way to a struggle for political equality in general and leading to the affirmation of the principle of equal concern, Stahl's romantic thought asserts that a constitution could only take place in the framework of a pluralist (in the sense of driven through unequal membership) social reality. Thus, Stahl's romantic philosophy of law shares with Romano's the same prejudice against political equality.

This is also the point where Hans Kelsen fails to render justice to modern constitutionalism. Kelsen's attempt to build a 'pure' science of law is well known, and need not be analysed here in depth. What we must consider here in some detail, however, is that Kelsen's 'opening move' is based on two main theoretical pillars. The first is a concept of rule that is seen not as a command or an imperative, but as a 'hypothetical judgment'. The second is a notion of the legal system as a 'dynamic order', a hierarchical structure of rules, where a central role is assigned to those norms that enable the production of all other norms. The legal system culminates in a master rule, the so-called *Grundnorm*, as is also discussed by Erik Eriksen in Chapter 3 of the present volume. The main peculiarity of this *Grundnorm* is that it is not a positive norm, but is merely hypothetical. In brief, the *Grundnorm* is an epistemological device intended to allow lawyers to conceive of legal norms as being part of a unitary system. Prima facie, this doctrine seems to bring about a full normativistic deconstruction of the state. The state should now be conceived solely as an agglomeration of norms without an internal substance. But a close reading of Kelsen's theses leads to a different conclusion. In the *Allgemeine Staatslehre*, his most representative public law treatise (Kelsen 1925: 248), we read that 'state function is law function'. By this, the Austrian legal theorist claims that the state exists in so far as there is a permanent process of production of norms, and a concretization of these norms. This is rendered possible by the working of a dynamic order, 'closed' at its summit by a fictitious master rule. Such a rule is the *real constitution* in a logical sense. Very interestingly, what we usually call the 'constitution' is such only 'in the sense of positive law'. Such a constitution cannot provide a unitary principle of legal order. This is so since the positive constitution can be changed, and is actually often changed. Therefore, it cannot offer stability and identity to the state. A proper, permanent identity can only be given by a constitution, which need not endure the contingencies of political conflict and historical developments. Rather the identities must be based on a purely logical or epistemological norm, with no substantive content except for the empowerment of those officials or 'organs' that produce the historical constitution, whatever its content.

The important implication of all this is that Kelsen moves from the need for a permanent state to an abstract, nearly empty notion of (logical) constitution, which he affirms as the truly supreme norm of the legal order. This leads him to reject any contractualist foundation for constitutionalism. To affirm that a constitution means a people's basic agreement is branded as a natural law thesis.[8] The latter affirms that the ultimate source of the law is not a normative figure (the *Grundnorm*), but a special event. This results in the violation of the sacrosanct purity of the legal normative domain.[9] Kelsen's approach does have serious normative consequences. In particular, Kelsen is led to state that the constitution as a written, formal document is a remnant of natural law ideas. His, then, is a view of the constitution as an expression of the legal order and state as based on a material agreement enshrined in a document to which an aura of sacrality is ascribed.[10] He thus ends up stating that the utility and opportunity of getting such a formal (sacral) document are to be doubted (Kelsen 1925: 253).

Such a statement is pregnant with far from pleasant consequences, and is indeed astonishing, given that Kelsen was the intellectual father of quite a number of formal constitutions.

The public law debate in Weimar

But if there was a constitution and a legal-theoretical debate on a constitution that had a major impact on the development of European public law, that was the Weimar Constitution and the legal-theoretical debate which focused on it. The constitutional and political experience of the Weimar Republic is a central one in constitutional and political history. First, the legal-theoretical debate which took place from 1919 to 1933 was extremely rich. Some of the seeds of the more fertile ideas of post-1945 constitutionalism, to which we will turn in the following section, were planted at this defining time. Second, the turbulent Weimar years and the final collapse of the Republic proved beyond any doubt that the time of classical legal positivism had come to an end, if only because classical legal positivism could not offer a concept of law that would be logically congruent with democratic ideals, or be minimally supportive of these. In particular, legal positivism was unable to react to the rise of *mass society* and the *social state* without endangering liberal culture. The Weimar Republic's breakdown led to the Third Reich monster, and to the ruin of Europe in World War II.

In fact, the entry into force of the Weimar Constitution of 1919 marked a new stage in the history of European constitutionalism. This was so for several reasons. First of all, the Constitution was the explicit product of a *constitutional moment*, an institutional act external to government itself, and allegedly authored by the people. The Preamble is telling in this respect: 'The German people [...] has given this constitution to itself.' Thus, we are not faced with a constitution *octroyée*, one that is a gracious concession by the powerful. Second, the Weimar Constitution contains a list of fundamental rights in the contemporary sense of the term. Moreover, the bill of rights is not a mere appendix to the text, but an integral and central element of the Constitution. Third, a strong principle of equality is affirmed at the core of the Constitution. Thus, equality is no longer reducible to formal equality before the law, but is *materialized*, so to speak. Fourth, the Weimar

Constitution allowed for the building of elements of constitutional justice or judicial review in the form of a Supreme Court (the *Staatsgerichtshof*), whose powers, however, remained a matter of doctrinal controversy (Stolleis 2003: 266ff.).

At one of the darkest times of history, Carl Schmitt published *Über die drei Arten des rechtswissenschaftlichen Denkens* (Schmitt 1934), a pamphlet in which he reconstructed the main legal-theoretical conceptions of the early twentieth century around three main types, namely *normativism, institutionalism* and *decisionism*. Whatever the assessment of Schmitt and of this specific work, it is quite appropriate to follow his three-fold categorization in our analysis of the legal-theoretical debates of Weimar.

First is *institutionalism*. Such an approach was quite popular in the 1920s, something not unrelated to its romantic origins and undertones. The most prominent spokesman of such an approach was Rudolf Smend, who, not unco-incidentally, was an admirer of Rudolf Kjellén's view of the state as *Lebensform* and Theodor Litt's phenomenological nationalism. According to Smend, the constitution is an act of self-production of a social body (*Selbstgestaltung*). For our present purposes, it is important to notice that the production of a social body was not conceived in discursive terms, that is, as an act of forging understanding and agreement among different conceptions of the good life, and hence making for an 'overlapping consensus'. Quite to the contrary, Smend actually despised such an approach, which would have probably deserved the qualification of 'contractualist', or, more explicitly and pejoratively, of 'individualist'. Constitutional *Selbstgestaltung* was rather a process of integration, or, what is the same, an irrational merging together of people around a collective myth. An integrative device according to Smend is, for instance, marching behind a flag or acclaiming a leader seen as a reflection of our culture and ethnic identity. In a similar vein, parliaments may also have integrative effects, but only if deprived of their rational and discursive character and functions, as laboratories for the production of myths and depositories of charisma. Institutionalism was, therefore, clearly at odds with a democratic conception of law.

Second, we must distinguish *decisionism*, which was often combined with some kind of communitarianism, as was arguably the case with Schmitt's own constitutional theory. *In abstracto*, decisionism seems closer to a democratic world-view. This is due to its overt voluntarism and to its explicit reference to a foundational constitutional moment. This structural reference to a *pouvoir constituant* helps create the conditions under which it is possible to render justice to the idea of government of the people by the people, that is, to the core tenet of democracy. There are nevertheless at least two major problems with decisionism, and especially with Weimar decisionist theories. Decisionism is incompatible with the idea of constitutional rules as a system of limits on power. The decisionist understanding of the constitution as an act of a *radically independent* subject is incompatible with the idea of the limiting of the very will whose expression the constitution actually is. To put it differently, decisionism can only conceptualize the constitution as the outcome of a supreme constituting power upon which no restraint can be laid. The *pouvoir constituant* always lies behind the constitutional arrangement, ready to act in a radically innovative way at any time. Accordingly, a constitution could hardly guarantee stability and security to social and political relationships without repudiating the primacy of the original *pouvoir constituant*. The obvious implication is that fundamental rights depend on the constituting power's whims, and cannot offer a basis for controlling legislation. Moreover, decisionism ends by affirming the supremacy of the state over the dignity of the constitution. Since the decisionist *pouvoir constituant* affirms itself as an existential collective entity, this must have a prior existence with regard to the constitution itself. Now, this entity, endowed with such a strong will of self-affirmation, cannot but be the (national) state. The (national) state was the only possible collective subject to which political homogeneity and effective will could be ascribed. This explains why, at the end of the day, the hard core of a constitution is not the bill of rights, but the provisions dealing with the form of the state, and its security.

A third important legal theoretical conception in Weimar Germany was Platonist constitutional theory, which conceived of political institutions as deduced from a higher moral order. Such a higher moral order could only be properly discerned by a restricted group of enlightened and virtuous statesmen, of the 'educated' (*Gebildeten*). Even if its theoretical impact was rather limited, the Platonist theory was deeply embedded in the spirit of the age, something which rendered its anti-democratic effluvia very influential. However, constitutional 'platonism' is not equivalent to normativism, whose paradigmatic expression remains Kelsen's pure theory.

None of the representatives of the now mentioned doctrines of constitutional law in Weimar was in a position (or even intended) to put forward a credible defence of democratic constitutionalism. Quite a few of them were openly critical of the liberal state and served as advocates for authoritarian reform plans. Both Smend's communitarianism and Schmitt's decisionism considered obsolete the question of the limits of political power. Moreover, they imbued their respective theories with a strong anti-individualistic pathos which made it quite difficult to think of the constitutional moment in terms of the affirmation of individual rights. They were also reluctant to defend seriously the need for a proper division of powers. Even if mostly developed by democrats, normativism à la Kelsen could not provide a strong normative justification for the democratic state. As has already been argued, normativism was handicapped in that respect by its emphasis on the scientific character of legal dogmatics. This explains its search for a pure object of analysis, and the consequent indifference to the normative features of positive law. As has also already been argued, the ultimate consequence of such an approach was the equation of any legal system with a constitutional system. But if any state is a legal and constitutional state, there is almost no room for any critique of attempts to re-shape the present state order in authoritarian terms. At any rate, there is no room for a non-relative, objective response founded on value-laden concepts.

The grounds of contemporary European constitutionalism

The German crisis leading to Hitler's seizure of power constitutes terrible evidence of the permanent failures and shortcomings of Weimar constitutional doctrines, and perhaps, more generally, of *classical legal positivism*. It could be said that contemporary European constitutionalism emerged out of the aim of overcoming those shortcomings and contradictions.

Such a new European constitutionalism could be seen as marked by five basic features. First, and most importantly, there is a rediscovery of the natural law tradition, a reconnection of constitutional law with natural law theories, which implies denying the absolute character of the opposition between positive law and natural law theories. This stands in stark contrast to the *radical positivism* of the authors discussed in the second section of this chapter. An outstanding representative of Spanish legal positivism expressed this idea in the following felicitous phrase: 'The question is establishing *within* the legal order a rule fulfilling functions previously ascribed to natural law' (de Otto 1987: 22, italics in the original). Second, and closely related, the central assumption of all European constitutions drafted after World War II is that human beings have a dignity which law cannot ignore, even less deny. Therefore, rights and their protection are seen as the *hard core* of the constitution. Third, the 'intangibility of the constitution', or, better, of its essential contents (*Wesensgehalt*), is strongly affirmed. The ordinary legislature should not be able to modify the contents of the constitution. Therefore, constitutional law needs to be neatly differentiated from ordinary law. Fourth, the conception of the constitution itself changes. In the nineteenth-century liberal states, the main task of the constitution was to limit the king's executive power, something which was done by means of the affirmation and protection of the legislative power of Parliament. Once the monarchical principle had been finally repudiated, the danger that unencumbered legislative power poses for constitutionalism became clear. The *constitutional taming* of the democratic legislator became one of the tasks of the constitution (Bin 2002: Chapter 1). Fifth, and finally, the constitution is reconceived as a programmatic societal agreement. This is paradigmatically expressed in the German *Grundgesetz* or the Italian republican constitution. Those two constitutions are long-term common projects for a better form of life. Their programmatic aspect takes a different meaning from the one which classical legal positivism attached to constitutions. More explicitly, the programmatic character of the constitution actually requires that it has *legal* effects, that is something else than a noble lie or a purely ethical programme. The constitution does not only limit political power, but also, and above all, prescribes ends and means for reaching them. This change of normative status is well mirrored – I believe – in the doctrine of fundamental rights as optimization commands defended by Professor Robert Alexy (Alexy 2002b).

It must be added that another major and somewhat paradoxical implication of postwar constitutionalism is the 'withering away' of the state. This was readily apparent in the works of the most distinguished European constitutional lawyers of the period. Costantino Mortati, once a Fascist public lawyer and the great theorist of the 'material constitution' – a theory originally intended to serve the purposes of the Fascist regime – was 'forced' to adapt his conception of the constitution to the new legal and political developments. His 'adapted' constitutional theory unexpectedly pointed towards the withering away of the state. While in the Fascist context the 'material constitution' referred to the Fascist monopolistic party structure and power claim, in the new postwar democratic republic it was meant both to reflect and to justify political and social pluralism. 'Material constitution' here is the outcome of the interplay of various groups within a pluralistic public sphere. Such interplay prevails over rigid, formal, legal forms, and also, and more importantly for us now, over the traditional state form itself. The constitution, in short, is the bedrock of a legal order, not of the state. Mortati's definition of a constitution is perhaps paradigmatic of postwar 'thick' constitutionalism, opposed to the nineteenth-century 'thin' positivistic version. The 'constitutive elements of the concept of constitution' are three-fold: (i) a people not as subject to an external supreme political power but as the 'unique holder of a power of producing in a unilateral way the constitutional order'; (ii) a solemn and formal procedure of drafting and writing down the constitutional charter as the supreme rule governing state agencies; and (iii) the overarching aim of safeguarding individual freedoms (Mortati 1962: 143).

A similar point is made by Konrad Hesse, probably the most influential German constitutional lawyer after 1945. His theory of *Wille zur Verfassung* is not very different from Costantino Mortati's pluralist reconsideration of the 'material constitution'. Once again, a previously tainted conception of the constitution – Nietzsche's controversial, decisionist and anti-democratic *Wille zur Macht* – is 'redeemed' through a bold reconceptualization. *Wille zur Verfassung* (Hesse 1959) means that it is true that a fundamental decision has to be taken, and that this is the legitimating ground for the constitutional state. However, such a decision is not incompatible with democracy, to the extent that the decision does not necessarily correspond to a pre-constitutional subject, that is, the state as a pre-constitutional entity. A state might be necessary, and perhaps even indispensable as an element of the constitutional order. But two caveats are in order. First, the scope of the constitutional order is wider than that of the state, as the constitutional order also comprises civil society, distinct and differentiated from the state (Hesse 1990: 10). Second, the state is necessary only if it is itself the product of a constitutional moment. 'There is as much state as it is produced by the constitution' (Häberle 1999: 52). The state is thus not a 'primary element' of a constitutional order. In short, within a constitutional order there is first a constitution, and only afterwards, eventually, we might have a state. This is why a legal philosopher of Ulrich Klug's calibre can boldly state that the fundamental principle of the constitutional rule of law is 'anarchy' (Klug 1981: 88ff.). This implies an explicit reconciliation of constitution, political autonomy and self-government or non-domination, which in a noble sense refers back to Klug's *anarchy*.

Moreover, postwar constitutionalism has affirmed itself as the law of 'fundamental rights'. Law is at the end of the day connected with *coercion*, but the substance of law is to be such that it will not contradict the substance and the free exercise of fundamental rights. Otherwise, law would lose its *normative legitimacy*. It can be added that the ultimate foundation of all fundamental rights is autonomy. It could be claimed that autonomy, at the individual level, plays the same role as does the constitutional moment at the public level. According to democratic constitutionalism, laws must respect the autonomy of the individual. Otherwise, the very origin of the constitutional structure would be undermined. The actual implementation of the constitutional order should lead to the 'social-ization of autonomy' and to the reproduction of the constitutional moment's originality. Autonomy socialized, extended to the community, is nothing less than self-government, the absence of political domination, or to quote Klug again, *anarchy*.

Therefore, we are once again confronted with a paradox. In democratic consti-tutionalism, law, an institution related to coercion, is rendered instrumental to the implementation of collective autonomy, that is, of 'anarchy'. Contemporary constitutional law accordingly requires a strong limitation not only of traditional *Herrschaft*, but also, and perhaps foremost, of coercion and violence. Law, once constitutionalized, is therefore required to be fully civilized, thoroughly human. This has been beautifully and intelligently expressed by the judge at the Italian Constitutional Court, Gustavo Zagrebelsky, with the expression *il diritto mite*, or *mild law* (Zagrebelsky 1992).

What was united in the *Rechtsstaat* as apparent from the works of those upholding a realist understanding of the constitution, the legal realists, has now become separated. This separation takes place especially on three levels: (i) sepa-ration of rights from legislative norms; (ii) separation of justice from positive law; and (iii) separation of principles from rules. What legal positivism through its reductionism united is, in the very end, revealed to be an immanent contradic-tion. One term of each pair, however, has to gain the upper hand: rights over statutes, justice over law, principles over rules (Zagrebelsky 1992: 49ff.). This once again speaks to a normative understanding of the constitution.

A constitution is not equivalent to constitutional laws or rules, as Zagrebelsky says, hence giving it a very different twist to that of Schmitt in his *Verfassungslehre*. A constitution is rather the outcome of an exceptional situation, a constitutional moment, where 'political actors will converge on a common purpose: to issue principles beyond everyone's particular interests to make possible a civic common life' (Zagrebelsky 1992: 156). A constitutional law is a 'mild law', first, in the sense that it is open to justification and that it implies argumentation and discourse; it is open to a 'a civil conversation'. But it is also mild in the sense that within its province – which is essentially discursive – the use of force and coer-cion is reduced as much as possible, in order to make it possible for collective autonomy, for 'anarchy', to daily express and reproduce the foundational 'will to the constitution' (*Wille zur Verfassung*). A 'will to the constitution' in fact is first and foremost a will to discourse, and this abhors violence and coercion. Here, there-fore, criminal law can only be 'minimal' and punishment will be mainly education into citizenship. The death penalty, for instance, cannot but be banned. It is not only an instance of unusual and cruel punishment, but it also represents the most serious infringement of the 'anarchy' requirement laid upon the constitutional rule of law, that is, the overwhelming and overarching respect for permanent individual and collective autonomy. Similar conclusions are affirmed by another influential German constitutional lawyer, Martin Kriele. After a critique of Hermann Heller's notion of sovereignty, he comes to the conclusion that 'in the constitutional state there is no sovereign' (Kriele 1981: 116). Fundamental and human rights do not allow for the embarrassing and menacing presence of an almighty centre of power (Kriele 1981: 116). Otherwise, fundamental rights would be, in the best case, pale reflexes of duties and obligations laid upon citizens by state agencies (*Reflexrechte*). Once rights are taken seriously, a constitution cannot but be subservient to them. This priority of rights over rules and duties changes the constitutional landscape and the very meaning of the constitution. Now, this 'is seen as a just political procedure which incorporates the equal political liberties and seeks to assure their fair value so that the processes of political decision are open to all on a roughly equal basis' (Rawls 1993b: 337).

Once invested by constitutional law, the old wild beast, Hobbesian Leviathan, the cold monster feared by Zarathustra, will hopefully be tamed. If it is still to be of use among humans, this will be in a new capacity, says Erhard Denninger (1990: 27–9), another German constitutional lawyer: that of a nice house pet.

Conclusions: towards a European constitution

From the short *aperçu* I have given of the evolution of European public law doctrine, a few important lessons can be drawn. First, we have seen that a modern, democratic constitution should be paradigmatically defined through three features, already enumerated in the famous Article 16 of the Declaration of the Rights of Man and the Citizen of 1789, and reaffirmed in post-1945 constitutionalism: (1) a constitution is an act of collective autonomy and a very special moment of public discourse: (2) a constitution deals with the whole of public powers, regulates and separates them; and (3) a constitution is founded on the fundamental rights which it is called to institutionalize and give protection to. Second, a modern, democratic constitution renders the traditional form of the state both contingent and obsolete, since it is the founding element of a new polity. This so because the state becomes a *contingent result* of a constitutional agreement; it has no essential substance which could eventually precede and outlive a given constitution. The state, moreover, is obsolete, since it consists of a specific form of polity whose two fundamental pillars are domination and monopoly of violence. Now, a constitution as collective repro-duction of individual autonomy could only be a form of self-government, of absence of domination, or, as we saw, anarchy. Its intrinsic discursivity does not tolerate a configuration of public power that in any sense supports violence and hierarchy or dependence.

If this is true, and the contemporary doctrine of constitutional law seems to confirm such an interpretation (as indicated in the previous section), a new and more promising scenario will become possible for an integrated European polity. To start with, there is no need to connect the validity of a European constitution to a correlative statehood. In fact, as has been argued, a constitution does not necessarily refer to a state. On the contrary, the constitution puts in motion a process by which the state is doomed to, so to speak, wither away. Accordingly, a polity which is not a form of statehood can perfectly well fit a constitutional moment. A European Union, which is not a state, nor a federation of states, could none the less be founded on a constitution.

Such a promising perspective could, still, be frustrated by the reaffirmation, at the European level, of the basic tenets of classical legal positivism. There are some hints of this drive towards Europe's legal past in the conceptions of law upheld by some legal and political analysts. Such conceptions have been far from isolated in the debates on and around the constitution of Europe. First, such conceptions were influential on the debates on the Charter of Fundamental Rights. This was so to the point that they were effective in shaping some of the actual provisions of the Charter, such as Article 17 on the right to private property. The literal tenor of such articles seems to have been heavily influenced by rather outdated conceptions of law (see a criticism in Grossi 2001; and also in Eriksen *et al.* 2003). Second, the tendency to associate the democratic surplus of the Laeken constitution-making process with the conveyance of the Convention on the Future of Europe, and to ignore the critical role to be played by the eventual public debates in the overlapping European public spheres, might also be said to be indicative of the renewed force of conceptions of law rather close to classical legal positivism, and, consequently, rather inattentive to the *democratic standards of legitimacy of constitution-making.*[11]

The aim of the second section of this chapter was to reveal the 'unholy alliance', so to speak, between such conceptions of law and quite undemocratic understandings of the constitution. To render explicit such implicit historical tendencies is not a mere antiquarian task, but rather a preliminary step in our dealings with the conceptions of law and constitution which compete to inform the future European constitution.

After all, it must be reaffirmed that once we accept modern constitutionalism and its purport (which, moreover, underpins the common constitutional traditions of the Member States), a constitution cannot but be an exercise in collective autonomy; hence, no European *octroyée* constitution will ever fulfil the requirements set for the legitimacy of a true constitutional moment. It is hard to argue that the political will of European citizens has been a major force in the process of writing a European constitution up to now, and, as already indicated, the conveyance of a Convention on the Future of Europe does not really give grounds to alter such an assessment (which does not rule out, of course, that a genuine public debate in overlapping European public spheres will take place at later stages of the process; but only then could we speak of a *democratically written constitution*). Third, since the constitution has as one of its main aims to institutionalize and perpetuate fundamental rights, such rights cannot but be considered a hard core of the constitution itself. However, such rights are co-original with the exercise of collective autonomy which the constitution consists of, and will not be fully constitutional if played against people's deliberation and public discourse (therefore, rights cannot be merely conceded either). A

European constitution, accordingly, cannot be given only through a European Charter of Fundamental Rights, but would have to rely on a more substantive context of collective debate and decision. The only sovereignty a modern constitution can support is one of principles and rights, which, however, though contributing to dissolve the state's ontological density, do not impede an exercise of public deliberation. Sovereignty is a *decisionistic* notion, related to an almighty and unreflective entity, the Supreme One. A constitution, however, is the author, not the product, of the relevant political unity. This cannot be presupposed, but only thematized through public discourse. Modern constitutionalism, of the kind to which European constitutionalism should aspire, can thus do without the embarrassing presence of that Supreme One, and accordingly be open to the multilateralism of plural, distinct, conventional legal orders. Moreover, it is only this pluralistic reading of modern constitutionalism which does justice to constitutional patriotism, as an alternative to nationalism and communitarianism. Otherwise, the former will but be a disguised form of the latter.

Notes

1 It might be too early to characterize the present moment as a 'constitutional moment', in a meaningful normative sense *à la* Ackerman. Thus the preference for a more neutral term.

2 Such a contrast is similarly established in Chapter 6, by Hauke Brunkhorst, and Chapter 7, by Agustín Menéndez.

3 Following the line of Habermas, Chapter 2 in this book.

4 Intellectual encouragement derives from the fact that many efforts have been made, especially in recent times, to redefine legal positivism. Such efforts are aimed at eschewing the bulk of conceptual and practical obstacles with which it has ever been confronted. Not all of these debates are to the point in this context. But to give the reader an idea of the difficulties which have to be confronted, it will suffice to say that the 'separability thesis', which draws a sharp dividing line between law and morality, used to be considered as the central thesis of legal positivism, but it would not be agreed upon by a few founding fathers of classical European positivism.

5 Normal citizens with their needs and their inclination to break the law or to protest can conveniently remain out of the picture.

6 For Kelsen – as is well known – only an order which may be considered 'as a whole (*im grossen und ganzen*)' as effective can be ascribed a 'fundamental norm' and thus legal validity. A similar strategic role is played by the so-called 'social fact thesis' within the Hartian jurisprudence and the notion of 'convention' in some post-Hartian theoretical developments; all of them centring on the idea of 'law as fact'. Here, once again, *ex facto oritur jus*.

7 It must be pointed that this constitutes a major difference with respect to Austin's work. In mainstream Continental public law, sovereignty is no longer a personal quality, but the attribute of a collective entity which acts through the law. A state and a state will are possible only in the form of law.

8 Which, it must be kept in mind, was the harshest possible criticism in Kelsen's terminology.

9 Curiously enough, natural law is seen as a herald of facticity, the triumph of which results in the defeat of normativity of the pure legal form (the norm).

10 Knowing how much Kelsen connected natural law with a notion of 'ideology', the conclusion of his argument might well be that a constitution essentially is an ideological device.
11 Something which is also criticized in several chapters of this book, especially Chapters 6 by Brunkhorst, 7 by Menéndez, 3 by Eriksen and 2 by Habermas.

10 Law, economics and politics in the constitutionalization of Europe

Christian Joerges and Michelle Everson

Introduction

The following chapter continues the effort (see Joerges 1994a, 1996a, 1996b; Everson 2003a) to trace a common path between the distinct disciplines of law and political science, to find the interdependence between the factual and the normative, to address facticity and validity within the integration process. This is no easy task. Law, we argue, must renew its perceptions of reality and open up its normative and dogmatic structures to factual demands. Political scientists engaged in integration research should, by the same token, take the law's normative structure seriously and open up their analytical and empirical models to this legal 'reality'. There are good reasons to undertake such efforts: Europe's constitution is too important to be left to lawyers; but it is also something that cannot be grasped by empirical and analytical approaches that are closed to consideration of this normative dimension within the 'real' world.

In the course of integration, as a European *body politique* has been formed and re-formed, Europe has repeatedly been 'constituted' anew. The law has consequently had to change; it has had to learn. The vital point underlying this process is the fact that the normative structures of the law have always had to adapt themselves to a moving target. Adaptation has never been a guarantee of its own success, but, looking back, we can usefully distinguish between distinct stages of legal renewal within Europe, as well as the rationales that contemporary commentators use to place such changes in their factual and normative context of integration:

1   From the founding of the EEC up to the Single European Act, law gave constitutional significance to the integration process, building up a 'supranational' body of law that claimed primacy over national law. This hierarchical, 'vertical constitutionalism' was often (in Germany) identified, both substantively and normatively, with a (politically neutral) European 'economic constitution'.

2   A second integration period, rooted in the Commission's 1985 'White Paper on Completion of the Internal Market' and the Single European Act (1987), and further consolidated by the Maastricht Treaty, drew the rapt attention

of political scholarship. The key political question was as follows: can the internal market be completed only at the cost of the welfare/social state? In turn, this question translated into two constitutional law problems: (a) to what degree do national constitutions limit integrationist assaults on statehood; and (b) which rule of law and standards of democracy must European integration respect?

3   Finally, although such issues have by no means been solved, the current renewed integration impetus provided by the Commission's 2001 White Paper on governance and by the Constitutional Convention set in motion by the Nice Treaty[1] and the Laeken Declaration of 2001 (European Council 2001a) determines that they are being addressed within a new context. On the whole, we might be optimistic about a new integrative phase that seems to address questions of governance from an explicitly constitutional background. Nonetheless, caution is urged upon the reader as governance reforms do not necessarily coincide with constitutionalization efforts.

This final point is determinative for us. Stages of integration have never been distinct and have always been controversial. Only ever incompletely captured by Treaty amendments or posited theories of the nature of the EU, a fluid European *body politique* has evolved mysteriously and incrementally. Deprived of clear normative direction on the nature of the polity, 'living law' has thus always engaged in legal learning. Entrusted with the task of upholding the legal basis for integration, it has responded both to the Commission's political programmes and to the many adjustments on which the 'Masters of the Treaty' have agreed, through a constitutionally sensitive and problem-related 'discovery process' of legal regeneration.

With the advent of the Constitutional Convention as completed on 10 July 2003,[2] however, and a presumption of a 'founding' of Europe, it might be assumed that the process of the legal definition and redefinition of the European polity is now drawing to a close. Instead, where the contours of the European polity have been politically drawn, law can withdraw to service its new European constitution in formalist isolation from consideration of adjustment to an ever-changing world. Nonetheless, patterns of European integration do remain – and here, the Commission's 2001 White Paper on governance is a clear case in point – which more closely reflect the historical incrementalism that has characterized the integration process. We may thus be confronted with a real paradox. Although the 'Constitution of Europe' is ever more visible, the legitimacy-mediating, constitutive role of European law is at risk. In this regard, then, law cannot close itself to consideration of empirical and analytical reality. Still less can political science dismiss the normative demands of the legal system from its methodologies. Governance within Europe must continue to be subject to a sensitive and fluid 'constitutionalism' which not only respects reality but also subjects that reality to the normative values inherent within law.

'Vertical constitutionalism': supremacy of European law and the theory of the economic constitution

Vertical constitutionalization: 'legal integration from above'

It is no coincidence that public law research into European law has dealt so intensively with differences between European law and international law. Nor is it a coincidence that the 'integration through law' methodology was spearheaded by the European Court of Justice (ECJ):

> Tucked away in the fairyland Duchy of Luxembourg and blessed, until recently, with benign neglect by the powers that be and the mass media, the Court of Justice of the European Communities has fashioned a constitutional framework for a federal-type Europe.
>
> (Stein 1981: 1)

The history of this Court-based constitiutionalization fascinates lawyers since it seems to confirm the existence of a legal culture of argumentation that is accepted over and above national legal systems. It is as fascinating for legal sociologists and political scientists as Baron von Münchhausen's tall claim that he pulled himself out of a swamp by his hair: can it really be true that, through its own efforts, the law was able to place itself above intergovernmental politics and impose its validity on sovereign states? What were the 'real' reasons – outside the law – for the law's success in the integration process?

Legal self-narratives

The interpretation of the EC system as a supranational legal community was an ingenious ECJ invention. Its jurisprudence has found – in the legal system and beyond – such widespread support that it can be regarded as the core of the dominant orthodoxy of Community law. The gradual construction of this legal architecture is a story that is often told and may be foreshortened here (Ipsen 1973: 97ff.; Weiler 1991: 2413ff.; Bogdandy 2001a: 11ff.).

The foundations were laid in 1963 with the doctrine of 'direct effect' of EC law (ECJ 1963). As long as they are sufficiently precise, the rules of the EEC Treaty are 'directly' binding on the Community and the Member States. They create individual rights; domestic courts must guarantee their protection as if they were the 'law of the land'. What we should not forget, however, is that this was anything but obvious at the time. Mirroring international law, Article 169 of the EEC Treaty (now Article 226 TEC) provided that the Commission would enforce the Treaty. Yet, or so we have come to believe, the preliminary rulings procedure of Article 177 (234) and the extensive law-making powers of the Community indicated that it was intended to be more than an international organization. These Treaty provisions were the reference point for the truly 'constitutional moment' proclaimed by the ECJ in its doctrine of direct effect (see ECJ 1963: 24f.). The second building block was of course the celebrated 'supremacy' principle as announced in *Costa* v. *ENEL* (see ECJ 1964: 1269f.).

'Direct effect' and 'supremacy' imply that Community law will 'pre-empt' Member States from taking legislative action, if and when the Community occupies a policy area. Equally, since Community law must be uniformly applied in all Member States, the ECJ must have the final competence to rule on the limits of its application (ECJ 1971). Case law inexorably expanding 'functional' Community competences – based on the objectives of the Treaty, as well as the doctrine of 'implied powers' – followed this judgment: even though the Treaty enumerates Community competences and therefore limits them (Art. 3b, now 4), they must nonetheless be treated 'purposively' and interpreted expansively.

Inevitably, the application of these principles posed and continues to pose difficult problems. But as long as these doctrines are accepted in principle, and as long as the ECJ can decide in cases of conflict, we are dealing with a supranational order that is fundamentally different from domestic or international law. Hence, we can denote the Community legal system a 'constitutional charter' (Stein 1981: 1; Weiler 1991: 2413; Pernice 1993: 449; and especially the Court's own Opinion: ECJ 1991).

Explanations

All ECJ statements on the quality and content of Community law are based on 'strictly juridical' operations. Nowhere can we find explications of methodological premises or theoretical deliberations as to the legitimacy of Europe's 'constitutional charter'. Is this the right way to go about creating and proclaiming a constitution?

What remains so remarkable and needs to be explained is the broad acceptance of this revolutionary jurisprudence. The ECJ could not muster national support for its landmark decisions (Stein 1981: 25). Equally, the Court had no recourse to sanctions. Instead, support came from Advocate-Generals, from the Commission, and, after some resistance, from national courts (Weiler 1993). Europe was built by a quiet and patient 'epistemic' community (cf. Höland 1993; Schepel and Wesseling 1997) of legal interpreters who adopted ECJ doctrines and used them as a framework for action.

How do political scientists narrate this 'Münchhausen' tale? In their account, the 'legal dialogue' between the ECJ and national courts was an important, if not *the* most important, 'dependent variable'. They also note the Commission's stubborn commitment to policy development and enforcement (Article 169, now 226) (Börzel 2001; Tallberg 2002). As a much noted interdisciplinary essay concluded, 'Law functions both as a mask and as a shield. It hides and protects the promotion of one particular set of objectives against contending objectives in the purely political sphere' (Burley and Mattli 1993: 72).

In such accounts, the normativity of law is an irrelevance. Did it matter what arguments the institutional actors used? Did it matter which *finalité* of the European project they invoked?

Ordo-*liberal economic constitution theory: Europe as* '*market without state*'

Asking whether the legal arguments used 'deserved' recognition might amount to a blurring of the borders between empirical and normative worlds. Nonetheless, they can be backed by normative 'facts': doctrinal reconstructions of European law were always accompanied, supported or criticized by meta-dogmatic justificatory discourses, by 'legal-science theories of integration', which dealt with the validity claims of law (Joerges 1996b). One justification for European law that continues to be important, and is far superior to the purely doctrinal notion of vertical constitutionalism, is given by the '*ordo*-liberal' theory of a supranational 'economic constitution'.

To understand the operational history of this theory we must return to the Weimar Republic. There, the founding fathers of *Ordo*-liberalism and *Ordnungspolitik*[3] advocated a conflicts framework, which was intended to guarantee economic freedoms, but, at the same time, to hold them in check through a system of law ensuring undistorted competition (Wiethölter 1989: 225ff.; Nörr 1999: 5–18). '*Ordo*-liberalism' also had an impact upon the young German Federal Republic, particularly because of its inclusion within the concept of a 'social market economy' (Nörr 1999: 58ff., 81ff.; Manow 2000). Its leading exponents – Walter Hallstein (1946; 1969), Franz Böhm (1946), Alfred Müller-Armack (1947) – committed themselves early and very successfully to Europe, bringing the core ideas of *ordo*-liberalism to bear there.

Conceptually, *ordo*-liberalism was particularly suited to integration. It could be used to justify the theorem of the primacy of European law and combine it with a precise 'economic constitutional' content, thereby also limiting it: the freedoms guaranteed in the EEC Treaty, the opening up of national economies, non-discrimination and competition rules were easily understood as a collective decision in favour of an economic constitution that matched *ordo*-liberal framework conditions for a market economic system (at least, to the degree that a blind eye could be turned to the original sin of the Common Agricultural Policy). The very fact that Europe had started its integrationist path as a mere economic community lent plausibility to *ordo*-liberal arguments: the interpretation of the European Community as a law-based order committed to guaranteeing economic freedoms gave it an 'apolitical' legitimacy of its own, independent from the institutions of the democratic constitutional state (see Müller-Armack 1966).

Ordo-liberalism's conception of economic and legal policy was significantly expanded, refined and altered in the seventies (for details, see Mussler 1998: 58ff., 91ff., 125ff.). But its core constitutional content remained unaffected: supranational economic constitutional law requires no on-going legitimation by the institutions of the constitutional state or political processes – and, for this very reason, must also confine its regulatory claims to the (competitive) order of the economy. Such a theory cannot easily be undermined by reality: if political practice does not concur with theory, then that practice is simply wrong. To be sure, once the positive-law underpinnings of the theory fall away – as happened with the Maastricht Treaty[4] – then the theory must withdraw, perhaps finding residual application to world trade law (Petersmann 1991, 1994).

Europe as 'regulatory state'? The 'Masters of the Treaties' as 'states without markets'?

Ordo-liberalism, however, was largely a child of private and economic law. German constitutional law and European law, by contrast, remained largely indifferent to the *ordo*-liberal credo. Dominant practice was instead functionalistic and technocratic and was given legal form early on by Hans Peter Ipsen, who denoted the (three) European Communities as 'purposive associations for functional integration' (Ipsen 1964; 1972). This understanding outlasted *ordo*-liberalism, experiencing a renaissance in the intense integration period beginning in the mid-eighties.

Although the concept of the 'special-purpose association' allowed the development of practices within Community law beyond the strict limits of *Ordnungspolitik*, it nonetheless did not require democratic legitimation of the Community. As a special-purpose association, Europe was to tackle 'technical' matters or administrative tasks that could properly be assigned to a supranational bureaucracy (Ipsen 1972: 176ff.). Working with Forsthoff's (1971) theory of the state and the constitution and American neo-functionalist integration theory, Ipsen rejected federal integration concepts and early interpretations of the Community as an international organization. For him, Community law formed a *tertium quid* between (federal) national law and international law, constituted and adequately legitimated through its 'specialized tasks' (Kaufmann 1997b: 312ff.; Bach 1999: 38ff.; Joerges 2002b). This technocratic view of the Community was adopted and renewed by the political scientist, Giandomenico Majone, who was to conceive of the Community as a 'fourth branch of government' (Majone 1994) and as a regulatory state (Majone 1996: 265ff.).

Factual developments

Eric Stein's view of European law, sketched out in 1981, was very close to reality at the time. Although European law was advancing steadily, the Community faced one political crisis after another and economic integration was stagnant. The institutional reasons for this were well known: 'legally', the 'functional' interpretation of Community powers to pursue the common market by adopting directives under Article 100 (now 94) or under Article 235 (now 308) was a potent force. In practice, however, the unanimity voting requirements of Article 100 ensured that each Member State could defend its own regulatory concepts and economic interests through its veto.

'Negative integration' and 'regulatory competition'

In the eighties, however, the now legendary internal market initiative (European Commission 1985) enabled a breakthrough (Joerges 1994a, 1994b;

Moravcsik 1998: 314ff.). Lawyers, economists and political scientists have different explanations for this. Economists cite the large degree of unofficial approval for economic rationality patterns: efficiency and competitiveness through de-regulation ('negative integration'), supplemented by 'regulatory competition', would keep welfare state policies in check. Or, was it 'political cunning' – personified by charismatic Commission President Jacques Delors – which made use of a neo-functionalist logic to bring together economic interests in a new European programme?

Prudent protagonists of the European project, however, felt that the legal principles developed by the ECJ provided the most steadfast integration impetus. As ever, the change upon which they relied was rooted in a trivial happening: the *Cassis de Dijon* case (ECJ 1979) saw the Court declare that a German ban on the marketing of a French liqueur with a lower alcohol content than its German counterparts was incompatible with the principle of free movement of goods (Article 30, now 28). From its convincing but trifling observation that confusion of German consumers could be avoided by disclosing alcohol content, the Court derived its far-reaching doctrine of 'mutual recognition'. It thus adopted a constitutional competence for itself to review national legislation and further market integration on the basis of primary law alone. In turn, the Commission adopted the ECJ's decision as the legal basis for the new harmonization policy that it developed in its White Paper on internal market policy (European Commission 1980; 1985). Whatever the economic, political and legal background, this policy found its way into the Single European Act, which came into force in 1987. It was further accompanied by other institutional innovations: the move to (qualified) majority decisions for all internal market decisions under Article 100A (now 95) was a change of fundamental importance – both for practical European policy *and* for its constitution.

'Re-regulation' instead of 'de-regulation'

Although a renewed integration project did not fulfil the *ordo*-liberal vision of a 'market without state', it did seem to confirm the existence of a supranational legal constitution that guaranteed economic freedoms for European market citizens and committed the Community and Member States to a competitive economic system (Mestmäcker 1987; Mussler 1998: 125ff.). Faster than supporters or critics of the internal market programme had foreseen, new regulatory and juridification trends evolved: intense regulation; new forms of cooperation amongst governmental and non-governmental actors; and a range of participation entitlements.

1   Regulatory interventions were intense, most particularly so in relation to consumer and health interests, which often also comprised safety-at-work and environmental concerns. Here, the provisions of Article 100a(3) SEA and the rights of Member States with high regulatory aspirations to 'go it alone' (Articles 100a(4), 118a(3), 130t) ensured that the opening of markets

was to come about only at the cost of a thoroughly modernized regulatory machinery (Joerges 1994b: 154ff.; Eichener 1997). But even in the domains of private and economic law, the 'completion' of the internal market was marked by the alienation of original mutual recognition goals, the growth and steady refinement of new economic regulation and consumer protection policies, and the coordination of Community and national oversight competences.

2   Without the resources and administrative powers to generate standards and apply them at national level, the Commission was forced to promote and coordinate national certification bodies and European standardization organizations. Further, it was forced to operate through a dense network of committees in which national administrative experts, independent scientists and representatives of economic and social interests were to collaborate.

Constitutional alternatives

This much is undisputed: the internal market programme has seen intense juridification.[5] Unloved by national governments, but unstoppable, how is it to be controlled? Two 'trans-disciplinary' alternatives arose.

Europe as regulatory 'state'

The sociologically trained lawyer, Ipsen, and the political scientist, Majone, are – though not very close! – relatives in spirit. Both see the strength of the integration project in the problem-solving capacity of European institutions. Ipsen's 'objective tasks' correspond to Majone's 'regulatory policies'. In both views, expert knowledge is needed to solve problems. Both also feel that tasks can only be completed properly in the absence of political influence. 'Non-majoritarian' institutions (including the Commission itself, and, most importantly for Majone, US-type independent agencies) will act at European level. Both views thus encompass 'constitutional' theories, since the integration project entails a commitment to a particular public goal, but is also limited 'politically' (Jachtenfuchs 2001). Here, however, closeness between Ipsen and Majone (confirmed by the latter *en passant* – 1994: 23) ends. Ipsen's 'purposive association' is far older than Majone's 'regulatory state' and was developed both before modern liberal regulatory patterns and in the absence of the social choice theories that inform Majone. Above all, Majone's regulatory state is concerned with market failure. He seeks to increase the economically defined welfare of consumers/citizens, whereas Ipsen's technocratic 'purposive association' simply furthers the infiltration of the state and its administration into society. Majone's *regulatory state* institutionalizes a 'fourth branch of government' which guards against possible 'regulatory failures' through its insulation from majoritarian and political influence. Yet this fourth branch should be held 'accountable' through indirect but effective control. Moreover, the non-majoritarian institutions of European regulatory politics and the majoritarian institutions of the Member

States do, in Majone's view, complement each other. In particular, distributive politics are said to be dependent on majoritarian legitimation and hence remain the domain of the nation-state.

We shall return to these questions below. For the moment, it suffices to say that even though the European regulatory state does not have comprehensive competences, it nonetheless entails disempowerment of the nation-state. This leaves us with a question: is such a disempowered state still a democratic constitutional state under its own constitution? The German Federal Constitutional Court addressed this issue in its judgment on the Maastricht Treaty of 12 October 1993. It sought to limit European integration in a manner surprisingly similar to Majone's.

The downgrading of Europe to an association of states: the German Constitutional Court's Maastricht judgment

The Maastricht Treaty, encompassing Economic and Monetary Union, a strengthening of Community industrial policy, new powers and an indistinct 'subsidiarity principle', created a Euro-critical public for the first time. Danes voted against, approval in France was by a slim majority, and in Germany, constitutional complaints were lodged against the new Treaty. Although Denmark finally signed up and the German Court rejected all complaints, life in Europe changed inexorably. The following deals only with the German decision, which raised the debate on Europe's constitution to a new level, and which remains interesting to us because of the Court's trans-disciplinary statements on integration and the relationship between legal and political science.

RESTRICTIONS ON 'VERTICAL' CONSTITUTIONALIZATION

The Maastricht judgment contains two clear shocks for European legal orthodoxy. First, the German justices seem to deny the supranationality of Europe, denoting it 'less than a Federation – even less than a Community' (BVerfGE 1993: 181; cf. 188ff.),[6] and settling on its description as an 'association of states' (*Staatenverbund*) that takes account of the 'national identity' of the Member States. Secondly, however, the Constitutional Court consistently distances itself from the principles of direct effect and the supremacy of European law. Certainly, the Court accepts majority decision-making (application of which the Maastricht Treaty had further enlarged) as a functional necessity of integration, but still seeks to limit it: '[Y]et the majority principle is limited – through the requirement for mutual respect – by the constitutional principles and fundamental interests of the Member States' (p. 184). With the requirement of 'mutual' respect, the Court promotes its own understanding of the term 'community of law' and thus limits the validity of European law through national law. The interests that are of 'fundamental interest' to Germany can only and should only be determined by Germany itself. The cohesiveness furnished by Community law supremacy breaks down into a 'disordered' heterarchical relationship. The Court responds to potential 'anarchy' by emphasizing 'cooperation'.

The Federal Constitutional Court does not view itself as the lower tier in a European judicial hierarchy, but prefers to define its link to the ECJ as a 'cooperative relationship' (p. 174). In particular, this wording refers to the Court's duty to protect basic or fundamental rights under the German Constitution. Equally, the Court reserves for itself a specific, non-transferable right of adjudicating on the assignment of competences. Should the Community misjudge the power to extend its competences unilaterally when, in fact, a Treaty revision is called for, then this process will not have a binding effect on Germany (p. 210).

BACK TO THE NATION-STATE

The Maastricht judgment has caused disquiet (Weiler 1995). In particular, concerns are raised about the Constitutional Court's understanding of the principle of democracy within the German Constitution. Certainly, the Court's concern that the exercise of sovereign rights must derive from 'the people of the state' (*Staatsvolk*, at p. 182), such that its Parliament must always possess 'sufficient powers of substantial political weight' (p. 207), can be seen as a neutral constitutional argument. It does not preclude German membership within the EU, but simply points out that the legitimacy of the German state, and of the EU, derives from its people(s) and their Parliament(s):

> If the peoples of the individual states (as is true at present) convey democratic legitimation via the national parliaments, then limits are imposed, by the principle of democracy, on the extension of the EC's functions and powers. State power in each of the states emanates from the people of that state. The states require sufficient areas of significant responsibility of their own, areas in which the *Staatsvolk* concerned may develop and express itself within a process of forming political will which it legitimizes and controls.
>
> (Bundersverfassungsgericht 1993: 86)

Nonetheless, the German Court's attempt to define democracy does potentially close the integration process. On the one hand, democracy is described as a fairly neutral process of social interaction: 'constant free debate among social powers, interests and ideas that encounter each other' (p. 185). On the other, however, 'a certain degree of social homogeneity' is also deemed a prerequisite for democracy. In this reading, the purpose of constitutional recognition for the democratic precedence of the *Staatsvolk* is to 'give legal expression to [...] that which spiritually, socially and politically links it [...] relatively homogeneously' (p. 186). This seeming prizing of the *ethnos* above the *demos* has drawn sharp critique (Pernice 1993; Bryde 1994: 311f.; Bogdandy 2000b: 295). Above all, the reference to Hermann Heller (1928: 427f.) would seem misplaced: the capacity of the nation-state to solve economic and social problems has been more thoroughly eroded – and, at the same time, a European capacity for peace made far stronger – than ever seemed conceivable in Heller's time.

THE 'MASTERS OF THE TREATIES' AS 'STATES WITHOUT
MARKETS': A PYRRHIC VICTORY OF GERMAN
ORDO-LIBERALISM

Far more problematic than the somewhat strange reference to Hermann Heller, however, was the Court's treatment of the primary concern of the complainant, Mr Brunner. Asserting that the ability of the constitutional state to secure the living conditions of its citizens would be reduced if it participated in Economic and Monetary Union, Mr Brunner was less concerned with democratic rights of participation and more with tying monetary policy inexorably to the German state.

The new Article 88(2), inserted into the Federal Bank Act by the Amending Act of 21 December 1992, provided for the transfer of the Bundesbank's tasks to a European Central Bank that is 'independent and which serves the primary objective of price stability'. The Federal Constitutional Court wholeheartedly endorsed this Article since the German Parliament had the right, before completion of monetary union, to examine the fulfilment of the Treaty criteria on price stability and convergence (pp. 202f.). Equally, should monetary union not follow the 'the agreed stability mandate', then German ratification law would no longer be valid (p. 205).[7]

The essential paradox in the Court's reasoning is readily apparent. First, it seeks to preserve the powers of the nation-state. However, economic integration is perceived as an apolitical phenomenon occurring autonomously outside the states, and European Monetary Union as a project given functional legitimacy by its commitment to a politically neutral notion of price stability. Economic integration, on this reading, would not be subject to on-going constitutional review for its democratic qualities. Europe would then become a 'market without a state' and the so-called 'Masters of the Treaties' would be left as 'states without markets'.[8]

Constitutionalization of governance in the European multi-level system

The debate about the above models of constitutionalization – legal supranationalism, the notion of an economic constitution, the regulatory state, the *Verbund* of states – has not been laid to rest either in law or in political science. But as debate develops, the object of discussion has also changed. To a degree, this change has been highly visible. But, and importantly so, a quieter change is on its way that may endanger the normative cohesiveness of European law.

Currently, we appear to be facing a millennial-type change in European law. Two projects in particular attract our attention. In October 2000, the Commission adopted its 'Working Programme' for a 'White Paper on the Governance of the European Union', bearing the programmatic subtitle 'Enhancing Democracy in the European Union' (European Commission 2000). At Nice – the Treaty was signed on 26 February 2001 – there followed the solemn Declaration on Human Rights (Charter of Fundamental Rights 2000), whereas Laeken saw the adoption of a Constitutional Convention, to begin work in December 2001[9] and which delivered its results in July 2003[10] (the original deadline was spring 2003).

From these latter achievements one might deduce that it is thus no longer the responsibility of the ECJ to mutate the Treaties into the 'Constitutional Charter' (ECJ 1991).[11] Apparently, Europe has become too important for its legal-constitutional progress to be left in the hands of the judiciary, and for its governance practices to be left to the Commission and national administrative bodies. To be sure, the decision to set up a Constitutional Convention takes account of the increasing importance of European governance; it is a reaction to pleas to place governance on a legitimate footing, by constituting it legally or by explicit constitutionalization. Yet, a different issue is what kind of expectations one might have of such a process. One should not, of course, view it in isolation and, at the same time, as the apex of a European constitutionalization process. But any prediction as to its future impact and any normative assessment would be premature, the more so since the Commission's governance project has been augmented by another hybrid, the much discussed open method of coordination (OMC – European Commission 2001), which seeks to correct and complement European economic integration. *Both* projects question the previous practice of integration politics.[12] The Commission's White Paper appears to shake itself free from legal and economic clutches in order to entrust itself to the leadership of political science and the prophecies of New Public Management (see section below). The Lisbon Summit 2000 introduced the OMC so as to initiate a new employment strategy at European level. It broke with the old 'Community method' for three reasons: first, it permitted the taking of action even outside the area of competences that had been expressly transferred to the Community; second, it upgraded the Council; third, it renounced the conventional 'juridification' of Community policies (see section 'The Open Method of Coordination' below).

It is the practice of 'governance', we assert, that demands renewed efforts to maintain legal openness to factual reality. Certainly, convention processes herald a welcome effort to constitute Europe politically. Nonetheless, they continue to coexist with a new institutional practice of governance, and it remains far from certain whether the current political constituting of Europe will be strong enough to stamp its character on institutional practice. In this case, the law cannot afford to withdraw to a formalist position, but must instead continue to blend the factual with the normative, imposing its questions and values on governance.

The Commission's White Paper on governance in Europe: a symptom of crisis

'Governance' has become a key concept in the European debate. In international relations theory, the term has been in vogue for a considerable time. In integration research, it refers, above all, to the decision-making processes that have been formed within the EU system (Jachtenfuchs 2001). It entered unofficial use within European politics when the President of the Commission, Romano Prodi, announced a White Paper in which the Commission would present new perspectives for a democratically reformed 'European Governance', and the creation of a 'Governance Team' to come up with proposals (European Commission 2000; see Joerges 2002b and 2002c).

Governance as the key concept of the European polity?

The adoption of the term 'governance' by the European Commission reflected lessons learnt during and after the 'completion' of the internal market, and above all an awareness that the internal market programme called for pro-active initiatives in ever wider areas and that permanent management of market integration was necessary in order to supervise its unforeseen economic and social implications (see section 'Factual Developments' above). The term 'governance' does indeed open up new perspectives. 'Governance' cannot be equated simply either with governmental or administrative acts, or with legal practice. It is all these things as well. But in ever more areas, particularly in all realms of regulatory politics, a specific feature of political action is that it builds upon social knowledge and the management capacities of enterprises and organizations. Politics in general – and the Commission in particular – cannot simply implement its objectives through command and control policy-making and policy implementation; however, to describe the cooperative arrangements between public and private actors as a 'delegation' of regulatory tasks to non-governmental actors would be misleading. Governance arrangements are a response to real social problems and to bottlenecks within the political system and its administrative machinery.[13] 'Governance' rather than 'government and administration': this is the outcome – but it is also the problem, the point at which law and political science inevitably must part company. In political science it is possible and necessary to distinguish between the efficiency of governance and its legitimacy (see, for instance, Jachtenfuchs 2001: 246); indeed, the analytical purpose of distinguishing dependent and independent variables is precisely to avoid entanglement within normative questions. Jurisprudence cannot copy that model. Even where lawyers act purely doctrinally, they are unavoidably confronted with the problems of legitimacy. They cannot simply ask whether governance arrangements are 'accepted', but must instead whether such governance *deserves* the recognition of the governed. The Commission's 'Governance Team' underestimated the weight of this legal-normative question. They responded to the legitimacy question with the metaphor of 'good governance' and developed principles (European Commission 2001: 10f.) and initiatives which, while individually worthwhile, merely reproduced the individual mechanics of administrative legitimacy and paid little if no attention to an overarching and coherent theory of constitutional legitimacy (Harlow 2002; Everson 2003b). The Commission's notion of governance ultimately remains a functionalist response to the problems of governing Europe and has, at best, only a functional legitimacy.

Back to the Community method?

The deficiency lies in a lack of effort to give 'good' European governance a new constitutional basis, to translate European praxis into a language of legitimacy as conveyed by law – and to expose it to such comprehensive legitimacy criteria. The example of regulatory politics demonstrates how important it would have been to build bridges between the disciplines: the concept of governance owes its attraction to the fact that it provides an 'appropriate' analysis for the practices of governance which have been developed for the management of the common market, and from which reformed normative perspectives can be derived. Conventional European law cannot properly recognize important elements of this praxis; they often appear illegal. It is this very reaction that one finds in the final version of the White Paper. That paper has suspended exploration of the normative validity of governance practices and returned to inherited legal categories; its language shifts from political science to law. 'Strengthening the Community method!' – this is the legal leitmotiv of the White Paper as adopted in July 2001 (European Commission 2001: 8). A simple legislative procedure, whereby Parliament and Council act as the legislature, is to be aspired to. The Commission is entrusted with 'implementing Community law' and is supported in this task by executive agencies (European Commission 2001: 24ff., 40). Paradoxically, the return to such 'empty' legal formulations undermines the analytical bases for renewed normative legitimacy that the governance method might have provided. The Commission represents the 'administration' of the internal market, as if its sole purpose was to implement the will of a European sovereign through the mobilization of expert support. The issues that this 'administration' must respond to are often economically weighty, politically sensitive and give rise to moral and ethical concerns. It is simply inexplicable how, based on the hands-on legal approach of the White Paper, the Commission hopes to reinforce the legitimacy of European governance. One window the White Paper points to is civil society (European Commission 2001: 14f.). But even then it leaves too many questions unanswered: what gives those actors and *expert communities* mentioned in the White Paper a political mandate? How do they represent affected interests? The answers in pertinent Commission documents remain vague or cautious.

The open method of coordination

The Treaty of Amsterdam saw the insertion of a new Title (VIII) on employment as well as a novel mode of governance, namely a national and Community coordination of employment strategies (Article 125). Since the European Council in Lisbon in 2000 also recommended this method for social policy, the 'OMC' has become the object of intensive discussion. Political scientists have high hopes of it on both sides of the Atlantic (cf., with many references, Eberlein and Kerwer 2002; Zeitlin and Trubek 2003). The OMC does indeed envisage a mode of governance that seeks to avoid the institutional bottlenecks in European law-making and administration, and that simultaneously opens up new perspectives for legitimizing the Union.

So far the effects of the OMC have not been easy to grasp in any of the fields in which it has been tried, and this is particularly true in the field of employment policy (Ashiagbor 2002). It is difficult to find reliable information on the mechanisms that define it: is the autonomy that nation-states enjoy in their search for means to achieve agreed-upon targets really being used innovatively? Have criteria been discovered and defined which enable a 'benchmarking' which competitors will find convincing? Do political and societal actors really expose themselves to learning processes that they then convert without further pressure? Or, does the OMC erode core principles of constitutionalism, such as the regulative idea that governance should adhere to legal principles and the rule of law? Whether this risk comes to pass depends on how the Member States synchronize their actions, and whether they find principles and rules to distinguish such coordination from pure political competition in a way that it gives us picture of 'democratic experimentalism' (Sabel 1994) and thus deserves approval.

Perspectives for constitutionalizing the European multi-level system

The Commission has not kept its promise to develop new perspectives for a democratization of European governance; it is doubtful whether the hopes which have been pinned on the coordination method recommended by the Council will be realized; the Constitutional Convention has completed its work, but the draft constitution as presented seems to offer little hope for an easy solution to continued and potentially illegitimate Community interpenetration into the lowlands of the economic, labour and social 'state of the (European) Union', or into the sensitive spheres of the risk society: none of this exactly sounds like good news. But we should not yet lose hope. The flexible history of law teaches us that there is a framework of analysis with the aid of which we can understand and treat the difficulties inherent in the approaches mentioned above. It also teaches us that the integration project has always found its own incremental paths out of impasses.

Constitutional incrementalism

Europe, so political-science integration research has been telling us for some years now, is to be understood as a 'multi-level system of governance *sui generis*' (Scharpf 1999; Jachtenfuchs and Kohler-Koch 2003). This qualification of the EU cannot be transferred to law that easily. But it points to problems that law must confront if it still wishes to ensure a legally mediated legitimacy for European governance. This is exemplified by the example of the demarcation of competences between the EU and the Member States and the legitimation of transnational, non-governmental governance.

COMPETENCE CONFLICTS AND 'DIAGONAL' DISPUTE SITUATIONS

Competence conflicts in the EU are distinguished by the fact that the Member State defending its autonomy itself belongs to the Community against whose power it is seeking to defend itself. In this sort of conflict, both the Member State concerned and the Community each bring their specific legitimacy to bear. Here, the principle of 'limited individual empowerment' (Articles 3–4, now 3–7), according to which the Community may act only in the areas explicitly allotted to it, is quite often dysfunctional: action on various technical problems may involve both Community and Member State powers. The resulting overlaps in practice compel Community and Member States *de facto* into complex mutual adjustments of their claims to act: each can block the other, but neither can arrive at solutions to problems alone (Scharpf 1988). This finding is very hard for case law to deal with because it treats the allotment of competences as both empowerments to action and restrictions on action that, at the same time, make political responsibilities transparent (for details, see Bogdandy and Bast 2001; Mayer 2001).

The ECJ is famous for its very broad interpretation of European competences. At the same time, however, it offers rich exemplary material for a prudent self-restriction in the practical treatment of the validity claims of the competences of European law (Furrer 1994). The institutional context compels the law to adopt 'procedural' conflicts settlements that take the regulatory concerns of the Member States seriously and still manage to harmonize them with the functional conditions of the EU system; solutions that prove to be 'protective of autonomy and compatible with the Community' (Scharpf 1994). One absolutely typical situation for the European multi-level system is the 'diagonal' conflict. In such cases, Community competence only extends to one sub-area of interdependent technical questions, whereas the Member States only possess partial powers and are also unable to arrive at autonomous solutions. As a result, these conflict situations force cooperation; they can then only be solved cooperatively, and, at best, in deliberative processes.

'DELIBERATIVE' SUPRANATIONALISM

The EU's *de facto* administrative weakness has strengthened the importance of these freedoms and engendered synergetic effects: it has promoted the development of autonomous transnational areas of governance that constitute neither mere modifications of the national polity nor supranational areas of administration. The hybrid rules of control that characterize the EU system, in which national and European, as well as public and non-governmental, actors collaborate, are responses to these institutional framework conditions. The perspectives on constitutionalization which tie up with these mechanisms of cooperation build on experiences in relatively well-known subsystems of risk regulation, and their normative content resembles the broader hopes associated with the OMC. They bank on regulatory policy remaining pluralistic – also in the sense of being responsive to societal differences in the internal market – during its 'implementation phase'. At the very least they expect regulatory policy to be structured in a manner that enables national bureaucracies to debate the positions of their counterparts in the neighbouring states such that:

- the interests and concerns of Member States are not disregarded;
- the still primarily nationally organized and oriented public spheres are induced to pool their interests, concerns and arguments in the decentralized communication relations of European politics;
- these public spheres are encouraged to mutually acknowledge each other;
- principles and rules deliberatively guarantee constructed solutions to problems which in turn legitimize these hybrid governance structures.

Conclusion

This tenacity of the European polity is reassuring, but no more than that. It does not, after all, guarantee that the incrementalist searching and learning process whereby Europe has 'constituted' itself can successfully continue; neither can it ensure a Third Way for the integration project between constitutionalization 'from above' and blind pragmatism. 'Constitutionalization', here, denotes the idea of a binding form of governance based upon the legal structuring of the processes of political opinion formation, such that decision-making is legitimated through legally secured 'deliberation' (Eriksen and Fossum 2000; Joerges 2002a). For this sort of programmatic re-attachment of the European project to the ideals of deliberative democracy, however, a formal constitutional text would be neither sufficient nor indispensable.

Acknowledgements

This essay has been through several pasts. It was begun as a contribution by Christian Joerges to Jachtenfuchs and Kohler-Koch 2003. In an ever-changing form it was presented in Mannheim, Oslo and Cambridge, before it was transformed into its present shape in a collective effort with Michelle Everson. There is no space here to acknowledge the many critical and constructive comments impacting on it. Particular thanks, however, to Armin von Bogdandy, Julia Chryssostalis, Jo Murkens and David Trubek.

Notes

1 Official Journal of the Communities C 80, 10 March 2001.
2 And submitted to the Council on 28 July 2003; accessible at http://european-convention.eu.int.
3 Both terms have no real equivalence in Anglo-Saxon jurisprudence and law. The pertinent Working Group VI of the European Convention has been called 'Economic Governance'. That 'translation', however, only very imperfectly conveys the connotations of *Ordnungstheorie* (cf. Gerber 1994; Sauter 1997: 26ff.; Manow 2000).
4 For an *ordo*-liberal critique of the Maastricht Treaty, cf. Streit and Mussler 1995; for a critique of *ordo*-liberal claims after the adoption of the Maastricht Treaty, cf. Sauter 1997: 31ff., 34ff.
5 According to a much quoted, but now rather hoary, statement by Jacques Delors (1988), the economic law in force in EC Member States is, to a large degree (80 per cent?), enacted or brought into being by the Community. Delors (1992) rejected complaints about the regulating mania of his bureaucracy: of 100 Community lawmaking initiatives, only 8 were truly to be attributed to the Commission: in 92 per

cent of cases, his officials were taking up the concerns of the Member States – and 70 per cent of cases saw the Community taking up the law-making concerns of the Federal Republic (Delors 1992: 12).

6 The term *Staatenverbund* (association of states) was used by the Second Senate's rapporteur, Paul Kirchhof, as a term for a form of organization 'between an alliance of states and the de-statization of the Member States', without combining this with any claim to a definitive legal substantive description (Kirchhof 1992: 859ff.). There has been much puzzlement over its meaning even in Germany (Möllers 2001a: 378ff.).

7 The Court again proved to be subsequently conciliatory; it has explicitly confirmed the constitutionality of the monetary union (BVerfGE 1998).

8 European law is a field for public lawyers. This may explain why even comprehensive analyses barely mention the ironic consequence of defending nation-state democracy brought out in the text, while the echoes of Schmitt have very much been taken seriously (cf. Bryde 1994; Weiler 1995; and Mayer 2000, on the one hand, and Ladeur 1997: 35ff. and Bogdandy 2000b, on the other).

9 The language setting it up was kept instructively vague:

> The question ultimately arises as to whether this simplification and reorganisation might not, in the long run, lead to the adoption of a constitutional text in the Union. [...] In order to pave the way for the next Intergovernmental Conference [...], the European Council has decided to convene a Convention. [...] [I]t will be the task of this Convention to consider the key issues arising for the Union's future and try to identify the various possible responses.
>
> (European Council 2001b)

Such caution has by now become unusual.

10 The text of the Draft Treaty Establishing a Constitution for Europe is accessible at http://european-convention.eu.int.

11 Cf. section 'Legal Self-narratives' above.

12 In our understanding of Europe's constitutionalization, the efforts to Europeanize private law, which are gaining ever more momentum, should be mentioned here; for a sceptical comment, cf. Joerges 2003.

13 The definition by the Commission is extraordinarily vague: (' "Governance" means rules, processes and behaviour that affect the way in which powers are exercised at European level, particularly as regards openness, participation, accountability, effectiveness and coherence'); see European Commission 2000: 4; and European Commission 2001: note 1.

Part III

How can it be made?

11 The Convention method and the transformation of EU constitutional politics

Carlos Closa

Introduction

Legal and political science scholars have for a long time propounded the notion that the EU has a constitution, even though both this notion and its connotations remain disputed. The European constitution resulted from a gradual process of interaction – between primary norms and the case law that interpreted them. The European Court of Justice (ECJ) acted as the leading 'constitutionalizing actor' by extracting constitutional principles from a body of law that also encompassed national constitutions. In parallel, Intergovernmental Conferences (IGCs) were largely treated as episodes of Treaty reform. The intellectual hegemony of 'liberal intergovernmentalism' in the explanation of Treaty changes, and its emphasis on a model of preference aggregation that came closer to the model of normal pluralistic politics (Moravcsik 1991, 1998), had the effect of removing their consideration from the prism of 'constitutional politics'.

The Convention on the Future of Europe has subtly modified this landscape. Nominally at least, the Convention has expressed a larger constitutional ambition, the most evident trait of which is the naming of its product a draft constitution. Leaving aside the exact reach and contents of its outcome, this chapter scrutinizes the Convention from the vantage-point of the notion of *constitutional moment*, as discussed in the introduction to this volume. Since other chapters (notably Chapter 12) review the Convention's procedures, this chapter pays specific attention to its representative quality in relation to its self-expressed claim of being a constitutional forum. The relevance of this inquiry derives from the fact that the Convention transcended its initial more limited – preparatory – mandate and endowed itself with a constitutional self-mandate (first section). The Convention's composition (second section) provides one set of grounds for its claiming a sort of constitutional legitimacy. However, this claim must be assessed in relation to the ambiguous nature of the Convention, which could be analysed from three different vantage-points – and which may also have provided the actors with alternative understandings (third section). This leads us to question its true 'constitutional' nature. The conclusion nevertheless argues that the Convention may not have changed the EU dramatically, but it has altered the nature of its constitutional politics.

The construction of a constitutional self-mandate

Constitutional politics are the processes of creation and modification of the fundamental norms, rules and institutions of the polity. Apart from the well-documented constitutive role of the ECJ, constitutional politics have proceeded through the mechanism of IGCs, from the Rome Treaty to the Nice Treaty. The choice of institutional setting for constitutional politics determines both procedures and outcomes. IGCs ensure that national governments are able to maintain tight control over outcomes and negotiations. Actors seek to maximize their benefits and to minimize their costs; the attendant logic of behaviour follows a strategy of bargaining: fixed preferences are exchanged through the calculus of effects. Not surprisingly, EU constitutional politics, synthesized in the successive treaties, could be depicted as an exercise in aggregating actors' concrete choices and preferences (Moravcsik 1991, 1998).

The shortcomings of this method are two-fold. The first relates to the legitimation of outcomes. Whilst the procedure produces pay-offs to all actors involved, it created a large gap between the insiders and the respective citizenries, a gap that at several times created 'explosions' in the ratification processes. The ratification of the Treaty of Maastricht saw the first such divergences between public opinion and national governments (in Denmark and France, but elsewhere too). Amsterdam posited similar problems and, finally, the Treaty of Nice process reached a plateau in the possible level of citizens' tolerance and acceptance. The negotiations at Nice prompted a public and political reaction against the Treaty, which was decisive in persuading European leaders to relax a method (the IGC) that 'fed the democratic deficit in the broadest sense of the term' (Dinan 2002: 31).[1] Against this background, an appealing line of explanation would argue that the drafting of a constitution would require infusing an 'Ackermanian' model of 'higher track' politics, in which the civic virtue instilled through deliberation will dominate over the strategic defence of specific interests.

But despite the appeal of this more emphatic and normatively oriented explanation, the Heads of State turned to the Convention method more as a device to circumvent deadlocks of IGCs. Several issues limited the efficiency of the Amsterdam and Nice IGCs (Hoffmann 2002). Firstly, the divisions among Member States increased in depth, and, in parallel, the EU institutions had a reduced or minimal influence; this applies in particular to the mediating role of the Commission. More decisively, the national governments adopted increasingly inflexible positions on issues that do not produce win-win situations for all parties involved. This was the case, in particular, with the issues confronted at Nice (namely the distribution of shares of power and votes). Realistically, it is debatable whether these issues could be settled through the automatic application of a constitutional principle (such as proportionality), rather than as the result of tough strategic bargaining and exchange between actors. In any case, the Nice negotiations, in particular, cast doubt on the capacity of 'top-level' negotiators defending national interests and guided only by strategic considerations to settle the kind of framework issues that define the fundamental design of the EU. And the forthcoming enlargement to 25 Member States made 'fundamental constitutional change' a pressing concern, not only a question of principle but also a question of necessity. Hence, efficiency considerations more or as much as a choice of democratic means led to the relinquishment of the traditional IGC mechanism. The limitations of the intergovernmental negotiations contrasted with the smooth and solemn elaboration (and subsequently proclamation) of the Charter of Fundamental Rights. This had the effect of translating a very positive perception of the outcome to the method that was used to draw up the Charter. Notwithstanding some initial scepticism, and even criticism, the comparison between the IGC and the Convention turned to the latter's advantage, which became considered as an attractive alternative to traditional diplomatic negotiations (Deloche-Gaudez 2001; De Schutter 2003). No doubt, the first Convention benefited from a number of factors, not least its strict and clear mandate, which facilitated the adoption of an 'identification' technique that also contributed to the success of the exercise.

This experience with the Convention on the Charter made it a paradigm of an efficient – and legitimate – mechanism to deal with preparation of constitutional issues. Even though the Convention did not secure a binding result and the Charter had an unresolved juridical status – the Charter was solemnly proclaimed with its incorporation into the Treaties and binding force postponed – this does not disprove the value of the Convention, since securing a binding result was far beyond its capability and competence. Part of the national governments' interest in the Convention model derives, precisely, from this ability to perform efficiently in conjunction with their final capability to decide on the outcome. The usual rhetorical references to democracy as the reason for convoking a Convention somehow disguised the additional 'instrumental' perception of European leaders. Many of the governments accepted the Convention on the Future of Europe because they expected a similar ability to produce results, as had been the case with the Charter Convention.

Thus, the decision to convene a Convention contained in the Laeken Declaration resulted in the need to resolve the pressing issues that IGCs have proved unable to fully tackle (see on this Ludlow 2002). The design of the Convention contained a compromise between the most ambitious reforming governments and the most sceptical ones. Next to its innovative and assembly-like profile, national governments introduced several mechanisms that preserved their room for manoeuvre to ensure control: national representatives outnumbered those from EU institutions (to keep any strong federalist coalition at bay); national governments had a semi-open mandate, and held control of several organizational devices (composition of the Praesidium, etc.); there was a directly appointed President (who had to report to the European Council); there was a large membership that might hinder the emergence of a strong self-organizing capability and would reinforce the role of the President; there were fixed time limits (including a cooling-off period); and, last but not least, national governments retained the power to accept and/or reject the outcome and decide on its binding force. Governments agreed because the process was unforeseeable, allowing them to hope they would be able to maximize their interests, while retaining the opportunity to minimize costs at the subsequent IGC.

Regardless of the intentions of national governments, the Convention skilfully exploited its self-regulative capability and, applying its own interpretations, turned some of these limitations to its own advantage. A number of agreements and procedures, such as the active role accorded to alternates, a certain steering capability of the time limits, and so on, served to modify the initial frame so as to suit the Convention's interest. Taken singly, the most important self-transformational action of the Convention was the subtle modification of its mandate, an action that transformed the initial nature of the Convention itself. The mandate of the European Council had asked the Convention to produce a final document that could adopt two different forms: it could either adopt a number of possible *options* on the various questions examined with an indication of the degree of support for each of these; or it could draft a list of *recommendations* in case of consensus. In any case, the IGC was not to be bound by the results of the Convention. The Laeken Declaration defined the status of the document produced as *the starting-point for the debates in the IGC together with national debates*. Whilst national governments had accepted the necessity of some changes in the status quo of constitutional politics, they obviously did not want to relinquish full control over the result, and an IGC guarantees at least a veto on any unwanted outcome, as well as offering the additional attraction of an arena for bargaining. From a strictly juridical point of view, the EU has limited room for a transformation of the constitutional procedure without a formal amendment of the rules guiding it (Art. 48 TEU) (Rodrigues 2001: 590).[2]

The process of modifying its mandate started subtly through two broadly shared agreements that emerged within the Convention. Firstly, the preference for the production of a *consensual* text (instead of a broad and loose mapping out of options) that could guarantee the success of the next IGC emerged quickly within the Convention.[3] Following Valéry Giscard d'Estaing's interpretation, the legitimacy deriving from the (however limited) democratic credentials of the Convention body, its procedures and the consensual character of an eventual text would sharply reduce in particular national governments' room for manoeuvre should a strong consensus on a precise text be achieved.

The second broadly shared agreement referred to the precise form of the consensual document. The Laeken Declaration mentioned the possibility of adopting a constitution in the long run, and this (together with the large number of declarations by European leaders) acted as a reference-point for the Convention, which, nevertheless, did not have an explicit constitutive mandate. Moreover, some national governments warned that even though the Union could endeavour towards a constitution in the future, the Convention should produce options and/or recommendations, since it does not have the legitimacy required to transform itself into a constituent assembly, and modification of the Treaties is reserved for an IGC.[4]

Instead of entering into a dispute on its role and mandate, the Convention moved pragmatically to a lower level. The broad understanding of its mandate borrowed the words of George Washington when he chaired the Philadelphia Convention: 'it can debate about everything, propose anything but decide nothing', and Convention members often quoted these words to legitimize their work. Using this understanding, Convention members generated, in constructivist fashion, a discourse that would allow shaping the outcome along the less ambitious reading of the Laeken mandate, but in a manner that could also fit the constitution model and terminology. In his opening speech, Giscard called for a broad consensus on a single text that might open the door to a European constitution. He proposed calling this a 'constitutional treaty' in order to avoid semantic disputes,[5] since this concept could be made into a synthesis of both a constitution and a treaty. Quite early in the debate, a majority of the Praesidium declared that the Convention objective should be to draft a 'Constitutional Treaty for Europe', and some Convention members endorsed this goal in plenary sessions.[6] Giscard himself repeated the view that Convention members are conscious that the Convention should propose the future Constitution of Europe (or Constitutional Treaty) (Giscard d'Estaing 2002), a view supported by a number of contributions.[7] In July 2002, 18 members and alternates submitted a motion for the preparation of a Constitutional Treaty that asked the Commission to prepare a text to be discussed in the October plenary session, on the basis of the European University Institute document and the Convention debates.[8] The first Praesidium draft at the end of October[9] already took the name *Constitutional Treaty*, and, from then onwards, successive drafts used this name.[10] The final draft is named the Draft Treaty Establishing a Constitution for Europe. To disprove those who underline that its true nature is a treaty under public international law, all provisions within it name the instrument (the treaty) the 'constitution'.

This attitude of naming the reality that they were constructing with a concept that did not totally reflect the juridical nature of the instrument was much helped by discharging the option of producing documents that contained lists of options and/or recommendations, and instead drafting fully fledged articles and legal provisions. This decision affected the activity of the Convention, its own style and the dynamics of interaction. In a nutshell, the Convention became a suitable institutional framework in order to forge consensus between federalists and anti-federalists on the conceptual designation of the EU as a constitutional entity. Thus, in name and form, the product of the Convention came closer to a constitution than could have been expected before it started its work. Naturally, the specific contents of the EU 'constitution' were poorer than the kind of substantial issues normally associated with an ideal type of constitution. Magnette (2003b) argues that the constitutionalization exercise basically amounts to one of simplification: once conflicts of interpretation and of opposing interests became evident, simplification became the label for the minimum compromise that could be attained. Materially, the constitution amounts to the following dimensions:

- the recognition of the legal personality of the Union;
- the elimination of the pillar structure;

- the recognition of the supremacy of EU law;
- reduction and simplification of the instruments for law-making and decision-making procedures, plus the introduction of a hierarchy of legal acts;
- a definition (albeit not conclusively clear) of the distribution of competences;
- the incorporation of the Charter of Fundamental Rights with binding force in the constitution (Part II);
- the generalization of qualified majority voting in the Council and the extension of co-decision;
- the consolidation of a model of 'constitutional politics' that differs from 'normal politics'.

The debate on whether or not this represents a true constitution is not the object of this chapter (see Chapter 13 in this volume). To some, the limited ability of the Convention to achieve much more than former treaties in substantive terms reduces its value, but a correct evaluation of the Convention requires an adequate placing of this body within EU constitutional politics. If we are to draw proper comparisons, it is necessary to underline that it is (formally) a preparatory body that has delivered the most thoroughly and thoughtfully elaborated and closed document ever faced by an IGC. Representatives of states will deal with a complete text that forms the only credible basis for negotiation (despite the rhetorical appeal to the value of national debates). Whether this conditions or limits their negotiating behaviour remains to be seen, but, in any case, the unchallenged consolidation of the Convention as the mechanism for constitutional reform (Art. I-7.2) proves its value.

Composition of the Convention: representation and legitimacy

Theorists of constitutional politics coincide in the importance of creating a functionally different institution separated from 'normal politics'. This releases 'constitutional choices' from pollution by 'normal politics' issues, increases the know-how basis available in the process, and, last but not least, creates a mechanism that infuses participants with a personal interest in a successful outcome (Ackerman 1992: 51–2; Schutze 2000: 22). The composition of this institution becomes a key issue, and more so in the EU, whose 'constitutional politics' have so far been a domain reserved for professional diplomats. The procedure followed to select the members of the Convention; the representation of two territorial levels; the equality of representation between states (including applicants); and the reflection of a broad ideological spectrum make the Convention a body with a strong representative basis – to an extent that might justify claims of legitimacy for constitutional outcomes. However, the Convention was a body with an ambiguous nature (as will be discussed in the third section).

Selection procedure

Avoiding a specific direct election, the European Council designed a number of nominating bodies (national parliaments and governments, the European Parliament and the Commission) each of which chose its own selection procedure, which differed greatly in transparency. The combination of diplomatic and political actors that resulted from this helped to prevent a setting exclusively oriented to negotiations and to steer it towards a more deliberative type of body. In particular, the presence of representatives from national opposition parties contributed to break down the impression of tightly and closely defined national interests. Additionally, the very large size of the Convention (the 105 members doubled *de facto* because of the progressive incorporation of alternates as full members) enlarged the possible number of alliances and, in this way, provided a mechanism for circumventing deadlocks.

Two-level representation: national and European

Its composition mirrors the criteria used for the former Convention (see Table 11.1). Two axes define the constituencies represented: territorial level and type of body represented. Territorial representation works on two levels, the EU and the Member States, which implies recognition of the European Union's dual sources of legitimacy. It is worth noting that for all the talk about distribution of competences among levels of governance and the defence of regions from any Union invasion of their competences, the third level of government has not been granted explicit representation, despite the regions' petitions. Regional presence was indirect through the representatives of a Union institution (the Committee of Regions) but only with observer status. Whilst federal states (Austria, Germany and Belgium) wanted regions with legislative powers to designate the three regional observers, France (and, implicitly, the Spanish government) objected. As a concession to federal and quasi-federal states, regions and cities with legislative powers have nominated these observers.

The states are represented through representatives from both the executive and the legislature. This specific shape reflects the compromise that was reached in the former Convention between those that wanted a purely parliamentary body (i.e. national and European MPs only – France) and those that wanted the inclusion of representatives from national governments (UK and Germany), although the latter, strictly speaking, are personal representatives of the Heads of State or Government. Representatives of national parliaments secure a link with the negotiating and decision-making stage, whilst the direct participation of national parliaments provides for an input of legitimacy (given the consensus on this issue within the EU). The latter formed the largest group within the Convention, although it was obviously the least cohesive. Lacking the capability to act as a single body, a common culture, and without personal assistants in Brussels, they were overburdened with commitments.

Table 11.1 Convention composition by nationality

	Presidency	Gov. reps	National MPs	MEPs	European Commission	Overall	Observers
Member states							
France	1	1 (1)	2 (2)	2 (2)	1	7 (5)	2
Italy	1	1 (1)	2 (2)	2 (1)	(1)	6 (5)	2
United Kingdom		1 (1)	2 (2)	3 (2)		6 (5)	
Germany		1 (1)	2 (2)	3 (1)		6 (4)	2
Portugal		1 (1)	2 (2)	1 (2)	1	5 (5)	1
Belgium	1	1 (1)	2 (2)	1 (0)		5 (3)	3
Austria		1 (1)	2 (2)	1 (2)		4 (5)	1
Denmark		1 (1)	2 (2)	1 (2)		4 (5)	
Spain		1 (1)	2 (2)	1 (1)		4 (4)	1
Netherlands		1 (1)	2 (2)	1 (0)		4 (3)	
Finland		1 (1)	2 (2)	0 (2)		3 (5)	1
Ireland		1 (1)	2 (2)	0 (1)	(1)	3 (5)	
Greece		1 (1)	2 (2)	0 (0)		3 (3)	
Luxembourg		1 (1)	2 (2)	0 (0)		3 (3)	
Sweden		1 (1)	2 (2)	0 (0)		3 (3)	
Subtotal	*3*	*15 (15)*	*30 (30)*	*16 (16)*	*2 (2)*	*66 (63)*	*13*
All candidate countries		1 (1)	2 (2)			3 (3)	
Subtotal		*13 (13)*	*26 (26)*			*39 (39)*	
Total	**3**	**28 (28)**	**56 (56)**	**16 (16)**	**2 (2)**	**105 (102)**	**13**

Source: Elaborated by Ben Crum (Centre for European Policy Studies).

Representatives of states outweighed representatives from EU institutions (which could be considered the representatives of the *European people*) by four to one. Even though this imbalance constructed a safeguard for national concerns, it did not automatically translate into strict compliance with the logic of national interest pursuit. Rather, EU institutions benefit from the kind of 'community skills' required for operating within the Convention setting. Members from EU institutions know each other, and they are used to working within the transnational environment on the same kinds of issues. Direct personal knowledge and shared experience eases the creation of networks in which they may well be able to impose the 'EU ethos' over a tight style of defence of national interests. Furthermore, some national representatives were former incumbents of EU posts. This is fertile ground for the emergence of a significant comparative capacity on the part of both the Commission and the European Parliament to shape proceedings and debates. They have expertise and a deep knowledge of EU affairs; they have material resources (background documents, staff, etc.); and both may more easily behave as a coherent group. The European Parliament and the Commission held internal debates on the issues discussed in the Convention, and these internal processes fed their representatives with skilful arguments and documents. Both have specific strategies with clear goals: the Commission aims at 'promoting the Community method in a legitimate, transparent and dialectic confrontation' (Vitorino 2002: 285), and the European Parliament's maximalist proposals are well known. However, the Parliament showed a larger cohesiveness than the Commission, whose internal discrepancies were openly aired.[11]

An additional leverage argument derives from their comparatively better presence in the Convention organs with 4 out of 12 members of the Praesidium (two Commissioners and two MEPs), the chair in 4 out of 11 Working Groups (which was particularly important given the power of the chairperson to set the agenda) and 2 out of 3 Discussion Circles. Both the Commission and the Parliament benefited from the continuity of key figures (Vitorino and Méndez de Vigo, respectively). The Commission, in particular, consolidated a central role, both in terms of posts and the ability to shape debate. Starting from an initially marginal position at the first convention (in which it was initially included as a mere observer and acted as a kind of legal watchdog), it now adopted a more proactive role, submitting regular contributions, and Commissioners took an active part in the debates. Additionally, the support it has lent to the Secretariat of the Convention (in the preparation of documents) added to the Commission's influence.

The principle of equality of states

The representation of states materialized around a basic principle of equality in representation, both regarding their relative territorial size and population, and with regard to current and would-be members (Turkey included). In addition, national debates in applicant countries will be considered on an equal footing with those in the current Member States.

Table 11.2 Composition by party affiliation

Party	Presidency	Gov. reps	Alternates	National MPs	Alternates	MEPs	Alternates	EU Commission	Subtotal
Current members									
PSE	1	4	3	13	7	5	5	1	39
PPE-DE	2	5	5	11	8	6	6	1	44
ELDR		3	1	3	3	1	1		12
UEN		2		1	3	1	1		8
GRN/ALE		1			5	1	1		8
GUE/ NGL					3	1	1		5
EDD						1	1		2
N/a			5	1					6
N/i			1	1 (FPÖ)	1 (FPÖ)				3
Subtotal	*3*	*15*	*15*	*30*	*30*	*16*	*16*	*2*	*127*
Applicant states									
PSE		2	2	6	7				17
PPE-DE		3	1	12	8				24

Table 11.2 Continued

					Total
ELDR	1		6	5	12
UEN					
GRN/ALE					
GUE/NGL			1		1
EDD					
Others					
N/a	7	10	2	5	24
Subtotal	*13*	*13*	*26*	*26*	*78*

Source: Own elaboration from data supplied by Ben Crum (Centre for European Policy Studies).

N/a: Not available; N/i: Not inscribed
PSE   Party of European Socialists
PPE-DE   European People's Party (Christian Democrats) and European Democrats
ELDR   European Liberal Democrat and Reform Party
UEN   Union for a Europe of Nations
GRN/ALE   Greens/European Free Alliance
GUE/NGL   Confederal Group of the European United Left/Nordic Green Left
EDD   Europe of Democracies and Diversities
FPÖ   Austrian Freedom Party

However, the original procedural rules introduced some inequalities between the two categories. Candidates were not supposed to prevent consensus from emerging among current members. Given the uncertainty surrounding the future status of applicant countries, this could be presented as a fair safeguard, although it also expresses a certain clubbishness with current rules serving to distribute gains between current members, while shifting costs to would-be members. Conversely, their subsequent full *de facto* inclusion testifies to the inclusive nature of the procedure and of the EU – in particular that it permits the forging of a possible constitution by states that are not formally members.[12]

In any case, candidates do not necessarily share *a priori* a common view on the future constitutional shape of the Union, leaving aside any mechanism attempting to sideline them. Of course, any final result that clearly discriminated between current and applicant members would have represented a failure for the process, with few chances for success, since these would be present at the 2003–2004 IGC and all 25 will have to ratify the Constitution.

The Convention redressed some other initial procedural and organizational inequalities: for instance, the Praesidium accepted the candidates' request to have at least one representative (with the status of guest of the meetings) on the Praesidium, which implied a partial modification of the design of the Laeken Council. Pursuing equality of treatment, the Secretariat hired a national from each of the candidate countries. However, these states did not obtain similar logistical support and the equal linguistic regime they had asked for.

Representativeness

The Convention model favours the emergence of political (i.e. ideological) affiliations whilst keeping the diplomatic orientation of some members. Political parties were not part of the explicit pattern of representation chosen. Unavoidably, though, European parties have become very active, and the European Liberal Democrat and Reform Party, the European People's Party (Christian Democrats) and European Democrats, and the Party of European Socialists organized meetings with all their members in the Convention (including commissioners, national MPs and MEPs). They also submitted documents with consensual proposals[13] that assisted in the articulation of ideological cleavages, although the ideological impact cannot be overemphasized. On the one hand, wide differences between national parties prevent the emergence of agreement on decisive issues, and proposals were vague and generic. On the other hand, leaders showed a marked preference for alternative settings to the Convention for party coordination and even for airing their views and preferences (Closa 2003).

A priori, party representation secured a wide and plural source of inputs, but the pattern within the Convention shows a leaning towards the two largest groups (see Table 11.2). The two main cleavages in EU politics (Europeanist/Eurosceptics and right/left) were represented (although Giscard and the Eurosceptics respectively noticed and complained of their under-representation) together with a variety of other concerns.

In other respects, though, the Convention showed a remarkably low degree of representativeness. From a gender point of view, it had just 17 women out of 104 full members (16.35 per cent), only a marginal improvement on the first convention (15 per cent), but this ratio worsens if directing positions are taken into account. Only two women belonged to the Praesidium (out of 12 members) and just one of them chaired one of the Working Groups (Gisella Stuart). Noticing this situation, Giscard wrote: 'They compensate for this situation of numerical inferiority with the strong personality of many among them [*sic*]' (Giscard d'Estaing 2002). Nor did the Convention accurately reflect the multicultural reality of many existing Member States, with virtually no presence of minorities. It is impossible not to agree with Jo Shaw (2003a), when she argues that these absences contradict the very constitutional objective of protecting minorities against the tyranny of the majority and ensuring that vulnerable groups receive enforceable protection.

The ambiguous nature of the Convention

Institutions shape the behaviour of actors, and the Convention has not been an exception to this rule. What are the institutional contours of the Convention? Giscard reflected the puzzlement that this question provoked when he said:

> We are not an intergovernmental conference, since we do not have a mandate to negotiate in the name of governments. Neither we are a Parliament, since we are not an institution elected by the citizens in order to draft legislative texts. We are a Convention. What does it mean?[14]

Its composition and performance made the Convention an ambiguous body that combined at least three functions from which actors could derive interpretations about their role and the role of the Convention itself. The Convention could be seen as simultaneously *an institutional arena for experts* (deriving from its original preparatory mandate); an '*embedded diplomatic conference*' (deriving from the membership with the presence of ministers as watchdogs of national interests) and a *constitutional assembly* (because of its representative character, its prevalent ethos and the final outcome).

The Convention as an institutional arena for experts

Clearly different from the Charter one, this Convention had explicit instructions to prepare a proposal for an IGC. Intergovernmental Conferences require preliminary groundwork for the reforms, a task until now usually carried out through *ad hoc* committees. Thus, the Delors Committee outlined at the end of the 1980s the stages and criteria required to reach Economic and Monetary Union, which was the initial core of the Maastricht reform. In addition, a Reflection Group (made up of diplomats) acted as suppliers of options for the Treaty of Amsterdam (through the Westendorpf Report). In this sense of preparation, the current round of reform is no different. Two sets of motivations facilitated the activity of groups of experts within the Convention. Firstly, it needed to produce outputs on a broad range of issues (those of the Laeken Declaration, plus those that found their way into the agenda) with different levels of concretization and definition. Secondly, the Convention accepted the challenge to produce these in legal form (i.e. as draft articles). Both tasks required substantial resources and skills, that is, legal and technical expertise. Whilst the Convention was so composed as to maximize representative and legitimacy criteria, actors selected according to these criteria did not necessarily have the required expertise or the knowledge of the often very complex institutional and legal implications of most issues under negotiation. This situation could give a large *a priori* role to EU institutions, such as the Commission or the European Parliament (Beach 2003); certainly, it opened a window of opportunity for specialized and technical groups working within the Convention. In particular, the processes of codification, merging of provisions and elimination of redundant ones – as part of the simplification exercise – required a kind of detailed acquaintance with the *acquis* of EU law and the Union's legal and political interactions, one particularly held by legal experts.

At the listening stage, political representatives could deal with specialized knowledge by directing issues to small Convention groups, that is, the *Working Groups*. Technical and legal expertise became indispensable in the drafting exercise. There, the *Secretariat*, which also had a decisive role in shaping the general debate by providing background documents, played a key role, together with an *ad hoc Group of Experts* and, to a lesser extent, *Discussion Circles*.

Working Groups

Working Groups bridged the gap between representatives' deliberation and in-depth analysis and advice. Lacking a previous definition of their function, the Praesidium and Giscard defined a low political profile for them. Above all, they should avoid fragmentation. In the words of Giscard, 'care should be taken to avoid [the Convention] being split up as a result of the creation of working groups'.[15] Because of this, he insisted, the Convention had to depart from the model of committee specialization characteristic of Parliaments.[16] Working Groups had a limited agenda: they examined particular issues already identified in the course of convention debates, and considered these in relation to specific mandates given by the Convention, which converted into question form the issues that had to be clarified. They also had a reporting task: to submit possible options to the plenary. No doubt, they served as basis for deeper and more focused and self-referred discussions than the ones at plenary sessions, not least because they could hear specialists from outside the Convention. Working Groups benefited from tighter contacts and the more permanent presence of their members, which contributed to improve their deliberative dynamics. But they were subject to strict time deadlines on their work, a limitation that restricted their ability to innovate and forced them to concentrate on their mandates. They were not generally open and transparent to the general public.

The influence of the Working Groups differs; those whose object of inquiry derived directly from the Laeken mandate and that had a more technical nature (simplification, juridical personality, subsidiarity or role of national parliaments)[17] provided recommendations that inspired some of the choices of the draft constitution. However, the more political ones that responded to political pressures within the Convention failed to produce consensual recommendations (social Europe and economic governance epitomize this trend).[18] Significantly, the Secretariat provided background expertise for the preparation of their mandate and (in almost all cases) it drafted their reports (Shaw 2003b).

The Secretariat

The Secretariat was conceived as a single-person organism, a role assumed by Sir John Kerr (former Head of the British Diplomatic Service). He was assisted by a Vice-Secretariat, a Spokesperson and a group of 11 'drafters' drawn from the General Secretariat of the Council, as well as officials from the European Parliament and the Commission, plus individuals seconded from national capitals. The composition of the Secretariat ensured that it acted as a bridge between existing secretariats and legal services, and this, in turn, served to secure a smooth flow of the current EU legal *acquis* within the Convention output and would prevent any (unlikely) revolutionary break. From its specific functions, the Secretariat derived a subtle influencing role: it drafted most of the documents, and these provided the basis for discussion: for instance, its proposals on rationalization and standardization of decision-making procedures;[19] on a systemic structure of legal acts or instruments;[20] on the functioning of Union institutions;[21] or on the various drafts of the Constitutional Treaty. These documents were essential in the emergence of a Convention substantive *acquis* and, despite their apparent descriptive line, these papers had the capacity to shape debates substantially because of their effective and detailed command of the issues and the legal status quo (Shaw 2003b). The Secretariat also drafted the summaries of amendments proposed,[22] which of course implied subtle selections.

Behind their technical appearance, these papers suggested important political choices. An excellent example of this is the discussion paper on simplification.[23] It not only outlined the components of the simplification exercise (consolidation, codification, merging of provisions and pillars, drawing up a basic treaty and revising the procedures for amending the treaties), but also hinted at ways to proceed with the exercise that, beneath its technical appearance, implied political options.[24] Thus, after suggesting a two-part treaty that separated constitutional from other provisions, the paper wonders: 'is the Convention the appropriate forum for carrying out this operation' (i.e. the drafting of Part II)? And it responds proposing two technical solutions. Option one implies postponing Part II to a later stage and the adoption (by the Convention) of a report outlining its contents. That operation (simplification) 'could be undertaken by a group of experts (comprising the legal departments of the [EU] institutions and the Convention secretariat?)', it wonders. The second option would be that the Convention drafts Part II. Then, it would instruct 'a group of experts (comprising the legal departments of the [EU] institutions and the Convention secretariat) to undertake in parallel a technical adaptation of the existing Treaty provisions. This approach', comments the paper, 'might, however, give rise to certain difficulties, such as persuading the Convention members not to touch the substance of certain policies (e.g. agriculture, structural funds, budget)'. In other words, the Secretariat suggests that the technical exercise of simplification (which is the best option to approach the *acquis* within the constitution-making process) requires the renouncing of deep debates on political choices on existing policies. Of course, this can barely be considered a technical recommendation.

The Group of Experts and Discussion Circles

Following these suggestions, the Praesidium decided that a Group of Experts from the legal services of the European Parliament, the Commission and the Council would prepare Part II (i.e. Part III in the final draft).[25] As a result, the group presented a document that listed the points that required substantive decisions; among these were the scope of the legislative procedure and the scope of qualified majority voting.[26] An additional mandate[27] to implement some of the solutions suggested increasing the reach of its work. Naturally, most actors (and representatives from national governments led the way) did not perceive simplification of Part III as a mere technical exercise, but rather as one with deep political implications.

Technical expertise was similarly invoked for the composition of the Discussion Circles, small groups of members of the Convention that examined in-depth three very specific issues: the role of the ECJ, the system of own resources, and the budgetary procedure. The first arose from plenary discussions and the two latter resulted from the Working Group on simplification, which asked for a deeper review of these issues. Their mandates explicitly stated that membership in such Discussion Circles should be restricted to the experience required for the matter.[28] Their composition, though, challenges the impression that only experts were involved, whilst, in parallel, the 'steering hand' of the Secretariat and the legal services can be felt in their outputs. In summary, they resembled mini-preparatory expert groups such as the ones operating under IGCs.

The Convention as an 'embedded diplomatic conference'

Individual Convention membership was based on the assumption of formal equality among all participants, but the preparatory character of the Convention and the decisive role assigned to the IGC gave automatic pre-eminence to representatives of national governments over the other constituencies represented at the Convention. They could waive an implicit threat of vetoing results, and this would make their opinions more practically relevant than those of other members of the Convention.

The backgrounds of these representatives demonstrate the importance that governments attached to the workings of the Convention. In contrast to the same group in the Charter Convention – largely made up of academics and lawyers – the Constitutional Convention shows the dominance of current incumbents in national governments (see Table 11.3). Out of a total of 28, 2 of these were deputy Prime Ministers, 14 were (Deputy) Ministers (for Foreign or European Affairs), 1 Political Director and 1 Adviser to the Prime Minister. Among the rest, five had assumed government offices (with two former Presidents or Prime Ministers). Only two representatives (those of Portugal and Finland) did not *a priori* seem to have strong government connections.

The initial batch of government representatives were of lower profile, perhaps because some governments then did not perceive the importance of the exercise. But once the proceedings of the Convention showed the real option of drafting a constitution, several governments moved to substitute their representatives. Of course, the group of personal representatives was in itself very prone to substitutions because of changing duties, re-shuffling of cabinets or elections

Table 11.3 Professional background of government representatives

		Member states		*Candidate countries*
Deputy Prime Minister	2	I, S	–	
(Deputy) Minister for Foreign/European Affairs	6	B, F*, UK, E*, IRL*, D*	8	PL, RO, LT, BG, LV, SK*, H*, TR*
MEP	2	L, GR	–	
Retired senior statesman	4	DK, NL*, A, P*	2	CY, EST
Academic/adviser	1	SF	1	M
Senior civil servant			2	SLO, CZ*

IRL*:	Roche replaced MacSharry
E*:	de Palacio became Minister of Foreign Affairs only later
P*:	Lopes replaced Joao de Vallera
NL*:	de Vries replaced van Mierlo
D*:	Fischer replaced Glotz
F*:	de Villepin replaced Moscovici
H*:	Balázs replaced Martonyi
CZ*:	Kohout replaced Kavan
TR*:	Yakiş replaced M. Yilmaz
SK*:	Korčok replaced Figel

(13 members were replaced during the Convention – Spanish and Turkish representatives twice). The timing of substitutions is highly indicative: half of the replacements happened between September and December 2002, when the Convention abandoned the 'listening' stage and entered the 'proposing' phase, that is, when the Convention moved closer to decision-making (with a stronger bargaining imprint).

Generally speaking, representatives of governments became the leading players because of their own 'importance', and the importance tacitly accepted by other Convention members, particularly at the last stages of the Convention. They had a key role in signalling issues and making those unacceptable visible to their respective governments. Giscard, willing to secure support for the IGC, made sure that the Convention's work reflected the opinions and ideas of national governments, especially those from the large Member States. The British government, in particular, through its representative Peter Hain, indicated very clearly on every issue the maximum concession that his government was prepared to yield. This gave Hain a prominent role that some equated with a 'shadow President of the Convention'. But this attitude of signalling maximum levels of acceptance was by no means exclusive to the British representative: Spanish, Polish, Benelux representatives, among others, clearly indicated the maximum their governments could accept on certain issues.

The pattern of government representatives' interaction provides further evidence of the underlying intergovernmental dynamic. Whilst some have argued that the Convention displayed a loose pattern of alliances, evidence of written contributions shows that representatives of national governments had a marked preference for associating with each other, as a mechanism for shaping discussions and identifying and defining governments' stances on each of the issues. Both the French–German proposal and the Spanish–British one on institutional issues exemplify this attempt to shape debates and outputs;[29] but these were by no means the only ones. In fact, institutional design mobilized the joint writing activity of governments' representatives: efficiency and effectiveness of the ECJ;[30] the strengthening of the Commission's role;[31] openness and good administration,[32] or the well-known Benelux contribution on the institutions.[33] They openly presented some of these as Benelux, Spanish–British or French–Dutch contributions in a clear breach of the Convention spirit, which asked Convention members to behave in a personal capability. Interestingly, all the formerly quoted contributions resulted from the association between representatives of governments of *current* Member States, with some minor exceptions.[34] Broad associations between members and non-members appeared to counteract Praesidium proposals,[35] and representatives of national governments very rarely teamed up with other Convention members from other constituencies.[36] The pattern of submissions of contributions from representatives of national governments reveals their underlying view of the Convention: they identified themselves reciprocally as the leading players and sought to ally among themselves or to build up large alternative coalitions to counteract proposals launched by the key governmental players. In this way, they implicitly conveyed an underlying dynamic of negotiation.

Not surprisingly, at the drafting stage, negotiation and bargaining gained pre-eminence. The orientation towards drafting concrete and specific legal provisions had a strong effect on actors. Changes affected both the behaviour of national government representatives and the dynamics of the Convention itself. Representatives of national governments sought wordings that would be closer to their preferences. They tended to interpret proposals as 'zero-sum' issues, which happened mainly around a large number of institutional questions that had been skilfully postponed by Giscard – institutional disagreements affected the composition of the Commission; the election mode for the Commission president; the Presidency of the European Council; the Presidency of the formations of the Council; the status of the new Foreign Affairs Minister; the number of MEPs; and the way of calculating qualified majority voting, among others.

A deep change took place in the register of government representatives' discourses. There was resort to defence of national interest and threats of using the veto: for instance, a Spanish proposal sought to impede the change of the Nice settlement on qualified-majority voting moved in this register – evidence of increasingly strategic behaviour. Then, the Convention witnessed some of the traditional bargaining mechanisms: building up of large coalitions of governments,[37] or bilateral top-level meetings.[38] Unavoidably, the outcome of the Convention, the constitution, reflects some provisions that could be interpreted as 'pay-offs': Germany pressed for (and obtained) the retention of the national veto on immigration policy; France retained the veto on the 'cultural exception' to external trade. The Presidency solution (reinforcement of the President of the Commission and election of the President of the European Council) seems a trade-off between strategically motivated actors.

However, the important aspect in the assessment of the behaviour of the representatives of national governments is the actual modification of their traditional bargaining attitude: they had to listen and talk to other Convention members and, in this sense, the institutional setting shaped their behaviour. To some extent, actors felt compelled to present normative justifications for their strategic goals. In this sense, the Convention ethos (what Giscard called the Convention spirit) conditioned the rationality of national government representatives. Even though they do not renounce their strategic goals, once actors have accepted the rules of the game, and as long as they hope to establish the legitimacy of their own point of view, they are forced to behave as if motivated by moral norms following the constraint that Elster (1998b) called the 'civilizing force of hypocrisy'. Although it was known that the IGC would be the decisive instance and they would have a voice in it, representatives of national governments tacitly accepted the importance of the outcome of the Convention. Consequently, they had to appeal to superior normative arguments in order to gain the support of other members of the Convention who were not so prone to strategic reasons, what has been called 'negotiation under the shadow of rhetoric' (Magnette 2003b). In a way, the Convention provided 'strong publics' for national representatives (i.e. an enlarged arena in which the discourse was tested in accordance with the rules of reason and reasonability). The Convention embedded diplomatic negotiations in an ethos and a method that neutralized much of the prevalent aggregative style of intergovernmental dealings. Observers wrote that the atmosphere and attitude within the Convention were entirely different from the petty diplomatic bargaining of previous IGCs (Temple Lang 2003: 9). In a similar vein, the Spanish minister and Convention member Ana Palacio called it a revolutionary method of creating public international law, which had a 'cathartic element': the change of opinions of the actors involved.

The Convention as a constitutional assembly

Next to being an institutional arena for expertise and an embedded diplomatic conference, the Convention also has traits that comply with the notion of a special-purpose assembly, a sort of constitutional assembly. The mere fact that its name resembles that of the Philadelphia *Convention* prompted some (among them, its President, Giscard d'Estaing) to compare the two constitutional bodies. In some respects, the European Convention compares satisfactorily: for instance, it seems that, so far, the European one has not required the kind of defence of its own legality espoused in *The Federalist* No. 40. The similarity creates a fertile ground for attempts at a parallel translation of the federalist's constitutional theory, in particular those characteristics that make the Convention part of a 'constitutional moment'.

In some respects, the European Convention fulfils expectations on representativity and legitimacy. It translated the dual legitimacy of the Union through its composition, and its large size allowed a broad representation of the ideological spectrum of European society. The Convention provided an excellent opportunity for the articulation of multiple non-permanent alliances and clusters of representatives around specific issues, which enhances its value as a representative of European society. Working procedures created a suitable environment for parliamentary deliberation. The Convention reproduced the parliamentary model of non-imperative mandate: members of the Convention did not have a mandate from their respective nominating institutions, and they could assert their autonomy. Autonomy of Convention members resulted essentially from deliberation, since the process of arguing and reasoning were not to be restricted by mandatory instructions. In this respect, the Convention compares very favourably with traditional IGCs. In these, the existence of a power of veto allows actors to stick to their mandatory instructions and, in this situation, the outcome results from bargaining between utility-maximizing actors.

Magnette observed that the autonomy of the members of the Convention has been essential for the emergence of a suitable context for deliberation and consensus: 'situated interests' are de-legitimated (i.e. representatives rarely speak on behalf of their respective bodies); a pragmatic discursive register dominates; and there is a clear absence of rigid and stable groups (see Chapter 12 in this book). Further, in typical assembly-like behaviour, the Convention adopted its own rules of procedures. It also determined that its proceedings would be public and that access to documents would be open to anyone through the

Convention's website. Openness reached further through the inclusion of civil society (although in very limited way, see Lombardo 2003).

Whilst many of these features would fit within the model of 'constitutional politics' drawn out from the experience of the Philadelphia Convention, the context of long-standing consolidated democracies in Europe imposes much higher standards on the European Convention. When viewed in this light, several shortcomings of the Convention appear. Firstly, the Convention lacked a direct mandate and, hence, it was imbued with indirect or derived legitimacy. The preparatory function of the Convention, or, in other words, its dependence upon the IGC, means that it may not *a priori* require direct legitimacy but it also means that the Convention's result could not circumvent the intervention of the IGC as decision-maker. Then, from the point of view of representativity, there was notable under-representation of some important constituencies: Euroesceptics, women, religious and ethnic minorities and regions. Equally important are the shortcomings from the point of view of receptiveness: the Convention has failed to engage European civil society in a constitutional debate, even though the constitutional dialogue has been greater than ever before. So far, the Convention has failed to produce the kind of mass civic mobilization required for a constitutional moment to materialize. This may be particularly important in the decisive stage of ratification: citizens' involvement might fall back into the sort of strategic reasoning and calculus that has historically militated against constitution-making politics in the EU and which has favoured aggregative politics. Convention members did not dedicate themselves fully to the constitutional enterprise, since almost all of them had other offices and tasks to attend to (which has practical and theoretical implications). The Convention also was imbued with some procedural shortcomings. It did not nominate its main organs, that is, its President and Vice-Presidents; these were named by an outside authority (the European Council) and, in fact, the President occasionally acted as mediator between the European Council and the Convention plenary. Then, the internal deliberations and dealings of the essential steering organ, the Praesidium, were not made subject to the requirement of openness. Some of the proceedings of the Working Groups were also kept behind closed doors. And, of course, the discrete discussions in private circles and restricted settings that dominated the last weeks of the Convention's work also marginalized the plenary sessions and undermined the transparency of the proceedings. Last but not least, the Convention did not decide on the duration of its work (although it did on the structure of proceedings).

The large representativity of the Convention, its ability to commit to a draft constitution that advances the resolution of pending issues much more than had been expected, combined with its working procedures, give it with a legitimacy that somehow transcends the preparatory dimension initially assigned to it. Despite the fact that the IGC remains unbound by the outcome of the Convention, it will be very difficult for national governments to go further than the re-negotiation of specific issues. Whilst the initial intention may have been a more representative and democratic preparatory stage, the final situation resembles one of transformation of EU constitutional politics. These transcend a diplomatic conference, and they are not exclusively based on the actors in normal EU politics. What remains an open issue for the future is the capability of future IGCs to impose their will against the results of new Conventions. For these, the deficiencies listed above provide a checklist if a future Convention is to be turned into something more akin to a constitutional assembly. In particular, their characteristic feature as 'strong publics' (institutionalized deliberation constrained by the logic of arguing and impartial justification that encompasses both opinion formation and decision making) (Fraser 1992) presupposes the fusion of the currently separate decision-making stage at the IGC with the deliberation that takes place within the Convention itself.

Concluding remarks

The Convention greatly improves the EU's constitutional politics by introducing a more representative body in the preparatory stage as well as deliberative procedures that enhance the search for common ground and shared understanding in a more efficient form than traditional IGCs. Whilst the initial rationale of the Convention may have responded as much – if not more – to considerations of efficiency as of democracy, in EU reform it has also advanced to a more representative and open model of constitutional politics. Its ambiguous nature served to accommodate different interpretations for the various actors, and its working procedures served to fit strategic negotiation within a 'constitutional' setting. Thus, the method has proved its worth, and the open question for the future is whether the decisional capability of the IGC can be incorporated into the Convention.

The limitations of the Convention are those of traditional EU constitutional politics. Although it has served to provide a common theme for the emerging European public sphere and it had the effect of stimulating national debates, its work remained largely aloof from public opinion. The Convention has so far not resolved the essential issue of the connection between its outcome and the will of the people. This failure becomes more pressing in the case of EU constitutional politics. Constitutional politics are performed in the name of a 'constituent' subject that should not be an 'essentialist' *demos*, but one that results from democratic praxis. Then, the first and most pressing task for improving the democratic credentials of the Convention model refers to its politicization by making its component electives and the outcome subject to ratification. In this way, both the Convention and the constitution would be more firmly anchored in the mechanisms that simultaneously legitimate the process and the outcome and that help to construct a democratic *demos* through praxis. If the EU aims towards some sort of constitution, then the legitimacy of this should be more firmly grounded on direct citizens' input.

Notes

Earlier arguments of this chapter were presented to the Joint Conference on Democracy and Accountability in the enlarged European Union, Berlin, 7–8 March 2003, and to the Conference on Prospects for a European Constitution – Prospects for more Legitimacy? at the Zentrum für Europäische Integrationforschung, Bonn, 14 May 2003. I am particularly grateful to the comments of M. Horeth and A. Maurer. See also Closa 2003.

1 The Irish referendum and anti-globalization demonstrations both in Gothenburg and at the G-7 meeting in Genoa reinforced the perception of rejection and aloofness from large sections of public opinion. In his speech at the inaugural session of the Convention, the President of the Council, Aznar, recognized explicitly that 'Nice is the reason why we are here today'. Speech to the opening session, 28 February 2002, Brussels; CONV 4/02.

2 The ECJ case-law established that a modification of the Treaties can only result from a revision in accordance with article 236 CEE (current 48 TEU). CJCE 8.4.76 Mlle Defrenne n. 43/75 Rec. 455.

3 Note on the plenary meeting – Brussels, 21 and 22 March 2002; CONV 14/02.

4 See the interview with the French Minister for European Affairs; Moscovici 2002.

5 Giscard, V. Speech at the opening session of the Convention 28 February 2002, CONV 04/02.

6 Note on the plenary meeting – Brussels, 21 and 22 March 2002, CONV 14/02.

7 Just at the very early stages, see the contributions by M. Haenel (CONV 12/02); A. Duff (CONV 22/02); E. Teufel (CONV 23/02); J. Trzcinski (CONV 34/02) and K.Hänsch and P. Berès (CONV 63/02). See also the Draft Constitution for the European Union drafted by Jo Leinen (European Parliament 2002).

8 Motion for a decision on the preparation of a Constitutional Treaty; CONV 181/02.

9 Preliminary Draft Constitutional Treaty, Brussels; CONV 369/02.

10 For example, Draft Articles 1 to 16 of the Constitutional Treaty, CONV 528/03.

11 The unilateral presentation by Romano Prodi of a draft constitution provoked angry reactions among his fellow Commissioners.

12 I owe this observation to John Erik Fossum and Agustín Menéndez.

13 The socialists presented the following two submissions: *The European Project of the Socialist: The New Federalism* (CONV 63/02) and *Proposals of the European Socialist* (CONV 182/02). During the summer (30 and 31 August) the socialists held a meeting in Birmingham that resulted in the manifesto *Priorities for Europe*, 3 October 2002, <http://europa.eu.int/futurum>. The PPE also presented its proposal *A Constitution for Europe* (CONV 325/02). Finally, the proposal of A. Duff, *A Model Constitution for a Federal Union of Europe* (CONV 234/02) can be regarded as the contribution of the Democrats and Reformists.

14 Speeches at the opening session of the Convention 28 February 2002, CONV 4/02.

15 Note on the plenary meeting – Brussels, 6 and 7 June 2002; CONV 97/02.

16 Note on the plenary meeting – Brussels, 23 and 24 May 2002; CONV 60/02.

17 See their final reports: subsidiarity (CONV 286/02); juridical personality (CONV 305/02); simplification (CONV 375/1/02); and role of national parliaments (CONV 353/02). As a token example, the Working Group on Juridical Personality recommended a structure of the new single Treaty in two parts: a fundamental one (composed by constitutional provisions, new or from the existing treaties) and a second part that would re-codify existing provisions. This was the one finally adopted (with changes to incorporate the Charter and the Final Provisions).

18 See their reports, respectively Definitive Report of Group VI 'Economic Governance' (CONV 357/02) (unable to agree on specific recommendations) and the Final Report of Group XI on Social Europe (CONV 516/1/03).

19 CONV 162/02.

20 CONV 216/02.

21 CONV 477/03.

22 For instance, CONV 821/03.
23 Secretariat discussion paper on the simplification and drawing up of a Constitutional Treaty (CONV 250/02).
24 Shaw (2003b) records that among the Secretariat members was Hervé Bribosa, whose previous work included acting as Rapporteur of the European University Institute's much quoted pre-Nice project on the simplification of the Treaties.
25 Praesidium decision of 29 January 2003 (CONV 529/03).
26 Report by the Working Party of Experts nominated by the legal services of the European Patliament, the Commission and the Council (CONV 618/03).
27 Complementary mandate CONV 682/03.
28 See, respectively, CONV 612/03 and CONV 654/03.
29 Respectively, Contribution by D. de Villepin and J. Fischer on the 'Institutional Architecture of the Union' (CONV 489/03) and Contribution by A. Palacio and P. Hain on 'The Union Institutions' (CONV 591/03).
30 CONV 620/03 (Dastis and de Vries).
31 CONV 664/03 (de Villepin and de Vries).
32 CONV 490/03 (Hjelm-Wallén, Tiilikainen and Roche).
33 CONV 732/03 (de Vries, Santer and Michel).
34 See, for instance, CONV 603/03 on 'Equality between Men and Women' (Hjelm-Wallén and Puwak) or CONV 826/03, Proposed Amendment on Article III.3 (Hjelm-Wallén, Tiilikanen, Hain, de Vries and Hololei.).
35 This is the case of the Spanish-sponsored reaction to the draft on the institutions. CONV 766/03 ('A Union Constitution for All': Dastis, E; Roche, IRL; Christophersen, DK; Hübner, PL; Farnleiter, A; Martinokis, LT; Attalaidis, CY; Hejlm-Wallén, S; Hain, UK; and Korčok, SK).
36 Articles III.59 and III.60 in the draft EU Constitutional Treaty (CONV 782/03).
37 The Benelux countries championed this tactic: at the Athens summit, the Benelux governments hosted a breakfast meeting of 18 Member States and would-be Member States, followed by a letter to the Convention supporting their institutional proposal (Contribution by the Benelux countries, presented by Mr Gijs de Vries, Mr Jacques Santer and Mr Louis Michel: 'The Union's Institutions', CONV 732/03). The letter argued that a majority of states at the informal European Council at Athens had endorsed their arguments. At the 15–16 May Plenary session, 16 representatives of national governments from small states gave Giscard a letter that warned that if the proposal of a Chair of the European Council was not amended they would not subscribe to the final consensus and they would force the production of alternative texts. The same representatives of small Member States and would-be Member States gathered in Vienna on 28 May and criticized the Draft.
38 For instance, the bilateral Blair–Giscard meeting in May 2003 that sought to diffuse any fear that the British government might have had regarding the constitution.

12 Deliberation or bargaining?

Coping with constitutional conflicts in the Convention on the Future of Europe

Paul Magnette

As acknowledged by most commentators, the creation of a 'Convention' to pave the way for the next round of institutional reform in the EU is a turning-point in the history of European integration (Shaw 2003a). First, this is because, so far, institutional choices have been piecemeal and instrumental decisions, primarily governed by the will of the Member States to protect their interests – and only partly influenced by a 'democratic ideology' (Pollack 1997; Moravcsik 1998). By contrast, the Convention was supposed to rethink the whole 'constitutional' setting of the Union. Second, while former reforms were adopted through closed negotiations between diplomatic representatives of the Member States,[1] the Convention involves a much broader range of actors, and is supposed to be a fully open process.

It is reasonable to believe that the transformation of the procedure could alter the process of constitution-making in the EU. Theoretical and empirical research on constitutional deliberation has indeed tried to show that 'the process matters'. Bargaining is usually defined as a process between (a) actors with stable interests who try to maximize their benefits (b) through promises and threats, leading to exchanges of concessions. By contrast, the advocates of deliberation argue that this process takes place among (a) actors who are ready to change their preferences in order to reach 'common interests' (b) through the exchange of rational arguments and mutual listening (Perelman and Olbrechts-Tyteca 1969; Cohen 1989; Habermas 1996; Elster 1998a; Dryzek 2000).

This dichotomy is based on analytical, but also normative, distinctions. From an analytical point of view, the advocates of deliberation argue that, in some instances, the actors tend to transform their preferences in the course of the process, and that this transformation can be explained by the practice of arguing. They do not assume that those who deliberate are motivated by impartial or altruistic motivations: an actor can be constrained to deliberate because he or she is unable to impose his/her point of view and therefore looks for means of agreement-building which are not based on force; because the depth of his/her disagreement with other actors makes strategic games impossible and requires 'dissonance reduction'; or because of a social norm conveyed by the context. In practice, ideal situations of deliberation, where equal actors argue freely and rationally to arrive at a rationally motivated consensus, are rare indeed. But the advocates of this concept argue that it is useful as a model which is sometimes approximated in real life. From a normative point of view, this praxis is said to be superior to bargaining. In terms of efficiency, it is supposed to produce 'integrative' results which go beyond the smallest common denominator. In terms of legitimacy, it purports to build more solid and better accepted solutions: after having argued, the actors not only agree on a norm, as in Rawls' 'overlapping consensus', but also on its justification (Habermas 1996). Those who haven't won at least have the satisfaction of having been heard, and do know why they have lost. The foundations of the agreement being clearer, later conflicts on the basic norms are less likely to occur. Moreover, if deliberation takes place in an open forum, ordinary citizens are given the opportunity to understand the raison d'être of the norms, and should therefore accept them more easily (Mill 1861; Manin 1997).

The major critique addressed to these assumptions is that they cannot be demonstrated empirically. Arguing can be a simple subterfuge, hiding an underground or parallel process of utilitarian negotiation (Mackie 1998; Przeworski 1998). And even if it could be demonstrated that the actors were sincere and that their arguments were not vitiated by misrepresentations, the added value of deliberation could still not be proved since we will never know what the outcome would have been if the parties had followed another procedure. Measuring the transformation of the actors' preferences is empirically very difficult, if not impossible (Checkel 2001).

This chapter will focus on the norms which governed the Convention's deliberations, so as to determine whether, why and to what extent this process differed from classic methods of intergovernmental negotiation in the EU. I will argue that the creation of the Convention itself, and the way its members have defined the rules governing their work, can be understood in deliberative terms.[2] This is not to say that the Convention fully broke with the tradition of interest-based negotiations. Comparative historical studies have shown that the members of a constitutional convention always combine arguing and bargaining (Elster 1994). My hypothesis is that this recent European experience confirms that a large part of the members of the Convention indeed tried to promote deliberative styles of negotiation in order to counter-balance the classic forms of bargaining. This experience also casts doubts, however, on the impact of the deliberative setting on the outcome: the *conventionnels* did comply with the rules of deliberation, but how much this affected the substance of the compromise remains unclear.[3]

Why a Convention?

Up to the late 1990s, nobody would have imagined that the governments would, before the 2004 Intergovernmental Conference (IGC), set up a mixed body including, besides their own representatives, members of the European Parliament and of the Commission, national parliamentarians and representatives of the candidate countries, and that they would give this preparatory body the vague mission to hold public debates on the finality of the Union over more than a year.

The governments have always been jealous to preserve their veto rights in these crucial issues. In 1996, the Westendorp Group, established to pave the way for the 1997 IGC, was composed of very disciplined delegates of the governments and only included two MEPs; as a result, its report simply fixed the disagreements among the Member States. Why did the governments suddenly change their minds during 2001? My hypothesis is that a majority of the governments, those of the smaller Member States, thought this process would give them the opportunity to overcome, or at least to reduce, the capacity of the large states to impose their views through threats and promises; and that the governments of the large states accepted this process because the context conveyed a quest for a different procedure, and because they believed they could control it. In other words, the creation of the Convention was not the result of a sudden transformation of the governments' preferences, but an ambivalent agreement. The Laeken Declaration nevertheless comprised procedures which could, at a later stage, promote deliberative styles of agreement-building.

The context

Since the beginning of the 1990s, the EU had entered a period of permanent institutional reform. The Maastricht Treaty had been judged unsatisfactory by some Member States, which had required another IGC five years later; the Amsterdam Treaty, in turn, was considered incomplete by some governments, and yet another IGC had been foreseen for the end of the decade. At Nice, in December 2000, the governments agreed again that their consensus was minimal and that other reforms would be necessary before the next wave of enlargement. In this context, the argument gained political ground that the process of the IGC itself was partly responsible for these repeated failures (Barbier 2002; Magnette 2002). The European Parliament recalled that it had long pleaded for other methods of constitutional reform – with which it would be associated – and some members of the Commission supported this argument, which was also widespread in academia and in transnational civil associations.

However, this is no evidence of a functionalist process: until the Nice Summit, most governments still considered that the IGC was the only possible path, from a political as well as from a legal point of view. But as the negotiations were slowly sinking under the French Presidency, some of the small Member States (Belgium and its Benelux partners, Portugal and Finland) began to realize that the Summit would not solve all the questions lying on its table, and started to think of an alternative formula to use to prepare the next round. The Summit itself was affected by very tough tensions when the governments came to address key questions of power (weighting of votes in the Council, number and repartition of Commissioners and MEPs) and it was understood by these same governments – and even by those of the larger Member States – as a caricature of intergovernmental bargaining. This context in itself did not produce any solution. But it convinced some governments that an original initiative had to be taken, and prepared the other ones to accept some modification of the IGC process.

The precedent

In the meantime, the Convention (originally called 'body') set up to codify the fundamental rights protected in the EU had concluded its work without major tensions, and had respected the deadline. When seen in contrast to the climate of the Nice Summit, it soon offered the blueprint of an alternative.

Proposed by the German government during its Presidency in 1999, this first Convention had been accepted by the other governments because they saw it as an innocuous process. First, the Convention was a preparatory organ, which was supposed to codify existing rights rather than rethink the EU's principles. Secondly, they agreed that the decision to adopt the result of this process, and to make it legally binding, would be taken by the governments themselves, according to the unanimity rule. Third, the most reluctant governments probably thought that, since it included representatives of all the governments, it would be constrained to state their disagreement on the most sensitive issues and would only agree on the smallest common denominator. At the end of its work, this first Convention, however, was broadly considered as a 'surprise' (the term was often used at that time). The governments of Britain and Denmark were irritated by what they saw as a *fait accompli* and the Charter was adopted *à la sauvette*, without being given a clear legal status (Braibant 2001). Those governments which, on the contrary, were looking for another process to reform the treaty soon presented the Convention as a 'model'.[4] The Belgian delegation, supported by its Benelux partners, obtained a declaration claiming a 'debate on the finality of the Union' during the Nice Summit. Though the then Belgian Prime Minister, Guy Verhofstadt, did not know precisely at that time what he would propose to his colleagues during the Belgian presidency, it was clear that he would suggest something inspired by this precedent.

An ambiguous agreement

It remains to be explained why the proposal to set up a new Convention (which included representatives of the governments, MEPs, commissioners, national parliamentarians and representatives of the candidate countries), and to give it a broad and vague mandate, was finally accepted by the other governments during the last month of the Belgian Presidency (December 2001). The European Parliament and the Commission supported this option, which would likely foster their interests, but their capacity to influence, let alone to constrain, the governments was nil. Apart from Germany, only Portugal and Finland initially supported the Belgian proposal. Those governments that had been irritated by the first experience had now learned that such a mixed organ could escape them. If the British Prime Minister, Tony Blair, or the French President, Jacques Chirac had told Guy Verhofstadt that there was no chance either would accept this new concession, and that either would oppose his veto if it were formally discussed during the Laeken Summit, it would probably have been buried at an early stage.

It remains difficult to explain the position of these reluctant governments. The use of bilateral negotiations by the Belgian Presidency so as to reduce opposition in a step-by-step fashion and avoid the formation of a sceptical front probably contributed to the slow progress of this idea. But, by its own, this classic diplomatic *savoir-faire* would not have been enough. The governments which were not enthusiastic about this prospect nevertheless accepted it for four reasons, which cannot be readily hierarchized.

First, in a liberal society, it is difficult for a political leader to refuse a 'broad debate' before an intergovernmental negotiation; it would, moreover, have ruined Tony Blair's efforts to convince his partners that Britain was now committed to Europe. The fact that the Belgian Presidency presented this 'broad debate' as a mixed process, combining a Convention, a forum of civil society organizations, and national debates, probably helped reduce the opposition of those who feared a Convention.[5]

Second, the prospect of the next wave of enlargement conveyed the impression that this would be the EU's last big institutional reform – the often repeated, though never demonstrated, argument being that, if reforms were difficult between 15 Member States, they would be impossible with 27 governments.[6] Many European leaders thought or pretended to think that this was Europe's 'last chance', and that what was needed was not just a cosmetic reform, but a deeper 'rationalization' of the EU. Interpreted in these terms, this reform was implicitly seen as a 'constitutional agenda'. In this intellectual context, the idea that parliaments should be associated with the process gained ground, for two reasons. First, whether they acknowledge it or not, European leaders are influenced by the formalistic reasoning of Europe's constitutional culture when they think about these kinds of issues (Kohler-Koch 2000; Costa and Magnette 2003).[7] Adopting the EU's 'constitution' through a classic IGC, without consulting the parliaments who are the formal bearers of sovereignty, and who would be asked to ratify the new treaty, sounded odd to many European leaders. On the other hand, in more realistic terms, a formula that associated the parliaments with a preliminary discussion, leaving the decision in the hands of the governments, could be seen as the lesser of two evils.

Third, the least enthusiastic governments – afraid of the impact the launch of a 'constitutional' debate could have on their national opinions – soon thought that if they could not refuse the discussion, they could nevertheless control it and reduce its impact: during the bilateral discussions with the Belgian Presidency, they focused on the content of the Laeken Declaration[8] and tried to limit the impact of the Convention by requiring strict deadlines and a period of reflection between the end of the Convention and the IGC, and by suggesting that the Convention's role should be limited to identifying options that would then be settled by the governments themselves during the IGC.[9] At the Laeken Summit, they again discussed the text of the Laeken Declaration rather than the creation of the Convention itself, and concentrated their negotiation on the nomination of the Convention's Chairman.

Finally, one could think that the reluctant governments, particularly the British, have thought that such an open body, with such a broad agenda, could launch a discussion on issues that would otherwise be considered taboo by the most orthodox governments. This would explain why, rather than refusing the Convention, they insisted on mentioning in the Laeken Declaration that it should discuss the strengthening of the Council, the reduction of the EU bureaucracy or the re-nationalization of some policies. The authorities of the most suspicious governments may have thought that a discussion in which they would be represented, and with the participation of national parliamentarians and of the representatives of the candidate countries – seen as less prone to further integration – could undermine the orthodoxy on questions such as the distribution of competencies, or the extent of the Community model. This is what the 'no taboo' leitmotiv of Tony Blair and Peter Hain's discourses seems to indicate. In other words, the governments agreed because, since the process would be highly unpredictable, they could all think that they would be able to maximize their interests – and otherwise they would still have the opportunity to minimize their costs as they retained their veto during the following IGC.

Thus the creation of the Convention is not the result of a sudden democratic conversion of European leaders. Only a minority of the governments – those of the small countries who thought that the influence of the large states could be diluted in such a hybrid organ – really supported this process, and they had to make concessions to reach a compromise. What matters to our analysis is that this compromise incorporates elements of both bargaining and deliberation. The fact that the Convention would be followed by a classic IGC, and that during its work it would be influenced by the governments from the inside – through their representatives – and from the outside – through the dialogue between its Chairman and the European Council – confirms that the praxis of intergovernmental negotiation remained crucial.[10] But the deliberative potential of the mandate defined at Laeken should not be underestimated.

First, the publicity of the debates could force the governments to publicly justify their positions[11] – some of them may have thought that this would actually give them the opportunity to demonstrate that their traditional reluctance was based not on a narrow defence of national interests or on prejudices, but on pragmatic reasoning.

Second, as all Member States were given the same number of representatives, it would have been very difficult, if not impossible, to vote in such an assembly: in the absence of a system of weighted votes, a majority could represent a very small minority of the European population. The Convention was thus condemned to decide by consensus, rendering the use of vetoes, blocking minorities or majoritarian coalitions very difficult. This, in turn, could preserve the fluidity of the assembly and, without precluding it, limit the resurgence of practices of bargaining dominated by the large states.

Finally, the fluidity of the body is also strengthened by its mixed composition: in an assembly composed of representatives of the national governments and parliaments – including those of the candidate countries – as well as MEPs and members of the Commission, the classic dividing lines of intergovernmental negotiations could be overcome by new, more flexible and unforeseen coalitions.

All this had been, moreover, illustrated by the experience of the Convention that had written the Charter of Fundamental Rights (Braibant 2001; Deloche-Gaudez 2001); governments could not say they were not aware of these potential effects of the rules they had defined. And they knew that all Conventions, in the history of modern politics, have always escaped their creators.

Setting the rules of deliberation

Such an open mandate, stating a long list of very vague questions, giving the Convention the opportunity to establish a draft treaty, and preserving its autonomy to organize its own work, offered many opportunities. They were soon exploited and institutionalized by the Convention, which was encouraged to do so by the President of the European Council himself.[12] The Praesidium – with the tacit or explicit support of the majority of the members – defined some basic rules and principles to affirm the autonomy of the Convention. Retrospectively, three orientations decided by the Praesidium, without opposition from the floor, appear to have shaped the work of the Convention.

First, President Giscard soon defined the 'final outcome' of this process. As a result of the compromise between the governments, the Laeken Declaration had left this crucial question open.[13] Immediately after the Summit, many voices – in the European Parliament, but also in some capitals – underlined the 'constitutional' nature of this exercise. Knowing that a vast majority of the Convention was willing to reach an ambitious agreement, Giscard affirmed during the first session – though he pretended to believe that 'it would be contrary to the logic of our approach to choose now' – that they should try to achieve 'broad consensus on a single proposal [...] [that] would thus open the way towards a Constitution for Europe'. The idea that its role would be limited to identifying options, which would then be settled by the IGC, was abandoned from the very beginning. This was a major decision, because it determined the organization of the Convention's work, and even the kind of arguments raised during the discussions. The first Convention had, under the impulse of its Chairman, decided to work 'as if' the result of its deliberations would be legally binding; in doing so, the Convention favored formal discussions moulded in legal terms – rather than vague debates on the EU's values and principles – and a neat organization of the Convention's agenda around quite clearly identified thematic issues. This decision was, retrospectively, interpreted by some key actors of this first Convention as its most important rule (Braibant 2001). Drawing the lessons of this precedent, Giscard made the same choice. This, in turn, led to the setting up of working groups to study the subjects which appeared, in the course of the discussions, to be the building blocks of the future treaty; and it facilitated a rapid agreement on the 'skeleton' of the 'constitution'. More generally, it probably convinced the members that, to be efficient, they should focus their arguments on precise points, and mould them in quasi-legal terms.

The second major decision made by the Praesidium was the clarification of the 'decision-making' rule. There again, Giscard affirmed during the first session

– with the tacit support of a vast majority of the members – that such an assembly could and should not vote. It could not vote, he explained in a press conference, because all Member States were on an equal footing – so that a majority of votes could be a tiny minority of the population. It should not vote, he argued, because 'there is no doubt that, in the eyes of the public, our recommendation would carry considerable weight and authority if we could manage to achieve broad consensus'. This sentence was the most applauded of his whole discourse – as he subtly noticed during the next session. He added, again during a press conference, that 'consensus does not mean unanimity'. In other words, as had been the case in the first Convention, a small minority would not be in a position to prevent the large majority of the Convention from adopting a common position – the precise size of this minority remained unclear. This principle is also crucial. When the members know that, if they cannot build a large front, their opposition will not be taken into consideration, they are encouraged to search for compromises that can be acceptable by the vast majority, even if this obliges them to depart from their initial preference.

Finally, President Giscard, supported by some active members, constantly defended what he called the 'Convention spirit'. In his introductory speech, he invited the members to embark on their task 'without preconceived ideas', and form their 'vision of the new Europe by listening constantly and closely' to all their partners. He added that 'the members of the four components of our Convention must not regard themselves simply as spokespersons for those who appointed them', and that if each member would remain 'loyal to his or her brief', he or she also had to 'make his or her personal contribution'.[14] This is, he argued, the key of the 'Convention spirit'. Paraphrasing the ideal-typical definition of deliberation, he concluded:

> If your contributions genuinely seek to prepare a consensus, and if you take account of the proposals and comments made by the other members of the Convention, then the content of the final consensus can be worked out step by step here within the Convention.

This, he added, was the crucial difference between the Convention and a classic IGC, which he defined as 'an arena for diplomatic negotiations between Member States in which each party sought legitimately to maximize its gains without regard for the overall picture',[15] paraphrasing, this time, the classic definition of bargaining. Later on, he often recalled this principle of independence and mutual listening when the positions tended to crystallize along national or party lines.[16]

True, these are simple exhortations. But their impact should not be neglected. First, as we will see in the next section, there are signs that the members understood that the attitudes that would violate these widely accepted 'social norms' would be seen as illegitimate. Second, these principles were also partly institutionalized in the organization of the Convention. Just to take two examples: when the socialist members of the European Parliament asked the Praesidium, before the first session, to be allowed to be seated by political groups, President

Giscard refused and imposed that they be seated in alphabetical order; he also decided that the order of the interventions would follow the demands – and would not be negotiated with the national or political groups, even if the Praesidium always tried to respect some balance. When, later on, some members required the creation of additional working groups, or asked the Praesidium to hold hearings with the Presidency of the Commission and of the Council, Giscard again refused, arguing that the Convention should avoid 'cutting itself into pieces' or adopt a 'parliamentary working method'.[17]

Criticisms were voiced by rank-and-file members against the Praesidium's leadership. Some of them – mainly the Eurosceptic members – denounced the lack of representativeness of the Convention itself, and of the organs it consulted.[18] Without contesting the representativeness of the assembly itself, others – mainly from the national parliaments and the smallest Member States – regretted the more generous chances given to the Commission and to the bigger Member States in the use of the floor. The most important and vivid criticism concerned the role of the Chairman. Giscard had tried, since the inception of the debates, to present himself as a neutral actor. He had refused to give his personal views on the issues discussed by the members, arguing that he did not want to prevent them from making up their own minds; and he had imposed a long 'listening phase'[19] (from March to July) dedicated to mutual listening among the members, and the consultation of NGOs, arguing that this would allow the members to define by themselves the issues that needed to be discussed. He, however, had soon taken the initiative to summarize the sessions. In doing so, he could privilege some issues,[20] and orient the following debates. This is the reason why his 'inductive role' gave rise to rather aggressive criticisms.[21] Behind these criticisms, one can read the fear (real or feigned) of some members – mainly MEPs – that the Convention was being manipulated by its Chairman, himself subject to the pressures of the European Council that nominated him, and particularly the largest Member States.[22] The purpose and the effect of these reactions were essentially symbolic: as they criticized Giscard's leadership, the opacity of the Praesidium or the complicity between the Chairman and the European Council, these members intended to demonstrate that they would protect the autonomy of the Convention from external pressures – which would have reintroduced a logic of intergovernmental negotiation.

'Deliberative effect' and its limits

Did this 'deliberative setting' influence the attitude of the members of the Convention? In this section I emphasize some indications that the *conventionnels* were indeed constrained by the norms the Convention had imposed upon its members. I also, however, indicate that it remains difficult to demonstrate that these norms have actually transformed the actors' preferences. I focus on three features of this process which can be seen as elements of an ideal-type deliberation: the de-legitimization of 'situated interests'; the domination of a 'pragmatic' discursive register over strategic games and passionate rhetoric; and the fluidity of the negotiation.[23]

The de-legitimization of 'situated interests'

The most visible effect of the deliberative setting on these discussions was the fact that, during the two first stages of the process at least, the members of the Convention usually presented their arguments as impartial views, as abstract reasoning seeking to define the 'common good'. It is empirically impossible to determine whether they were sincerely seeking to reach a common view, or if they simply disguised their interests. Adopting an 'impartial' attitude may be, and often is, a simple subterfuge. The advocates of deliberation argue that such hypocritical behaviour does not reduce the exchange of arguments to a mere comedy (Elster 1998b): when an actor believes that she needs to disguise her private interests and talk the language of the general interest – because of the 'social constraint' of the forum, or because, in strategic terms, she thinks this is the most efficient register – she pays tribute to the deliberative setting and paves the way for a rational exchange of arguments. This is supposed to be a virtuous circle: the actors who think they have to respect the deliberative setting to be efficient tend to strengthen the 'social constraint' of impartial reasoning, and to adapt their own preferences.

The Laeken Convention does not seem to confirm this hypothesis, known after Elster (1995) as the 'civilizing force of hypocrisy'. First, the members have violated this principle, stating their interest very bluntly.[24] Secondly, as the *conventionnels* were aware of the interests of their colleagues, they were rarely duped by the apparent impartiality of their discourse. A double standard often governed the deliberation: the public arguments were easily decoded by the *conventionnels*, who privately reasoned in crude realistic terms – as all those who have had 'off the record' discussions with *conventionnels* realized.[25]

The members were torn between three sets of interests: they represented the states of which they were nationals, the institution by which they were nominated (national or European parliament, government, Commission), and they shared the views of their political family (political party). Though the Chairman tried to avoid a rigid structuration of these identities, their organization was not formally prohibited. The major political families held meetings before the plenary sessions, in order to coordinate their position, and they organized seminars to draw common lines during the summer.[26] The members also met as 'components' before the sessions, and, albeit this was more rarely made public, all governments organized some sort of coordination between their nationals – be they representative of the government or not, member of the majority or not. The Rousseauist ideal of a purely atomistic deliberation between free and equal actors was thus far from being realized.

True, when they took the floor, the members rarely made reference to these identities, and the interests associated with them. This testifies to the weight of the 'social norm' which rendered the naked expression of interests problematic. But whether the translation of their interest into seemingly impartial views led to a transformation of their preferences remains to be proved. As far as *national interests* are concerned, the members often openly presented their position as their government's line, notably during the discussions on the intergovernmental pillars (common foreign and security policy, defence, criminal and judicial cooperation) and on institutional matters. The Chairman recalled that 'this isn't about articulating from a national viewpoint [...]. We must expect a European expression from the *conventionnels*',[27] but this did not really convince the members to change their attitudes. *Ideological identities* were often mentioned too, particularly (as could be expected) on policy questions. Some members even justified this open expression of their ideological bias, arguing that this was a 'contribution to the formation of a consensus'.[28] In other words, they implicitly defended an organic conception of consensus-making – by opposition to the classic Rousseauist atomistic version – in order to legitimize the expression of 'situated interests'. The identity associated with an *institution* was more rarely expressed. But this is due to tactics rather than to the will to be regarded as an impartial player. Those members who stated that they presented the official point of view of their government actually referred to 'national interests' rather than to the functionally based identity of the executive bodies. If the MEPs and commissioners tended to mould their arguments in terms of the 'European interest', they merely wanted to avoid being seen as advocates of the corporate interest of their institution.[29]

The restriction of the discursive register

The Convention also showed signs that its members were willing to be seen as 'rational' actors, avoiding strategic and passionate registers. One can think that, as much as the social norms of deliberation, it is the lack of efficiency of rhetorical registers playing on fears and emotions which convinced them to adopt this strategy: in the absence of a common history and of a shared civic culture, arguments based on a passionate appeal to history and traditional symbols of identity would not have impressed the members who did not share these references.[30] True, the members could have quoted their common history – the experience of the war and of the resistance, and the history of European integration itself. But they did not seem to be willing to do so. In his introductory speech, Giscard made several references to the 'cruel confrontations of the past', to the 'European legacy' (reason, humanism and freedom), and he quoted the founding fathers.[31] But the members did not follow his example. When some of them quoted the precedent of Philadelphia, they did it to emphasize, by contrast, the originality of this experience.[32] The history of European integration was very rarely mentioned.[33]

Doctrinal concepts were very rarely used too. Apart from the Eurosceptics, who sometimes used this kind of register, they were nearly absent from the debates.[34] The time when Condorcet asked the Assemblée Constituante 'to shelter from those hasty resolutions, snatched sometimes in the name of liberty, sometimes in the name of Roman history'[35] seemed to be very remote. The members of this Convention were definitely more 'rational': their language was usually very technical – using the jargon of public and Community law – and their arguments were generally empiricist or pragmatic – trying to demonstrate the realistic or unrealistic nature of an option on the basis of experience and/or hypothetical experimentation.[36]

Threats were not openly used either. According to Elster, the deliberative setting constrains the actors to present them as 'warnings' – to avoid the opprobrium associated with the use of 'force'. Examples of this phenomenon can be found in the deliberations of the Convention. When an actor knew that his position was not supported by a majority, and he wouldn't be able to oppose his veto, warning was the only strategy available to try to convince the audience to come closer to his point. The discussions on the Union's foreign policy on 12 July 2002 offer a good example of this mechanism. Against those who had suggested the extension of the Community method to these spheres, the representative of the British government, Peter Hain, repeatedly used this kind of register: 'communitization will simply not work', 'That is the truth. If you do not recognize that truth you will not get a serious foreign policy', 'A serious policy must be based on governments. You will simply not get it otherwise', 'If you do not have the confidence of the heads of government, you will not get a common voice. That is the brutal truth'. In the framework of an IGC, he could simply have vetoed this kind of proposal. Here, he needed to combine warnings and empiricist arguments. But the *conventionnels* easily understood that what the representative of the British government meant was that an 'agreement' that would bypass those lines would be vetoed by his government during the next IGC. Paying tribute to the deliberative setting, Mr Hain nevertheless punctuated his speech with concessions softening his position when he added 'I am open to ideas from Mr. Duff', 'We are not approaching this with a fixed mind', 'Those are my concerns, but I am not shutting the door on it'.

The mixed impression left by the deliberations of this Convention is due to the duality of its standards. Apparently, the members were constrained by the 'deliberative setting', and they adopted attitudes that did not violate the principles of rationality and impartiality. In fact, the members have never forgotten that they were just a preparatory body, and that their compromise would be renegotiated by the governments in the next IGC. They knew, and often publicly stated, that if they reached a very ambitious compromise, but did not take into account the governments' positions, they would be disavowed by the negotiators of the IGC. The *conventionnels* were induced to anticipate the IGC, and this limited their ambition.[37] Deliberation took place, but under the shadow of the veto.

The absence of rigid and stable structures

The absence of stable and rigid groups is also considered as a factor which can favour deliberation. Deliberation is possible between a small number of actors, but it is easier when the assembly is cross-cut by different kinds of cleavages: in such a fluid forum it will indeed be more difficult in practice to follow a logic of bargaining (Elster 1998b); moreover, the risk of group polarization (a tendency like-minded persons can have, when they deliberate, to radicalize their prejudice rather than searching for new solutions) is more limited in a diverse body (Sunstein 2002).

No obvious signs of stable coalition-building and log-rolling could be noticed in this Convention: if the views of representatives of the Central and Eastern European countries, the small nations or the national parliaments have sometimes been convergent, they did not constitute permanent and coherent groups. The members belonging to the same party federation tried to coordinate their positions, but the discussion was not dominated by ideological cleavages. And the members often disagreed with their fellow-citizens. As could be expected, in a complex and hybrid assembly, the dividing lines varied according to the subject of the debate. On socio-economic matters, a left–right cleavage emerged, albeit a nationalist left did not support further integration and a federalist right was inclined to accept more coordination. On institutions, discussions were first dominated by the old quarrel between the federalist and the intergovernmentalist visions of the EU, before being overshadowed by a less ideological and more strategic opposition between small and large countries. These cross-cutting cleavages prevented the emergence of a majoritarian division, but this was due to the state of the preferences, not to the process of deliberation. As the MEPs, the national parliamentarians and the representatives of the candidate countries did not form coherent groups, and were divided by the same lines that had divided former IGCs, the mixed composition of the Convention did not really alter the dynamics of negotiation.

The formal equality of the members, however, influenced the form of the debate, if not its content or its outcome. Formally, the deliberations of this Convention were not dominated by the governments. The plenary sessions gave rise to discussions that were structured by the interventions of four types of 'leaders', who gradually emerged in the course of the debates. First, the '*big interests*': when Peter Hain, Peter Glotz, Gianfranco Fini (all representatives of national governments, British, German and Italian, respectively), and so on, took the floor, the audience usually paid attention to their positions. It must be added that their interventions elicited a considerable number of replies on the side of other *conventionnels*. This testifies to the weight of intergovernmental reasoning among the members. But the discussions were also channelled by other types of 'leaders'. A second group of actors was made up of the *radicals*: the Eurosceptics soon adopted a very critical and vivid language which also drew the attention of the other members. The *dialecticians* form a third category. Some members – most of whom were MEPs like Olivier Duhamel, Andrew Duff or Johannes Voggenhuber – chose to focus a large part of their intervention on the process of deliberation itself: they sometimes questioned the Chairman on his role, and sometimes underlined conflicts and disagreements between the previous speakers in order to stimulate contradictory debates. A fourth category comprised the *facilitators*: some members (this is particularly the case of the two commissioners) generally used their turn to explain elements of the Union – and reduce the dissonance due to a lack of understanding – to suggest possible compromises and to ask the other members to reason in pragmatic terms.

The debates were dominated by the role played by these leaders, while most other members could be seen as laggards, who mainly reacted to the positions expressed by these dominant actors. But if these leaders influenced the dynamics of deliberation, it remains difficult to demonstrate that they affected its contents. The pattern of these debates can be summarized as follows: the *big interests* presented their positions (usually in terms of 'public interest') without, in most cases, underlining their agreement or disagreement with other opinions; the *dialecticians* emphasized these lines of agreement or conflict; while the *radicals* denounced – and maybe thereby paradoxically strengthened – the pro-European consensus; the *facilitators* then tried to reduce the 'cognitive dissonance' through explanations, and suggested compromises. The interventions of the other members between those of the 'leaders' simply tended to confirm the weight of the different positions. Whether the dialecticians and the facilitators managed to convince the other members to adopt integrative solutions rather than simple give-and-take concessions remains to be seen. It is reasonable to believe that, on questions which do not alter the balance of power too openly – such as the merging of the Treaties, the simplification of the norms and procedures, the incorporation of the Charter, etc. – these actors were able to overcome former divisions by explaining, fostering formal reasoning and suggesting compromise. But this hypothesis requires further investigation.[38]

Conclusion

This Convention was undeniably inspired by a deliberative ideal. The rhetoric of constitutionalization, and the formalist pattern of thought of most politicians, convinced them that a new process was needed.

The mandate of the Convention, albeit resulting from a quite classic intergovernmental negotiation, incorporated some elements of a 'deliberative setting': the hybrid nature of the organ, its broad mandate, the publicity of its work, were potentialities that could be used by the Convention. The majority of the *conventionnels* managed to translate these principles into – merely informal – rules which have governed its working method. The early – and largely implicit – decision to try to reach a broad consensus on a quasi-constitutional text, and the insistence of the Praesidium on the 'Convention spirit', largely correspond to the ideal-type definition of deliberation.

The Convention's work was apparently influenced by this 'deliberative setting': the de-legitimization of discourses based on 'situated interests' or on threats and passionate rhetoric, and the absence of stable coalitions, seem to confirm the impact of these rules. On the other hand, the *conventionnels* knew and acknowledged that their experience would be followed by a classic IGC, and tended to anticipate it. They deliberated, but under the shadow of the veto. As a result, the strength of arguments proved unable to counter-balance the weight of interests in many instances. Discussions were governed by the same dividing lines as those which had constrained former IGCs. As a result, the *conventionnels* did not manage to reach a really innovative compromise.

This might seem very disappointing for those who believe in the strength of deliberation. But the legitimating effect of this exercise should not be neglected. Firstly, this is because after the Convention, two classic sets of criticisms will lose their appeal. The argument of those who had criticized the Treaties because they had been negotiated in closed and restricted fora of diplomats will no longer be be valid. Moreover, those non-founding Member States who had long criticized the EU, and its institutions, on the grounds that they had had to accept the whole package when they became members, in spite of the fact that they disagreed with some aspects of the Treaties, will have to acknowledge that they have now taken part in a broad debate, where everything was on the table. If they support the new treaty, this will amount to a confirmation of their acceptance. The very hostile campaign of the British Eurosceptic press against the Convention's constitutional proposal, and the efforts made by the British government to explain why they accepted reforms they had long rejected earlier (suppression of the pillars, extension of qualified majority voting and co-decision, incorporation of the Charter, etc.), show that this confirmation is not a strictly formal event.

Secondly, the impact of form should not be underestimated. Since the Convention managed to write a relatively simple, clear and understandable text – compared to the *status quo ex ante* and to national standards – the consensus might grow.[39] Modern political thoughts are forged by formal categories, and the conformity of the Union's basic text to the canons of western law could make it more acceptable.

This experience has not confirmed, however, the 'educative' potentialities of public deliberation. Inside the Convention, the exchange of arguments was facilitated by the formation of a 'common language' and the progressive sharing of cognitive and normative frameworks among the *conventionnels*. After a period of 'listening' dominated by vague rhetoric, the *conventionnels* have opted for pragmatic reasoning, and moulded their arguments around the legal and technical terms of Euro-jargon. This might have helped them reach a consensus, as conflicts based on misunderstandings and passions were reduced. But this also tends to weaken the 'external promise' of deliberation. When debates are cast in technical terms, deprived of passionate rhetoric and remote from citizens' common sense, they do not draw the attention of the general public and do not help citizens understand the issues at stake (Magnette 2003a). The fact that the Convention has been largely ignored by the European press, and the absence of public debate outside the small circles of 'Europeanized' citizens, are clear illustrations of the limits of this 'public' deliberation.

It should not be forgotten, however, that most constitutional deliberations in history only take place during the ratification process, after the end of the Convention itself. The French Assemblée Constituante was a noticeable – if not very encouraging – exception. It cannot be excluded that a larger part of the citizenry will listen to arguments about the Convention's work after the IGC, as was the case with the debates generated by the Maastricht Treaty in France and Denmark, or by the Nice Treaty in Ireland. Advocates of public deliberation

warn that '[t]he success of public deliberation should be measured reconstruc-
tively – that is in light of the historical development of democratic institutions
and practices' (Bohman 1996: 241). In the short term, the impact of deliberation
on public opinion is probably very limited. In the long term, it may play some
role in the formation of a common civic culture. The new constitutional treaty,
and its commentaries, might become something like the *Federalist Papers*, read by
generations of politicians, constitutional judges, lawyers and students, and often
used as a reference to interpret the US Constitution. Since the interpretation of
the founding fathers – 'la volonté du constituant' in French – is an important
element of western legal culture, the records of this deliberation might become,
in the long term, a key to interpret the European constitutional treaty in political
and judicial fora; as such, they would be an element of these 'conceptual
resources' that Rawls (1993b) presents as a necessary condition of any 'overlapping consensus'.

Notes

A preliminary version of this chapter was presented at the First Pan-European
Conference of the ECPR Standing Group on European Integration in Bordeaux in
September 2002 and at the Minda de Gunzburg Center of European Studies at
Harvard University in January 2003. I would like to thank the participants and other
colleagues for their comments, and most particularly Carlos Closa, John Fossum,
Justine Lacroix, Andrew Moravcsik, Kalypso Nicolaïdis, Fritz Scharpf, Vivien
Schmidt and David Trubek.

1   Even when IGCs only consecrated inter-institutional agreements or accepted practices, as was the case for example with the reforms of the European Parliament's
powers during the negotiations of the Amsterdam Treaty, the process remained
rather discrete and limited to a narrow range of actors.
2   Other aspects of the EU's decision-making processes have been analysed in terms of
deliberation. See Joerges and Neyer 1997; Costa 2001; Eriksen and Fossum 2000;
Joerges 2001; Smismans 2000.
3   This chapter was written before the end of the Convention's work (May 2003). The
emphasis is thus on the impact of deliberation in the course of the process.
4   The European Parliament adopted a report calling for another Convention before the
next IGC in October 2000, but at that time this was not noticed by the governments.
There is no evidence that this report influenced them, though one can hypothesize
that the governments which are inclined to support the European Parliament, such as
that of Germany, may have accepted in part because it was defended by the
Parliament.
5   The text of the Laeken Declaration itself reduces the potential impact of the
Convention when it states that '*together with the outcome of national debates on the future of
the Union*, the final document [drawn up by the Convention] will provide a starting-
point for discussions in the Intergovernmental Conference' (emphasis added).
6   Negotiation theories show that, in some circumstances, the process is easier when the
number of parties is higher, because this reduces frontal oppositions and increases the
number of possible winning coalitions.
7   Moravcsik argues that 'democratic ideology' plays a certain role on symbolic and
unforeseeable issues. See Moravcsik 1998; Moravcsik and Nicolaïdis 1998.
8   The French and British delegations insisted that the diagnosis of the Union should be
less pessimistic, and a sentence mentioning the 'deadlocks of unanimity' be

suppressed. They also asked for the reformulation of a question concerning the direct election of the Commission's President – because they found the initial sentence sounded like a positive answer; and required the introduction of other questions concerning the re-nationalization of some policies and the strengthening of the Council. This process explains why the Laeken Declaration is the most open document ever adopted by the governments.

9 The text of the Laeken Declaration is marked by this negotiation. Some redundancies (on the role of national parliaments notably) and the lack of coherence of the text are due to the amendments required by some governments. The non-decisional nature of the Convention is neatly affirmed: the text says that 'it will be the task of that Convention to *consider* the key issues arising for the Union's future development and try to *identify the various possible options*' (emphasis added); the final document is said to 'provide a starting-point for discussions in the Intergovernmental Conference, which will take the ultimate decisions'.

10 The geographic and political balance of the Praesidium also corresponds to a classic intergovernmental logic. The fact that the Secretariat of the Convention was chaired by a British diplomat was also part of the Laeken deal.

11 Theories of deliberation show that the principle of publicity can have perverse effects, in that the actors may be tempted to use rhetoric to convince the external audience (Elster 1998a). But this did not occur in a Convention that was largely ignored by the general public.

12 In his inaugural speech, Jose Maria Aznar (CONV 4/02) argued that 'Nice is the reason why we are here today'. Partly rewriting history, he added that '[i]mmediately thereafter, the Heads of State and Government convened the Convention that is starting now, in the knowledge that *the new stage calls for new forms of operation and deliberation* in order to continue to create "more Europe"' (emphasis added).

13 The Laeken Declaration says: 'The Convention will consider the various issues. It will draw up a final document which may comprise either different options, indicating the degree of support which they received, or recommendations if consensus is achieved.'

14 Inaugural speech, pp. 8 and 13. He added during a press conference that the term 'representative' was an 'error of drafting', since 'they are not representatives; when they talk, they do not speak for one or the other component' (Agence Europe, 28 March 2002), p. 6. Jose Maria Aznar, as President of the European Council, had, on the contrary, argued that the members had to follow the views of the organs they represented.

15 Ibid., p. 13.

16 In a press conference after the session of 22 March, Giscard said he found it 'normal that big European sensitivities harmonize their points of view', while, however, warning against any 'excessive structuring' of the Convention (*Bulletin quotidien Europe*, 23 March 2002). In his opinion published by *Le Monde* in July (Giscard d'Estaing 2002), he said about the representatives of the governments:

> Their situation is somewhat ambiguous: do they participate at the meetings and interrogations of the Convention as individuals or do they rather attend the meetings in order to express the points of view of the governments that appointed them? Following an initial doubt, my impression was that their 'conventional' character prevailed.

17 Plenary session, 23 May 2002.

18 Jens-Peter Bonde (Danish Eurosceptic MEP) and David Heathcoat-Amory (British Conservative MP) particularly criticized the organization of the hearings with the civil society and the Youth Convention, in June and July 2002, arguing that these private bodies, often supported by the Commission and the European Parliament, were not objective and did not represent the Eurosceptic elements of European public opinion.

19 This was not Giscard's personal idea. He had initially envisaged examining the positions of the Member States and the EU institutions (as is acknowledged by his suggestions in his introductory speech), but he was convinced by a majority in the Praesidium that this could fix the positions and that a larger and less structured debate would help prevent an early structuration of the Convention.

20 After the first session, he already insisted on the EU's external role – a priority he had long defended – though this had not really been discussed. He also argued that the members had not asked for new competencies for the EU on internal matters, and insisted on the need for clarification and simplification. See his synthesis at the beginning of the third session and his speech in Stuttgart in May 2002. The same lines are defended in his opinion published by *Le Monde* in July (Giscard d'Estaing 2002) and in his report before the European Council in June 2002. They have not evolved in the following months.

21 Regretting that he had not mentioned that many members had asked for the integration of the Charter in the future treaty, the Austrian MEP Johannes Voggenhuber asked: 'Will we be allowed to draw a consensus which does not correspond to your preference', while the Belgian MP Elio Di Rupo stated, after Giscard had presented the synthesis he had given to the European Council, 'this is only your report, which does not regard us' (24 June 2002).

22 This is what the German MEP Elmar Brok meant when he called Giscard the 'grand architecte' (23 May 2002), or when another German MEP (Jo Leinen) denounced in a press conference the 'secret consultations' between Giscard and the Heads of State and Government (see Agence Europe, 17 June 2002).

23 These are revised versions of the elements of a 'deliberative setting' as identified by Elster 1998b.

24 See notably this very clear and blunt answer to the President of the Commission, Romano Prodi, by the representative of the British government, Peter Hain, on 5 December 2002:

> There is no prospect at all of common foreign and security policy being communitarized, as proposed by the Commission. There is no prospect at all of that except in those areas where it already exists. [...] Frankly, there is no prospect of the Commission agenda being accepted by the British Government or, from what they have said, by the Governments of France, Spain, Italy, Sweden and Ireland, at least not in this respect.

25 The author has attended most of the plenary sessions of this Convention, and has discussed these issues with many *conventionnels* during the coffee breaks.

26 The three largest political groupings have nominated a 'representative' among their members: Elmar Brok for the European People's Party (Christian Democrats) and European Democrats, Giuliano Amato for the Party of European Socialists and Andrew Duff for the European Liberal Democrat and Reform Party.

27 ' ... il ne s'agira pas de s'exprimer d'un point de vue national [...]. Nous attendons des conventionnels une expression européenne' (12 July 2002).

28 See notably the interventions of the British Liberal MEP Andrew Duff (whose position may also be explained by the fact that he represents the pro-European minority of a still largely Eurosceptic country). This organic conception of consensus-making was also justified by Giuliano Amato during a press conference, when he explained that a good final document could only be a balance between the visions of the largest political families – a very consociative logic, which governed the making of the Italian Constitution after World War II. See *Bulletin quotidien Europe*, 16 April 2002. The same argument was made by Pat Cox and Andrew Duff (*Bulletin quotidien Europe*, 5 April 2002).

29 See Giscard's intervention after the representative of the Commission had supported
    Prodi's line, on 5 December 2002:

>   I would only like to remind you of an ethical point of the Convention, Mr
>   Ponzano. This is not about a discussion between the institutions, the European
>   Parliament and the governments. Everybody speaks for himself. For example,
>   regarding the members of the Commission, we know that Mr Barnier or Mr
>   Vitorino are members of the Commission when they express their opinions.
>   However, they do not express the points of view of the Commission. The
>   Commission expresses itself in its own right through the appropriate channels.
>   We are here at a meeting of conventionnels, where everybody expresses their
>   personal opinions, as Mr Fischer will do in a minute.

30 This kind of register was sometimes, though rarely, used by some members. But they
    seemed to target external audiences.
31 He again played on this register later on. On 23 May 2002 he recalled the memory of
    'our friend Altierri [*sic*]' (actually Altierro Spinelli); on 24 June he asked one minute of
    silence in memory of Pierre Werner. The other members rarely followed his example.
32 Valéry Giscard d'Estaing, on the contrary, argued in several conferences before and
    during the Convention that this European experience was not substantially different
    from the Philadelphia precedent.
33 The failure of the European Defence Community and the Fouchet plans were
    mentioned once during the discussion on CFSP, on 12 July 2002.
34 The notion of 'sovereignty' was mentioned several times during the discussion on the
    intergovernmental pillars, but it usually referred to the legal definition of the state's
    prerogatives, rather than to abstract notions of independence.
35 'de se mettre à l'abri de ces résolutions précipitées qu'on lui arrache, tantôt au nom
    de la liberté, tantôt au nom de l'histoire romaine'.
36 Giovanni Sartori distinguishes rationalist (based on concepts and logical deduction),
    empiricist (based on historical experience) and pragmatic (based on experimentation)
    patterns of constitutional thought. See Sartori 1965, and also Olsen 2002.
37 On each and every subject, the British government drew lines in the sand: it very
    clearly indicated, through its representative within the Convention, the limits it would
    not be ready to bypass. President Giscard implicitly encouraged this attitude by giving
    Peter Hain a key position in the debates – so that some observers called him the
    'shadow President' of the Convention.
38 This is the subject of another paper. A provisional version is available on
    <http://www.arena.uio.no/cidel/workshopZaragoza/PMagnette.pdf>.
39 Rawls notes that 'constitutional essentials' must not be too detailed and that their
    principles must be 'made visible' in the institutions in order to benefit from a large
    support (Rawls 1993b: VI, §6, 1).

13 Still a Union of deep diversity?

The Convention and the Constitution for Europe

John Erik Fossum

Introduction

The European Union, as noted in the Laeken Declaration, is at a critical crossroads (European Council 2001a). This notion of crossroads pertains to three critical dimensions. The first is the geographical scope of the future Union, where several stages of enlargement will make it a much larger and more diverse EU. The second is its institutional-constitutional status. Under the shadow of enlargement, the EU has launched a broad and deep review process on the fundamental aspects of the Union, so as to help it grapple with the challenges ahead. The third is the normative dimension and pertains to the political justifications and basis of legitimacy that the entity can and should draw upon. The Convention on the Future of Europe, it is here claimed, offers a unique contribution to the assessment as to whether, or the extent to which, the three dimensions have converged in its work and results.

What have the Convention's efforts at forging a constitutional and institutional framework resulted in with regard to our conception of the nature of the polity and the fundamental principles that this is to be based upon? This question is squarely located in the constitutional debate – with particular attention to the peculiar nature and status of the entity that makes up the EU. It has long been acknowledged that the European Community has developed a legal order that in many respects is unique and is something more than an international legal order. The EU is clearly also more than an economic arrangement. It is widely held to possess a material constitution. In legal dogmatic terms, the Treaties make up the 'constitution of the Union'. This constitutional arrangement, several prominent analysts assert, is based on a set of principles, organizational arrangements and modes of allegiance, and also lays claim to a normative justification. To Joseph Weiler, the core legitimating principle of this system is *constitutional tolerance* (Weiler 2001a, 2001b, 2002). It permeates, and is embedded within, an institutional system that is a complex mixture of supranational and intergovernmental traits and whose basis of allegiance is not one *demos* but *multiple demoi*. This position not only recognizes, but also lauds, the fact that there is no European people upon which to base the EU. I will argue that in allegiance terms, such a system can be termed as marked by *deep diversity* (Taylor 1993).[1]

There is also a second constitutional vision. This vision of the EU is informed by a full-fledged constitution on a par with that of the democratic constitutional state; its attendant mode of allegiance is *constitutional patriotism*; and it also rests on a set of rather specific institutional-constitutional arrangements (see chapters by Habermas, Eriksen and Menéndez in this book). The EU has embraced many of the core principles of this arrangement, and has throughout its history experienced several defunct attempts to establish such a European democratic constitution. It is widely acknowledged that the EU falls well short of the standards of the democratic constitutional state or that there is a deep gap between these standards and its legal-institutional – and constitutional – makeup.[2]

Given the presence of two visions, and in particular the fact that the present EU represents an aberration from conventional constitutional thought, the question is: what is the nature of the constitutional doctrine with regard to allegiance formation that we can discern from the Convention? Does the Convention depart from the system in place and embrace a mainstream type of constitutional doctrine that presupposes the creation of *one* demos, or does it seek to retain the present system of multiple *demoi*?

To this end I first spell out the two constitutional doctrines, which I label *deep diversity* and *constitutional patriotism*. In the third part each of these is briefly assessed against the Convention, its work and its results (delimited to its draft). The point here is to establish the direction of change, and the relative salience of one doctrine as opposed to the other. A clear determination requires that the provisions in the complex document be put into effect and tested against the complex European reality (a task clearly beyond the scope of this work). The assessment of the direction of change presented here is nevertheless important to shed light on (a) the magnitude of change suggested by the Convention; (b) the Convention's underlying constitutional thinking; and (c) the prospects for a post-national European democratic constitution. The final part of the chapter holds the conclusion.

Deep diversity and constitutional patriotism

Deep diversity is here such construed as to provide a set of standards for the assessment of the political-institutional underpinnings and the sociological-anthropological character of allegiance that is relevant to the question of identity in contemporary Europe, not the least perhaps because it refers to a wide range of allegiances, well beyond national identity. A Union of deep diversity might even be an apt description of the system in place.

Deep diversity

Deep diversity refers to a situation where a 'plurality of ways of belonging [are] acknowledged and accepted' (Taylor 1993: 183) within the same state or polity. Acceptance entails that special political-legal, and even constitutional, measures have been devised to preserve and promote it. Communitarianism is the philosophical basis of deep diversity. This position underlines that rights and constitutional arrangements are inadequate as means of fostering a sense of community and belonging. The law and rights are always steeped within a particular cultural setting that provides people with deep-seated cues as to who they are and what is good and valuable (Taylor 1989, 1994, 1995a, 1995b).[3]

Legal-political arrangements thus offer only a partial intake to people's actual allegiances, albeit it is possible to spell out some core conditions under which deep diversity will occur. The following extrapolation and application of this principle contains some adaptations from Taylor's description, to suit the European case.

A political system whose hallmark is deep diversity can be federal but cannot be based on one nation-state. Deep diversity does not presuppose a constitutional *demos*, and the constitutional arrangement, therefore, does not need an explicit popular endorsement on a par with that of a full-fledged constitution. The first condition that we can use to assess the work and results of the Convention in relation to deep diversity refers to the nature of the constitution: deep diversity presupposes that the entity is based not on a full-fledged constitution (with the underlying recognition of a unified popular will), but on a compact, which at most can be characterized as a constitutional treaty. It acknowledges the existence of separate national popular wills, but establishes a set of common institutions and principles based on a constitutional treaty, not a full-fledged constitution.

Second, the society contains *several and different* collective conceptions of its cultural or national or linguistic or ethnic make-up, and there is thus *no overarching agreement on what the country is for*.

Third, the existence of different collective goals is not only an acknowledged and accepted fact, but also something that is accommodated through differentiated citizenship, and other means, through which collectives try to maintain their sense of difference. Deep diversity presumes that a group's sense of belonging to the overarching entity passes through its belonging to another smaller and more integrated community. Citizenship in the overarching entity is thus differentiated because it must reflect the nature of this relation and the character of the smaller and more integrated community. Additional provisions are needed to protect the unique history, culture, language and identity of each such national (and other distinct) community. At the same time, an overarching system of provisions, laws and institutions is needed to ensure that the basic concerns and interests of *non-nationals* are systematically taken into account. Such a system could be marked by the lack of a clear normative hierarchy and perhaps even sanctioning means; acceptance and subordination could thus at least in principle be voluntary. Deep diversity is hence also compatible with provisions for voluntary exit of individual states or sub-units from the polity.

Fourth, deep diversity presumes that each Member State and other relevant cultural actors have veto over treaty or constitutional change.

The present-day EU – a Union of deep diversity?[4]

Deep diversity, as noted, presumes a wider approach to allegiance than that presented in legal documents. Its relevance must therefore be established with reference to central traits of the EU. How compatible is deep diversity with the central tenets of the present-day EU? The EU is a particularly complex multinational and poly-ethnic entity, with a wide range of sources of difference and diversity. As noted, the sheer range of diversity and the strong sense of *national* identity have prompted many analysts and even decision-makers to conclude that there is *no European demos*.[5]

Deep diversity assumes that this respect for difference is central to the entity's constitutional ethos. It is a normative good. The constitutional term for such an entity would be constitutional treaty (Grimm, Chapter 5 in this book; Weiler 2001a, 2001b, 2002). At the same time, deep diversity presupposes a set of institutions that can undertake common tasks and foster the respect and tolerance necessary for democratic and peaceful coexistence.

In line with the second and third criteria listed above, Joseph Weiler argues that the EU has developed a unique federal arrangement, the normative hallmark of which is the *principle of constitutional tolerance*. This is based on two core components. The first is the consolidation of democracy within and among Member States. The second is the explicit rejection of the One Nation ideal and the recognition that

> the Union […] is to remain a union among distinct peoples, distinct political identities, distinct political communities. […] The call to bond with those very others in an ever closer union demands an internalization – individual and societal – of a very high degree of tolerance.
>
> (Weiler 2001a: 68)

As Weiler notes in a more recent article,

> in the Community, we subject the European peoples to constitutional discipline even though the European polity is composed of distinct peoples. It is a remarkable instance of civic tolerance to be bound by precepts articulated, not by 'my people', but by a community composed of distinct political communities: a people, if you wish, of 'others'.
>
> (Weiler 2002: 568)

The EU, therefore, is accepting of different conceptions and visions of what the polity is, and ought to be.

In its strongest and most pronounced form, deep diversity is incompatible with a constitutionally entrenched Charter of Rights, if such leads to uniform citizenship and helps eradicate difference. However, a Charter (that is incorporated in the constitution) might still support deep diversity, provided the following requirements are met:

- the Constitutional Treaty contains provisions on differentiated citizenship and other means of acknowledging cultural and national and other forms of difference;
- the scope of application of the Charter is limited and only applies to issues that do *not* affect the propounding of such forms of difference.

In a Union of deep diversity, each national community would be seen as the locus of primary and deeper attachments. This condition is reflected in many aspects of the EU, such as the notion of Member States as the Masters of the Treaties, unanimity requirements, division of powers and European citizenship provisions – where access to European citizenship is conditional on national citizenship.

The Union of deep diversity's Constitutional Treaty cannot be based on the notion of final, ultimate authority, or on a single, founding norm. In the EU, the overarching entity is equipped with a constitutional authority, but the acceptance of its authority is, at least in principle, 'an autonomous voluntary act, endlessly renewed on each occasion, of subordination, in the discrete areas governed by Europe to a norm which is the aggregate expression of other wills, other political identities, other political communities' (Weiler 2001a: 53). The supranational level is intended to fulfil a specified set of tasks that the lower-level entities confer on it. Further, there are provisions to ensure that the authority conferred, and the resources granted, are properly put to those tasks.

Deep diversity does not require a full-fledged representative democratic system based on majority rule. That could amount to a nation-state. Deep diversity could instead be based on *audit democracy*,[6] which is based on the principle of accountability, and supplemented with representation. The core concern is to maintain the conditions for voluntary acceptance of the structure in place. Since the structure affects both states and citizens directly, the higher-level institutions will have to have institutions that can accommodate both sets of concerns. All higher-level institutions, courts, legislative, executive and administrative bodies would have to account for how they have expended with the powers and prerogatives granted to them to the fulfilment of certain goals defined in the Constitutional Treaty (this is akin to output legitimacy). This is one element of accountability – in relation to both goals/purposes and institutional/constitutional provisions. It does not provide adequate assurance against growth in functions through issue-linkages and spill-over. Neither does it offer an adequate *democratic* sanctioning of the system in place, not in the sense of citizens as the authors of the laws but as the stewards of the treaty goals and accountability criteria.[7] Audit democracy presupposes popularly elected bodies at both levels that are endowed with specific responsibilities for the monitoring and stock-taking of the Union's principles, institutional arrangements and activities and for the ensuring that these resonate with popular needs. The present-day EU is imbued with the logic of audit democracy but it also has traits – albeit weaker – of representative democracy.

The last criterion of deep diversity is that of Member State (and other relevant diversities) veto over constitutional change. To protect nationally based difference, the Constitutional Treaty is a seamless web in that no part is open to majority decisions. This provision is necessary to ensure that the states are in legal and symbolic terms the Masters of the Treaties. The present system of treaty change/amendment in the EU complies with these requirements. In sum, the present EU system can to a large extent be labelled a Union of deep diversity.

Constitutional patriotism

Habermas has written extensively on constitutional patriotism. In his chapter in this book, he outlines the institutional conditions for a European federation. His prescriptions are clearly consonant with the core components of constitutional patriotism, as set out here. In the chapter Habermas uses the term 'federation of nation-states'. This term might carry with it the connotation of multiple *demoi*. The version of constitutional patriotism that I present here is also federal but more explicitly *post-national*, and based on the notion of one constitutional *demos*.[8]

Constitutional patriotism elicits a *post-national* and rights-based type of allegiance, a sense of allegiance that is derived not from pre-political values and attachments steeped in a culture, tradition or a way of life, but from a set of principles and values that are universal in their orientation, albeit contextualized. Constitutional patriotism is a mode of allegiance; it elicits support and emotional attachment, because the universalistic principles are *embedded in a particular context*. People's attachments are derived from the manner in which a set of universal principles are interpreted and entrenched within a particular institutional setting. The principles are fused with a set of values that are steeped in a particular geographical setting, and embedded within a particular set of traditions. The universal principles help entrench a set of procedures that, when made to operate within a particular context, render this self-reflective, and, hence, responsive to change. Constitutional patriotism thus provides one set of answers or recommendations for how to reconcile universal values with context-specific ones, whilst also retaining sensitivity to difference and diversity.

There are four central components to how we might think that constitutional patriotism, as based on universal rights steeped within a particular legal and communicative community, can be fostered through the work and results of the Convention. The first relates to the putative status of the draft constitution, the second to rights, the third to institutional conditions, and the fourth to provisions for constitutional change/amendment.

On the first, the status of the constitution, in the European setting, an unambiguous expression of constitutional patriotism is found in the explicit pronouncement of a *European constitution*, and not a European constitutional treaty, and one that is both fully recognized and acknowledged as 'higher' law. Constitutional patriotism presupposes a democratic constitution. A necessary aspect of this is an explicit popular endorsement.

With regard to the second, rights, constitutional patriotism presupposes a firm commitment to individual autonomy. This applies to both public *and* private autonomy – as both are required for democracy, that is, political participatory rights as well as private protective rights. The two sets of autonomy are mutually dependent on each other and presuppose each other (Habermas 1994, 1996). Those who are the addressees of the law, to be truly autonomous, and to act as the authors of the law, also need to participate in the actual process of law-making.

Social rights are also important. They help ensure autonomy and also foster a deeper sense of solidarity. Certain cultural rights are also required, as part of a commitment to, and provisions for, the respect for diversity, albeit in conditional rather than absolute form. The underlying principle is the notion of 'the reciprocal recognition of different cultural forms of life' (Habermas 1998: 118–19). In both substantive and symbolic terms, the framers' inclusion of a strong and comprehensive commitment to rights in the constitution serves to direct subsequent constitutional interpreters to ensure that these provisions are heeded and also that the other provisions in the constitution are made to cohere with this strong commitment to rights. The most explicit way of doing so is to entrench a Charter or a Bill of Rights in the constitution, that is, one that contains the full range of rights. That lends high visibility and unambiguous status to rights as intrinsic parts of 'higher' law. Not only must the spirit of constitutional patriotism permeate the result of the process of constitution-making, the method of forging the constitution also has to be transparent, deliberative and widely representative. If not, citizens would have little or no assurance that their rights would be protected in the resultant text.

Third, constitutional patriotism presupposes that the constitution contain a set of institutional prescriptions that ensure that citizens can see themselves as the ultimate authors of the law. In other words, representative bodies are required that can transform popular deliberations in the public sphere into binding decisions in a manner consistent with the spirit of these deliberations. This also relates to the division of competences, congruence and accountability. In complex, federal-type, entities the vertical and horizontal division of competences must be so construed as to ensure that the basic criteria of congruence and accountability are maintained. This should be achieved not through excessive centralization but through a vertical division that is consistent with the location of problems and the means to their solution.

Fourth, and in an extension of the above, constitutional patriotism presupposes that the constitution is sanctioned through direct popular consultation. This entails a commitment to some majoritarian formula. No single Member State can have veto power over constitutional change. Otherwise the ensuing constitution would lack this critical component of popular sovereignty, and citizens would not in any meaningful way conceive of themselves as the authors of the law.

The Convention's work and results: an assessment[9]

Was the Convention intended to forge a European constitution or to consolidate the structure in place? The Laeken Declaration (December 2001), which contained the decision to set up a Convention and also spelled out its mandate and composition, did not designate it as a Constitutional Convention. It was presented as a *preparatory body* with the task of forging one – or several – proposals for the forthcoming Intergovernmental Conference (IGC), which was the body formally in charge of treaty change (according to Art. 48 TEU).

The democratic credentials of this idea were weak. The Convention idea was not carried forward by a strong popular movement or a pan-European movement, which is characteristic of constitutional moments. Neither was there a process of obtaining a popular mandate for a European constitution through election or other direct consultation. The push for a Convention came from the European Parliament and national parliamentarians. There was no explicit mandate for the Convention to forge a European constitution.

This could be construed as an effort merely to consolidate the structure in place. However, the mandate did instruct it to consider the constitutional question. The Convention, as expressed by its President in his inaugural speech, took upon itself to produce a constitutional proposal and succeeded in producing a complete constitutional draft within the eventual deadline set by the European Council. This draft was accepted by the European Council meeting in Thessaloniki on 19–20 June 2003 as the basis for its work.

The draft is officially labelled the Draft Treaty Establishing a Constitution for Europe. This term is suggestive of the result as formally a treaty, hence lending support to the first criterion of deep diversity and not to the first criterion of constitutional patriotism. But the term also seems to suggest that it might serve as a launching-pad for a subsequent constitution. The following assessment will also touch on the merits of such an assertion.[10]

As is revealed in several of the contributions to this book (e.g. Closa, Chapter 11; Magnette, Chapter 12), the process of preparing the draft (the Convention process) was so different as to raise the expectation that the existing Constitutional Treaty could be turned into a constitution proper.

A constitution of states or of citizens?

The present structure of the EU has strong traits of deep diversity. This is also reflected in the ambiguous coupling of the notion of the Member States as the Masters of the Treaties, with the principles of European law supremacy and direct effect. A move from the present situation to one consistent with constitutional patriotism would require a constitution that is – and is portrayed as – explicitly derived from its citizens.

Article I-1 states that, '[r]eflecting the will of the citizens and States of Europe to build a common future, this Constitution establishes the European Union, on which the Member States confer competences to attain objectives they have in common' (CONV 850/03: 5). This statement can be construed as equipping the Union with a dual basis of legitimacy: a Union of citizens and of states (European Parliament 2003). The constitution emanates from both, but the draft retains the notion of attributed competence. The citizens thus have to convey their will to the Union through the power of conferral that rests with the Member States. On its part, the Union must ensure that it has the necessary competence before it can seek to realize the citizens' will. The explicit founding of the Union on the dual principle of legitimation is a clear step in the direction of constitutional patriotism, though the retention of the Member States in a privileged position does indicate that much of the old structure of state-privileged deep diversity may be retained. It is noteworthy, however, that there was movement on this question during the Convention's work. In the first draft of the relevant provisions (CONV 528/03), the reference was to 'the will of the peoples and the States of Europe', a statement that is far closer to the spirit of deep diversity. This change from peoples to citizens is important in symbolic terms. It highlights Europe as a collection of individuals over that of peoples' communities. It further privileges states over peoples, and awards a greater role to states to ensure deep diversity. The net effect might be to highlight that form of diversity that we associate with state-based national identity.

A democratic Union, a Christian Union or a European Union of nations?

Does this apparent privileging of the Member States signal that the Union is based on several and different collective conceptions of its cultural, national, linguistic and ethnic make-up? Is there no overarching agreement on what the EU is for (both of which are critical components of deep diversity)?

The values (as expressed in Art. I-2) that the Union is founded on are basically the same universal values as were presented at Amsterdam, and reiterated on numerous occasions, namely human dignity, liberty, democracy, the rule of law and respect for human rights. In addition, equality was added in the final draft, after great pressure by numerous members of the Convention. This article further notes that '[t]hese values are common to the Member States in a society of pluralism, tolerance, justice, solidarity and non-discrimination' (CONV 850/03: 5). Central to the Union's objectives is to 'promote peace, its values and the well-being of its peoples' (I-3). The values referred to in Part I, Title I, and that spell out the definition and objectives of the Union, are universal in their orientation. There is no reference to an explicit *European* value basis. Neither does the preamble make such a reference, although it does emphasize the

> cultural, religious and humanist inheritance of Europe, the values of which, still present in its heritage, have embedded within the life of society the central role of the human person and his or her inviolable and inalienable rights, and respect for law.
>
> (CONV 850/03: 3)

These values are highly consonant with the spirit of constitutional patriotism. How consonant they will be depends on how they become embedded in institutional and cultural form, as constitutional patriotism refers both to universal values and to their contextualization.

In the Convention there were strong efforts to carve out a clearer and more restrictive set of values. Some, including Giscard, were concerned with how the values would inform the more specific criteria for membership and the use of internal sanctions (CONV 601/03: 4). Others were concerned with giving the constitutional edifice a much clearer ethical – and even religious – foundation. Some also wanted to include religious criteria in the membership requirements. A number of Convention members, strongly supported by the Pope, and much of the European People's Party, sought to have a reference inserted to Europe's religious foundation – through a reference to God modelled on the Polish Constitution, or to Christianity, or to Europe's Judaeo-Christian roots, or to Graeco-Roman roots.[11] The debates on the value basis in the Convention proceeded along at least four dimensions: those that sought to base the Union on a set of universal and secular values; those that sought a mention of religion but without confining it to a specific religion; those that sought to highlight the role of Christianity; and those that sought to highlight national (and regional) identity. The two former groups could be seen as exponents of some variant of constitutional patriotism. The third group could be seen as championing either a European community spirit or that of deep diversity – due to the sheer multitude of different confessional orientations in Europe. The fourth group could be seen as championing a Union of deep diversity. The resultant draft basically retains the universal value orientation that has marked the EU, albeit grafted onto a set of provisions that speak to the need for the Union to 'respect its rich cultural and linguistic diversity' (I-3.3).

That the Union has a strong nation-state presence, and that its retention is valuable, was made clear in Article 1–5, which stated that: 'The Union shall respect the national identities of its Member States […] '. This provision is retained from the TEU. In the Convention's deliberations, opinions had differed on this. Federalists wanted this struck (Duff and four other members). Many Convention members sought reference to national identities as reflective of the states' institutional and constitutional structures (57 members and observers), including regional and local levels, whereas others stressed the need to link national identity with cultural heritage and the cultural and linguistic diversity of Europe. It is the latter position that is the closest to deep diversity. A clear majority in the Convention stressed the institutional over the cultural emphasis, and this was also the result, as is spelled out in Article I-5; hence the deep diversity position was not pursued to the full. This raises the interesting scenario of propounding constitutional patriotism at the national level, whilst propounding national diversity at the European level. But it could also be argued that the result might serve as a restriction on the pursuit of diversity and serve as a *de facto* further vehicle of ensuring the inclusiveness necessary to sustain European cooperation.

Another indication of the Convention's conception of the Union's value basis can be inferred from the regulations regarding admission of new members and the question of boundaries. The Convention members differed in terms of values versus principles, and whether *European* location should be privileged over basic principles, as expressed in the constitution. Article I-1 stated that: 'The Union shall be open to all European states which respect its values and are committed to promoting them together.' The referral to European states serves as a clear restriction, whereas the values otherwise referred to are universal. This provision is an explication of Union practice, a practice where, over time, the Union has strengthened the onus on basic rights, the rule of law and democracy (Sjursen and Smith 2001).

To sum up, in value terms the Convention, in the draft, ended up appealing to the same complex of universality and difference as is found in the most recent treaties. The question is whether the draft also contained the same particular mixture of such, how these would be embedded in institutional shape, and which institutions would carry or sustain them. One critical issue here is whether the Convention, in its work and in the draft, brought the EU closer to an agreement of the type of entity it was and what it would be for.

In the Convention there appeared to be consensus that the present-day EU is not a state, but no consensus on precisely what type of entity it is. An earlier formulation (CONV 528/03) included the following reference: 'shall administer certain common competences on a federal basis', which sparked a lot of debate and proposals. Thirty-four members of the Convention wanted to have the reference to 'federal basis' struck, but their reasons differed, in line with their different conceptions of the EU. Some wanted it struck because it conflicted with their largely intergovernmental notion of a Union derived from the Member States. The majority of the UK and Scandinavian contingent associated the word 'federal' with centralization and a European state. Others wanted it struck because they saw it as linking the EU too closely to the notion of state and hence downplaying its unique character as polity. Even those propagating its role did not agree on the resultant entity. The upshot was that the 'federal' reference was struck, and replaced with 'the Community way'. This latter term is open-ended: it could be seen to depict an entity *sui generis*, but it does not foreclose the development of a full-fledged European state. Somewhat ironically, 'federal' does not necessarily designate 'state' (cf. Elazar 1987: 230). The Convention left it to others to develop further the vocabulary to depict the entity.

In sum, the Convention experience revealed the continued presence of widely different conceptions of Europe and what the EU should be for. At the same time it is important to underline that the Convention, in its debates, its documents and its proposals, amplified the *political* character of the Union. If its draft is accepted, people will be hard put to label it as merely an economic Union.

Chartered Citizenship – European or differentiated?

The Convention, by agreeing to make the Charter of Fundamental Rights in the EU legally binding,[12] has greatly raised the symbolic role and visibility of individual rights. Community law has long taken individual rights into account, but the Charter signals that they are an intrinsic part of the EU constitutional edifice. The very notion of a Charter of Rights is laden with constitutional symbolism. A resolve on the part of the EU to make a Charter could be seen as an important stepping stone towards a proper European constitution, or it could simply serve to consolidate the structure in place, provided the Charter is confined in the ways prescribed by deep diversity.[13]

The underlying philosophical orientation of the Charter is that of constitutional patriotism (Fossum 2003b). The values listed in the preamble of the Charter (which was retained in the draft, hence leaving the draft with two preambles, one for the whole constitution and one for the Charter) refer to a conception of the EU as based on a set of universal principles. Its commitment is to the principles and values of democracy and the rule of law, and not to a set of specific and uniquely European values.

The Charter is neither different from nor more constrained in its scope of rights than conventional state-based Charters or Bills of Rights. It is also more updated. Further, the strong onus on solidarity and social rights in the Charter could – if pursued to the full – provide the EU with a more explicit ethical foundation.

Having said that, there are aspects of its drafting and its perceived role in the EU that affect its salience as a vehicle for propounding constitutional patriotism. The Convention that drafted the Charter wrote it *as if* it were to be binding. Its provisions draw heavily from existing EU law. This is significant in the sense that the Convention decided not to reopen the contents of the Charter. The Working Group in the Convention specifically devoted to the Charter dealt with how it could be incorporated, not with its substantive contents. The Charter, including its preamble, was directly included in Part II of the draft constitution. This means that the weak provisions on citizens' public autonomy[14] in the Charter were carried into the draft constitution. The Charter therefore does not abrogate the aspect of differentiated citizenship that inheres from the fact that access to EU citizenship is conditional on national citizenship and subject to national rules of incorporation, but it might narrow it considerably. Another possible constraint relates to the restrictive rules of legal standing for direct actions, and the European Court of Justice's enormous workload, which might reduce the applicability of the Charter (Craig 2003: 5). Further, the horizontal clauses (and to some extent the onus on interpreting it in line with the explanations provided by the Charter Convention) clearly restrict its scope of application. The setting in which the Charter is to be included is one highly protective of nationally based identities and values.

To sum up, the Charter is imbued with the spirit of constitutional patriotism, but its ability to foster such will likely be hampered by several important restrictions, some of which were explicitly injected by those seeking to retain a Union of deep nationally based diversity.

Representative or audit democracy?

The present Constitutional Treaty structure of the EU is more akin to the audit democracy of deep diversity than to the representative democracy associated with constitutional patriotism (although the trend over time has been towards representative democracy). Audit democracy highlights accountability over representation, and is consistent with the privileging of nationally based democracy, characteristic of a constitutional treaty. Such accountability is ensured among other things through conferral of authority onto the Union by the Member States, as set out in the Treaties; through the fixed allotment of money and careful monitoring of its use; and through the democratic auditing role played by bodies such as the European Parliament – probably more of a democratic auditor than a full-fledged representative assembly. However, even now because of its decision-making powers, the European Parliament has acquired a role beyond that envisaged in a Constitutional Treaty marked by deep diversity.

Does the draft constitution contain such provisions as to move the EU from this extended auditing democratic role to a full-fledged representative democracy role, in line with the requirements of a democratic constitution? Article I-45 states: 'The working of the Union shall be founded on the principle of representative democracy.' Article I-46 spells out the principle of participatory democracy. Article I-44 ('The Principle of Democratic Equality') states: 'In all its activities, the Union shall observe the principle of the equality of citizens. All shall receive equal attention from the Union's Institutions.' The question is whether these provisions, their specific definitions and the relevant institutional provisions to ensure their operation can be construed so as to think of the EU as a system of self-legislating citizens. Another relevant question is whether the EU will be endowed with the means (fiscal and other) that this notion presupposes.

The definitions provided in Part I, Title VI on 'The Democratic Life of the Union' (Articles I-45–51) make clear that the conception of representative and participatory democracy is more akin to the accountability requirements of audit democracy than to the participatory requirements of representative democracy.[15] For instance, Article I-45.3 states: 'Every citizen shall have the right to participate in the democratic life of the Union. Decisions shall be taken as openly as possible and as closely as possible to the citizen.' The mode of participation referred to (Article I-46) is 'opportunity to make known and publicly exchange their views', engage in 'an open, transparent and regular dialogue', be involved in consultations carried out by the Commission, and seek a Commission initiative through a citizens' initiative. These definitions reveal a clear willingness to involve citizens, but they are not unambiguously reflective of the notion of citizens as self-legislative. The citizens have a stake in the institutions but the institutions are not unambiguously framed as 'theirs'. This corresponds to the weak notion of public autonomy in the Charter, as noted above.

On the other hand, the provisions in Title VI, and in particular I-45, are sufficiently strongly framed so as not to *exclude* citizens from seeing themselves as the ultimate authors of the law. The crux of the matter is the nature of the institutional provisions, and in particular the role of representative bodies such as the European Parliament and national parliaments within the larger institutional system of the EU.

Several of the institutional proposals will – if adopted – increase the democratic quality of the EU. The resolve to institute co-decision as the main legislative procedure (Art. I-33, with reference to Art. III-302), coupled with a greatly increased use of qualified majority voting in the Council (cf. Art. I-24) and the abolition of the pillar system (albeit far from completely in practice), will help greatly amplify the role of the European Parliament in the EU institutional system. These reforms will go quite far in establishing the Parliament as a legislative chamber on a par with the Council. An improved clarification of the distinction between legislative and executive acts has the 'implication that any executive act requires a legislative (or constitutional) mandate. This means that, except for constitutionally provided exceptions, the European Parliament acting as a full legislator enjoys a veto-power over any delegation of executive powers in the Union' (Crum 2003: 8). Heightened transparency requirements (Arts I-49, III-304, 305) help improve individual and inter-institutional lines of accountability.

The proposal moves the EU closer to a parliamentary model in that the role of the European Parliament is strengthened but this is not an unambiguous strengthening. For one, although the Commission shall be responsible to the Parliament (Art. I-25.5, with reference to Art. III-243), the Commission does not emanate from Parliament, as it would do in a full-fledged parliamentary system. The European Council proposes a candidate for President of the Commission to the Parliament, who is adopted or rejected by the Parliament. As John Pinder notes, however:

> the European Council is required to take into account the results of the European Elections and to decide on this candidate 'after appropriate consultations'; and if the candidate is not approved by a majority of the Parliament's members, the European Council must follow the same procedures before proposing a new candidate. Thus the Parliament should be able to convert the procedure into one of virtual co-decision with the European Council, which should be optimal, given the need for a Commission that is acceptable to the states as well as to the citizens' representatives; and the citizens will be able to see that their votes in the European Elections help to determine the character of the executive as well as of the legislature.
>
> (Pinder 2003: 2)

The Union Minister for Foreign Affairs is appointed by the European Council (with the agreement of the President of the Commission), and can be replaced by the same. The Minister is only accountable to the European Parliament when handling those aspects of the Union's external relations that he/she handles within the Commission (cf. Art. I-27.3). The Council President is elected by the Council and neither the President nor the Council is accountable to the Parliament. The Council is both an executive and a legislative body, with the specific division of tasks still unclear. The specific delineation of tasks and functions between the Commission and the Council as executive is also not entirely clear. The institutional system that is devised is one of complex and quite ambiguous lines of accountability.

The draft also amplifies the role and salience of national parliaments in that they are able to give inputs into European policy-making.[16] Such amplification could serve as an institutional guarantor for deep diversity, in that it could help protect democracy at the national level, as well as providing an additional check on the system that those issues deemed critical for the maintenance of nationally based identities were retained at the national level. On national democracy, increased use of qualified majority voting in the Council could, however, reduce nationally based lines of accountability (Crum 2003), although this could be somewhat modified by heightened transparency requirements. On national identity, the early warning system could serve such a purpose, but it is not clear from the provisions how important this concern will be.

The net upshot of the Convention's proposal is to strengthen the European-level democratic institutions and to involve national ones more directly in the process. The proposal clearly moves the EU institutions from an onus on audit democracy to one on representative democracy, but far from all the way. These institutions still do not comply with the requirements of a democratic constitution. The proposals are also not internally consistent so as to pull the EU in one coherent direction. They do not in an unambiguous way support the notion that the Union derives its legitimacy from its citizens. But they weaken the notion that the Member States are the Masters of the Treaties.

Institutional coherence versus institutional diversity?

Deep diversity is wholly compatible with the logic of a pillar structure (such as that set down in the Maastricht Treaty): to protect or shield certain areas deemed vital for the protection of national identity from the gravitational force of integration. An obvious question in this connection is whether the *present* pillar structure is consistent with deep diversity. The short-hand answer is that the pillar structure matters to the preservation of deep diversity, but many of the areas important to the preservation of national and other identities are not in pillars II and III. In the present system, some of the important factors for the protection of national (and other forms of relevant) identity are the division of competences, the notion that the Union needs a basis in the Treaties to act, unanimity as voting procedure, national implementation, economic dependence on the Member States, and that the Member States – acting unanimously – are in charge of treaty change. These serve, in institutional terms, to help sustain an important imprint of deep diversity on the Union.

A democratic constitution consistent with constitutional patriotism presupposes a coherent institutional structure. In other words, for the Convention to have moved the EU in the direction of constitutional patriotism, it would have to abolish many of the traits listed above and replace these with the institutional prescriptions for constitutional patriotism. Was this done?

The Convention decided to equip the EU with *legal personality* (cf. I-6: 7). The EEC earlier had personality. But this change paves the way for a merging of the Treaties and it gives greater coherence to the Union's constitutional architecture (cf. CONV 305/02: 4). This does entail the abolition of the pillar structure (although, as will be seen below, some of this is retained through other provisions).

Other institutional provisions point in the same direction of coherence-inducing simplification. The endorsement of co-decision (symbolically elevated to 'the ordinary legislative procedure') and qualified majority voting in the Council, as general principles, could be seen as further steps of de-pillarization. The general embrace of these two principles should strengthen the Community method and lend greater coherence to the institutional system of the EU. The draft introduces a simpler set of requirements for its operation (these will not be operational until 2009, however). The question is whether these changes will amount to more than ensuring a functioning institutional system in an EU of 25+, as qualified majoity voting is often depicted as necessary to prevent dead-lock in an enlarged EU.

What aspects of the diversity of Europe – even in a Europe of 25 – will be retained with these decision-making procedures in place? Note first that the Convention did not adopt qulaified majority voting or co-decision across the board.[17] Unanimity was retained in the areas of foreign and defence policy, tax policy, and in most aspects of social policy. The unanimity requirement on tax effec-tively keeps the present system, where the Union is at the mercy of the Member States with regard to its funding. Other institutional mechanisms also entrench a continued strong Member State dominance within the foreign policy and defence areas.

On the division of competences, the draft retains the notion of Union competences as 'governed by the principle of conferral' (Art. I-9: 9). This means that

> the Union shall act within the limits of the competences conferred upon it by the Member States in the Constitution to attain the objectives set out in the Constitution. Competences not conferred upon the Union in the Constitution remain with the Member States.

As noted, this principle is one means for the Member States to protect their uniqueness.

In the draft, Union exclusive competences are identified and singled out (mone-tary policy, common commercial policy, customs union and conservation of marine biological resources, cf. Art. I-12). This list is very short, and does not include the four freedoms, which are placed in the next category: shared competence. The list of shared competences is very long,[18] and Craig (2003: 7) notes that this is now the default position between exclusive competence and its supporting and coordinating role (in such areas as education and culture [Art. I-16]).

This way of dividing competences leaves large scope for the interweaving of levels through the very large number of – and scope for – issue areas within the shared competence category; hence raising questions as to the status of the prin-ciple of conferral. Although this certainly raises the spectre of further unleashing the teleology inbuilt in the common market and/or provides the Union with means of further aggregating powers, the overall picture is more complex. The levels are not only tightly interwoven; the manner in which they are woven together varies considerably from one issue to the next. These are spelled out in the detailed provisions in Part III (Craig 2003: 7).

The flexibility clause (Art. I-17) offers the possibility of Union action in areas listed in Part III, where the Union does not have powers. The provision can enable the Union to obtain such, subject to unanimous Council approval and European Parliamentary consent. The provisions on enhanced cooperation (I-43 and III-322–9) permit at least a third of the Member States to avail themselves of the Union institutions to pursue closer cooperation in specified fields. The conditions for such are spelled out and are to serve as a last resort, rather than as a procedure that can be easily triggered.

The draft also contains a provision that permits voluntary withdrawal from the Union (I-59). It is left to the applying state itself to determine how such an initiative comes about. The Union does not, for instance, impose a popular consultation requirement. The Union bodies decide in favour of or against such a proposal. This threshold is lower than, for instance, in Canada, the only other entity with provisions for voluntary withdrawal. Voluntary withdrawal is clearly compatible with the basic tenets of deep diversity.

In sum, the draft does propose a more coherent institutional structure for the EU than is the case at present. The abolition of the pillars and the steps towards harmonization of decision rules are important to that end. At the same time, the significant competence overlap and the large scope for Union action within a very wide range of policy fields raises questions as to the salience of the principle of conferral of powers. Its operation is clearly dependent on the complex system of detailed rules in Part III. Of considerable importance, then, is whether these provisions can easily be changed, or whether they are quite resilient to change.

Constitutional amendment or treaty change?

The system in place is based on the deep diversity provision of national veto. Midway through in the Convention's work, Convention Vice-President Giuliano Amato noted:

> If the current procedures for amending Union treaties are retained, the projected constitution would be such only in name. On the other hand, should the adopted amendment procedure require that future amendments be decided at the level of the European Parliament and be enforced only if subsequently approved by four-fifths of the national parliaments, the treaty would be constitutional in substance.
>
> (Amato 2003: 362; see also Weiler 2002)

The proposed mechanism is spelled out in Article IV-7, 'Procedure for Revising the Treaty Establishing the Constitution' (CONV 850/03). This mechanism is marked by the following traits. First, it embodies the key traits of what may now be termed the Laeken model (cf. Fossum and Menéndez 2003). Second, it is a procedure for the whole Constitutional Treaty, that is, there is no formal differentiation between the different parts of the constitution, as was considered during the Convention debate. Third, it is a very elaborate procedure in that it greatly formalizes the process. Fourth, the European Parliament is more directly included in this model than in the IGC model, that is, the pre-Laeken model. The Parliament may submit a proposal to the Council. This means that the procedure provides institutional space for a popular movement organized around the Parliament to ask for a constitutional change. But there is no real or strong provision for such a popular movement to come about, as the procedure still largely privileges the institutions, and the *executive* component of these. Fifth, the model opens up the possibility for the reconvening of a Convention, but this is *not* a mandatory requirement.

The mechanism has what may be labelled as several thresholds. The first threshold is the power of initial initiative, which includes the European Parliament. The present system in place does not. The draft also states that national parliaments shall be notified: that is, if they want to take an initiative, they must still submit this to their government or to the EU institutions. If they do, they are faced with a choice as to whether a Convention should be set up. Here the requirement is a simple majority in the European Council, after a round of consultation among the three EU institutions. The decision on whether to use the Convention option is based on a substantive assessment of the 'extent of the proposed amendments'. The next step is the Convention's assessment of proposals and ability to forge a consensus on these. The second threshold is determination by common accord of the conference of representatives of the governments of the Member States. The third threshold is ratification – the requirement is unanimity, and each state decides according to its constitutional requirements. There is no uniform procedure for ratification. Subsection 4 provides a set of guidelines to be followed should all governments not have ratified the amendments. The failure of a state to ratify will after two years be referred to the European Council, but there is no explicit procedure for how the Council is to handle this. This is an important new provision and its specific contents and operation will likely be the subject of considerable debate.

The Convention vehicle is *not* a mandatory part of constitutional change. Whether this raises or lowers the threshold for subsequent constitutional change is less certain. The final version of the text (CONV 850/03), after significant pressure from the European Parliament and national parliamentarians, included an insert to the effect that a decision not to establish a Convention had to be approved by the Parliament.

The wording used to initiate the Convention procedure differs from one amendment to the next. The Convention's draft (CONV 850/03) uses 'extent of the proposed amendments', whereas an earlier version (CONV 728/03) uses 'should this not be justified by the tenor of the proposed amendments'. The explanatory note uses 'the scale of the amendments'. These are quite different justifications. When the Convention option is *not* used, the draft states that the

European Council must spell out the terms of reference for the conference of representatives of the governments of the Member States (CONV 850/03).

The draft contains an elaborate procedure, which essentially provides each Member State with the power of veto, but there are some important changes from the present system. The draft does include the European Parliament more directly and also many of the different stages – this is an important difference from the current arrangement. This means that there is much more scope for popular mobilization through an open initial part of the process – the initiative and proposal stages – whereas the decision-making and ratification stages are more closed and narrowed through national vetoes.

The elaborate procedure might also make the system rigid and resilient to change. However, it is important to recall that the draft does contain scope for change without recourse to this procedure. Consider the flexibility clause (I-17), the provisions on enhanced cooperation, and the so-called *passerelle* in Article I-24.4. This clause permits the European Council, acting unanimously, to take issue areas under special legislative procedures and subject them to the Community method.

Conclusion

The Convention's mandate was to develop proposal(s) for the IGC to consider, and not to serve as a constitutional convention. However, the mandate did not exclude a broader – and constitutional – role in that it asked the Convention to discuss the question of a European constitution, and the Convention did seize the opportunity. Commentators and participants have been struck with the progress that the Convention has been able to make. It has moved ahead on a number of issues, where the IGCs had previously failed to reach agreement, albeit the end result of this process of course does hinge on the outcome of the IGC.

At the outset, two constitutional visions for the EU were presented. The use of two visions served several purposes, not the least to avoid the fallacy of confusing 'the juridical presupposition of a constitutional *demos* with political and social reality. In many instances, constitutional doctrine presupposes the existence of that which it creates [...]' (Weiler 2001b: 56). The present-day EU is said to actually favour a multiple *demoi* constitutional doctrine. But there is also a partial commitment to an alternative doctrine that propounds the need to found the EU on constitutional patriotism.

These doctrines were assessed in relation to the existing structure of the EU and the Convention's work and results. It was found that the Convention has taken a number of decisions that appear to weaken the multiple constitutional *demoi* doctrine and that – if adopted – seem to move the EU closer to one based on constitutional patriotism. In this context, the symbolic value of the explicit pronouncement that the EU is based on the citizens and the states of Europe should not be ignored. Having said that, the wording that runs through the text and that appeared from the Convention's debates is far from an explicit endorsement of constitutional patriotism.

The result does reflect an effort to take a further step in the process of forging a viable political entity in Europe, and to do more than merely simplify and consolidate the structure in place. The Convention's very use of the terminology associated with constitution could be potentially significant as a rallying call to bring institutional reality in line with constitutional aspirations. But there is more than one set of aspirations. Further, it is less clear that the treaty has laid the institutional groundwork so as to *establish* a subsequent constitution, even if fully adopted. Aspects that might support such a further process are, first, the Charter, which might empower citizens to think of themselves as Europeans and inspire them to take actions that breach the distance between the new treaty and a full-fledged constitution. Second, such a process could be reinforced through the strengthened role of the European Parliament – and national parliaments – and perhaps also the abolition of the pillar structure, co-decision and qualified majority voting. On the other hand is the cumbersome and still largely intergovernmental revision procedure, which *might* act as a significant brake on any such attempt. Might is rightly emphasized here because of the more prominent presence of the European Parliament – coupled with the option of a Convention. Both could inject a strong popular input into subsequent amendment processes. How this procedure will work in the future will become clearer once the present process has come to an end.

There is also a real risk that the new structure in a Union of 25 might contain an overly high threshold for subsequent change. This risk is twofold: over-reliance on constitutional terminology and symbolism to create something that does not have the proper preconditions; and the setting up of an apparatus and procedures bent on, and almost premised on, the ongoing approach to constitution-making that is characteristic of the EU but now having to operate within a setting of overly high thresholds.

Nevertheless, perhaps it could be argued that the main contribution of the draft and the Convention's work is to open up and leave open the question as to whether Europe should be based on multiple constitutional *demoi* or one constitutional *demos*. The Convention has not resolved the constitutional question. The hopefuls may say that it has given this discussion a major boost and also furnished future constitution-makers with better tools to push the process further. The doubters may say that the Convention abrogated its responsibility to act as a true constitution-maker and instead left the question in the hands of citizens, but without giving them the proper tools. What the citizens themselves and their representatives will make out of this remains to be seen.

Notes

The author is grateful for constructive comments and suggestions to an earlier draft from Ben Crum, Paul Magnette and Justus Schönlau.

1 For applications to the EU see Fossum 2003b, 2003c. This overlaps with but is not the same as Weiler's constitutional tolerance.
2 For a small sample of assessments of the EU's democratic quality and the nature of the gap, see Beetham and Lord 1998; Weale and Nentwich 1998; Scharpf 1999; Weiler 1999c; Eriksen and Fossum 2000; Schmitter 2000.

3 This is a standard communitarian argument.
4 Other terms to capture its complex nature are *condominio*, *consortio* (cf. Schmitter 1996), a multi-level polity (Marks *et al.* 1996), mixed commonwealth (Bellamy and Castiglione 1997), post-national entity (Curtin 1997; Habermas 1998, 2000), *objet politique nonidentifié* (Schmitter 2000), cooperative confederation (Bulmer 1996) and quasi-federal entity (Sbragia 1992).
5 The German Constitutional Court's ruling, in the famous Maastricht case, was premised on the notion that there is no European *demos*. See Weiler 1995. European Convention, Contribution by Mr. Jens-Peter Bonde, 'The Convention about the Future of Europe', CONV 277/02: 45.
6 For a definition of this term explicitly applied to the European Parliament, see Eriksen and Fossum 2002. The definition used here is developed further and in relation to the requirements of deep diversity, as I try to reconstruct it here.
7 Weiler lauds the EU for explicitly having rejected the full-fledged federal state option, yet criticizes it for its democratic inadequacies. The EU thus both presents democratic theory with a challenge as well as having to meet the democratic challenge properly (cf. Weiler 2001a: 54).
8 This also appears to be consistent with the tenet of other of Habermas's writings. See Habermas 1996, 1998, 2000. See also Eriksen and Weigård 2003.
9 This assessment is based on Convention documents, academic analyses, interviews with Convention members and others who followed the Convention process, and personal attendance at debates in the Convention and in the European Parliament.
10 Note that during the process of forging the draft, it has been referred to as both constitution and constitutional treaty. The first draft was termed a constitutional treaty (CONV 369/02) and set the stage for a constitutional treaty for Europe, not a full-fledged constitution. In the subsequent proposals for articles, the terms 'constitution' and 'constitutional treaty' were used interchangeably on the Convention website – there is no clear logic as to what term is used where.
11 There were also similar attempts in the Charter Convention and the German-language version of the Charter deviates from the rest with its reference to Europe's *religious* rather than *spiritual* heritage (cf. Schönlau 2003: 130).
12 See I-7: 'Fundamental Rights', which states: 'The Union shall recognize the rights, freedoms and principles set out in the Charter of Fundamental Rights which constitutes Part II of the Constitution' (CONV 850/03: 8).
13 For a small sample of assessments of the Charter see Feus 2000; Lenaerts and de Smijter 2001; Weiler 2001 and Chapter 4 in this book; Eriksen *et al.* 2003.
14 Some of the well over 30 constitutional proposals that have been submitted to the Convention contain citizenship provisions that could rectify this. See, for instance, MEP Jo Leinen's draft proposal (European Parliament 2002).
15 A total of 235 amendments were submitted to these proposed articles. An earlier version (CONV 650/03: 08) contained an even weaker set of formulations, but these were changed in response to strong pressure from Convention members. In a proposed amendment 19 members and alternates proposed to delete the entire title (proposed articles 33–7), as 'Title VI is an inadequate advertisement of the Union's true democratic underpinnings. It reads like an apology [...] it diminishes the visibility and impact of the true democratic bases of the Union's decision-making institutions.':
   (<http://European-convention.eu.int/Docs/Treaty/pdf/600/global600.pdf>)
16 See CONV 353/02 for the recommendations from the Working Group (WG IV) and an analysis of the protocol on national parliaments (CONV 611/03).
17 Maurer (2003) notes that qualified majority voting accounts for 175 and unanimity for 78 issue areas in the 27 June draft proposal (CONV 820/1/03REV and 848/03) (as compared to 137 for EU/EC in Nice). Co-decision applies to 82 issue-areas, as compared to 45 in the Nice Treaty.

18 The list includes: the internal market; the area of freedom, security and justice; agriculture and fisheries excluding conservation; transport and trans-European networks; energy; social policy; economic, social and territorial cohesion; the environment; consumer protection; and common safety concerns in public health matters (cf. Art. I-13.2). The Union also has competence to act in other areas, such as research, technological development and space (I-13.3), development cooperation and humanitarian aid (I-13.4).

Bibliography

Abromeit, H. (2002) 'Ein neuer Minimalismus', mimeo, Darmstadt.

Ackerman, B. (1991) *We the People: Foundations*, Cambridge, Mass.: Harvard University Press.

—— (1992) *The Future of Liberal Revolution*, New Haven: Yale University Press.

—— (1998) *We the People: Transformations*, Cambridge, Mass.: Harvard University Press.

Ackerman, B. and Alstott, A. (1999) *The Stakeholder Society*, New Haven and London: Yale University Press.

Ackerman, B. and Fishkin, J. (2004) *Deliberation Day*, New Haven and London: Yale University Press.

Alexy, R. (1993) *A Theory of Constitutional Rights*, Oxford: Oxford University Press.

—— (1996) 'Discourse Theory and Human Rights', *Ratio Juris*, Vol. 9, No. 3: 209–35.

—— (2002a) *An Argument from Injustice*, Oxford: Oxford University Press.

—— (2002b) *A Theory of Constitutional Rights*, Oxford: Oxford University Press.

Allan, T.R.S. (1993) *Law, Liberty and Justice: The Legal Foundations of British Constitutionalism*, Oxford: Clarendon Press.

Alston, P. and Weiler, J.H.H. (1999) 'An "Ever Closer Union" in Need of a Human Rights Policy: The European Union and Human Rights', in P. Alston, M.S. Bustelo and J. Heenan (eds) *The EU and Human Rights*, Oxford: Oxford University Press. Also available as Harvard Jean Monnet Working Paper 1/99 at: <http://www.law.harvard.edu/programs/JeanMonnet/>.

Alter, K.J. (1996) 'The European Court's Political Power', *West European Politics*, Vol. 19, No. 3: 458–87.

—— (1998) 'Who Are the "Masters of the Treaty"?: European Governance and the European Court of Justice', *International Organization*, 52: 121–47.

—— (2001) *Establishing the Supremacy of European Law: The Making of an International Rule of Law in Europe*, Oxford: Oxford University Press.

Alter, K.J. and Meunier-Aitsahalia, S. (1994) 'Judicial Politics in the European Community. European Integration and the Pathbreaking "Cassis de Dijon" Decision', *Comparative Political Studies*, Vol. 26, No. 4: 535–61.

Amato, G. (2003) 'The European Convention: First Achievements and Open Dilemmas', *International Journal of Constitutional Law*, Vol. 1, No. 2: 355–63.

Angelino, L. (2003) *Le forme dell'Europa*, Genoa: Il Melangolo.

Apel, K.O. (1998) *Auseinandersetzungen in Erprobung des transzendental-pragmatischen Ansatzes*, Frankfurt: Suhrkamp.

Arendt, H. (1963) *On Revolution*, New York: Viking Press.

—— (1974) *Über die Revolution*, Munich: Hanser.

—— (1986) *The Origins of Totalitarianism* (1951), New York: Meridian Books.

Arndt, A. (1963) 'Umwelt und Recht', *Neue Juristische Wochenschrift*: 24–6.

Asch, R.G. (1997) 'Das Common Law als Sprache und Norm der politischen Kommunikation in England', in H. Duchhardt and G. Melville (eds) *Im Spannungsfeld von Recht und Ritual*, Cologne: Böhlau.

Ashiagbor, D. (2002) 'Soft Harmonization: Labour Law, economic Theory and the European Employment Strategy', Ph.D. thesis, European University Institute, Florence.

Augustin, A. (2000) *Das Volk der Europäischen Union*, Berlin: Duncker und Humblot.

Austin, J. (1954) *The Province of Jurisprudence Determined*, ed. H.L.A. Hart, London: Weidenfeld & Nicolson.

Bach, M. (1999) *Die Bürokratisierung Europas. Verwaltungseliten, Experten und politische Legitimation in Europa*, Frankfurt: Campus Verlag.

Ball, T. and Hanson, T. (eds) (1989) *Political Innovation and Conceptual Change*, Cambridge: Cambridge University Press.

Baquero Cruz, J. (2002) *Between Competition and Free Movement*, Oxford: Hart.

Barbier, C. (2002) *La Convention européenne: Genèse et premiers débats*, Brussels: Courrier hebdomadaire du CRISP, 1776–1777.

Barendt, E. (1998) *An Introduction to Constitutional Law*, Oxford: Oxford University Press.

Beach, D. (2003) 'Towards a New Method of Constitutional Bargaining? The Role and Impact of EU Institutions in the IGC and the Convention Method Treaty Reform', *Federal Trust Papers*, <http://www.fedtrust.co.uk/uploads/constitution/13_03.pdf>.

Beard, C.A. (1913) *An Economic Interpretation of the Constitution of the United States*, New York: Macmillan.

Beetham, D. and Lord, C. (1998) *Legitimacy and the EU*, London: Longman.

Bellamy, R. and Castiglione, D. (1997) 'Building the Union: The Nature of Sovereignty in the Political Architecture of Europe', *Law and Philosophy*, 16: 421–45.

Bessette, J.M. (1994) *The Mild Voice of Reason*, Chicago: University of Chicago Press.

Bickel, A. (1962) *The Least Dangerous Branch*, New Haven: Yale University Press.

Bin, R. (2002) *Capire la costituzione*, Rome-Bari: Laterza.

Blichner, L. (2000) 'Interparliamentary Discourse and the Quest for Legitimacy', in E.O. Eriksen and J.E. Fossum (eds) *Democracy in the European Union – Integration through Deliberation?*, London: Routledge.

Böckenförde, E.-W. (1991) *Staat, Verfassung, Demokratie: Studien zur Verfassungstheorie und zum Verfassungsrecht*, Frankfurt: Suhrkamp.

—— (1997) *Welchen Weg geht Europa?*, Munich: Siemens-Stiftung.

Bogdandy, A. von (1999) *Supranationaler Föderalismus als Wirklichkeit und Idee einer neuen Herrschaftsform*, Baden-Baden: Nomos.

—— (2000a) *Gubernative Rechtsetzung*, Tübingen: Mohr.

—— (2000b) 'Das Leitbild der dualistischen Legitimation für die europäische Verfassungsentwicklung', *Kritische Vierteljahresschrift für Gesetzgebung und Rechtswissenschaft*, 83: 284–97.

—— (2001a) 'Beobachtungen zur Wissenschaft vom Europarecht. Strukturen, Debatten und Entwicklungsperspektiven der Grundlagenforschung zum Recht der Europäischen Union', *Der Staat*, 39: 3–43.

—— (2001b) 'Comunità di Diritti Fondamentali come meta dell'integrazione? I Diritti Fondamentali e la natura dell'Unione Europea', *Diritto Pubblico*, 7: 849–99.

Bogdandy, A. von and Bast, J. (2001) 'Die vertikale Kompetenzordnung der Europäischen Union. Rechtsdogmatischer Bestand und verfassungspolitische Reformperspektiven', *Europäische Grundrechte Zeitschrift*, 28: 441–58.

Böhm, F. (1946) 'Die Bedeutung der Wirtschaftsordnung für die politische Verfassung', *Süddeutsche Juristen-Zeitung*, 1: 141–9.

Bohman, J. (1996) *Public Deliberation: Pluralism, Complexity and Democracy*, Cambridge, Mass.: MIT Press.

Bohman, J. and Rehg, W. (eds) (1997) *Deliberative Democracy – Essays on Reason and Politics*, Cambridge, Mass.: MIT Press.

Boldt, H. (1975) *Deutsche Staatslehre im Vormärz*, Düsseldorf: Droste.

Börzel, T. (2001) 'Non-Compliance in the European Union', *Journal of European Public Policy*, 8: 803–24.

Braibant, G. (2001) *La charte des droits fondamentaux de l'Union européenne*, Paris: Le Seuil.

Brand, M. (2002) 'Towards the Definitive Status of the Charter of Fundamental Rights of the European Union: Political Document or Legally Binding Text?', *German Law Journal*, Vol. 4, No. 4: 395–409.

Brandom, R.B. (2000) *Articulating Reasons*, Cambridge, Mass.: Harvard University Press.

Brandt, H. (1968) *Landständische Repräsentation im Vormärz*, Neuwied: Luchterhand.

Brennan, W.J. (1989) 'Why Have a Bill of Rights?', *Oxford Journal of Legal Studies*, Vol. 9, No. 4: 425–40.

Brunkhorst, H. (1999) 'Menschenrechte und Souveränität – ein Dilemma?', in H. Brunkhorst, W.R. Köhler and M. Lutz-Bachman (eds) *Recht auf Menschenrechte*, Frankfurt: Suhrkamp.

—— (2002a) 'Verfassung ohne Staat? – Das Schicksal der Demokratie in der europäischen Rechtsgenossenschaft', *Leviathan*, 4: 530–43.

—— (2002b) *Solidarität. Von der Bürgerfreundschaft zur globalen Rechtsgenossenschaft*, Frankfurt: Suhrkamp.

—— (2002c) 'Globalizing Democracy Without a State: Weak Public, Strong Public, Global Constitutionalism', *Millennium: Journal of International Studies*, Vol. 31, No. 3: 675–90.

—— (2003) 'Evolution und Revolution – Hat die Evolution des politischen Systems eine normative Seite?', in K.-U. Hellmann, K. Fischer and H. Bluhm (eds) *Das System der Politik. Niklas Luhmanns politische Theorie*, Opladen: Westdeutscher Verlag.

Bryde, B.-O. (1994) 'Die bundesrepublikanische Volksdemokratie als Irrweg der Demokratietheorie', *Staatswissenschaften und Staatspraxis*, 5: 305–30.

Bulmer, S.J. (1996) 'The European Council and the Council of the European Union: Shapers of a European Confederation', *Publius*, Vol. 26, No. 4: 17–42.

Burdeau, G., Hamon, F. and Troper, M. (1997) *Droit constitutionnel*, Paris: L.G.D.J.

Burke, E. (1774) 'Speech to the Electors of Bristol', in D. Bromwich (ed.) *On Empire Liberty and Reform. Speeches and Letters of Edmund Burke*, New Haven: Yale University Press, 2000.

—— (1790) *Reflections on the Revolution in France*, ed. J.C.D. Clark, Palo Alto: Stanford University Press, 2001.

Burley, A.-M. and Mattli, W. (1993) 'Europe before the Court: A Political Theory of Legal Integration', *International Organization*, 47: 41–76.

Carré de Malberg, R. (1984) *La loi, expression de la volonté générale: étude sur le concept de la loi dans la Constitution de 1875* (1931), Paris: Economica.

Cassese, S. (1991) 'La Costituzione Europea', *Quaderni Costituzionali*, 11: 487–508.

Checkel, J.T. (2001) 'Taking Deliberation Seriously', ARENA Working Paper 01/14, Oslo: ARENA.

Classen, C.D. (1994) 'Europäische Integration und demokratische Legitimation', *Archiv des öffentlichen Rechts*, 119: 238–60.

—— (2001) 'Einführung', in *Europa-Recht*, Munich: dtv.

Closa, C. (2003) 'Improving EU Constitutional Politics? A Preliminary Assessment of the Convention', Constitutionalism Web-Papers, ConWEB No. 1/2003: <http://les1.man.ac.uk/conweb/>.

Cohen, J. (1989) 'Deliberation and Democratic Legitimacy', in A. Hamlin and P. Pettit (eds) *The Good Polity*, Oxford: Blackwell.

Cohen, J. and Sabel, C. (1997) 'Directly-Deliberative Polyarchy', *European Law Journal*, Vol. 3, No. 4: 313–42.

Corwin, E.S. (1936) 'The Constitution as Instrument and as Symbol', *American Political Science Review*, XXX: 1071.

Costa, O. (2001) *Le Parlement européen, assemblée délibérante*, Brussels: Éditions de l'Université de Bruxelles.

Costa, O. and Magnette, P. (2003) 'Pourquoi les gouvernements ont-ils constamment renforcé le Parlement européen? Idées, institutions et interest dans les politiques institutionelles de l'Union européenne', *Politique européenne*, 9: 49–75.

Craig, P. (2003) 'What Constitution Does Europe Need? The House that Giscard Built: Constitutional Rooms with a View', London: The Federal Trust, August.

Crum, B. (2003) ' "Throwing the Rascals Out": The European Convention and the Prospects for Representative Democracy', paper presented at CIDEL Workshop 'Deliberative Constitutional Politics in the EU', Albarracín, Spain, 20–1 June.

Curtin, D. (1997) *Postnational Democracy: The European Union in Search of a Political Philosophy*, The Hague: Kluwer Law.

Dahl, R. (1989) *Democracy and Its Critics*, New Haven: Yale University Press.

Däubler, W. (2000) 'In bester Verfassung: Zur Verabschiedung der europäischen Grundrechte-Charta', *Blätter für deutsche und internationale Politik*, Heft 11, November: 1315–21.

de Búrca, G. (2001) 'The drafting of the European Union Charter of Fundamental Rights', *European Law Review*, 26: 126–38.

Deloche, F. (2002) 'La Convention pour l'élaboration de la charte des droits fondamentaux: une méthode constituante?', in R. Dehousse (ed.) *Une constitution pour l'Europe?*, Paris: Presses de sciences-po.

Deloche-Gaudez, F. (2001) *The Convention on a Charter of Fundamental Rights: A Method for the Future?*, Groupement d'Études et de Recherches Notre Europe, Research and Policy Paper No. 15.

Delors, J. (1988) 'Speech in the European Parliament on 4.7.1988', *EC Bulletin* 1988, 7/8: 124.

—— (1992) 'Europa im Umbruch. Vom Binnenmarkt zur Europäischen Union, in Kommission der EG', *Europäische Gespräche*, Heft 9 (Bonn).

den Boer, P. (1998) 'Europe as an Idea', *European Review*, October: 395–402.

Denninger, E. (1990) *Der gebändigte Leviathan*, Baden-Baden: Nomos.

de Otto, I. (1987) *Derecho constitucional. Sistema de fuentes*, Barcelona: Ariel.

Derrida, J. (2001) *L'université sans condition*, Paris: Gallimard.

de Schutter, O. (2001) 'La contribution de la Charte des droits fondamentaux de l'Union européenne à la garantie des droits sociaux dans l'ordre juridique communautaire', *Revue Universelle des Droits de L'Homme*, 12: 33–47.

—— (2003) 'Civil Society in the Constitution for Europe', in E.O. Eriksen, J.E. Fossum and A.J. Menéndez (eds) *The Chartering of Europe*, Baden-Baden: Nomos.

de Souza Santos, B. (1999) 'The GATT of Law and Democracy: (Mis)Trusting the Global Reform of Courts', in J. Feest (ed.) *Onati Papers 7: Globalization and Legal Cultures*, Onati: IISL 1999: 49–86.

de Tocqueville, A. (1851) *The Ancient Régime and the French Revolution*, London: Collins, 1966.

Dewey, J. (1984) 'The Public and its Problems', in *The Later Works 2*, Carbondale: Southern Illinois University Press.

De Witte, B. (1986) 'Retour à Costa. La primauté du droit communitaire à la lunière du droit international', in W. Maihofer (ed.) *Noi si mura. Selected Working Papers of the European University Institute*, Florence: European University Institute.

Dicey, A.V. (1959) *Introduction to the Study of the Law of the Constitution*, 10th edn, London: Macmillan.

Diez-Picazo, L.M. (2002) 'What Does it Mean to be a State within the European Union?', *Rivista Italiana di Diritto Pubblico Communitario*, Anno XII, Fasc. 4: 651–71.

Di Fabio, U. (1991) *Offener Diskurs und geschlossene Systeme*, Berlin: Duncker und Humblot.

Dinan, D. (2002) 'Institutions and Governance 2001–2002: Debating the EU's Future', *Journal of Common Market Studies: Annual Review*, 40: 29–43.

Dryzek, J. (2000) *Deliberative Democracy and Beyond: Liberals, Critics, Contestations*, Oxford: Oxford University Press.

Duff, A. (2000) 'Towards a European Federal Society', in K. Feus (ed.) *The EU Charter of Fundamental Rights*, London: Kogan Page.

Durkheim, É. (1893) *Über soziale Arbeitsteilung. Studie über die Organisation höherer Gesellschaften*, Frankfurt: Suhrkamp, 1988.

Dworkin, R. (1996) *Freedom's Law: The Moral Reading of the American Constitution*, Cambridge, Mass.: Harvard University Press.

Eberlein, B. and Kerwer, D. (2002) 'Theorizing the New Modes of EU Governance', *European Integration Online Papers*, Vol. 6, No. 5: <http://eiop.or.at>.

Eckhout, P. (2000) 'The Proposed EU Charter of Fundamental Rights: Some Reflections of Its Effects in the Legal Systems of the EU and of Its Member States', in K. Feus (ed.) *The EU Charter of Fundamental Rights*, London: Kogan Page.

Economist (2003) 'The Germ of a Good Idea', 10 April.

Eichener, V. (1997) *Das Entscheidungssystem der Europäischen Union. Institutionelle Analyse und demokratietheoretische Bewertung*, Opladen: Leske und Budrich.

Elazar, D.J. (1987) *Exploring Federalism*, Tuscaloosa, AL: University of Alabama Press.

Eleftheriadis, P. (1998) 'Begging the Constitutional Question', *Journal of Common Market Studies*, 36: 255–72.

Elkin, S.L. (1993) 'Constitutionalism's Successor', in S.L. Elkin and K.E. Sotan (eds) *A New Constitutionalism: Designing Political Institutions*, Chicago: University of Chicago Press.

Elkins, S.M. and McKitrick, E.L. (1993) *The Age of Federalism*, Oxford: Oxford University Press.

Elster, J. (1991) 'Arguing and Bargaining in Two Constituent Assemblies', unpublished copy, Chicago.

—— (1994) 'Argumenter et négocier dans deux assemblées constituantes', *Revue française de science politique*, Vol. 44, No. 2: 187–256.

—— (1995) 'Strategic Uses of Argument', in K. Arrow, R.H. Mnookin, L. Ross, A. Tversky and R. Wilson (eds) *Barriers to the Negotiated Resolution of Conflict*, New York: Norton.

—— (ed.) (1998a) *Deliberative Democracy*, Cambridge: Cambridge University Press.

—— (1998b) 'Deliberation and Constitution Making', in J. Elster (ed.) *Deliberative Democracy*, Cambridge: Cambridge University Press.

Epstein, R.A. (1995) *Simple Rules for a Complex World*, Cambridge, Mass.: Harvard University Press.

Eriksen, E.O. (2001) ' "Governance or Democracy? The White Paper on European Governance", No. 6/01, Symposium: Responses to the European Commission's White Paper on Governance', in C. Joerges, Y. Mény and J.H.H. Weiler (eds) *Mountain or a Molehill?*, New York: Harvard Law School Working Paper Series.

—— (2003) 'Why a Charter of Fundamental Rights in the EU?', *Ratio Juris*, Vol. 16, No. 3: 352–73.

Eriksen, E.O. and Fossum, J.E. (eds) (2000) *Democracy in the European Union – Integration through Deliberation?*, London: Routledge.

—— (2002) 'Democracy through Strong Publics in the European Union', *Journal of Common Market Studies*, Vol. 40, No. 3: 401–24.

—— (2004) 'Europe at a Crossroads – Government or Transnational Governance?', in C. Joerges, I.-J. Sand and G. Teubner (eds) *Constitutionalism and Transnational Governance*, London: Hart.

Eriksen, E.O. and J. Weigård (2003) *Understanding Habermas: Communicative Action and Deliberative Democracy*, London: Continuum.

Eriksen, E.O., Fossum, J.E., and Menéndez, A.J. (eds) (2003) *The Chartering of Europe*, Baden-Baden: Nomos.

Esser, J. (1999) 'Der cooperative Nationalstaat im Zeitalter der "Globalisierung" ', in D. Döring (ed.) *Sozialstaat in der Globalisierung*, Frankfurt: Suhrkamp.

Estlund, D. (1993) 'Making Truth Safe for Democracy', in D. Copp, J. Hampton and J. Roemer (eds) *The Idea of Democracy*, Oxford: Oxford University Press.

—— (1998) 'The Insularity of the Reasonable: Why Political Liberalism Must Admit the Truth', *Ethics*, 108: 252–75.

European University Institute (2000a) *Reorganization of the European Treaties*, available at <http://www.iue.it/RSCAS/Research/Institutions/EuropeanTreaties.shtml>.

—— (2000b) *A Basic Treaty for the European Union. A Study of the Reorganization of the Treaties*, Florence: European University Institute.

Everson, M. (1999) 'The Constitutionalization of European Administrative Law: Legal Oversight of a Stateless Internal Market', in C. Joerges and E. Vos (eds) *EU Committees: Social Regulation, Law and Politics*, Oxford: Hart.

—— (2003a) 'Social Pluralism and the European Court of Justice: A Court Between a Rock and a Hard Place', *Journal of Legislative Studies*, Vol. 8, No. 4.

—— (2003b) 'Accountability and Law in Europe: Towards a New Public Legal Order?', *Modern Law Review* (forthcoming).

Feus, K. (ed.) (2000) *An EU Charter of Fundamental Rights – Text and Commentaries*, London: Federal Trust.

Finer, S.E. (1997) *The History of Government from the Earliest Times*, Vol. III, Oxford: Oxford University Press.

Fioravanti, M. (1996) *Los derechos fundamentales: apuntes de historia de las constituciones*, Madrid: Editorial Trotta.

—— (2001) *Constitucion. De la Antigüedad a nuestros días*, Madrid: Editorial Trotta.

Fioravanti, M. and Mannoni, S. (2001) 'Il Modelo Constituzionale Europeo. Tradizione e prospettive', in G. Bonacchi (ed.) *Una Constituzione senza stato?*, Bologna: Il Mulino.

Fischer, J. (2000) 'Vom Staatenverbund zur Föderation', speech at Humboldt University on 12 May 2000, in C. Joerges, Y. Mény and J.H.H. Weiler (eds) *What Kind of Constitution for What Kind of Polity? – Responses to Joschka Fischer*, San Domenico: European University Institute.

Forsthoff, E. (1971) *Der Staat der Industriegesellschaft. Dargestellt am Beispiel der Bundesrepublik Deutschland*, 2nd edn, Munich: C.H. Beck.

Fossum, J.E. (2000) 'Constitution-Making in the European Union', in E.O. Eriksen and J.E. Fossum (eds) *Democracy in the European Union – Integration through Deliberation?*, London: Routledge.

—— (2001) 'The European Union – In Search of an Identity', unpublished copy, Oslo: ARENA.

—— (2003a) 'The Transformation of the Nation-State: Why Compare the EU and Canada?', unpublished copy, ARENA, 16 January.

—— (2003b) 'The European Union in Search of an Identity', *European Journal of Political Theory*, Vol. 2, No. 3: 319–40.

—— (2003c) 'The European Charter – Between Deep Diversity and Constitutional Patriotism', in E.O. Eriksen, J.E. Fossum and A.J. Menéndez (eds) *The Chartering of Europe: The Charter of Fundamental Rights and Its Constitutional Implications*, Baden-Baden: Nomos.

Fossum, J.E. and Menéndez, A.J. (2003) 'The Constitution's Gift: A Deliberative Democratic Analysis of Constitution-Making in the European Union', paper presented at CIDEL Workshop 'Deliberative Constitutional Politics in the EU', Albarracín, Spain, 20–1 June.

Foucault, M. (1997) *Il faut défendre la société*, Paris: Gallimard.

Fraenkel, E. (1991) *Deutschland und die westlichen Demokratien*, Frankfurt: Suhrkamp.

Fraser, N. (1992) 'Rethinking the Public Sphere: A Contribution to the Critique of Actually Existing Democracy', in C. Calhoun (ed.) *Habermas and the Public Sphere*, Cambridge, Mass.: MIT Press.

Furet, F. (1978) *Penser la Révolution française*, Paris: Gallimard.

Furrer, A. (1994) *Die Sperrwirkung des sekundären Gemeinschaftsrechts auf die nationalen Rechtsordnungen*, Baden-Baden: Nomos.

Galtung, J. (1973) *The European Community: A Superpower in the Making*, London: George Allen.

—— (1975) 'The Lome Convention and Neo-Capitalism', *Prio Papers*, No. 20, Oslo: PRIO.

Gerber, C.F. von (1880) *Grundzüge des deutschen Staatsrechts*, Leipzig: Bernard Tauchnitz.

Gerber, D.J. (1994) 'Constitutionalizing the Economy: German Neo-liberalism, Competition Law and the "New" Europe', *American Journal of Comparative Law*, 42: 25–84.

Gerstenberg, O. (1997) *Bürgerrechte und Demokratie*, Frankfurt: Suhrkamp.

Giscard d'Estaing, V. (2002) 'La dernière chance de l'Europe unie', Le Monde, 22 July.

Gneist, R. von (1879) *Der Rechtsstaat und die Verwaltungsgerichte in Deutschland*, 2nd edn, Berlin: Springer.

Grande, E. (1996) 'Post-National Democracy in Europe', in M. Greven and L. Pauly (eds) *Democracy beyond the State?*, Lanham, Md: Rowman & Littlefield.

—— (2000) 'Demokratische Legitimation und europäische Integration', *Leviathan*, 24: 339–60.

Grande, E. and Risse, T. (2000) 'Bridging the Gap', *Zeitschrift für internationale Beziehungen*, 7: 235–66.

Griffiths, R.T. (2001) *Europe's First Constitution*, London: Kogan Page.

Grimm, D. (1995) 'Does Europe Need a Constitution?', *European Law Journal*, Vol. 1, No. 3: 282–302.

—— (1997) 'Vertrag oder Verfassung?', in D. Grimm, J.J. Hesse, R. Jochimsen and F.W. Scharpf (eds) *Zur Neuordnung der Europäischen Union. Die Regierungskonferenz 1996–97*, Baden-Baden: Nomos.

—— (2001a) 'Braucht Europa eine Verfassung?', in *Die Verfassung und die Politik. Einsprüche in Störfällen*, Munich: C.H. Beck.

—— (2001b) 'Vom Rat zur Staatenkammer', in *Die Verfassung und die Politik. Einsprüche in Störfällen*, Munich: C.H. Beck.

—— (2003) 'Die grösste Erfindung unserer Zeit – Als weltweit anerkanntes Vorbild braucht Europa keine Verfassung', *Frankfurter Allgemeine Zeitung*, 16 June.

Grossi, P. (2001) 'Pagina introduttiva: storia e cronostoria dei "Quaderni Fiorentini"', *Quaderni Fiorentini*, 30: 1–12.

Grözinger, G. (2004) 'Die "vereinigten Parlamente von Europa" und weitere Über- legungen zur subsidiären demokratie', forthcoming in C. Offe (ed.) *Erneuerung der Demokratie*.

Guéhenno, J.-M. (1994) *Das Ende der Demokratie*, Munich: Artemis.

—— (1996) 'Europas Demokratie erneuern', in W. Weidenfeld (ed.) *Demokratie am Wendepunkt: Die demokratische Frage als Projekt des 21. Jahrhunderts*, Berlin: Siedler.

Günther, K. (1988) *Der Sinn für Angemessenheit – Anwendungsdiskurse in Moral und Recht*, Frank- furt: Suhrkamp.

Haas, E.B. (1961) 'International Integration: The European and the Universal Process', *International Organization*, 15: 366–92.

Häberle, P. (1999) 'Lo Stato costituzionale europeo', in *Sovranità, rappresentanza, democrazia. Rapporti tra ordinamento comunitario e ordinamenti nazionali*, proceedings of a conference held in Naples, 25–6 June, Naples: Jovene.

Habermas, J. (1986) *Philosophical-Political Profiles*, Cambridge: Polity.

—— (1990) *Die nachholende Revolution*, Frankfurt: Suhrkamp.

—— (1992) *Faktizität und Geltung*, Frankfurt: Suhrkamp.

—— (1994) 'Struggles for Recognition in the Democratic Constitutional State', in C. Taylor and A. Gutmann (eds) *Multiculturalism*, Princeton, NJ: Princeton University Press.

—— (1996) *Between Facts and Norms: Contributions to a Discourse Theory of Law and Democracy*, Cambridge, Mass.: MIT Press.

—— (1998) *The Inclusion of the Other*, Cambridge, Mass.: MIT Press.

—— (2000) *The Postnational Constellation*, Cambridge, Mass.: MIT Press.

—— (2001) 'Constitutional Democracy: A Paradoxical Union of Contradictory Prin- ciples', *Political Theory*, Vol. 29, No. 6: 766–81.

Hallstein, W. (1946) 'Wiederherstellung des Privatrechts', *Süddeutsche Juristen-Zeitung*, 1.

—— (1969) *Der unvollendete Bundesstaat*, Düsseldorf: Econ.

Haltern, U. (2003a) 'Pathos and Patina: The Failure and Promise of Constitutionalism in the European Imagination', *European Law Journal*, Vol. 9, No. 1: 14–44.

—— (2003b) 'Das Politische in Europa', unpublished manuscript.

Hanschmann, F. (2003) 'Sprachliche Homogenität und europäische Demokratie – Zum Zusammenhang von Sprache, Öffentlichkeit und Demokratie', unpublished copy.

Harlow, C. (2002) *Accountability in the European Union*, Oxford: Oxford University Press.

Hart, H.L.A. (1961) *The Concept of Law*, Oxford: Oxford University Press.

Hauser, R. and Becker, I. (1999) 'Wird unsere Einkommensverteilung immer ungleicher? Einige Forschungsergebnisse', in D. Döring (ed.) *Sozialstaat in der Globalisierung*, Frank- furt: Suhrkamp.

Heintzen, M. (1994) 'Die "Herrschaft" über die europäischen Gemeinschaftsverträge', *Archiv des öffentlichen rechts*, 119: 564–89.

Held, D. (1995) *Democracy and the Global Order*, Cambridge: Polity.

Heller, H. (1928) 'Politische Demokratie und soziale Homogenität', *Gesammelte Schriften*, Vol. 2, Tübingen: Mohr Siebeck, 1971.

Henkin, L. (1994) 'Revolutionen und Verfassungen', in U.K. Preuss (ed.) *Zum Begriff der Verfassung*, Frankfurt: Fischer.

Hennis, W. (1968) *Verfassung und Verfassungswirklichkeit. Ein deutsches Problem*, Tübingen: J.C.B Mohr/Paul Siebeck.

Hespanha, A.M. (1999) *Introduzione alla storia del diritto europeo*, Bologna: Il Mulino.

Hesse, K. (1959) *Die normative Kraft der Verfassung*, Tübingen: Mohr Siebeck.

—— (1990) *Grundzüge des Verfassungsrechts der Bundesrepublik Deutschland*, Heidelberg: C.F. Müller.

Hoffmann, L. (2002) *The Convention on the Future of Europe – Thoughts on the Convention-Model*, Jean Monnet Working Paper 11/02: <http://www.jeanmonnetprogram.org/papers/papers02.html>.

Hofmann, H. (1995) 'Geschichtlichkeit und Universalitätsanspruch des Rechtsstaats', *Der Staat*, Vol. 34, No. 1: 1–32.

—— (1998) *Das Recht des Rechts, das Recht der Herrschaft und die Einheit der Verfassung*, Berlin: Duncker und Humblot.

—— (2000) 'Von der Staatssoziologie zu einer Soziologie der Verfassung?', in H. Dreier (ed.) *Rechtssoziologie am Ende des 20. Jahrhunderts*, Tübingen: Mohr Siebeck.

Höland, A. (1993) 'Die Rechtssoziologie und der unbekannte Kontinent Europa', *Zeitschrift für Rechtssoziologie*, 14: 177–89.

Holmes, S. (1995) *Passions and Constraints: On the Theory of Liberal Democracy*, Chicago: University of Chicago Press.

Hsü, D.-L. (1932) *Die Verfassungswandlung*, Berlin: de Gruyter.

Ipsen, H.P. (1964) 'Der deutsche Jurist und das Europäische Gemeinschaftsrecht', *Deutscher Juristentag*, 43, Vol. II, No. 14 (Munich).

—— (1972) *Europäisches Gemeinschaftsrecht*, Tübingen: Mohr.

—— (1973) 'Über Supranationalität', in H.P. Ipsen (ed.) *Europäisches Gemeinschaftsrecht in Einzelstudien*, Baden-Baden: Nomos.

—— (1983) 'Die Verfassungsrolle des Europäischen Gerichtshofs für die Integration', in J. Schwarze (ed.) *Der Europäische Gerichtshof als Verfassungsgericht und Rechtsschutzinstanz*, Baden-Baden: Nomos.

—— (1987) 'Die Bundesrepublik Deutschland in den Europäischen Gemeinschaften', in J. Isensee and P. Kirchhof (eds) *Handbuch des Staatsrechts der Bundesrepublik Deutschland*, Heidelberg: Müller.

Jachtenfuchs, M. (2001) 'The Governance Approach to European Integration', *Journal of Common Market Studies*, 39: 245–64.

Jachtenfuchs, M. and Kohler-Koch, B. (eds) (2003) *Europäische Integration*, 2nd edn, Opladen: Leske und Budrich.

Jellinek, G. (1887) *Gesetz und Verordnung. Staatsrechtliche Untersuchungen aurechtsgeschichtlicher und rechtsvergleichender Grundlage*, Freiburg: B. Mohr.

—— (1906) *Verfassungswandlung und Verfassungsänderung*, Berlin: O. Häring.

—— (1979) *System der subjektiven öffentlichen Rechte*, Aalen: Scientia.

Jesch, D. (1961) *Gesetz und Verwaltung*, Tübingen: Mohr.

Joerges, C. (1994a) 'Economic Law, the Nation-State and the Maastricht Treaty', in R. Dehousse (ed.) *Europe after Maastricht: an Ever Closer Union*, Munich: C.H. Beck.

—— (1994b) 'Rationalisierungsprozesse im Recht der Produktsicherheit: Öffentliches Recht und Haftungsrecht unter dem Einfluß der Europäischen Integration', *Jahrbuch für Umwelt- und Technikrecht*, 14: 141–78.

—— (1996a) *The Market without a State? States without Markets? Two Essays on the Law of the European Economy*, EUI Working Paper Law 1/96, San Domenico di Fiesole: EUI, available at <http://eiop.or.at/eiop>.

—— (1996b) 'Taking the Law Seriously: On Political Science and the Role of Law in the Process of European Integration', *European Law Journal*, 2: 105–35.

—— (1996c) 'Das recht im Prozezz der europäischen Integration', in M. Jachtenfuchs and B. Kohler-Koch (eds) *Europäische Integration*, Opladen: Leske.

—— (1996d) 'Rechtswissenschaftliche Integrationstheorien', in B. Kohler-Koch and W. Woyke (eds) *Die Europäische Union. Lexikon der Politik*, Vol. 5, Munich: C.H. Beck.

—— (2001) 'In Defense of Deliberative Supranationalism', *European Integration Online Papers*, 5/4.

—— (2002a) ' "Deliberative Supranationalism" – Two Defences', *European Law Journal*, 8: 133–51.

—— (2002b) ' "Economic Order" – "Technical Realization" – "the Hour of the Executive": Some Legal Historical Observations on the Commission White Paper on European Governance', in C. Joerges, Y. Mény and J.H.H. Weiler (eds) *Mountain or a Molehill?* New York: Harvard Law School Working Paper Series. Available at <http://www.iue.it/RSC/Governance/>.

—— (2002c) 'The Commission's White Paper on Governance in the EU: A Symptom of Crisis?' (Guest Editorial), *Common Market Law Review*, 39: 441–5.

—— (2003) 'Zur Legitimität der Europäisierung des Privatrechts. Überlegungen zu einem Recht-Fertigungs-Recht für das Mehrebenensystem der EU', in C. Joerges and G. Teubner (eds) *Rechtsverfassungsrecht: Recht-Fertigungen zwischen Privatrechtsdogmatik und Gesellschaftstheorie*, Baden-Baden: Nomos.

Joerges, C. and Everson, M. (2000) 'Challenging the Bureaucratic Challenge', in E.O. Eriksen and J.E. Fossum (eds) *Democracy in the European Union – Integration through Deliberation?*, London: Routledge.

Joerges, C. and Neyer, J. (1997) 'From Intergovernmental Bargaining to Deliberative Political Processes: The Constitutionalization of Comitology', *European Law Journal*, Vol. 3, No. 2: 273–9.

Joerges, C. and Vos, E (eds) (1999) *EU Committees: Social Regulation, Law and Politics*, Oxford: Hart.

Joerges, C., Mény, Y. and Weiler, J.H.H. (eds) (2000) *What Kind of Constitution for What Kind of Polity? – Responses to Joschka Fischer*, San Domenico: European University Institute.

Kant, I. (1785) 'Groundwork of the Metaphysics of Morals', in M.J. Gregor (ed.) *Practical Philosophy*, Cambridge: Cambridge University Press, 1996.

—— (1798) 'The Metaphysics of Morals', in M.J. Gregor (ed.) *Practical Philosophy*, Cambridge: Cambridge University Press, 1996.

Kaufmann, M. (1997a) 'Permanente Verfassungsgebung und verfassungsrechtliche Selbstbindung im europäischen Staatenverbund', *Der Staat*, 4: 521–46.

—— (1997b) *Europäische Integration und Demokratieprinzip*, Baden-Baden: Nomos.

Kelsen, H. (1921) *Wesen und der Wert der Demokratie*, reprint of 2nd edn, Aalen: Scientia, 1981.

—— (1925) *Allgemeine Staatslehre*, Berlin: Springer.

—— (1944) *Peace through Law*, Chapel Hill: University of North Carolina Press.

—— (1945) *General Theory of Law and State*, Cambridge, Mass.: Harvard University Press.

—— (1970) *The Pure Theory of Law*, Berkeley: University of California Press.

—— (1992) *Introduction to the Problems of Legal Theory*, Oxford: Clarendon Press.

Kirchhof, P. (1992) 'Der deutsche Staat im Prozeß der europäischen Integration', in J. Isensee and P. Kirchhof (eds) *Handbuch des Staatsrechts der Bundesrepublik Deutschland*, Vol. VII, Heidelberg: C.F. Mueller.

Kirste, S. (1998) *Die Zeitlichkeit des positiven Rechts und die Geschichtlichkeit des Rechtsbewusstseins*, Berlin: Duncker und Humblot.

Kitzinger, U.W. (1960) 'Europe: The Six and Seven', *International Organization*, 14: 20–36.

Kleger, H. (1998) 'Wie is Mehrfachidentität lebbar? Deutschland zwishen Sub- und Transnationalität', in R. Voigt (ed.) *Der Neue Nationalstaat*, Baden-Baden: Nomos.

Kloppenberg, J.T. (2000) 'Demokratie und Entzauberung der Welt: Von Weber und Dewey zu Habermas und Rorty', in H. Joas (ed.) *Philosophie der Demokratie*, Frankfurt.

Klug, U. (1981) 'Die geordnete Anarchie als philosophisches Leitbild des freiheitlichen Rechtsstaates', in *Skeptische Rechtsphilosophie und humanes Strafrecht*, Vol. 1, Berlin: Springer.

Kohler-Koch, B. (2000) ' "Framing": The Bottleneck of Constructing Legitimate Institutions', *Journal of European Public Policy*, Vol. 7, No. 4: 513–31.

Korioth, S. (1990) *Integration und Bundesstaat*, Berlin: Duncker und Humblot.

Koskenniemi, M. (2001) *The Gentle Civilizer of Nations – The Rise and Fall of International Law 1870–1960*, Cambridge: Cambridge University Press.

Krajewsky, M. (2001) 'Democratic Legitimacy and Constitutional Perspectives of WTO Law', *Journal of World Trade*, Vol. 35, No. 1: 167–90.

Kramnick, I. (1987) *Federalist*, Edition 12, Harmondsworth: Penguin.

Kraus, P. (2000a) 'Von Westfalen nach Kosmopolis. Die Problematiks kultureller Identität in der Europäischen Politik', *Berliner Journal für Soziologie*, 2: 203–18.

—— (2000b) 'Political Unity and Linguistic Diversity in Europe', *Archives européennes de sociologie*, 41: 138–63.

Kriele, M. (1981) *Einführung in die Staatslehre*, Opladen: Westdeutscher Verlag.

Laband, P. (1911) *Das Staatsrecht des Deutschen Reiches*, Vol. 1, Tübingen: Mohr.

Ladeur, K.-H. (1997) 'Towards a Legal Theory of Supranationality: The Viability of the Network Concept', *European Law Journal*, 3: 33–54.

Langer, S. (1994) *Grundlagen einer internationalen Wirtschaftsverfassung*, Munich: C.H. Beck.

Lassalle, F. (1862) *Über Verfassungswesen*, Berlin: Cassirer, 1919.

La Torre, M. (2003) 'The German Impact on Fascist Public Law Doctrine – Constantino Mortati's Material Constitution', in C. Joerges and N. Singh Ghaleigh (eds) *Darker Legacies of Law in Europe*, Oxford: Hart.

Lenaerts, K. and de Smitjer, E. (2001) 'A "Bill of Rights" for the European Union', *Common Market Law Review*, 38: 273–300.

Lenaerts, K. and Van Nuffel, P. (1999) *Constitutional Law of the European Union*, London: Sweet and Maxwell.

Lepsius, M.R. (1993) 'Die Europäische Gemeinschaft und die Zukunft des Nationalstaats', in *Demokratie in Deutschland: soziologisch-historische Konstellationsanalysen: ausgewählte Aufsätze*, Göttingen: Vandenhoeck & Ruprecht.

Lepsius, O. (1997) *Verwaltungsrecht unter dem Common Law*, Tübingen: Mohr/Siebeck.

—— (2000) ' "Staatstheorie und Demokratiebegriff" in der Weimarer Republik', in C. Gusy (ed.) *Demokratischer Denken in der Weimarer Republik*, Baden-Baden: Nomos.

Llorente, F.R. (2003) 'A Charter of Dubious Utility', *Oxford University Press and New York Unversity School of Law*, Vol. 1, No. 3: 405–25.

Lombardo, E. (2003) 'The Participation of Civil Society in the Debate on the Future of Europe: Rhetorical or Action Frames in the Discourse of the Convention?', Working Paper, <http://www.unizar.es/union_europea/files/workPapers3_UE.pdf>.

Löwenstein, K. (1967) *Staatsrecht und Staatspraxis von Grossbritannien*, Berlin: Springer.

—— (1997) *Verfassungslehre*, Tübingen: Mohr.

Ludlow, P. (2002) The Laeken Council EuroComment, *European Council Commentary*, Vol. 1, No. 1, Brussels.

Luhmann, N. (1987) *Rechtssoziologie*, Opladen: Westdeutscher Verlag.

—— (1988) *Macht*, 2nd edn, Stuttgart: Enke.

—— (1990) 'Verfassung als evolutionäre Errungenschaft', *Rechtshistorisches Journal*, 9: 176–220.

—— (1993) *Das Recht der Gesellschaft*, Frankfurt: Suhrkamp.

—— (1997) *Die Gesellschaft der Gesellschaft*, Frankfurt: Suhrkamp.

MacCormick, J. (1950) *The Flag in the Wind*, London: Wackburg.

MacCormick, N.D. (1978) 'Does the United Kingdom have a Constitution? Reflections on *MacCormick* vs. *Lord Advocate*', *Northern Ireland Legal Quarterly*, 29: 1–20.

Mackie, G. (1998) 'All Men are Liars: Is Democracy Meaningless?', in J. Elster (ed.) *Deliberative Democracy*, Oxford: Oxford University Press.

Madison, J., Hamilton, A. and Jay, J. (1788) *The Federalist Papers*, New York: McLean.

Maduro, M.P. (2000) *Europe and the Constitution: What If This Is As Good As It Gets?*, CON-WEB Working Papers 5.

Magnette, P. (ed.) (2002) *La Constitution de l'Europe*, Brussels: Éditions de l'Université de Bruxelles.

—— (2003a) 'European Governance and Civic Participation: Beyond Elitist Citizenship?', *Political Studies*, Vol. 52, No. 1: 139–56.

—— (2003b) 'In the Name of Simplification. Constitutional Rhetoric in the Convention on the Future of Europe', paper presented at CIDEL Workshop 'Deliberative Constitutional Politics in the EU', Albarracín, Spain, 20–1 June: <http://www.arena.uio.no/cidel/workshopZaragoza/PMagnette.pdf>.

Maitland, F.W. (1908) *The Constitutional History of England*, reprint, Cambridge, Cambridge University Press, 1961.

Majone, G. (1994) 'The European Community. An "Independent Fourth Branch of Government"?', in G. Brüggemeier (ed.) *Verfassungen für ein ziviles Europa*, Baden-Baden: Nomos.

—— (1996) *Regulating Europe*, London: Routledge.

Mancini, G.F. (1998) 'Europe: The Case for Statehood', *European Law Journal*, Vol. 4, No. 1: 29–43.

Manin, B. (1997) *Principles of Representative Government*, Cambridge: Cambridge University Press.

Manow, P. (2000) '*Modell Deutschland' as an Inter-denominational Compromise. Program for the Study of Germany and Europe*, Working Paper No. 003. Center for European Studies, Harvard University, Cambridge, Mass.

Marjolin, R. (1986) *Le travail d'une vie*, Paris: Robert Laffon.

Marks, G., Scharpf, F.W., Schmitter, P. and W. Streek (1996) *Governance in the European Union*, London: Sage.

Marquand, D. (1979) *A Parliament for Europe*, London: Jonathan Cape.

Martin, R. (1993) *A System of Rights*, Oxford: Oxford University Press.

Maurer, A. (2003) 'Schliesst sich der Kreis? Der Konvent, nationale Vorbehalte und die Regierungskonferenz. Teil II – Datenbasis und Detailanalyse', CONVEU 30, SWP, Berlin.

Maus, I. (1989) 'Die Trennung von Recht und Moral als Begrenzung des Rechts', *Rechtstheorie*, 20: 191–210.

—— (1992) *Zur Aufklärung der Demokratietheorie*, Frankfurt: Suhrkamp.

—— (1994) 'Volk und Nation im Denken der Aufklärung', *Blätter für deutsche und internationale Politik*.

—— (2001) 'Nationalstaatliche Grenzen und das Prinzip der Volkssouveränität', unpublished copy, Frankfurt.

Mayer, F.C. (2000*) Kompetenzüberschreitung und Letztentscheidung. Das Maastricht-Urteil des Bundesverfassungsgerichts und die Letztentscheidung über Ultra vires-Akte in Mehrebenensystemen*, Munich: C.H. Beck.

—— (2001) 'Die drei Dimensionen der Europäischen Kompetenzdebatte', *Zeitschrift für ausländisches öffentliches Recht und Völkerrecht*, 61: 577–640.

Maynor, J. (2003) *Republicanism in the Modern World*, Cambridge: Polity.

Menéndez, A. J. (2001) *Justifying taxes*, Dordrecht: Kluwer.

—— (2002) 'Chartering Europe. Legal Status and Policy Implications of the Charter of Fundamental Rights of the European Union', *Journal of Common Market Studies*, 40: 471–90.

—— (2003a) 'Taxing Europe – Two Cases for a European Power to Tax', ARENA Working Paper No. 3/03.

—— (2003b) ' "Rights to Solidarity". Balancing Solidarity and Economic Freedoms', in E.O. Eriksen, J.E. Fossum and A.J. Menéndez (eds) *The Chartering of Europe. The European Charter of Fundamental Rights and Its Constitutional Implications*, Baden-Baden: Nomos.

Mestmäcker, E.-J. (1987) 'Auf dem Wege zu einer Ordnungspolitik für Europa', in E.-J. Mestmäcker, H. Möller and H.P. Schwartz (eds) *Eine Ordnungspolitik für Europa. Festschrift für Hans v.d. Groeben*, Baden-Baden: Nomos.

Meyer, H. (1997) 'Diskussionsbeitrag', in *Kontrolle aiswärtiger Gewalt – Veröffentlichungen der Vereinigung der Deutschen Staatsrechtslehrer*, Heft 56, Berlin: de Gruyter.

Meyer, J. (ed.) (2003) *Kommentar zur Charta der Grundrechte der Euopäischen Union*, Baden-Baden: Nomos.

Michelman, F.I. (1997) 'How can the People ever Make the Laws? A Critique of Deliberative Democracy', in J. Bohman and W. Rehg (eds) *Deliberative Democracy*, Cambridge, Mass.: MIT Press.

—— (1998) 'Constitutional Authorship', in L. Alexander (ed.) *Constitutionalism: Philosophical Foundations*, Cambridge: Cambridge University Press.

—— (1999) 'Bedürfen Menschenrechte demokratischer Legitimation?', in H. Brunkhorst, W.R. Köhler and M. Lutz-Bachman (eds) *Recht auf Menschenrechte*, Frankfurt: Suhrkamp.

Mill, J.S. (1861) 'Considerations on Representative Government', in *On Liberty and Other Essays*, Oxford: Oxford University Press, 1991.

Möllers, C. (2001a) *Staat als Argument*, Munich: C.H. Beck.

—— (2001b) 'Globalisierte Jurisprudenz: Einflüsse relativierter Nationalstaatlichkeit auf das Konzept des Rechts und die Funktion seiner Theorie', *Archiv für Rechts- und Sozialphilosophie Beiheft*, 79: 41–60.

—— (2002) 'Policy, Polities oder Politische Theorie', unpublished copy, Heidelberg (on the White Paper of the European Commission on Governance).

—— (2003a) 'Verfassungsgebende Gewalt – Verfassung – Konstitutionalisierung. Begriffe der verfassung in Europa', in A. von Bogdandy (ed.) *Europäisches Verfassungsrecht*, Berlin: Springer.

—— (2003b) 'Verfassung – Verfassunggebung – Konstitutionalisierung', in A. von Bogdandy (ed.) *Europäisches Verfassungsrecht*, Berlin: Springer.

Moral Soriano, L. (2003) 'How Proportionate Should Anti-Competitive State Intervention Be?', *European Law Review*, 28: 112–23.

Moravcsik, A. (1991) 'Negotiating the Single Europan Act: National Interests and Conventional Statecraft in the European Community', *International Organization*, Vol. 45, No. 1: 19–56.

—— (1998) *The Choice for Europe: Social Purpose and State Power from Messina to Maastricht*, Ithaca, NY: Cornell University Press.

Moravcsik, A. and Nicolaïdis, K. (1998) 'Keynote Article: Federal Ideals and Constitutional Realities in the Treaty of Amsterdam', *Journal of Common Market Studies: Annual Review*, 36: 13–38.

Mortati, C. (1962) 'Costituzione (dottrine generali)', in *Enciclopedia del Diritto*, Vol. 11, Milan: Giuffrè.

—— (1998) *La Constituzione in senso materiale*, Milan: Giuffré.

Moscovici, P (2002) 'Interview', *Revue du Marché commun et l'Union européenne*, March, No. 456: 145–7.

Mouffe, C. (2002) 'For an Antagonistic Public Sphere', in O. Enzewor (ed.) *Democracy Unrealized*, Kassel: Hatje Cantz.

Müller, F. (1997) *Wer ist das Volk? Eine Grundfrage der Demokratie, Elemente einer Verfassungstheorie VI*, Berlin: Duncker und Humblot.

Müller-Armack, A. (1947) *Wirtschaftslenkung und Marktwirtschaft*, 2nd edn, Hamburg: Verlag für Wirtschaft und Sozialpolitik.

—— (1966) 'Die Wirtschaftsordnung des Gemeinsamen Marktes', in *Wirtschaftsordnung und Wirtschaftspolitik*, Freiburg: Rombach.

Mussler, W. (1998) *Die Wirtschaftsverfassung der Europäischen Gemeinschaft im Wandel. Von Rom nach Maastricht*, Baden-Baden: Nomos.

Neves, M. (1992) *Verfassung und positives Recht in der peripheren Moderne*, Berlin: Duncker und Humblot.

—— (1998) *Symbolische Konstitutionalisierung*, Berlin: Duncker und Humblot.

—— (2000) *Zwischen Themis und Leviathan: Eine schwierige Beziehung*, Baden-Baden: Nomos.

Niess, F. (2000) 'Das "F-Wort" ', *Genetics*, September: 1105–15.

Nörr, K.W. (1999) *Die Republik der Wirtschaft. Teil I: Von der Besatzungszeit bis zur Großen Koalition*, Tübingen: Mohr Siebeck.

O'Donnell (1994) 'Delegative Democracy', *Journal of Democracy*, 1: 55–68.

Oeter, S. (1995) 'Souveränität und Demokratie als Probleme in der "Verfassungsentwicklung" der Europäischen Union', *Zeitschrift für ausländisches öffentliches Recht und Völkerrecht* 55: 659–712.

—— (1999) 'Allgemeines Wahlrecht und Ausschluss von Wahlberechtigung: Welche Vorgaben enthält das Grundgesetz', in U. Davy (ed.) *Politische Integration der ausländischen wohnbevölkerung*, Baden-Baden: Nomos.

—— (2002) 'Ansichten zur Gemeinschaftsverfassung', in *EuR*, Beiheft 3, FS Nicolaysen: 43–69.

Offe, C. (2000) 'Is There, or Can There Be, a European Society?', unpublished manuscript, Berlin.

Olsen, J.P. (2002) 'Coping with Conflict in Constitutional Moments', paper prepared for a conference in honour of James G. March, Lucca, Italy, 4–6 June.

Ost, F. (1999) *Le Temps du Droit*, Paris: Dalloz.

Perelman, C. and Olbrechts-Tyteca, L. (1969) *The New Rhetoric: A Treatise of Argumentation*, Notre Dame, IN: Notre Dame University Press.

Pernice, I. (1993) 'Maastricht, Staat und Demokratie', *Die Verwaltung*, 26: 449–88.

—— (1999) 'Which Institutions for What Kind of Europe?', unpublished manuscript.

Peters, A. (2001) *Elemente einer Theorie der Verfassung Europas*, Berlin: Duncker und Humblot.

Petersmann, E.U. (1991) 'Constitutionalism, Constitutional Law and European Integration', *Aussenwirtschaft*, 46: 247–80.

—— (1994) 'Grundprobleme der Wirtschaftsverfassung der EG', *Aussenwirtschaft*, 48: 389–414.

Pettit, P. (1997) *Republicanism: A Theory of Freedom and Government*, Oxford: Oxford University Press.

Pinder, J. (2003) 'Editorial: Really Citizens?', *EU Constitution Project Newsletter*, Vol. 1, No. 4: 1–2.

Pitkin, H.F. (1972) *The Concept of Representation*, Berkeley: University of California Press.

Pizzorusso, A. (2002) *Il patrimonio costituzionale europeo*, Bologna: Il Mulino.

Pocock, J.G.A. (1957) *The Ancient Constitution and the Feudal Law*, Cambridge: Cambridge University Press, 1987.

Pollack, M. (1997) 'Delegation, Agency and Agenda Setting in the European Community', *International Organization*, Vol. 51, No. 1: 99–134.

Poscher, Ralf (2003) 'Recht und Gewalt', unpublished manuscript, Berlin.

Post, R. (1995) *Constitutional Domains: Democracy, Community, Management*, Cambridge, Mass.: Harvard University Press.

Preuss, U.K. (1994) *Revolution, Fortschritt und Verfassung*, Frankfurt: Fischer.

—— (1996) 'Prospects of a Constitution for Europe', *Constellations*, Vol. 3, No. 2: 209–24.

Przeworski, A. (1998) 'Deliberation and Ideological Domination', in J. Elster (ed.) *Deliberative Democracy*, Oxford: Oxford University Press.

Putnam, H. (1991a) 'Interview', in G. Borradori *The American Philosopher*, Chicago: University of Chicago Press.

—— (1991b) 'A Reconsideration of Deweyan Democracy', in M. Brint and W. Weaver (eds) *Pragmatism in Law and Society*, Boulder, Colo.: Westview Press.

Rawls, J. (1971) *A Theory of Justice*, Oxford: Oxford University Press.

—— (1993a) 'The Law of the Peoples', in S. Shute and S. Hurley (eds) *On Human Rights*, New York: Basic Books.

—— (1993b) *Political Liberalism*, New York: Columbia University Press.

Raz, J. (1998) 'On the Authority and Interpretation of Constitutions: Some Preliminaries', in L. Alexander (ed.) *Constitutionalism: Philosophical Foundations*, Cambridge: Cambridge University Press.

Reinhard, W. (1999) *Geschichte der Staatsgewalt*, Munich: C.H. Beck.

Richmond, C. (2000) 'Perspectives on Law', Ph.D. thesis, European University Institute, Florence.

Rodrigues, S. (2001) 'La réforme de l'Union Européenne: changement de méthode? À propos du débat sur l'avenir de l'Europe au Conseil Européenne de Gand', *Revue du Marché commun et de l'Union européenne*, 452: 588–93.

Romano, S. (1933) *Corso di diritto costituzionale*, Padua: CEDAM.

Ross, G. (1995) *Jacques Delors and European Integration*, Cambridge: Polity.

Rousseau, D. (2000) 'Pour une constitution européenne', *Le Débat*, January–February: 54–73.

Rousseau, J.-J. (1762) *The Social Contract*, Oxford: Oxford University Press, 1994.

Sabel, C.F. (1994) 'Learning by Monitoring: The Institutions of Economic Development', in N.J. Smelser and R. Swedberg (eds) *The Handbook of Economic Sociology*, Princeton, NJ: Princeton University Press.

Santiago Nino, C. (1989) *Ética y derechos humanos*, Barcelona: Ariel.

Sartori, G. (1964) 'Constitutionalism, A Preliminary Discussion', *American Political Science Review*, 56: 853–64.

—— (1965) *Democratic Theory*, New York: Praeger.

Sauter, W. (1997) *Competition Law and Industrial Policy in the EU*, Oxford: Clarendon.

Sbragia, A. (ed.) (1992) *EuroPolitics: Institutions and Policymaking in the 'New' European Community*, Washington, DC: Brookings Institution.

Scharpf, F.W. (1988) 'The Joint-Decision Trap: Lessons from German Federalism and European Integration', *Public Administration*, 66: 239–78.

—— (1993), in M.R. Lepsius (ed.) *Demokratie in Deutschland: soziologisch-historische Konstellationsanalysen: ausgewählte Aufsätze*, Göttingen: Vandenhoeck & Ruprecht.

—— (1994) 'Community and Autonomy: Multi-Level Policy Making in the European Union', *Journal of European Public Policy*, 1: 219–38.

—— (1999) *Governing in Europe – Effective and Democratic?*, Oxford: Oxford University Press.

—— (2000) 'The Viability of Advanced Welfare States in the International Economy', *Journal of European Public Policy*, 7: 190–228.

—— (2002) 'Regieren im europäischen Mehrebenensystem – Ansätze zu einer Theorie', *Leviathan*, 1: 65–92.

Schepel, H. and Wesseling, R. (1997) 'The Legal Community: Judges, Lawyers, Officials and Clerks in the Writing of Europe', *European Law Journal*, 3: 165–88.

Schlesinger, P. and Kevin, D. (2000) 'Can the European Union Become a Sphere of Publics?', in E.O. Eriksen and J.E. Fossum (eds) *Democracy in the European Union: Integration through Deliberation?*, London: Routledge.

Schmalz-Bruns, R. (1999) 'Deliberativer Supranationalismus', *Zeitschrift für internationale Beziehungen*, 2: 185–243.

Schmidt, S. (1998) *Die Liberalisierung Europa. Die Rolle der Europäischen Kommission*, Frankfurt: Campus.

Schmitt, C. (1927) *Verfassungslehre*, Munich: Duncker und Humblot.

—— (1934) *Über die drei Arten des rechtswissenschaftlichen Denkens*, Hamburg: HAVA.

—— (1989) *Verfassungslehre*, Berlin: Duncker und Humblot.

Schmitter, P. (1996) 'Imagining the Future of the Euro-Polity', in G. Marks and F. Scharpf (eds) *Governance in the European Union*, London: Sage.

—— (2000) *How to Democratize the European Union … And Why Bother?*, Lanham, Md: Rowman and Littlefield.

Schönberger, C. (1997) *Das Parlament im Anstaltsstaat*, Frankfurt: Klostermann.

—— (1999) 'Der "Staat" der Allgemeinen Staatslehre: Anmerkungen zu einer eigenwilligen Disziplin im Vergleich mit Frankreich', in O. Beaud and E.V. Heyen (eds) *Eine deutsch–französische Rechtswissenschaft?/ Une science juridique franco-allemande?*, Baden-Baden: Nomos.

—— (2003) 'Die Europäische Union als Bund – Zugleich ein Beitrag zur Verabschiedung des Staatenbund-Bundesstaat-Schemas', unpublished copy, Freiburg.

Schönlau, J. (2003) 'New Values for Europe? Deliberation, Compromise, and Coercion in Drafting the Preamble to the EU Charter of Fundamental Rights', in E.O. Eriksen, J.E. Fossum and A.J. Menéndez (eds) *The Chartering of Europe*, Baden-Baden: Nomos.

Schuppert, G.F. (2000) 'Anforderungen an eine Europäische Verfassung', in H.-D. Klingmann and F. Neidhardt (eds) *Zur Zukunft der Demokratie. Herausforderungen im Zeitalter der Globalisierung*, WZB-Jahrbuch 2000, Berlin: Sigma.

Schutze, R.O. (2000) 'Constitutional Reform as a Process', in R.O Schutze and R. Sturm (eds) *The Politics of Constitutional Reform in North America. Coping with New Challenges*, Opladen: Leske und Budrich.

Schwarze, J. (2000) 'Die Entstehung einer europäischen Verfassungsordnung', in J. Schwarze (ed.) *Die Entstehung einer europäischen Verfassungsordnung*, Baden-Baden: Nomos.

Sewell, W.H., Jr. (1994) *A Rhetoric of Bourgeois Revolution*, Durham, NC: Duke University Press.

Shaw, J. (2003a) 'Process, Responsibility and Inclusion in EU Constitutionalism', *European Law Journal*, Vol. 9, No. 1: 45–68.

—— (2003b) *What's in a Convention? Process and substance in the project of European Constitution-Building*, Institute for Advanced Studies, Vienna, Working Paper 89: <http://www.ihs.ac.at/index.php3?id=450>.

Siedentop, L. (2000) *Democracy in Europe*, London: Allen Lane.

Sieyès, E.J. (1789) 'Was is der dritte Stand? (1789)', in *Politische Schriften 1788–1790*, 2nd edn, Munich: Oldenbourg, 1981.

Simpson, B. (2001) *Human Rights and the End of Empire*, Oxford: Oxford University Press.

Sjursen, H. and Smith, K. (2001) 'Justifying EU Foreign Policy: The Logics Underpinning EU Enlargement', ARENA Working Paper 01/1, Oslo: ARENA.

Smend, R. (1928) *Verfassung und Verfassungsrecht*, Munich: Duncker und Humblot.

Smismans, S. (2000) 'The European Economic and Social Committee: Towards Deliberative Democracy in a Functional Assembly', *European Integration Online Papers*, Vol. 4, No. 12.

Stahl, F.J. (1878) *Die Philosophie des Rechts nach geschichtlicher Ansicht*, Vol. 2, Tübingen: Mohr.

Stein, E. (1981) 'Lawyers, Judges, and the Making of a Transnational Constitution', *American Journal of International Law*, 75: 1–27.

Stevenson, C.L. (1938) 'Persuasive Definitions', *Mind*, 47: 331–50.

Stolleis, M. (1995) 'Das "europäische Haus" und seine Verfassung', *Kritische Vierteljahresschrift für Gesetzgebung und Rechtswissenschaft*, 78: 275–97.

—— (2003) 'Judicial Review, Administrative Review, and Constitutional Review in the Weimar Republic', *Ratio Juris*, 16: 266–80.

Stourzh, G. (1977) 'Staatsformenlehre und Fundamentalgesetze in England und Nordamerika im 17. und 18. Jahrhundert', in R. Vierhaus (ed.) *Herrschaftsvertäge, Wahlkapitulationen, Fundamentalgesetze*, Göttingen: Vandenhoeck & Ruprecht.

Streit, M.E. and Mussler, W. (1995) 'The Economic Constitution of the European Community: From "Rome" to Maastricht', *European Law Journal*, 1: 5–30.

Sunstein, C. (2002) *Designing Democracy: What Constitutions Do*, Oxford: Oxford University Press.

Tallberg, J. (2002) 'Paths to Compliance: Enforcement, Management, and the European Union', *International Organization*, Vol. 56 No. 3: 609–43.

Taylor, C. (1989) *Sources of the Self: The Making of the Modern Identity*, Cambridge, Mass.: Harvard University Press.

—— (1993) *Reconciling the Solitudes: Essays on Canadian Federalism and Nationalism*, Montreal and Kingston: McGill-Queen's University Press.

—— (1994) 'The Politics of Recognition', in C. Taylor and A. Gutmann (eds) *Multiculturalism*, Princeton, NJ: Princeton University Press.

—— (1995a) *Philosophical Arguments*, Cambridge, Mass.: Harvard University Press.

—— (1995b) *Identitet, frihet och gemenskap: Politisk-filosofiska texter i urval av Harald Grimen*, Gothenburg: Daidalos.

Telò, M. and Magnette, P. (2001) 'Social Justice and Solidarity', in F. Cerutti and E. Rudolph (eds) *A Soul for Europe. On the Political and Cultural Identity of the Europeans. A Reader*, Vol. 1, Leuven: Peeters.

Temple Lang, J. (2003) 'The Convention on the Future of Europe – So far', *Federal Trust Papers*, <http://www.fedtrust.co.uk/uploads/constitution/18_03.pdf>.

Thayer, J.B. (1893) 'The Origin and Scope of the American Doctrine of Constitutional Law', *Harvard Law Review*, 7: 129.

Therborn, G. (2001) 'Europe's Break with Itself', in F. Cerutti and E. Rudolph (eds) *A Soul for Europe. On the Cultural and Political Identity of the Europeans. An Essay Collection*, Vol. 2, Leuven: Peeters.

Tomuschat, C. (1997) 'Diskussionsbeitrag', in *Kontrolle aiswärtiger Gewalt – Veröffentlichungen der Vereinigung der Deutschen Staatsrechtslehrer*, Heft 56, Berlin: de Gruyter.

Triepel, H. (1899) *Völkerrecht und Landesrecht*, Leipzig: Hirschfield.

van Aaken, A. (2002) 'Deliberative institutional economics, or Does "Homo oeconomicus" Argue?', *Philosophy & Social Criticism* 4: 361–94.

Van Caenegem, R.C. (1995) *An Historical Introduction to Western Constitutional Law*, Cambridge: Cambridge University Press.

—— (2001) *European Law in the Past and the Future*, Cambridge: Cambridge University Press.

Viroli, M. (2002) *Republicanism*, New York: Hill and Wang.

Vitorino, A. (2002) 'Interview', *Revue du Marché commun et l'Union Européene*, 485: 285–90.

Vobruba, G. (2000) 'Actors in Processes of Inclusion and Exclusion', *Social Policy and Administration*, 32: 603–13.

von Beyme, K. (1968) *Die verfassunggebende Gewalt des Volkes*, Tübingen: Mohr.

Vorländer, H. (1999) *Die Verfassung. Idee und Geschichte*, Munich: C.H. Beck.

Wahl, R. (1981) 'Der Vorrang der Verfassung', *Der Staat*, 20: 485–516.

Walker, N. (1998) 'Sovereignty and Differentiated Integration in the European Union', *European Law Journal*, Vol. 4, No. 4: 355–88.

—— (2001) ' The Idea of Constitutional Patriotism', unpublished copy, Florence.

Weale, A. and Nentwich, M. (eds) (1998) *Political Theory and the European Union. Legitimacy, Constitutional Choice and Citizenship*, London and New York: Routledge.

Weber, M. (1921) 'Parlament und Regierung im neugeordneten Deutschland', in *Gesammelte politische Schriften*, Munich: Siebek.

Weiler, J.H.H. (1991) 'The Transformation of Europe', *Yale Law Journal*, 100: 2403–83.

—— (1993) 'Journey to an Unknown Destination: A Retrospective and Prospective of the European Court of Justice in the Arena of Political Integration', *Journal of Common Market Studies*, Vol. 31, No. 4: 417–46.

—— (1995) 'Does Europe Need a Constitution? Reflections on Demos, Telos and the German Maastricht Decision', *European Law Journal*, 1: 219–58.

—— (1997) 'To be a European citizen – Eros and civilization', *Journal of European Public Policy*, Vol. 4, No. 4: 495–519.

—— (1998) 'Europe: The Case Against the Case for Statehood', *European Law Journal*, Vol. 4, No. 1: 43–62.

—— (1999a) 'Epilogue: "Comitology" as Revolution – Infranationalism, Constitutionalism and Democracy', in C. Joerges and E. Vos (eds) *EU Committees: Social Regulation, Law and Politics*, Oxford: Hart.

—— (1999b) 'The Constitution of the Common Market Place: Text and Context in the Evolution of the Free Movement of Goods', in P. Craig and G. De Burca (eds) *The Evolution of EU Law*, Oxford: Oxford University Press.

—— (1999c) *The Constitution of Europe*, Cambridge: Cambridge University Press.

—— (2001a) 'European Democracy and the Principle of Toleration: The Soul of Europe', in F. Cerutti and E. Rudolph (eds) *A Soul for Europe. On the Political and Cultural Identity of the Europeans. A Reader*, Vol. 1, Leuven: Peeters.

—— (2001b) 'Federalism without Constitutionalism: Europe's Sonderweg', in K. Nicolaïdis and R. Howse (eds) *The Federal Vision*, Oxford: Oxford University Press.

—— (2002) 'A Constitution for Europe: Some Hard Choices?', *Journal of Common Market Studies*, 40: 563–80.

Wellmer, A. (1998) 'Menschenrechte und Demokratie', in S. Gosepath and G. Lohmann (eds) *Philosophie der Menschenrecthe*, Frankfurt: Suhrkamp.

—— (1999) 'Hannah Arendt über die Revolution', in H. Brunkhorst, W.R. Köhler and M. Lutz-Bachmann (eds) *Recht auf Menschenrechte*, Frankfurt: Suhrkamp.

Wiethölter, R. (1989) 'Franz Böhm (1895–1977)', in B. Diestelkamp and M. Stolleis (eds) *Juristen an der Universität Frankfurt a.M.*, Baden-Baden: Nomos.

Wolf, K.D. (2000) *Die neue Staatsräson – Zwischenstaatliche Kooperation als Demokratieproblem der Weltgesellschaft*, Baden-Baden: Nomos.

Wood, G.S. (1969) *The Creation of the American Republic*, New York: Norton.

Zagrebelsky, G. (1992) *Il diritto mite*, Turin: Einaudi.

Zeitlin, J. and Trubek, D.M. (eds) (2003) *Governing Work and Welfare in a New Economy: European and American Experiments*, Oxford: Oxford University Press.

Zuleeg, M. (1997) 'The European Constitution under Constitutional Constraints: The German Scenario', *European Law Review*, 22: 19–29.

Zürn, M. (1996) 'Zum Verhältnis von Globalisierung, politischer Integration und politischer Fragmentierung', in *Jahrbuch Arbeit und Technik*, Bonn: Dietz.

—— (1999) 'The State in the Post-National Constellation – Societal Denationalization and Multi-Level Governance', ARENA Working Paper 99/35, Oslo: ARENA.

Official documents

BVerfGE/ Bundesverfassungsgericht (German Federal Constitutional Court) (1967) *European Community regulations – Art. 24 GG*, BVerfGE 22, 293.

—— (1974) *Solange 1 judgment*, BVerfGE 37, 271.

—— (1986) *Mutlangen*, BverfGE 73, 306.

—— (1993) *Urteil v.12.10.1993* – 2 BvR 2134/92 u. 2 BvR 2159/92, BVerfGE 89, 155.

—— (1998) *Beschluß v. 31.3.1998*, 2 BvR 1877/97, 2 BvR 50/98, BVerfGE 97, 350.

—— (2000) BVerfGE 2, BvL 1/97, 6 June.

Charter of Fundamental Rights (2000) *Charter of Fundamental Rights of the European Union*, Official Journal of the European Communities 2000/C 346/01–22.

Convention on the Charter (2000) *Record of the first meeting of the Body to draw up a draft Charter of Fundamental Rights of the European Union (held in Brussels, 17 December 1999)*, CHARTE 4105/00, Brussels, 13 January 2000.

Court of Session (Scotland) (1953) *John MacDonald MacCormick vs. Lord Advocate*, SC 396.

European Commission (1980) Commission Communication on the effects of the ECJ judgment of 20 February 1979 in 120/78 ('Cassis de Dijon'), OJ C 256, 3 October, 2–3.

—— (1985) Commission White Paper to the European Council on Completion of the Internal Market, COM (85) 310 final, 14 June.

—— (2000) A White Paper on European Governance – 'Enhancing Democracy in the European Union', Work programme, SEC (2000) 1547/7 final, 11 October.

—— (2001) European Governance. A White Paper, COM (2001) 428 final of 25 July.

European Convention (2002) CONV 4/02, *Speeches delivered at the inaugural meeting of the Convention on 28 February 2002*, Brussels, 5 March.

—— (2002) CONV 12/02, *CONTRIB 1 – Contribution from Mr Hubert Haenel, member of the Convention*, Brussels, 19 March.

—— (2002) CONV 14/02, *Note on the plenary meeting – Brussels, 21 and 22 March 2002*, Brussels, 25 March.

—— (2002) CONV 22/02, *CONTRIB 6 – Contribution from Mr Andrew Duff, member of the Convention*, Brussels, 8 April.

—— (2002) CONV 23/02, *CONTRIB 7 – Contribution from Minister-President Erwin Teufel, member of the Convention*, Brussels, 9 April.

—— (2002) CONV 34/02, *CONTRIB 17 – Contribution from Mr Janusz Trzcinski, alternate member of the Convention*, Brussels, 17 April.

—— (2002) CONV 60/02, *Note on the plenary meeting – Brussels, 23 and 24 May 2002*, Brussels, 29 May.

—— (2002) CONV 63/02, *CONTRIB 32 – Contribution from Ms Pervenche Berès and Mr Klaus Hänsch, members of the Convention*, Brussels, 23 May.

—— (2002) CONV 97/02, *Note on the plenary meeting – Brussels, 6 and 7 June 2002*, Brussels, 19 June.

—— (2002) CONV 162/02, *The legal instruments: present system*, Brussels, 13 June.

—— (2002) CONV 181/02, *Motion for a decision on the preparation of a Constitutional Treaty*, Brussels, 10 July.

—— (2002) CONV 182/02, *CONTRIB 62 – Contribution from Mr René van der Linden, member of the Convention, and Mr Wim van Eekelen, alternate member of the Convention: 'The role of national parliaments: an example of a good practice'*, Brussels, 11 July.

—— (2002) CONV 216/02, *Legislative procedures (including the budgetary procedure); current situation*, Brussels, 24 July.

—— (2002) CONV 234/02, *CONTRIB 82 – Contribution by Mr Andrew Duff, member of the Convention: 'A model constitution for a Federal Union of Europe'*, Brussels, 3 September.

—— (2002) CONV 250/02, *Simplification of the Treaties and drawing up of a constitutional treaty*, Brussels, 10 September.

—— (2002) CONV 277/02, *CONTRIB 96 – Contribution by Mr Jens-Peter Bonde, member of the Convention: 'The Convention about the Future of Europe'*, Brussels, 1 October.

—— (2002) CONV 286/02, *WG I 15 – Conclusions of Working Group I on the Principle of Subsidiarity*, Brussels, 23 September.

—— (2002) CONV 305/02, *WG III 16 – Final report of Working Group III on Legal Personality*, Brussels, 1 October.

—— (2002) CONV 325/02, *CONTRIB 111 – Contribution by Mr Brok, member of the Convention: 'Constitution of the European Union'*, Brussels, 8 October.

—— (2002) CONV 353/02, *WG IV 17 – Final Report of Working Group IV on the role of national parliaments*, Brussels, 22 October.

—— (2002) CONV 357/02, *WG VI 17 – Final report of Working Group VI on Economic Governance*, Brussels, 21 October.

—— (2002) CONV 369/02, *Preliminary Draft Constitutional Treaty*, Brussels, 28 October.

—— (2002) CONV 375/1/02 REV 1, *WG V 14 – Final report of Working Group V on Complementary Competencies*, Brussels, 4 November.

—— (2003) CONV 477/03, *The Functioning of the Institutions*, Brussels, 10 January.

—— (2003) CONV 489/03, *CONTRIB 192 – Contribution submitted by Mr Dominique de Villepin and Mr Joschka Fischer, members of the Convention*, Brussels, 16 January.

—— (2003) CONV 490/03, *CONTRIB 193 – Contribution by Ms Lena Hjelm-Wallén, Ms Teija Tiilikainen, Mr Dick Roche, members of the Convention: 'A Constitutional Treaty: Openness and good administration in the EU institutions'*, Brussels, 16 January.

—— (2003) CONV 516/1/03 REV 1, *WG XI 9 – Final report of Working Group XI on Social Europe*, Brussels, 4 February.

—— (2003) CONV 528/03, *Draft of Articles 1 to 16 of the Constitutional Treaty*, Brussels, 6 February.

—— (2003) CONV 529/03, *Remit of the working party of experts nominated by the Legal Services*, Brussels, 6 February.

—— (2003) CONV 591/03, *CONTRIB 264 – Contribution by Mrs Ana Palacio and Mr. Peter Hain, members of the Convention: 'The Union institutions'*, Brussels, 28 February.

—— (2003) CONV 601/03, *Summary report on the plenary session – Brussels 27 and 28 February 2003*, Brussels, 11 March.

—— (2003) CONV 603/03, *CONTRIB 270 – Contribution submitted by Mrs Lena Hjelm-Wallén and Ms Hildegard Puwak, members of the Convention: 'Equality between men and women'*, Brussels, 10 March.

—— (2003) CONV 611/03, *Reactions to the draft protocol on the role of National Parliaments in the European Union – Analysis*, Brussels, 12 March.

—— (2003) CONV 612/03, *'Discussion circle' on the budgetary procedure*, Brussels, 13 March.

—— (2003) CONV 618/03, *Part Two of the Constitution. Report by the working party of experts nominated by the Legal Services of the European Parliament, the Council and the Commission*, Brussels, 17 March.

—— (2003) CONV 620/03, *CONTRIB 277 – Contribution by Mr Alfonso Dastis and Mr Gijs De Vries, members of the Convention: 'Proposals to guarantee greater efficiency and effectiveness in the working methods of the Court of Justice and the Court of First Instance'*, Brussels, 13 March.

—— (2003) CONV 650/03, *The democratic life of the Union*, Brussels, 2 April.

—— (2003) CONV 654/03, *Discussion circle on own resources*, Brussels, 31 March.

—— (2003) CONV 664/03, *CONTRIB 295 – Franco-Netherlands contribution from Mr Gijs de Vries and Mr Dominique de Villepin: 'Strengthening the Commission's role'*, Brussels, 2 April.

—— (2003) CONV 682/03, *Complementary mandate for the working party of experts nominated by the Legal Services*, Brussels, 11 April.

—— (2003) CONV 728/03, *Draft text of Part IV, with comments*, Brussels, 26 May.

—— (2003) CONV 732/03, *CONTRIB 320 – Contribution by the Benelux countries, presented by Mr Gijs de Vries, Mr Jacques Santer and Mr Louis Michel: 'The Union's institutions'*, Brussels, 8 May.

—— (2003) CONV 766/03, *CONTRIB 343 – Contribution by the representatives of the Heads of State or Government of several States: 'A Union Constitution for all. A success for the Convention'*, Brussels, 28 May.

—— (2003) CONV 782/03, *CONTRIB 353 – Contribution by Mr Peter Hain, Ms Lena Hjelm-Wallén, Ms Danuta Hübner, Mr Ivan Korčok, Mr Dick Roche, Mr Tunne Kelam, Mr Rein Lang; members of the Convention – Mr Henrik Hololei, Mr Bobby McDonagh, Ms Ana Palacio, Mr Robert Žile, Mr Pat Carey, Mr Kenneth Kvist, Mr Urmas Reinsalu, Lord Tomlinson, Mrs Liina Tonisson; alternate members of the Convention: Articles III 59 and III 60 in the draft EU constitutional treaty*, Brussels, 3 June 2003.

—— (2003) CONV 820/1/03 REV.

—— (2003) CONV 821/03, *Reactions to draft text CONV 802/03 – Analysis*, Brussels, 27 June.

—— (2003) CONV 826/03, *CONTRIB 381 – Contribution of Ms Lena Hjelm-Wallén; Ms Teija Tiilikainen; Mr Peter Hain; Mr Gijs de Vries, members of the Convention – Mr Henrik Hololei, alternate member of the Convention: 'Suggestion for amendement of Article III 3'*, Brussels, 8 July.

—— (2003) CONV 848/03, *Draft Constitution, Volume II*, Brussels, 9 July.

—— (2003) CONV 850/03, *Draft Treaty Establishing a Constitution for Europe*, Brussels, 18 July.

European Council (1995a) *Reflection Group on the 1996 Intergovernmental Conference – Interim report*, SN S09/2/95 Rev. 2.

—— (1995b) *Reflection Group on the 1996 Intergovernmental Conference – Report of 5 December 1995*, SN S20/95 (Reflex 21).

—— (1999) *Decision on the drawing up of a Charter of Fundamental Rights of the European Union*, Annex IV to the Conclusions of the European Council in Cologne 3–4 June.

—— (2000) *Declaration on the Future of the Union*, Annex to the Treaty of Nice, Official Journal of the European Communities c 80/85-86, 10 March 2001.

—— (2001a) *Laeken Declaration on the Future of the European Union*, SN 273/01, Laeken, 15 December.

—— (2001b) *Presidency Conclusions*, European Council Meeting in Laeken, Belgium, 14 and 15 December, SN 300/01.

ECJ/ European Court of Justice (1956) *Fé de char*, Case 8/55, ECR 292.

—— (1963) *Van Gend en Loos*, Case 26/62, ECR 1.

—— (1964) *Costa v. ENEL*, Case 6/64, ECR 1251.

—— (1969) *Stauder*, Case 29/69, ECR 419.

—— (1970) *Internationale Handelsgesellschaft*, Case 11/70, ECR 1125.

—— (1971) *Commission v. Council*, Case 72/70, ECR 263 – AETR.

—— (1979) *Cassis de Dijon*, Case 120/78, ECR 649.

—— (1986) *Parti écologiste 'Les Verts' v. European Parliament*, Case 294/83, ECR 1357.

—— (1991) *Opinion 1/91 – Delivered pursuant to the second sub-paragraph of Article 228(1) of the EEC Treaty: draft agreement between the Community, on the one hand, and the countries of the European Free Trade Association, on the other, relating to the creation of the European Economic Area*, ECR I 6079, EEA Opinon.

European Parliament (1984) *Draft Treaty Establishing a European Union ('Spinelli Report')*, 14 February 1984, Official Journal of the European Communities C77/33.

—— (1994) *Resolution on the Constitution of the European Union ('Herman Resolution')*, A3–0064/94, Official Journal of the European Communities C61/155–170.

—— (2002) MEP Jo Leinen's draft proposal entitled *Draft Constitution of the European Union*, Brussels, October.

—— (2003) Committee on Constitutional Affairs, *Draft Report on the Draft Treaty on the European Constitution and EP Opinion on the Convocation of the Intergovernmental Conference* (IGC), PROVISIONAL 2003/0902(CNS), Par 1, 5 August.

House of Lords (2000) *Eighth Report: The EU Charter of Fundamental Rights*, House of Lords European Union Committee, Session 1999–2000.

Index